HISTORY OF ENGLISH LITERATURE

This text was originally published in the USA on the year of 1889.
The text is in the public domain.
The edits and layout of this version are Copyright © 2024+
by Century Bound.

This publication has no affiliation with the original Author or publication company.

The publishers have made all reasonable efforts to ensure this book is indeed in the Public Domain in any and all territories it has been published, and apologise for any omissions or errors made. Corrections may be made to future printings or electronic publications.

CENTURY BOUND

Printed or published to the highest ethical standard

History of English Literature

Volume 3

By Hippolyte Taine

Translated by
Henri Van Laun

Published by Century Bound

First Published
1872

CONTENTS

BOOK III.— THE CLASSIC AGE (CONTINUED) 1
   Chapter Seventh. The Poets 1

BOOK IV— MODERN LIFE 32
   Chapter First. Ideas and Productions 32
   Chapter Second. Lord Byron 82
   Chapter Third. The Past and Present 127
      Part I.— The Past 127
      Part II.— The Present 133

BOOK V— MODERN AUTHORS 150
   Introductory Note 150
   Chapter First. The Novel.— Dickens 152
      Part I.— The Author 153
      Part II.— The Public 167
      Part III.— The Characters 172
   Chapter Second. The Novel (Continued)— Thackeray 182
      Part I.— The Satirist 183
      Part II.— The Artist 205
   Chapter Third. Criticism and History— Macaulay 219
   Chapter Fourth. Philosophy and History— Carlyle 254
      Part I.— Style and Mind 254
      Part II— Vocation 270
      Part III.— Philosophy, Morality, and Criticism 276
      Part IV.— Conception of History 286
   Chapter Fifth. Philosophy— Stuart Mill 298
      Part I.— Experience 301
      Part II.— Abstraction 323
   Chapter Sixth. Poetry— Tennyson 341

DETAILED HISTORICAL CONTEXT 368

BOOK III.—THE CLASSIC AGE (*CONTINUED*)

CHAPTER SEVENTH. THE POETS

Section I—The Domination of the Classical Spirit

When we take in at one view the vast literary region in England, extending from the restoration of the Stuarts to the French Revolution, we perceive that all the productions, independently of the English character, bear a classical impress, and that this impress, special to this region, is met with neither in the preceding nor in the succeeding time. This dominant form of thought is imposed on all writers from Waller to Johnson, from Hobbes and Temple to Robertson and Hume: there is an art to which they all aspire; the work of a hundred and fifty years, practice and theory, inventions and imitations, examples and criticism, are employed in attaining it. They comprehend only one kind of beauty; they establish only the precepts which may produce it; they rewrite, translate, and disfigure on its pattern the great works of other ages; they carry it into all the different kinds of literature, and succeed or fail in them according as it is adapted to them or not. The sway of this style is so absolute that it is imposed on the greatest, and condemns them to impotence when they would apply it beyond its domain. The possession of this style is so universal that it is met with in the weakest authors, and raises them to the height of talent when they apply it in its domain.[1] This it is which brings to perfection prose, discourse, essay, dissertation, narration, and all the productions which form part of conversation and eloquence. This it is which destroyed the old drama, debased the new, impoverished and diverted poetry, produced a correct, agreeable, sensible, colorless, and narrow-minded history. This spirit, common to England and France, impressed its form on an infinite diversity of literary works, so that in its universal manifest ascendancy we cannot but recognize the presence of one of those internal forces which bend and govern the course of human genius.

In no branch was it displayed more manifestly than in poetry, and at no time did it appear more clearly than in the reign of Queen Anne. The poets have just attained to the art which they had before dimly discerned. For sixty years they were approaching it; now they possess it, handle it; they use and exaggerate it. The style is at the same time finished and artificial. Let us open the first that comes to hand, Parnell or Philips, Addison or Prior, Gay or Tickell, we find a certain turn of mind, versification, language. Let us pass to a second, the same form reappears; we might say that they are imitations of one another. Let us go on to a third; the same diction, the same apostrophes, the same fashion of arranging an epithet and rounding a period. Let us turn over the whole lot; with little individual differences, they seem to be all cast in the same mould; one is more epicurean, another more moral, another more biting; but a noble language, an oratorical pomp, a classical correctness, reign throughout; the substantive is accompanied by its adjective, its knight of honor; antithesis balances its symmetrical architecture; the verb, as in Lucan or Statius, is displayed, flanked on each side by a noun decorated by an epithet; we would say that it is of a uniform make, as if fabricated by a machine; we forget what it wishes to make known; we are tempted to count the measure on our fingers; we know beforehand what poetical ornaments are to embellish it. There is a theatrical dressing, contrasts, allusions, mythological elegance, Greek or Latin quotations. There is a scholastic solidity, sententious maxims, philosophic commonplaces, moral developments, oratorical exactness. We might imagine ourselves to be before a family of plants; if the size, color, accessories, names differ, the fundamental type does not vary; the stamens are of the same number, similarly inserted around similar pistils, above leaves arranged on the same plan: a man who knows one knows all; there is a common organism and structure which involves the uniformity of the rest. If we review the whole family we will doubtless find there some characteristic plant which displays the type in a clear light, whilst all around it and by degrees it alters, degenerates, and at last loses itself in the surrounding families. So here we see classical art find its centre in the neighbors of Pope, and above all in Pope himself, then, after being half effaced, mingle with foreign elements until it disappears in the poetry which succeeded it.[2]

Section II.—Alexander Pope.—His Education and Mode of Life

In 1688, at a linen draper's in Lombard Street, London, was born a little, delicate, and sickly creature, by nature artificial, constituted beforehand for a studious existence, having no taste but for books, who from his early youth derived his whole pleasure from the contemplation of printed books. He copied the letters, and thus learned to write. He passed his infancy with them, and was a verse-maker as soon as he knew how to speak. At the age of twelve he had written a little tragedy out of the Iliad, and an "Ode on Solitude." From thirteen to fifteen he composed a long epic of four thousand verses, called "Alcander." For eight years shut up in a little house in Windsor Forest, he read all the best critics, almost all the English, Latin, and French poets who had a reputation, Homer, the Greek poets, and a few of the great ones in the original, Tasso and Ariosto in translations, with such assiduity that he nearly died from it. He did not search in them for passions, but style: there was never a more devoted adorer, never a more precocious master of form. Already his taste showed itself: amongst all the English poets his favorite was Dryden, the least inspired and the most classical. He perceived his career. He states that Mr. Walsh told him there was one way left of excelling. "We have several great poets," he said, "but we never had one great poet that was correct; and he advised me to make that my study and aim."[3] He followed this advice, tried his hand in translations of Ovid and Statius, and in recasting parts of old Chaucer. He appropriated all the poetic elegances and excellences, stored them up in his memory; he arranged in his head a complete dictionary of all happy epithets, all ingenious turns of expression, all sonorous rhythms by which a poet may exalt, render precise, illuminate an idea. He was like those little musicians, infant prodigies, who, brought up at the piano, suddenly acquire a marvellous touch, roll out scales, brilliant shakes, make the octaves vault with an agility and accuracy which drive off the stage the most famous performers. At seventeen, becoming acquainted with old Wycherley, who was sixty-nine, he undertook, at his request, to correct his poems, corrected them so well that the other was at once charmed and mortified. Pope blotted out, added, recast, spoke frankly, and eliminated firmly. The author, in spite of himself, admired the corrections secretly, and tried openly to make light of them, until at last his vanity, wounded at owing so much to so young a man, and at finding a master in a scholar, ended by breaking off an intercourse by which he profited and suffered too much. For the scholar had at the outset carried the art beyond any of the masters. At sixteen[4] his Pastorals bore witness to a correctness which no one had possessed, not even Dryden. When people observed these choice words, these exquisite arrangements of melodious syllables, this science of division and rejection, this style so fluent and pure, these graceful images rendered still more graceful by the diction, and all this artificial and many-tinted garland of flowers which Pope called pastoral, they thought of the first eclogues of Vergil. Mr. Walsh declared "that it is not flattery at all to say that Vergil had written nothing so good at his age."[5] When later they appeared in a volume, the public was dazzled. "You have only displeased the critics," wrote Wycherley, "by pleasing them too well."[6] The same year the poet of twenty-one finished his "Essay on Criticism," a sort of "Ars Poetica"; it is the kind of a poem a man might write at the end of his career, when he has handled all modes of writing and has grown gray in criticism; and in this subject, of which the treatment demands the experience of a whole literary life, he was at the first onset as ripe as Boileau.

What will this consummate musician, who begins by a treatise on harmony, make of his incomparable mechanism and his science as a teacher? It is well to feel and think before, writing: a full source of living ideas and real passions is necessary to make a genuine poet, and in him, seen closely, we find that everything, to his very person, is scanty and artificial; he was a dwarf, four feet high, contorted, hunchbacked, thin, valetudinarian, appearing, when he arrived at maturity, no longer capable of existing. He could not get up himself, a woman dressed him; he wore three pairs of stockings, drawn on one over the other, so slender were his legs; "when he rose, he was invested in bodices made of stiff canvas, being scarce able to hold himself erect till they were laced, and he then put on a flannel waistcoat;"[7] next came a sort of fur doublet, for the least thing made him shiver; and lastly, a thick linen shirt, very warm, with fine sleeves. Over all this he wore a black garment, a tye-wig, a little sword; thus equipped, he went and took his place at the table of his great friend, the Earl of Oxford. He was so small that he had to be raised on a chair of his own; so bald that when he had no company he covered his head with a velvet cap; so punctilious and exacting that the footman evaded going his errands, and the Earl had to discharge several "for their resolute refusal of his messages." At dinner he ate too much; like a spoiled child, he would have highly seasoned dishes, and thus "would oppress his stomach with repletion." When cordials were offered him, he got angry, but did not refuse them. He had all the appetite and whims of an old child, an old invalid, an old author, an old bachelor. We are prepared to find him whimsical and susceptible. He often, without saying a word, and without any known cause, quitted the house of Lord Oxford, and the footman had to go repeatedly with messages to bring him back. If Lady Mary Wortley, his former poetical divinity, were unfortunately at table, there was no dining in peace; they would not fail to contradict, peck at each other, quarrel; and one or other would leave the room. He would be sent for and would return, but he brought his hobbies back with him. He was as crafty and malignant as a nervous abortion, which he was; when he wanted anything, he dared not ask for it plainly; with hints and contrivances of speech he induced people to mention it, to bring it forward, after which he would make use of it. "Thus he teased Lord Orrery till he obtained a screen. He hardly drank tea without a stratagem. Lady Bolingbroke used to say that 'he played the politician about cabbages and turnips.'"[8]

The rest of his life is not much more noble. He wrote libels on the Duke of Chandos, Aaron Hill, Lady Mary Wortley, and then lied or equivocated to disavow them. He had an ugly liking for artifice, and played a disloyal trick on Lord Bolingbroke, his greatest friend. He was never frank, always acting a part; he aped the *blasé* man, the impartial great artist, a contemner of the great, of kings, of poetry itself. The truth is, that he thought of nothing but his phrases, his author's reputation, and "a little regard shown him by the Prince of Wales melted his obduracy."[9] When we read his correspondence, we find that there are not more than about ten genuine letters; he is a literary man even in the moments when he opened his heart; his confidences are formal rhetoric; and when he conversed with a friend he was always thinking of the printer, who would give his effusions to the public. Through this very pretentiousness he grew awkward, and unmasked himself. One day Richardson and his father, the painter, found him reading a pamphlet that Cibber had written against him. "These things," said Pope, "are my diversion. They sat by him while he perused it, and saw his features writhing with anguish; and young Richardson said to his father, when they returned, that he hoped to be preserved from such diversion."[10] After all, his great cause for writing was literary vanity: he wished to be admired, and nothing more; his life was that of a coquette studying herself in a glass, painting her face, smirking, receiving compliments from anyone, yet declaring that compliments weary her, that paint makes her dirty, and that she has a horror of affectation. Pope has no dash, no naturalness or manliness; he has no more ideas than passions; at least such ideas as a man feels it necessary to write, and in connection with which we lose thought of words. Religious controversy and party quarrels resound about him; he studiously avoids them; amidst all these shocks his chief care is to preserve his writing-desk; he is a very lukewarm Catholic, all but a deist, not well aware of what deism means; and on this point he borrows from Bolingbroke ideas whose scope he cannot see, but which he thinks suitable to be put into verse. In a letter to Atterbury (1717) he says: "In my politics, I think no further than how to prefer the peace of my life, in any government under which I live; nor in my religion, than to preserve the peace of my conscience in any church with which I communicate. I hope, all churches and governments are so far of God, as they are rightly understood and rightly administered; and where they err, or may be wrong, I leave it to God alone to mend or reform them."[11] Such convictions do not torment a man. In reality, he did not write because he thought, but thought in order to write; manuscript and the noise it makes in the world, when printed, was his idol; if he wrote verses, it was merely for the sake of doing so.

This is the best training for versification. Pope gave himself up to it; he was a man of leisure, his father had left him a very fair fortune; he earned a large sum by translating the Iliad and Odyssey; he had an income of eight hundred pounds. He was never in the pay of a publisher; he looked from an eminence upon the beggarly authors grovelling in their free and easy life, and, calmly seated in his pretty house at Twickenham, in his grotto, or in the fine garden which he had himself planned, he could polish and file his writings as long as he chose. He did not fail to do so. When he had written a work he kept it at least two years in his desk. From time to time he re-read and corrected it; took counsel of his friends, then of his enemies; no new edition was unamended; he altered without wearying. His first outburst became so recast and transformed that it could not be recognized in the final copy. The pieces which seem least retouched are two satires, and Dodsley says that in the manuscript "almost every line was written twice over; I gave him a clean transcript, which he sent some time afterwards to me for the press, with almost every line written twice over a second time."[12] Dr. Johnson says: "From his attention to poetry he was never diverted. If conversation offered anything that could be improved, he committed it to paper; if a thought, or perhaps an expression, more happy than was common, rose to his mind, he was careful to write it; an independent distich was preserved for an opportunity of insertion; and some little fragments have been found containing lines, or parts of lines, to be wrought upon at some other time."[13] His writing-desk had to be placed upon his bed before he rose. "Lord Oxford's domestic related that, in the dreadful winter of 1740, she was called from her bed by him four times in one night to supply him with paper, lest he should lose a thought."[14] Swift complains that he was never at leisure for conversation, because he "had always some poetical scheme in his head." Thus nothing was lacking for the attainment of perfect expression; the practice of a lifetime, the study of every model, an independent fortune, the company of men of the world, an immunity from turbulent passions, the absence of dominant ideas, the facility of an infant prodigy, the assiduity of an old man of letters. It seems as though he were expressly endowed with faults and good qualities, here enriched, there impoverished, at once narrowed and developed, to set in relief the classical form by the diminution of the classical depth, to present the public with a model of a worn-out and accomplished art, to reduce to a brilliant and rigid crystal the flowing sap of an expiring literature.

Section III.—Eloisa to Abelard.—The Rape of the Lock.—The Dunciad

It is a great misfortune for a poet to know his business too well; his poetry then shows the man of business, and not the poet. I wish I could admire Pope's works of imagination, but I cannot. In vain I read the testimony of his contemporaries, and even that of the moderns, and repeat to myself that in his time he was the prince of poets; that his epistle from "Eloisa to Abelard" was received with a cry of enthusiasm; that a man could not then imagine a finer expression of true passion; that to this very day it is learned by heart, like the speech of Hippolyte in the "Phèdre" of Racine; that Johnson, the great literary critic, ranked it amongst "the happiest productions of the human mind"; that Lord Byron himself preferred it to the celebrated ode of Sappho. I read it again and am bored; this is not as it ought to be; but, in spite of myself, I yawn, and I open the original letters of Eloisa to find the cause of my weariness.

Doubtless poor Eloisa is a barbarian, nay worse, a literary barbarian; she puts down learned quotations, arguments, tries to imitate Cicero, to arrange her periods; she could not do otherwise, writing a dead language, with an acquired style; perhaps the reader would do as much if he were obliged to write to his mistress in Latin.[15] But how does true feeling pierce through the scholastic form! "Thou art the only one who can sadden me, console me, make me joyful.... I should be happier and prouder to be called thy mistress than to be the lawful wife of an emperor.... Never, God knows, have I wished for anything else in thee but thee. It is thee alone whom I desire; nothing that thou couldst give; not marriage, not dowry: I never dreamt of doing my own pleasure or my own will, thou knowest it, but thine." Then come passionate

BOOK III.— THE CLASSIC AGE (CONTINUED)

words, genuine love words,[16] then the unrestrained words of a penitent, who says and dares everything, because she wishes to be cured, to show her wound to her confessor, even her most shameful wound; perhaps also because in extreme agony, as in child-birth, modesty vanishes. All this is very crude, very rude; Pope has more wit than she, and how he endues her with it! In his hands she becomes an academician, and her letter is a repertory of literary effects; portraits and descriptions; she paints to Abelard the nunnery and the landscape:

> "In these lone walls (their days eternal bound),
> These moss-grown domes with spiry turrets crowned,
> Where awful arches make a noon-day night,
> And the dim windows shed a solemn light....
> The wandering streams that shine between the hills,
> The grots that echo to the tinkling rills,
> The dying gales that pant upon the trees,
> The lakes that quiver to the curling breeze."[17]

Declamation and commonplace: she sends Abelard discourses on love and the liberty which it demands, on the cloister and the peaceful life which it affords, on writing and the advantages of the post.[18] Antitheses and contrasts, she forwards them to Abelard by the dozen; a contrast between the convent illuminated by his presence and desolate by his absence, between the tranquillity of the pure nun and the anxiety of the sinful nun, between the dream of human happiness and the dream of divine happiness. In fine, it is a *bravura*, with contrasts of *forte* and *piano*, variations and change of key. Eloisa makes the most of her theme, and sets herself to crowd into it all the powers and effects of her voice. Admire the *crescendo*, the shakes by which she ends her brilliant *morceaux*; to transport the hearer at the close of the portrait of the innocent nun, she says:

> "How happy is the blameless vestal's lot!
> The world forgetting, by the world forgot:
> Eternal sunshine of the spotless mind!
> Each prayer accepted and each wish resigned;
> Labour and rest, that equal periods keep;
> 'Obedient slumbers that can wake and weep;'
> Desires composed, affections ever even;
> Tears that delight, and sighs that waft to heav'n.
> Grace shines around her with serenest beams,
> And whisp'ring angels prompt her golden dreams.
> For her, th' unfading rose of Eden blooms,
> And wings of seraphs shed divine perfumes,

> For her the spouse prepares the bridal ring,
> For her white virgins hymeneals sing,
> To sounds of heavenly harps she dies away,
> And melts in visions of eternal day."[19]

Observe the noise of the big drum; I mean the grand contrivances, for so may be called all that a person says who wishes to rave and cannot; for instance, speaking to rocks and walls, praying the absent Abelard to come, fancying him present, apostrophizing grace and virtue:

> "O grace serene! O virtue heavenly fair!
> Divine oblivion of low-thoughted care!
> Fresh-blooming hope, gay daughter of the sky!
> And faith, our early immortality!
> Enter, each mild, each amicable guest;
> Receive, and wrap me in eternal rest!"[20]

Hearing the dead speaking to her, telling the angels:

> "I come! I come! Prepare your roseate bow'rs,
> Celestial palms, and ever-blooming flow'rs."[21]

This is the final symphony with modulations of the celestial organ. I presume that Abelard cried "Bravo" when he heard it.

But this is nothing in comparison with the art exhibited by her in every phrase. She puts ornaments into every line. Imagine an Italian singer trilling every word. O what pretty sounds! how nimbly and brilliantly they roll along, how clear, and always exquisite! it is impossible to reproduce them in another tongue. Now it is a happy image, filling up a whole phrase; now a series of verses, full of symmetrical contrasts; two ordinary words set in relief by strange conjunction; an imitative rhythm completing the impression of the mind by the emotion of the senses; the most elegant comparisons and the most picturesque epithets; the closest style and the most ornate. Except truth, nothing is wanting. Eloisa is worse than a singer, she is an author: we look at the back of her epistle to Abelard to see if she has not written on it "For Press."

Pope has somewhere given a receipt for making an epic poem: take a storm, a dream, five or six battles, three sacrifices, funeral games, a dozen gods in two divisions; shake together until there rises the froth of a lofty style. We have just seen the receipt for making a love-letter. This kind of poetry resembles cookery; neither heart nor genius is necessary to produce it, but a light hand, an attentive eye, and a cultivated taste.

BOOK III.— THE CLASSIC AGE (CONTINUED)

It seems that this kind of talent is made for light verses. It is factitious, and so are the manners of society. To make pretty speeches, to prattle with ladies, to speak elegantly of their chocolate or their fan, to jeer at fools, to criticise the last tragedy, to be good at insipid compliments or epigrams— this, it seems, is the natural employment of a mind such as this, but slightly impassioned, very vain, a perfect master of style, as careful of his verses as a dandy of his coat. Pope wrote the "Rape of the Lock" and the "Dunciad"; his contemporaries went into ecstasies about the charm of his badinage and the precision of his raillery, and believed that he had surpassed Boileau's "Lutrin" and "Satires."

That may well be; at all events the praise would be scanty. In Boileau there are, as a rule, two kinds of verse, as was said by a man of wit;[22] most of which seem to be those of a sharp schoolboy in the third class, the rest those of a good schoolboy in the upper division. Boileau wrote the second verse before the first: this is why once out of four times his first verse only serves to stop a gap. Doubtless Pope had a more brilliant and adroit mechanism; but this faculty of hand does not suffice to make a poet, even a poet of the boudoir. There, as elsewhere, we need genuine passion, or at least genuine taste. When we wish to paint the pretty nothings of conversation and the world, we must at least like them. We can only paint well what we love.[23] Is there no charming grace in the prattle and frivolity of a pretty woman? Painters, like Watteau, have spent their lives in feasting on them. A lock of hair raised by the wind, a pretty arm peeping from underneath a great deal of lace, a stooping figure making the bright folds of a petticoat sparkle, and the arch half-engaging, half-mocking smile of the pouting mouth— these are enough to transport an artist. Certainly he will be aware of the influence of the toilet, as much so as the lady herself, and will never scold her for passing three hours at her glass; there is poetry in elegance. He enjoys it as a picture; delights in the refinements of worldly life, the grand quiet lines of the lofty, wainscoted drawing-room, the soft reflection of the high mirrors and glittering porcelain, the careless gayety of the little sculptured Loves, locked in embrace above the mantelpiece, the silvery sound of these soft voices, buzzing scandal round the tea-table. Pope hardly if at all rejoices in them; he is satirical and English amidst this amiable luxury, introduced from France. Although he is the most worldly of English poets, he is not enough so: nor is the society around him. Lady Mary Wortley Montague, who was in her time "the pink of fashion" and who is compared to Mme de Sévigné, has such a serious mind, such a decided style, such a precise judgment, and such a harsh sarcasm, that we would take her for a man. In reality the English, even Lord Chesterfield and Horace Walpole, never mastered the true tone of the *salon*. Pope is like them; his voice is out of tune, and then suddenly becomes biting. Every instant a harsh mockery blots out the graceful images which he began to awaken. Consider "The Rape of the Lock" as a whole; it is a buffoonery in a noble style. Lord

Petre had cut off a lock of hair of a fashionable beauty, Mrs. Arabella Fermor; out of this trifle the problem is to make an epic, with invocations, apostrophes, the interventions of supernatural beings, and the rest of poetic mechanism; the solemnity of style contrasts with the littleness of the events; we laugh at these bickerings as at insects quarrelling.

Such has always been the case in England; whenever Englishmen wish to represent social life, it is with a superficial and assumed politeness; at the bottom of their admiration there is scorn. Their insipid compliments conceal a mental reservation; let us observe them well, and we will see that they look upon a pretty, well-dressed, and coquettish woman as a pink doll, fit to amuse people for half an hour by her outward show. Pope dedicates his poem to Mrs. Arabella Fermor with every kind of compliment. The truth is, he is not polite; a Frenchwoman would have sent him back his book, and advised him to learn manners; for one commendation of her beauty she would find ten sarcasms upon her frivolity. Is it very pleasant to have it said: "You have the prettiest eyes in the world, but you live in the pursuit of trifles"? Yet to this all his homage is reduced.[24] His complimentary emphasis, his declaration that the "ravish'd hair... adds new glory to the shining sphere,"[25] all his stock of phrases is but a parade of gallantry which betrays indelicacy and coarseness. Will she

> "Stain her honor, or her new brocade,
> Forget her pray'rs or miss a masquerade,
> Or lose her heart, or necklace at a ball?"[26]

No Frenchman of the eighteenth century would have imagined such a compliment. At most, that bearish Rousseau, that former lackey and Geneva moralist, might have delivered this disagreeable thrust. In England it was not found too rude. Mrs. Arabella Fermor was so pleased with the poem that she gave away copies of it. Clearly she was not hard to please, for she had heard much worse compliments. If we read in Swift the literal transcript of a fashionable conversation, we shall see that a woman of fashion of that time could endure much before she was angry.

But the strangest thing is, that this trifling is, for Frenchmen, at least, no badinage at all. It is not at all like lightness or gayety. Dorat, Gresset, would have been stupefied and shocked by it. We remain cold under its most brilliant hits. Now and then at most a crack of the whip arouses us, but not to laughter. These caricatures seem strange to us, but do not amuse. The wit is no wit: all is calculated, combined, artificially prepared; we expect flashes of lightning, but at the last moment they do not descend. Thus Lord Petre, to "implore propitious heaven, and every power,"

BOOK III.– THE CLASSIC AGE (CONTINUED)

> "To Love an altar built
> Of twelve vast French romances, neatly gilt.
> There lay three garters, half a pair of gloves,
> And all the trophies of his former loves;
> With tender billets-doux he lights the pyre,
> And breathes three am'rous sighs to raise the fire."[27]

We remain disappointed, not seeing the comicality of the description. We go on conscientiously, and in the picture of Melancholy and her palace find figures much stranger:

> "Here sighs a jar, and there a goose-pye talks;
> Men proved with child, as pow'rful fancy works,
> And maids turned bottles, call aloud for corks."[28]

We say to ourselves now that we are in China: that so far from Paris and Voltaire we must be surprised at nothing, that these folk have ears different from ours, and that a Pekin mandarin vastly relishes kettle-music. Finally, we comprehend that, even in this correct age and this artificial poetry, the old style of imagination exists; that it is nourished as before, by oddities and contrasts; and that taste, in spite of all culture, will never become acclimatized; that incongruities, far from shocking, delight it; that it is insensible to French sweetness and refinements; that it needs a succession of expressive figures, unexpected and grinning, to pass before it; that it prefers this coarse carnival to delicate insinuations; that Pope belongs to his country, in spite of his classical polish and his studied elegances, and that his unpleasant and vigorous fancy is akin to that of Swift.

We are now prepared and can enter upon his second poem, "The Dunciad." We need much self-command not to throw down this masterpiece as insipid, and even disgusting. Rarely has so much talent been spent to produce greater tedium. Pope wished to be avenged on his literary enemies, and sang of Dulness, the sublime goddess of literature, "daughter of Chaos and eternal Night,... gross as her sire, and as her mother grave,"[29] queen of hungry authors, who chooses for her son and favorite, first Theobald and afterwards Cibber. There he is, a king, and to celebrate his accession she institutes public games in imitation of the ancients; first a race of booksellers, trying to seize a poet; then the struggle of the authors, who first vie with each other in braying, and then dash into the Fleet-ditch filth; then the strife of critics, who have to undergo the reading of two voluminous authors, without falling asleep.[30] Strange parodies, to be sure, and, in truth, not very striking. Who is not deafened by these hackneyed and bald allegories, Dulness, poppies, mists, and Sleep? What if I entered into details, and described the poetess offered for a prize, "with cow-like udders, and with ox-like eyes"; if I related the plunges of the authors, the floundering in the Fleet-ditch, the vilest sewer in the town; if I transcribed all the extraordinary verses in which

> "First he relates, how sinking to the chin,
> Smit with his mien, the mud-nymphs suck'd him in:
> How young Lutetia, softer than the down,
> Nigrina black, and Merdamante brown,
> Vied for his love in jetty bow'rs below."...[31]

I must stop. Swift alone might have seemed capable of writing some passages, for instance, that on the fall of Curll. We might have excused it in Swift; the extremity of despair, the rage of misanthropy, the approach of madness, might have carried him to such excess. But Pope, who lived calm and admired in his villa, and who was only urged by literary rancor! He can have had no nerves! How could a poet have dragged his talent wantonly through such images, and so constrained his ingeniously woven verses to receive such dirt? Picture a pretty drawing-room basket, destined only to contain flowers and fancy work sent down to the kitchen to be turned into a receptacle for filth. In fact, all the filth of literary life is here; and heaven knows what it then was! In no age were hack-writers so beggarly and so vile. Poor fellows, like Richard Savage, who slept during one winter in the open air on the cinders of a glass manufactory, lived on what he received for a dedication, knew the inside of a prison, rarely dined, and drank at the expense of his friends; pamphleteers, like Tutchin, who was soundly whipped; plagiarists, like Ward, exposed in the pillory and pelted with rotten eggs and apples; courtesans, like Eliza Heywood, notorious by the shamelessness of their public confessions; bought journalists, hired slanderers, venders of scandal and insults, half rogues, complete roisterers, and all the literary vermin which haunted the gambling-houses, the stews, the gin-cellars, and at a signal from a bookseller, stung honest folk for a crownpiece. These villanies, this foul linen, the greasy coat six years old, the musty pudding, and the rest, are to be found in Pope as in Hogarth, with English coarseness and precision. This is their error, they are realists, even under the classical wig; they do not disguise what is ugly and mean; they describe that ugliness and meanness with their exact outlines and distinguishing marks; they do not clothe them in a fine cloak of general ideas; they do not cover them with the pretty innuendoes of society. This is the reason why their satires are so harsh. Pope does not flog the dunces, he knocks them down; his poem is hard and malicious; it is so much so that it becomes clumsy; to add to the punishment of dunces, he begins at the deluge, writes historical passages, represents at length the past, present, and future empire of Dullness, the library of Alexandria burned by Omar, learning extinguished by the invasion of the barbarians and by the

BOOK III.– THE CLASSIC AGE (CONTINUED)

superstition of the Middle Ages, the empire of stupidity which extends over England and will swallow it up. What paving-stones to crush flies!

> "See skulking Truth to her old cavern fled,
> Mountains of casuistry heap'd o'er her head!
> Philosophy, that leaned on Heav'n before,
> Shrinks to her second cause, and is no more.
> Physic of Metaphysic begs defence,
> And Metaphysic calls for aid on sense!...
> Religion blushing veils her sacred fires,
> And unawares Morality expires.
> Nor public flame, nor private, dares to shine,
> Nor human spark is left, nor glimpse divine!
> Lo! thy dread empire, Chaos! is restored;
> Light dies before thy uncreating word:
> Thy hand, great anarch! lets the curtain fall;
> And universal darkness buries all."[32]

The last scene ends with noise, cymbals and trombones, crackers and fireworks. As for me, I carry away from this celebrated entertainment only the remembrance of a hubbub. Unwittingly I have counted the lights, I know the machinery, I have touched the toilsome stage property of apparitions and allegories. I bid farewell to the scene-painter, the machinist, the manager of literary effects, and go elsewhere to find the poet.

Section IV.—Pope's Descriptive Talent.—His Didactic Poems

However, a poet exists in Pope, and to discover him we have only to read him by fragments; if the whole is, as a rule, wearisome or shocking, the details are admirable. It is so at the close of every literary age. Pliny the younger, and Seneca, so affected and so stiff, are charming in small bits; each of their phrases, taken by itself, is a masterpiece; each verse in Pope is a masterpiece when taken alone. At this time, and after a hundred years of culture, there is no movement, no object, no action, which poets cannot describe. Every aspect of nature was observed; a sunrise, a landscape reflected in the water,[33] a breeze amid the foliage, and so forth. Ask Pope to paint in verse an eel, a perch, or a trout, he has the exact phrase ready; we might glean from him the contents of a "Gradus." He gives the features so exactly, that at once we think we see the thing; he gives the expression so copiously, that our imagination, however obtuse, will end by seeing it. He marks everything in the flight of a pheasant:

> "See! from the brake the whirring pheasant springs
> And mounts exulting on triumphant wings....

> Ah! what avail his glossy, varying dyes,
> His purple crest, and scarlet-circled eyes,
> The vivid green his shining plumes unfold,
> His painted wings, and breast that flames with gold?"[34]

He possesses the richest store of words to depict the sylphs which flutter round his heroine, Belinda:

> "But now secure the painted vessel glides,
> The sunbeams trembling on the floating tides:
> While melting music steals upon the sky,
> And softened sounds along the waters die;
> Smooth flow the waves, the zephyrs gently play,
> The lucid squadrons round the sails repair:
> Soft o'er the shrouds the aerial whispers breathe,
> That seemed but zephyrs to the train beneath.
> Some to the sun their insect-wings unfold,
> Waft on the breeze, or sink in clouds of gold;
> Transparent forms, too fine for mortal sight,
> Their fluid bodies half dissolved in light.
> Loose to the wind their airy garment flew,
> Thin glitt'ring textures of the filmy dew,
> Dipped in the richest tincture of the skies,
> Where light disports in ever-mingling dyes;
> While ev'ry beam new transient colors flings,
> Colors that change whene'er they wave their wings."[35]

Doubtless these are not Shakespeare's sylphs; but side by side with a natural and living rose, we may still look with pleasure on a flower of diamonds, as they come from the hand of the jeweller, a masterpiece of art and patience, whose facets make the light glitter, and cast a shower of sparkles over the filagree foliage in which they are embedded. A score of times in a poem of Pope's we stop to look with wonder on some of these literary adornments. He feels so well in what the strong point of his talent lies, that he abuses it; he delights to show his skill. What can be staler than a card party, or more repellent to poetry than the queen of spades or the king of hearts? Yet, doubtless for a wager, he has recorded in the "Rape of the Lock" a game of ombre; we follow it, hear it, recognize the dresses:

> "Behold four kings in majesty revered,
> With hoary whiskers and a forky beard;
> And four fair queens whose hands sustain a flower,
> Th' expressive emblem of their softer power;

> Four knaves in garb succinct, a trusty band;
> Caps on their heads and halberts in their hand;
> And parti-coloured troops, a shining train,
> Drawn forth to combat on the velvet plain."[36]

We see the trumps, the cuts, the tricks, and instantly afterwards the coffee, the china, the spoons, the fiery spirits (to wit, spirits of wine); we have here in advance the modes and periphrases of Delille. The celebrated verses in which Delille at once employs and describes imitative harmony are translated from Pope.[37] It is an expiring poetry, but poetry still: an ornament to put on a mantelpiece is an inferior work of art, but still it is a work of art. To descriptive talent Pope unites oratorical talent. This art, proper to the classical age, is the art of expressing ordinary general ideas. For a hundred and fifty years men of both the thinking countries, England and France, employed herein all their study. They seized those universal and limited truths, which, being situated between lofty philosophical abstractions and petty sensible details, are the subject-matter of eloquence and rhetoric, and form what we nowadays call commonplaces. They arranged them in compartments; methodically developed them; made them obvious by grouping and symmetry; disposed them in regular processions, which with dignity and majesty advanced well disciplined, and in a body. The influence of this oratorical reason became so great that it was imposed on poetry itself. Buffon ends by saying, in praise of certain verses, that they are as fine as fine prose. In fact, poetry at this time became a more affected prose subjected to rhyme. It was only a higher kind of conversation and more select discourse. It is powerless when it is necessary to paint or represent an action, when the need is to see and make visible living passions, large genuine emotions, men of flesh and blood; it results only in college epics like the "Henriade," freezing odes and tragedies like those of Voltaire and Jean-Baptiste Rousseau, or those of Addison, Thomson, Dr. Johnson, and the rest. It makes them up of dissertations, because it is capable of nothing else but dissertations. Here henceforth is its domain; and its final task is the didactic poem, which is a dissertation in verse. Pope excelled in it, and his most perfect poems are those made up of precepts and arguments. Artifice in these is less shocking than elsewhere. A poem— I am wrong, essays like his upon "Criticism," on "Man" and the "Government of Providence," on the "Knowledge and Characters of Men," deserve to be written after reflection; they are a study, and almost a scientific monograph. We may, we even ought, to weigh all the words, and verify all the connections: art and attention are not superfluous, but necessary; the question concerns exact precepts and close arguments. In this Pope is incomparable. I do not think that there is in the world a versified prose like his; that of Boileau is not to be compared to it. Not that its ideas are very worthy of attention; we have worn them out, they interest us no longer. "The

Essay on Criticism" resembles Boileau's "Epitres" and "L'Art Poétique," excellent works, no longer read but in classes at school. It is a collection of very wise precepts, whose only fault is their being too true. To say that good taste is rare; that we ought to reflect and learn before deciding; that the rules of art are drawn from nature; that pride, ignorance, prejudice, partiality, envy, pervert our judgment; that a critic should be sincere, modest, polished, kindly— all these truths might then be discoveries, but they are so no longer. I suppose that in the time of Pope, Dryden, and Boileau, men had special need of setting their ideas in order, and of seeing them very distinctly in very clear phrases. Now that this need is satisfied, it has disappeared: we demand ideas, not arrangement of ideas; the pigeon-holes are manufactured, fill them. Pope was obliged to do it once in the "Essay on Man," which is a sort of "Vicaire Savoyard,"[38] less original than the other. He shows that God made all for the best, that man is limited in his capacity and ought not to judge God, that our passions and imperfections serve for the general good and for the ends of Providence, that happiness lies in virtue and submission to the divine will. We recognize here a sort of deism and optimism, of which there was much at that time, borrowed, like those of Rousseau, from the "Théodicée" of Leibnitz,[39] but tempered, toned down, and arranged for the use of respectable people. The conception is not very lofty: this curtailed deity making his appearance at the beginning of the eighteenth century, is but a residuum: religion having disappeared, he remained at the bottom of the crucible; and the reasoners of the time, having no metaphysical inventiveness, kept him in their system to stop a gap. In this state and at this place this deity resembles classic verse. He has an imposing appearance, is comprehended easily, is stripped of power, is the product of cold argumentative reason, and leaves the people who attend to him very much at ease; on all these accounts he is akin to an Alexandrine. This poor conception is all the more wretched in Pope because it does not belong to him, for he is only accidentally a philosopher; and to find matter for his poem, three or four systems, deformed and attenuated, are amalgamated in his work. He boasts of having tempered them one with the other, and having "steered between the extremes."[40] The truth is, that he did not understand them, and that he jumbles incongruous ideas at every step. There is a passage in which, to obtain an effect of style, he becomes a pantheist; moreover he is bombastic, and assumes the supercilious, imperious tone of a young doctor of theology. I find no individual invention except in his "Moral Essays"; in them is a theory of dominant passion which is worth reading. After all he went farther than Boileau, for instance, in the knowledge of man. Psychology is indigenous in England; we meet it there throughout, even in the least creative minds. It gives rise to the novel, dispossesses philosophy, produces the essay, appears in the newspapers, fills current literature, like those indigenous plants which multiply on every soil.

BOOK III.– THE CLASSIC AGE (CONTINUED)

But if the ideas are mediocre, the art of expressing them is truly marvellous: marvellous is the word. "I chose verse," says Pope in his "Design of an Essay on Man, because I found I could express them (ideas) more shortly this way than in prose itself." In fact, every word is effective: every passage must be read slowly; every epithet is an epitome; a more condensed style was never written; and, on the other hand, no one labored more skilfully in introducing philosophical formulas into the current conversation of society. His maxims have become proverbs. I open his "Essay on Man" at random, and fall upon the beginning of his second book. An orator, an author of the school of Buffon, would be transported with admiration to see so many literary treasures collected in so small a space:

> "Know then thyself, presume not God to scan,
> The proper study of mankind is man.
> Placed on this isthmus of a middle state,
> A being darkly wise, and rudely great:
> With too much knowledge for the sceptic side,
> With too much weakness for the stoic's pride;
> He hangs between; in doubt to act, or rest;
> In doubt to deem himself a God or beast;
> In doubt his mind or body to prefer;
> Born but to die, and reas'ning but to err;
> Alike in ignorance, his reason such,
> Whether he thinks too little or too much;
> Chaos of thought and passion, all confused;
> Still by himself abused or disabused;
> Created half to rise, and half to fall;
> Great lord of all things, yet a prey to all;
> Sole judge of truth in endless error hurled,
> The glory, jest, and riddle of the world."[41]

The first verse epitomizes the whole of the preceding Epistle, and the second epitomizes the present Epistle, it is, as it were, a kind of staircase leading from one temple to another, regularly composed of symmetrical steps, so aptly disposed that from the first step we see at a glance the whole building we have left, and from the second the whole edifice we are about to visit. Have we ever seen a finer entrance, or one more conformable to the rules which bid us unite our ideas, recall them when developed, pre-announce them when not yet developed? But this is not enough. After this brief announcement, which premises that he is about to treat of human nature, a longer announcement is necessary, to paint beforehand, with the greatest possible splendor, this human nature of which he is about to treat. This is the proper oratorical exordium, like those which Bossuet places at the beginning of his funeral orations; a sort of elaborate portico to receive the audience on their entrance, and prepare them for the magnificence of the temple. The antitheses follow each other in couples like a succession of columns; thirteen couples form a suite; and the last is raised above the rest by a word, which concentrates and combines all. In other hands this prolongation of the same form would become tedious; in Pope's it interests us, so much variety is there in the arrangement, and the adornments. In one place the antithesis is comprised in a single line, in another it occupies two; now it is in the substantives, now in the adjectives and verbs; now only in the ideas, now it penetrates the sound and position of the words. In vain we see it reappear; we are not wearied, because each time it adds somewhat to our idea, and shows us the object in a new light. This object itself may be abstract, obscure, unpleasant, opposed to poetry; the style spreads over it its own light; noble images borrowed from the grand and simple spectacles of nature illustrate and adorn it. For there is a classical architecture of ideas as well as of stones: the first, like the second, is a friend to clearness and regularity, majesty and calm; like the second, it was invented in Greece, transmitted through Rome to France, through France to England, and slightly altered in its passage. Of all the masters who have practised it in England, Pope is the most skilled.

After all, is there anything in the lines just quoted but decoration? Translate them literally into prose, and of all those beauties there remains not one. If the reader dissects Pope's arguments, he will hardly be moved by them; he would instinctively think of Pascal's "Pensées," and remark upon the astonishing difference between a versifier and a man. A good epitome, a good bit of style, well worked out, well written, he would say, and nothing further. Clearly the beauty of the verses arose from the difficulty overcome, the well-chosen sounds, the symmetrical rhythms; this was all, and it was not much. A great writer is a man who, having passions, knows his dictionary and his grammar; Pope thoroughly knew his dictionary and his grammar, but stopped there.

People will say that this merit is small, and that I do not inspire them with a desire to read Pope's verses. True; at least I do not counsel them to read many. I would add, however, by way of excuse, that there is a kind in which he succeeds, that his descriptive and oratorical talents find in portraiture matter which suits them, and that in this he frequently approaches La Bruyère; that several of his portraits, those of Addison, Lord Hervey, Lord Wharton, the Duchess of Marlborough, are medals worthy of finding a place in the cabinets of the curious, and of remaining in the archives of the human race; that when he chisels one of these heads, the comprehensive images, the unlooked-for connections of words, the sustained and multiplied contrasts, the perpetual and extraordinary conciseness, the incessant and increasing impulse of all the strokes of eloquence brought to bear upon the same spot, stamp upon the memory an impress which we never forget. It is better to repudiate these partial apologies, and frankly to avow that, on the whole, this great poet, the glory of his age, is wearisome— wearisome to us. "A woman of forty," says Stendhal, "is only beautiful to those who have loved her in their youth." The poor muse in question is not forty years old for us; she is a hundred and forty. Let us remember, when we wish to judge her fairly, the time when we made French verses like our Latin verse. Taste became transformed an age ago, for the human mind has wheeled round; with the prospect the perspective has changed; we must take this change of place into account. Nowadays we demand new ideas and bare sentiments; we care no longer for the clothing, we want the thing. Exordiums, transitions, peculiarities of style, elegances of expression, the whole literary wardrobe, is sent to the old-clothes shop; we only keep what is indispensable; we trouble ourselves no more about adornment, but about truth. The men of the preceding century were quite different. This was seen when Pope translated the Iliad; it was the Iliad written in the style of the "Henriade": by virtue of this travesty the public admired it. They would not have admired it in the simple Greek guise; they only consented to see it in powder and ribbons. It was the costume of the time, and it was very necessary to put it on. Dr. Johnson, in his commercial and academical style, affirms even that the demand for elegance had increased so much, that pure nature could no longer be borne.

Good society and men of letters made a little world by themselves, which had been formed and refined after the manner and ideas of France. They adopted a correct and noble style at the same time as fashion and fine manners. They held by this style as by their coat; it was a matter of propriety or ceremony; there was an accepted and unalterable pattern; they could not change it without indecency or ridicule; to write, not according to the rules, especially in verse, effusively and naturally, would have been like showing one's self in the drawing-room in slippers and a dressing-gown. Their pleasure in reading verse was to try whether the pattern had been exactly followed, originality was only permitted in details; a man might adjust here a lace, there some embroidered stripe, but he was bound scrupulously to preserve the conventional form, to brush everything minutely, and never to appear without new gold lace and glossy broadcloth. The attention was only bestowed on refinements; a more elaborate braid, a more brilliant velvet, a feather more gracefully arranged; to this were boldness and experiment reduced; the smallest incorrectness, the slightest incongruity, would have offended their eyes; they perfected the infinitely little. Men of letters acted like these coquettes, for whom the superb goddesses of Michael Angelo and Rubens are but milk-maids, but who utter a cry of pleasure at the sight of a ribbon at twenty francs a yard. A division, a displacing of verses, a metaphor delighted them, and this was all which could still charm them. They went on day by day embroidering, bedizening, narrowing the bright classic robe, until at last the human mind, feeling fettered, tore it, cast it away, and began to move. Now that this robe is on the ground the critics pick it up, hang it up in their museum of ancient curiosities, so that everybody can see it, shake it, and try to conjecture from it the feelings of the fine lords and of the fine speakers who wore it.

Section V.—The Poets Prior, Gay and Thomson

It is not everything to have a beautiful dress, strongly sewn and fashionable; a man must be able to get into it easily. Reviewing the whole train of the English poets of the eighteenth century, we perceive that they do not easily get into the classical dress. This gold-embroidered jacket, which fits a Frenchman so well, hardly suits their figure; from time to time a too powerful, awkward movement makes rents in the sleeves and elsewhere. For instance, Matthew Prior seems at first sight to have all the qualities necessary to wear the jacket well; he has been an ambassador to the French court, and writes pretty French impromptus; he turns off with facility little jesting poems on a dinner, a lady; he is gallant, a man of society, a pleasant storyteller, epicurean, even sceptical like the courtiers of Charles II, that is to say, as far as and including political roguery; in short, he is an accomplished man of the world, as times went, with a correct and flowing style, having at command a light and a noble verse, and pulling, according to the rules of Bossu and Boileau, the string of mythological puppets. With all this, we find him neither gay enough nor refined enough. Bolingbroke called him wooden-faced, stubborn, and said there was something Dutch in him. His manners smacked very strongly of those of Rochester, and the well-clad scamps whom the Restoration bequeathed to the Revolution. He took the first woman at hand, shut himself up with her for several days, drank hard, fell asleep, and let her make off with his money and clothes. Amongst other drabs, ugly enough and always dirty, he finished by keeping Elizabeth Cox, and all but married her; fortunately he died just in time. His style was like his manners. When he tried to imitate La Fontaine's "Hans Carvel," he made it dull, and lengthened it; he could not be piquant, but he was biting; his obscenities have a cynical harshness; his raillery is a satire; and in one of his poems, "To a Young Gentleman in Love," the lash becomes knock-down blow. On the other hand, he was not a common roisterer. Of his two principal poems, one on "Solomon" paraphrases and treats of the remark of Ecclesiastes, "All is vanity." From this picture we see forthwith that we are in a Biblical land: such an idea would not then have occurred to a boon companion of the Duke of Orleans, Regent of France. Solomon relates how he in vain "proposed his doubts to the lettered Rabbins," how he has been equally unfortunate in the hopes and desires of love, the possession of power, and ends by trusting to an "omniscient Master, omnipresent King." Here we have English gloom and English conclusions.[42] Moreover, under the rhetorical and uniform composition of his verses, we perceive warmth and passion, rich painting, a sort of magnificence, and the profusion of an overcharged imagination. The sap in England is always stronger than in France; the sensations there are deeper, and the thoughts more original. Prior's other poem, very bold and philosophical, against conventional truths and pedantries, is a droll discourse on the seat of the soul, from which Voltaire has taken many ideas and much foulness. The whole armory of the sceptic and materialist was built and furnished in England, when the French took to it. Voltaire has only selected and sharpened the arrows. This poem is also wholly written in a prosaic style, with a harsh common-sense and a medical frankness, not to be terrified by the foulest abominations.[43] "Candide" and the "Earl of Chesterfield's Ears," by Voltaire, are more brilliant but not more genuine productions. On the whole, with his coarseness, want of taste, prolixity, perspicacity, passion, there is something in this man not in accordance with classical elegance. He goes beyond it or does not attain it.

This dissonance increases, and attentive eyes soon discover under the regular cloak a kind of energetic and precise imagination, ready to break through it. In this age lived Gay, a sort of La Fontaine, as near La Fontaine as an Englishman can be, that is, not very near, but at least a kind and amiable good fellow, very sincere, very frank, strangely thoughtless, born to be duped, and a young man to the last. Swift said of him that he ought never to have lived more than twenty-two years. "In wit a man, simplicity a child," wrote Pope. He lived, like La Fontaine, at the expense of the great, travelled as much as he could at their charge, lost his money in South Sea speculations, tried to get a place at court, wrote fables full of humanity to form the heart of the Duke of Cumberland,[44] and ended as a beloved parasite and the domestic poet of the Duke and Duchess of Queensberry. He had little of the grave in his character, and neither many scruples nor manners. It was his sad lot, he said, "that he could get nothing from the court, whether he wrote for or against it." And he wrote his own epitaph:

"Life is a jest; and all things show it,
I thought so once; but now I know it."[45]

This laughing, careless poet, to revenge himself on the minister, wrote the "Beggars' Opera," the fiercest and dirtiest of caricatures. In this Opera they cut the throat of men in place of scratching them; babes handle the knife like the rest. Yet Gay was a laugher, but in a style of his own, or rather in that of his country. Seeing "certain young men of insipid delicacy,"[46] Ambrose Philips, for instance, who wrote elegant and tender pastorals, in the manner of Fontenelle, he amused himself by parodying and contradicting them, and in the "Shepherd's Week" introduced real rural manners into the metre and form of the visionary poetry; "Thou wilt not find my shepherdesses idly piping on oaten reeds, but milking the kine, tying up the sheaves, or if the hogs are astray, driving them to their styes. My shepherd... sleepeth not under myrtle shades, but under a hedge, nor doth he vigilantly defend his flocks from wolves, because there are none."[47] Fancy a shepherd of Theocritus or Vergil, compelled to put on hobnailed shoes and the dress of a Devonshire cowherd; such an oddity would amuse us by the contrast of His person and his garments. So here "The Magician, The Shepherd's Struggle," are travestied in a modern guise. Listen to the song of the first shepherd, "Lobbin Clout":

> "Leek to the Welch, to Dutchmen butter's dear,
> Of Irish swains potatoe is the chear;
> Oat for their feast, the Scotish shepherds grind,
> Swetet turnips are the food of Blouzelind.
> While she loves turnips, butter I'll despise,
> Nor leeks, nor oatmeal, nor potatoe prize."[48]

The other shepherd answers in the same metre; and the two continue verse after verse, in the ancient manner, but now amidst turnips, strong beer, fat pigs, bespattered at will by modern country vulgarities and the dirt of a northern climate. Van Ostade and Tenies love these vulgar and clownish idyls; and in Gay, as well as with them, unvarnished and sensual drollery has its sway. The people of the north, who are great eaters, always liked country fairs. The vagaries of toss-pots and gossips, the grotesque outburst of the vulgar and animal mind, put them into good humor. A man must be a genuine man of the world or an artist, a Frenchman or an Italian, to be disgusted with them. They are the product of the country, as well as meat and beer; let us try, in order that we may enjoy them, to forget wine, delicate fruits, to give ourselves blunted senses, to become in imagination compatriots of such men. We have become used to the pictures of these drunken boobies, whom Louis XIV called "baboons," to these red-faced cooks who clean fish, and to the like scenes. Let us get used to Gay; to his poem, "Trivia, or the Art of Walking the Streets of London"; to his advice as to dirty gutters, and shoes "with firm, well-hammer'd soles"; his description of the amours of the goddess Cloacina and a scavenger, whence sprang the little shoe-blacks. He is a lover of the real, has a precise imagination, does not see objects wholesale and from a general point of view, but singly, with all their outlines and surroundings, whatever they may be, beautiful or ugly, dirty or clean. The other literary men act likewise, even the chief classical writers, including Pope. There is in Pope a minute description, with high-colored words, local details, in which comprehensive and characteristic features are stamped with such a liberal and sure hand, that we would take the author for a modern realist, and would find in the work an historical document.[49] As to Swift, he is the bitterest positivist, and more so in poetry than in prose. Let us read his eclogue on "Strephon

BOOK III.— THE CLASSIC AGE (CONTINUED)

and Chloe," if we would know how far men can debase the noble poetic drapery. They make a dishclout out of it, or dress clodhoppers in it; the Roman toga and Greek chlamys do not suit these barbarians' shoulders. They are like those knights of the Middle Ages, who, when they had taken Constantinople, muffled themselves for a joke in long Byzantine robes, and went riding through the streets in these disguises, dragging their embroidery in the gutter.

These men will do well, like the knights, to return to their manor, to the country, the mud of their ditches, and the dunghill of their farm-yards. The less man is fitted for social life, the more he is fitted for solitary life. He enjoys the country the more for enjoying the world less. Englishmen have always been more feudal and more fond of the country than Frenchmen. Under Louis XIV and Louis XV the worst misfortune for a nobleman was to go to his estate in the country and grow rusty there; away from the smiles of the king and the fine conversation of Versailles, there was nothing left but to yawn and die. In England, in spite of artificial civilization and the charms of polite society, the love of the chase and of bodily exercise, political interests and the necessities of elections brought the nobles back to their estates. And there their natural instincts returned. A sad and impassioned man, naturally self-dependent, converses with objects; a grand gray sky, whereon the autumn mists slumber, a sudden burst of sunshine lighting up a moist field, depress or excite him; inanimate things seem to him instinct with life; and the faint light, which in the morning reddens the fringe of heaven, moves him as much as the smile of a young girl at her first ball. Thus is genuine descriptive poetry born. It appears in Dryden, in Pope himself, even in the writers of elegant pastorals, and shines in Thomson's "Seasons." This poet, the son of a clergyman, and very poor, lived, like most of the literary men of the time, on donations and literary subscriptions, on sinecures and political pensions; for lack of money he did not marry; wrote tragedies, because tragedies brought in plenty of money; and ended by settling in a country house, lying in bed till midday, indolent, contemplative, but a simple and honest man, affectionate and beloved. He saw and loved the country in its smallest details, not outwardly only, as Saint Lambert,[50] his imitator; he made it his joy, his amusement, his habitual occupation; a gardener at heart, delighted to see the spring arrive, happy to be able to add another field to his garden. He paints all the little things, without being ashamed, for they interest him, and takes pleasure in "the smell of the dairy." We hear him speak of the "insect armies," and "when the envenomed leaf begins to curl,"[51] and of the birds which, foreseeing the approaching rain, "streak their wings with oil, to throw the lucid moisture trickling off."[52] He perceives objects so clearly that he makes them visible: we recognize the English landscape, green and moist, half drowned in floating vapors, blotted here and there by violet clouds, which burst in showers at the horizon, which they darken, but where the light is delicately dimmed by the fog, and the clear heavens show at intervals very bright and pure:

> "Th' effusive South
> Warms the wide air, and o'er the void of heaven
> Breathes the big clouds with vernal showers distent.[53]...
> Thus all day long the full-distended clouds
> Indulge their genial stores, and well-showered earth
> Is deep enriched with vegetable life;
> Till in the western sky, the downward sun
> Looks out, effulgent, from amid the flush
> Of broken clouds, gay-shifting to his beam.
> The rapid radiance instantaneous strikes
> The illumined mountain; through the forest streams;
> Shakes on the floods; and in a yellow mist,
> Far smoking o'er the interminable plain,
> In twinkling myriads lights the dewy gems.
> Moist, bright, and green, the landscape laughs around."[54]

This is emphatic, but it is also opulent. In this air and this vegetation, in this imagination and this style, there is a heaping up, and, as it were, an impasto of effaced or sparkling tints; they are here the glistening and lustrous robe of nature and art. We must see them in Rubens— he is the painter and poet of the teeming and humid clime; but we discover it also in others; and in this magnificence of Thomson, in this exaggerated, luxuriant, grand coloring, we find occasionally the rich palette of Rubens.

Section VI.—The Beginnings of the Modern Age

All this suits ill the classical embroidery. Thomson's visible imitations of Vergil, his episodes inserted to fill up space, his invocations to spring, to the muse, to philosophy, all these pedantic relics and conventionalisms, produce incongruity. But the contrast is much more marked in another way. The worldly artificial life, such as Louis XIV had made fashionable, began to weary Europe. It was found meagre and hollow; people grew tired of always acting, submitting to etiquette. They felt that gallantry is not love, nor madrigals poetry, nor amusement happiness. They perceived that man is not an elegant doll, or a dandy the masterpiece of nature, and that there is a world beyond the drawing-room. A Genevese plebeian (J. J. Rousseau), a Protestant and a recluse, whom religion, education, poverty, and genius had led more quickly and further than others, spoke out the public secret aloud; and it was thought that he had discovered or rediscovered the country, conscience, religion, the rights of man, and natural sentiments. Then appeared a new personality, the idol and model of his time, the man of feeling who, by his grave character and liking for nature, contrasted with the man at court. Doubtless the man of feeling has not escaped the influence of the places he has frequented. He is refined and insipid, melting at the sight of the young lambs nibbling the newly grown grass, blessing the little birds, who give a concert to celebrate their happiness. He is emphatic and wordy, writes tirades about sentiment, inveighs against the age, apostrophizes virtue, reason, truth, and the abstract divinities, which are engraved in delicate outline on frontispieces. In spite of himself, he continues a man of the drawing-room and the academy; after uttering sweet things to the ladies, he utters them to nature, and declaims in polished periods about the Deity. But after all, it is through him that the revolt against classical customs begins; and in this respect, he is more advanced in Germanic England than in Latin France. Thirty years before Rousseau, Thompson had expressed all Rousseau's sentiments, almost in the same style. Like him, he painted the country with sympathy and enthusiasm. Like him, he contrasted the golden age of primitive simplicity with modern miseries and corruption. Like him, he exalted deep love, conjugal tenderness, the union of souls and perfect esteem animated by desire, paternal affection, and all domestic joys. Like him, he combated temporary frivolity, and compared the ancient republics with modern States:

"Proofs of a people, whose heroic aims
Soared far above the little selfish sphere
Of doubting modern life."[55]

Like Rousseau, he praised gravity, patriotism, liberty, virtue; rose from the spectacle of nature to the contemplation of God, and showed to man glimpses of immortal life beyond the tomb. Like him, in short, he marred the sincerity of his emotion and the truth of his poetry by sentimental vapidities, by pastoral billing and cooing, and by such an abundance of epithets, personified abstractions, pompous invocations and oratorical tirades, that we perceive in him beforehand the false and ornamental style of Thomas,[56] David,[57] and the first French Revolution.

Other authors follow in the same track. The literature of that period might be called the library of the man of feeling. First there was Richardson, the puritanic printer, with his Sir Charles Grandison, a man of principles, an accomplished model of a gentleman, a professor of decorum and morality, with a soul into the bargain. There is Sterne too, a refined and sickly blackguard, who, amidst his buffooneries and oddities, pauses to weep over an ass or an imaginary prisoner. There is, in particular, Henry Mackenzie, "the Man of Feeling," whose timid, delicate hero weeps five or six times a day; who grows consumptive through sensibility, dares not broach his love till at the point of death, and dies in broaching it. Naturally, praise induces satire; and in the opposite camp we see Fielding, a valiant roisterer, and Sheridan, a brilliant but naughty fellow, the one with Blifil, the other with Joseph Surface, two hypocrites, especially the second, not coarse, red-faced, and smelling of the vestry, like Tartuffe, but worldly, well-clad, a fine talker, loftily serious, sad and gentle from excess of tenderness, who, with his hand on his heart and a tear in his eye, showers on the public his sentences and periods whilst he soils his brother's reputation and debauches his neighbor's wife. When a man of feeling has been thus created, he soon has an epic made for him. A Scotsman, a man of wit, of too much wit, having published on his own account an unsuccessful rhapsody, wished to recover his expenses, visited the mountains of his country, gathered picturesque images, collected fragments of legends, plastered over the whole an abundance of eloquence and rhetoric, and created a Celtic Homer, Ossian, who with Oscar, Malvina, and his whole troop, made the tour of Europe, and, about 1830, ended by furnishing baptismal names for French *grisettes* and *perruquiers.* Macpherson displayed to the world an imitation of primitive manners, not over-true, for the extreme rudeness of barbarians would have shocked the people, but yet well enough preserved or portrayed to contrast with modern civilization, and persuade the public that they were looking upon pure nature. A keen sympathy with Scottish landscape, so grand, so cold, so gloomy, rain on the hills, the birch trembling to the wind, the mist of heaven and the vague musing of the soul, so that every dreamer found there the emotions of his solitary walks and his philosophic sadness; chivalric exploits and magnanimity, heroes who set out alone to engage an army, faithful virgins dying on the tomb of their betrothed; an impassioned, colored style, affecting to be abrupt, yet polished; able to charm a disciple of Rousseau by its warmth and elegance: here was something to transport the young enthusiasts of the time; civilized barbarians, scholarly lovers of nature, dreaming of the delights of savage life, whilst they shook off the powder which the hairdresser had left on their coats.

Yet this is not the course of the main current of poetry; it runs in the direction of sentimental reflection; the greatest number of poems, and those most sought after, are emotional dissertations. In fact, a man of feeling breaks out in excessive declamations. When he sees a cloud, he dreams of human nature and constructs a phrase. Hence at this time among poets, swarm the melting philosophers and the tearful academicians; Gray, the morose hermit of Cambridge, and Akenside, a noble thinker, both learned imitators of lofty Greek poetry; Beattie, a metaphysical moralist, with a young girl's nerves and an old maid's hobbies; the amiable and affectionate Goldsmith, who wrote the "Vicar of Wakefield," the most charming of Protestant pastorals; poor Collins, a young enthusiast, who was disgusted with life, would read nothing but the Bible, went mad, was shut up in an asylum, and in his intervals of liberty wandered in Chichester cathedral, accompanying the music with sobs and groans; Glover, Watts, Shenstone, Smart, and others. The titles of their works sufficiently indicate their character. One writes a poem on "The

Pleasures of Imagination," another odes on the "Passions" and on "Liberty"; one an "Elegy Written in a Country Churchyard" and a "Hymn to Adversity," another a poem on a "Deserted Village," and on the character of surrounding civilizations (Goldsmith's "Traveller"); one a sort of epic on "Thermopylæ," and the other the moral history of a young minstrel. They were nearly all grave, spiritual men, impassioned for noble ideas, with Christian aspirations or convictions, given to meditating on man, inclined to melancholy, to description, invocation, lovers of abstraction and allegory, who, to attain greatness, willingly mounted on stilts. One of the least strict and most noted of them was Young, the author of "Night Thoughts," a clergyman and a courtier, who, having vainly attempted to enter Parliament, then to become a bishop, married, lost his wife and children, and made use of his misfortunes to write meditations on "Life, Death, Immortality, Time, Friendship, The Christian Triumph, Virtue's Apology, A Moral Survey of the Nocturnal Heavens," and many other similar pieces. Doubtless there are brilliant flashes of imagination in his poems; seriousness and elevation are not wanting; we can even see that he aims at them; but we discover much more quickly that he makes the most of his grief, and strikes attitudes. He exaggerates and declaims, studies effect and style, confuses Greek and Christian ideas. Fancy an unhappy father, who says:

> "Silence and Darkness! Solemn sisters! Twins
> From ancient Night! I to Day's soft-ey'd sister pay my court,...[58]
> (Endymion's rival!) and her aid implore;
> Now first implor'd in succour to the Muse."[59]

And a few pages further on he invokes heaven and earth, when mentioning the resurrection of the Saviour. And yet the sentiment is fresh and sincere. Is it not one of the greatest of modern ideas to put Christian philosophy into verse? Young and his contemporaries say beforehand that which Chateaubriand and Lamartine were to discover. The true, the futile, all is here forty years earlier than in France. The angels and the other celestial machinery long figured in England before appearing in Chateaubriand's "Génie du Christianisme" and the "Martyrs." Atala and Chactas are of the same family as Malvina and Fingal. If Lamartine read Gray's odes and Akenside's reflections, he would find there the melancholy sweetness, the exquisite art, the fine arguments, and half the ideas of his own poetry. And nevertheless, near as they were to a literary renovation, Englishmen did not yet attain it. In vain the foundation was changed, the form remained. They did not shake off the classical drapery; they write too well, they dare not be natural. They have always a patent stock of fine suitable words, poetical elegances, where each of them thought himself bound to go and pick out his phrases. It boots them nothing to be impassioned or realistic; like Shenstone, to dare to describe a schoolmistress, and the very part on which she whips a young rascal; their simplicity is conscious, their frankness archaic, their emotion formal, their tears academical. Ever at the moment of writing, an august model starts up, a sort of schoolmaster, weighing on each with his full weight, with all the weight which a hundred and twenty years of literature can give his precepts. Their prose is always the slave of the period: Dr. Johnson, who was at once the La Harpe and the Boileau of his age, explains and imposes on all the studied, balanced, irreproachable phrase; and classical ascendancy is still so strong that it domineers over nascent history, the only kind of English literature which was then European and original. Hume, Robertson, and Gibbon, were almost French in their taste, language, education, conception of man. They relate like men of the world, cultivated and well-informed, with charm and clearness, in a polished, rhythmic, sustained style. They show a liberal spirit, an unvaried moderation, an impartial reason. They banish from history all coarseness and tediousness. They write without fanaticism or prejudice. But, at the same time, they attenuate human nature; comprehend neither barbarism nor loftiness; paint revolutions and passions, as people might do who had seen nothing but decked drawing-rooms and dusted libraries; they judge enthusiasts with the coldness of chaplains or the smile of a sceptic; they blot out the salient features which distinguish human physiognomies; they cover all the harsh points of truth with a brilliant and uniform varnish. At last there started up an unfortunate Scotch peasant (Burns), rebelling against the world, and in love, with the yearnings, lusts, greatness, and irrationality of modern genius. Now and then, behind his plough, he lighted on genuine verses, verses such as Heine and Alfred de Musset have written in our own days. In those few words, combined after a new fashion, there was a revolution. Two hundred new verses sufficed. The human mind turned on its hinges, and so did civil society. When Roland, being made a minister, presented himself before Louis XVI in a simple dress-coat and shoes without buckles, the master of the ceremonies raised his hands to heaven, thinking that all was lost. In reality, all was changed.

---

[1] Paul Louis Courier (1772-1825) says, "a lady's maid, in Louis XIV's time, wrote better than the greatest of modern writers."

[2] The Rev. Whitwell Elwin, in his second volume of the works of Alexander Pope, at the end of his introduction to "An Essay on Man," p. 338, says: "M. Taine asserts that from the Restoration to the French Revolution, from Waller to Johnson, from Hobbes and Temple to Robertson and Hume, all our literature, both prose and verse, bears the impress of classic art. The mode, he says, culminated in the reign of Queen Anne, and Pope, he considers, was the extreme example of it.... Many of the most eminent authors who flourished between the English Restoration wrote in a style far removed from that which M. Taine calls classical... The verse differs like the prose,

BOOK III.— THE CLASSIC AGE (CONTINUED)

though in a less degree, and is not 'of a uniform make, as if fabricated by a machine.'... Neither is the substance of the prose and verse, from the Restoration to the French Revolution, an invariable common-sense mediocrity.... There is much truth in his (M. Taine's) view, that there was a growing tendency to cultivate style, and in some writers the art degenerated into the artificial."— Tr.

[3] R. Carruthers, "Life of Alexander Pope," 2d ed. 1857. ch. I. 33.

[4] It is very doubtful whether Pope was not older than sixteen when he wrote the Pastorals. See on this subject, Pope's Works, ed. Elwin, London, 1871, I. 230 et passim.— Tr.

[5] Ibid. 233.

[6] Pope's Works, ed. Elwin, I. 242.

[7] Johnson, "Lives of the Most Eminent English Poets." 3 vols. ed. Cunningham, 1854. A. Pope, III. 96.

[8] Johnson. "Lives of the Most Eminent English Poets"; A. Pope, III. 99.

[9] Boswell's "Life of Johnson," ch. LXXI. 670.

[10] Carruthers's "Life of Pope," ch. X. 377.

[11] Carruthers's "Life of Pope," ch. IV. 164.

[12] Johnson, "The Lives of the English Poets"; Alexander Pope, III. 114.

[13] Ibid. III. 111.

[14] Ibid. III. 105.

[15] Rev. W. Elwin, in his edition of Pope's Works, II. 224, says: "The authenticity of the Latin letters has usually been taken for granted, but I have a strong belief that they are a forgery.... It is far more likely that they are the fabrication of an unconcerned romancer, who speaks in the name of others with a latitude which people, not entirely degraded, would never adopt towards themselves. The suspicion is strengthened when the second party to the correspondence, the chief philosopher of his generation, exhibits the same exceptional depravity of taste."— Tr.

[16] "Vale, unice."

[17] Pope's Works, ed. Elwin; "Eloisa to Abelard," II. 245, lines 141-160.

[18] Ibid. II. 240, lines 51-58.

"Heav'n first taught letters for some wretch's aid,
Some banished lover, or some captive maid;
They live, they speak, they breathe what love inspires,
Warm from the soul, and faithful to its fires,
The virgin's wish without her fears impart,
Excuse the blush, and pour out all

the heart,
Speed the soft intercourse from soul
to soul,
And waft a sigh from Indus to the
Pole."

    [19]Ibid. II. 249, lines 207-222.
    [20]Ibid. 255, line 317.
    [21]"Eloisa to Abelard," II. 254, lines 297-302.
    [22]M. Guillaume Guizot.
    [23]Goethe sings:
"Liebe sei vor alien Dingen,
Unser Thema, wenn wir singen."
    [24]See his "Epistle of the Characters of Women." According to Pope, this character is composed of love of pleasure and love of power.
    [25]"Rape of the Lock," c. V. 181, line 141.
    [26]Ibid. c. II. 153, lines 37-42.
    [27]Ibid. c. IV. 169, line 52.
    [28]Ibid. c. II. 156, line 107.
    [29]Pope's Works, "The Dunciad," bk. I.
    [30]Ibid. bk. II.
    [31]"The Dunciad," bk. II.
    [32]"The Dunciad," the end.
    [33]Pope's Works, I. 352; "Windsor Forest," line 211.
"Oft in her glass the musing shepherd
spies
The headlong mountains and the
downward skies,
The wat'ry landscape of the pendant
woods,
And absent trees that tremble in the
floods."
    [34]Ibid. I. 347; "Windsor Forest," lines 111-118.
    [35]Ibid. II. 154; "The Rape of the Lock," c. 2, lines 47-68.
    [36]Pope's Works, II. 160, "The Rape of the Lock," c. 3, 160, lines 37-44.
    [37]"Peins-moi légèrement l'amant léger
de Flore,
Qu'un doux ruisseau murmure en
vers plus doux encore."
    [38]A tale of J. J. Rousseau, in which he tries to depict a philosophical clergyman.— Tr.
    [39]The "Théodicée" was written in French, and published in 1710.— Tr.
    [40]These words are taken from the "Design of an Essay on Man."
    [41]Pope's Works, II.; "An Essay on Man," Ep. II. 375, lines 1-18.

[42] Prior's Works, ed. Gilfillan, 1851: "In the remotest wood and lonely grot,
Certain to meet that worst of evils,
thought."

[43] "Alma," canto II. lines 937-978: "Your nicer Hottentots think meet
With guts and tripe to deck their feet;
With downcast looks on Totta's legs
The ogling youth most humbly begs,
She would not from his hopes remove
At once his breakfast and his
love....
Before you see you smell your toast,
And sweetest she who stinks the
most."

[44] The same duke who was afterwards nicknamed "the Butcher."

[45] "Poems on Several Occasions," by Mr. John Gay, 1745, 2 vols. II. 141.

[46] Ibid. The Poem to "The Shepherd's Week." I. 6.

[47] Ibid. I. 66.

[48] Gay's Poems, "The Shepherd's Week"; first pastoral, "The Squabble," p. 80.

[49] "Epistle to Mrs. Blount, on Her Leaving the Town."

[50] A French pastoral writer (1717-1803), who wrote, in imitation of Thomson, "Les Saisons."— Tr.

[51] Poetical Works of T. Thomson, ed. R. Bell, 1855, 2 vols.; II. "Spring," 18.

[52] Ibid. 19.

[53] Ibid. 20.

[54] Ibid.

[55] Poetical Works of Thomson, "Liberty," part I. 102.

[56] Anthony Léonard Thomas (1732-1785) wrote memoirs and essays on the character of celebrated men in highly oratorical and pompous style.— Tr.

[57] See the paintings of David, called "Les Fêtes de la Révolution."

[58] Young's "Night Thoughts." Night the First: On Life, Death, and Immortality.

[59] Ibid. Night the Third: Narcissa.

BOOK IV—MODERN LIFE

CHAPTER FIRST. IDEAS AND PRODUCTIONS

Section I—Rise of Democracy

On the eve of the nineteenth century the great modern revolution began in Europe. The thinking public and the human mind changed, and whilst these changes took place a new literature sprang up.

The preceding age had done its work. Perfect prose and classical style put within reach of the most backward and the dullest minds the notions of literature and the discoveries of science. Moderate monarchies and regular administrations had permitted the middle class to develop itself under the pompous aristocracy of the court, as useful plants may be seen shooting up beneath trees which serve for show and ornament. They multiply, grow, rise to the height of their rivals, envelop them in their luxuriant growth, and obscure them by their dense clusters. A new world, a world of citizens and plebeians, henceforth occupies the ground, attracts the gaze, imposes its form on manners, stamps its image on minds. Towards the close of the century a sudden concourse of extraordinary events brings it all at once to the light, and sets it on an eminence unknown to any previous age. With the grand applications of science, democracy appears. The steam-engine and spinning-jenny create in England towns of from three hundred and fifty thousand to five hundred thousand souls. The population is doubled in fifty years, and agriculture becomes so perfect that, in spite of this enormous increase of mouths to be fed one-sixth of the inhabitants provide from the same soil food for the rest; imports increase threefold, and even more; the tonnage of vessels increases sixfold, the exports sixfold and more.[60] Comfort, leisure, instruction, reading, travel, whatever had been the privilege of a few, became the common property of the many. The rising tide of wealth raised the best of the poor to comfort, and the best of the well-to-do to opulence. The rising tide of civilization raised the mass of the people to the rudiments of education, and the mass of citizens to complete education. In 1709 appeared the first daily newspaper,[61] as big as a man's hand, which the editor did not know how to fill, and which, added to all the other papers, did not circulate to the extent of three thousand numbers in the year. In 1844 the Stamp Office showed that seventy-one million newspapers had been printed during the past year, many as large as volumes, and containing as much matter. Artisans and townsfolk, enfranchised, enriched, having gained a competence, left the low depths where they had been buried in their narrow parsimony, ignorance, and routine; they made their appearance on the stage now, doffed their workman's and supernumerary's dress, assumed the leading parts by a sudden irruption or a continuous progress, by dint of revolutions, with a prodigality of labor and genius, amidst vast wars, successively or simultaneously in America, France, the whole of Europe, founding or destroying states, inventing or restoring sciences, conquering or acquiring political rights. They grew noble through their great deeds, became the rivals, equals, conquerors of their masters; they need no longer imitate them, being heroes in their turn: like them, they can point to their crusades; like them, they have gained the right of having a poetry; and like them, they will have a poetry.

In France, the land of precocious equality and completed revolutions, we must observe this new character— the plebeian bent on getting on; Augereau, son of a green-grocer; Marceau, son of a lawyer; Murat, son of an innkeeper; Ney, son of a cooper; Hoche, formerly a sergeant, who in his tent, by night, read Condillac's "Traité des Sensations"; and chief of all, that spare young man, with lank hair, hollow cheeks, eaten up with ambition, his heart full of romantic fancies and grand roughhewn ideas, who, a lieutenant for seven years, read twice through the whole stock of a bookseller at Valence, who about this time (1792) in Italy, though suffering from itch, had just destroyed five armies with a troop of barefooted heroes, and gave his government an account of his victories with all his faults of spelling and of French. He became master, proclaimed himself the representative of the Revolution, declared "that a career is open to talent," and impelled others along with him in his enterprises. They follow him, because there is glory, and above all, advancement, to be won. "Two officers," says Stendhal, "commanded a battery at Talavera; a ball laid low the captain. 'So!' said the lieutenant, 'François is dead, I shall be captain. Not yet,' said François, who was only stunned, and got on his feet again." These two men were neither enemies nor wicked; on the contrary, they were companions and comrades; but the lieutenant wanted to rise a step. Such was the sentiment which provided men for the exploits and carnage of the Empire, which caused the Revolution of 1830, and which now, in this vast stifling democracy, compels men to vie with each other in intrigues and labor, genius and baseness, to get out of their primitive condition, and raise themselves to the summit, of which the possession is given up to their rivalry or promised to their toil. The dominant character nowadays is no longer the man of the drawing-room, whose position in society is settled and whose fortune is made: elegant and careless, with no employment but to amuse himself and to please; who loves to converse, who is gallant, who passes his life in conversation with finely dressed ladies, amidst the duties of society and the pleasures of the world: it is the man in a black coat who works alone in his room or rushes about in a cab to make friends and protectors; often envious, feeling himself always above or below his station in life, sometimes resigned, never satisfied, but fertile in invention, not sparing his labor, finding the picture of his blemishes and his strength in the drama of Victor Hugo and the novels of Balzac.[62]

This man has also other and greater cares. With the state of human society, the form of the human mind has changed. It changed by a natural and irresistible development, like a flower growing into fruit, like fruit turning to seed. The mind renews the evolution which it had already performed in Alexandria, not as then in a deleterious atmosphere, amidst the universal degradation of enslaved men, in the increasing decadence of a disorganized society, amidst the anguish of despair and the mists of a dream; but lapt in a purifying atmosphere, amidst the visible progress of an improving society and the general ennobling of lofty and free men, amidst the proudest hopes, in the wholesome clearness of experimental sciences. The oratorical age which declined, as it declined in Athens and Rome, grouped all ideas in beautiful commodious compartments, whose subdivisions instantaneously led the gaze towards the object which they define, so that thenceforth the intellect could enter upon the loftiest conceptions, and seize the aggregate which it had not yet embraced. Isolated nations, French, English, Italians, Germans, drew near and became known to each other through the upheaving of the first French Revolution and the wars of the Empire, as formerly races divided from one another, Greeks, Syrians, Egyptians, Gauls, by the conquests of Alexander and the domination of Rome: so that henceforth each civilization, expanded by the collision with neighboring civilizations, can pass beyond its national limits, and multiply its ideas by the commixture of the ideas of others. History and criticism spring up as under the Ptolemies; and from all sides, throughout the universe, in all directions, they were engaged in resuscitating and explaining literatures, religions, manners, societies, philosophies: so that thenceforth the intellect, enfranchised by the spectacle of past civilizations, can escape from the prejudices of its century, as it has escaped from the prejudices of its country. A new race, hitherto torpid, gave the signal: Germany communicated to the whole of Europe the impetus to a revolution of ideas, as France to a revolution of manners. These simple folk who smoked and warmed themselves by a stove, and seemed only fit to produce learned editions, became suddenly the promoters and leaders of human thought. No race has such a comprehensive mind; none is so well adapted for lofty speculation. We see it in their language, so abstract, that away from the Rhine it seems an unintelligible jargon. And yet, thanks to this language, they attained to superior ideas. For the specialty of this revolution, as of the Alexandrian revolution, was that the human mind became more capable of abstraction. They made, on a large scale, the same step as the mathematicians when they pass from arithmetic to algebra, and from ordinary calculation to the computation of the infinite. They perceived that beyond the limited truths of the oratorical age, there were deeper unfoldings; they passed beyond Descartes and Locke; as the Alexandrians went beyond Plato and Aristotle: they understood that a great operative architect, or round and square atoms, were not causes; that fluids, molecules, and monads were not forces; that a spiritual soul or a physiological secretion would not account for thought. They sought religious sentiment beyond dogmas, poetic beauty beyond rules, critical truths beyond myths. They desired to grasp natural and moral powers as they are, and independently of the fictitious supports, to which their predecessors had attached them. All these supports, souls and atoms, all these fictions, fluids and monads, all these conventions, rules of the beautiful and of religious symbols, all rigid classifications of things natural, human and divine, faded away and vanished. Thenceforth they were nothing but figures; they were only kept as an aid to the memory, and as auxiliaries of the mind; they served only provisionally, and as starting-points. Through a common movement along the whole line of human thought, causes draw back into an abstract region, where philosophy had not been to search them out for eighteen centuries. Then appeared the disease of the age, the restlessness of Werther and Faust, very like that which in a similar moment agitated men eighteen centuries ago; I mean discontent with the present, the vague desire of a higher beauty and an ideal happiness, the painful aspiration for the infinite. Man suffered through doubt, yet he doubted; he tried to seize again his beliefs, they melted in his hand: he would settle and rest in the doctrines and the satisfactions which sufficed for his predecessors, and he does not find them sufficient. He launches, like Faust, into anxious researches through science and history, and judges them vain, dubious, good for men like Wagner,[63] learned pedants and bibliomaniacs. It is the "beyond" he sighs for; he forebodes it through the formulas of science, the texts and confessions of the churches, through the amusements of the world, the intoxication of love. A sublime truth exists behind coarse experience and transmitted catechisms; a grand happiness exists beyond the pleasures of society and family joys. Whether men are sceptical, resigned, or mystics, they have all caught a glimpse of or imagined it, from Goethe to Beethoven, from Schiller to Heine; they have risen towards it in order to stir up the whole swarm of their grand dreams; they will not be consoled from falling away from it; they have mused upon it, even during their deepest fall; they have instinctively dwelt, like their predecessors the Alexandrians and Christians, in that splendid invisible world in which, in ideal peace, slumber the creative essences and powers; and the vehement aspiration of their heart has drawn from their sphere the elementary spirits, "film of flame, who flit and wave in eddying motion! birth and the grave, an infinite ocean, a web ever growing, a life ever glowing, ply at Time's whizzing loom, and weave the vesture of God."[64]

Thus rises the modern man, impelled by two sentiments, one democratic, the other philosophic. From the shallows of his poverty and ignorance he exerts himself to rise, lifting the weight of established society and admitted dogmas, disposed either to reform or to destroy them, and at once generous and rebellious. These two currents from France and Germany at this moment swept into England. The dykes there were so strong, they could hardly force their way, entering more slowly than elsewhere, but entering nevertheless. They made for themselves a new channel between the ancient barriers, and widened without bursting them, by a peaceful and slow transformation which continues till this day.

Section II.—Robert Burns

ROBERT BURNS

The new spirit broke out first in a Scottish peasant, Robert Burns: in fact, the man and the circumstances were suitable; scarcely ever was seen together more of misery and talent. He was born January, 1759, amid the hoar frost of a Scottish winter, in a cottage of clay built by his father, a poor farmer of Ayrshire; a sad condition, a sad country, a sad lot. A part of the gable fell in a few days after his birth, and his mother was obliged to seek refuge with her child, in the middle of a storm, in a neighbor's house. It is hard to be born in Scotland; it is so cold there, that in Glasgow on a fine day in July, whilst the sun was shining, I did not feel my overcoat too warm. The soil is wretched; there are many bare hills, where the harvest often fails. Burns's father, no longer young, having little more than his arms to depend upon, having taken his farm at too high a rent, burdened with seven children, lived parsimoniously, or rather fasting, in solitude, to avoid temptations to expense. "For several years butchers' meat was a thing unknown in the house." Robert went barefoot and bareheaded; at "the age of thirteen he assisted in thrashing the crop of corn, and at fifteen he was the principal laborer on the farm." The family did all the labor; they kept no servant, male or female. They had not much to eat, but they worked hard. "This kind of life— the cheerless gloom of a hermit, with the unceasing toil of a galley slave— brought me to my sixteenth year," Burns says. His shoulders were bent, melancholy seized him; "almost every evening he was constantly afflicted with a dull headache, which at a future period of his life was exchanged for a palpitation of the heart, and a threatening of fainting and suffocation in his bed in the night-time. The anguish of mind which we felt," says his brother, "was very great." The father grew old; his gray head, careworn brow, temples "wearing thin and bare," his tall bent figure, bore witness to the grief and toil which had spent him. The factor wrote him insolent and threatening letters which "set all the family in tears." There was a respite when the father changed his farm, but a lawsuit sprang up between him and the proprietor: "After three years' tossing and whirling in the vortex of litigation, my father was just saved from the horrors of a gaol by consumption, which after two years' promises kindly stepped in." In order to snatch something from the claws of the lawyers, the two sons were obliged to step in as creditors for arrears of wages. With this little sum they took another farm. Robert had seven pounds a year for his labor; for several years his whole expenses did not exceed this wretched pittance; he had resolved to succeed by dint of abstinence and toil: "I read farming books, I calculated crops, I attended markets;... but the first year, from unfortunately buying bad seed, the second from a late harvest, we lost half our crops." Troubles came apace; poverty always engenders them. The master-mason Armour, whose daughter was Burns's sweetheart, was said to contemplate prosecuting him, to obtain a guarantee for the support of his expected progeny, though he refused to accept him as a son-in-law. Jean Armour abandoned him; he could not give his name to her child. He was obliged to hide; he had been publicly admonished by the church. He said: "Even in the hour of social mirth, my gayety is the madness of an intoxicated criminal under the hands of the executioner." He resolved to leave the country; he agreed with Dr. Charles Douglas for thirty pounds a year to be bookkeeper or overseer on his estate in Jamaica; for want of money to pay the passage, he was about to "indent himself," that is, become bound as apprentice, when the success of a volume of poetry he had published put a score of guineas into his hands, and for a time brought him brighter days. Such was his life up to the age of twenty-seven, and that which succeeded was little better.

Let us fancy in this condition a man of genius, a true poet, capable of the most delicate emotions and the loftiest aspirations, wishing to rise, to rise to the summit, of which he deemed himself capable and worthy.[65]

Ambition had early made itself heard in him: "I had felt early some stirrings of ambition, but they were the blind groping of Homer's Cyclops around the walls of his cave.... The only two openings by which I could enter the temple of fortune were the gate of niggardly economy, or the path of little chicaning bargain-making. The first is so contracted an aperture, I never could squeeze myself into it; the last I always hated— there was contamination in the very entrance."[66] Low occupations depress the soul even more than the body; man perishes in them— is obliged to perish; of necessity there remains of him nothing but a machine: for in the kind of action in which all is monotonous, in which throughout the very long day the arms lift the same flail and drive the same plough, if thought does not take this uniform movement, the work is ill done. The poet must take care not to be turned aside by his poetry; to do as Burns did, "think only of his work whilst he was at it." He must think of it always, in the evening unyoking his cattle, on Sunday putting on his new coat, counting on his fingers the eggs and poultry, thinking of the kinds of dung, finding a means of using only one pair of shoes, and selling his hay at a penny a truss more. He will not succeed if he has not the patient dulness of a laborer, and the crafty vigilance of a petty shopkeeper. How could poor Burns succeed? He was out of place from his birth, and tried his utmost to raise himself above his condition.[67] At the farm at Lochlea, during mealtimes, the only moments of relaxation, parents, brothers, and sisters, ate with a spoon in one hand and a book in the other. Burns, at the school of Hugh Rodger, a teacher of mensuration, and later at a club of young men at Tarbolton, strove to exercise himself in general questions, and debated *pro* and *con* in order to see both sides of every idea. He carried a book in his pocket to study in spare moments in the fields; he wore out thus two copies of Mackenzie's "Man of Feeling. The collection of songs was my *vade mecum*. I pored over them driving my cart, or walking to labor, song by song, verse by verse, carefully noting the true, tender, sublime, or fustian." He maintained a correspondence with several of his companions in the same rank of life in order to form his style, kept a commonplace-book, entered in it ideas on man, religion, the greatest subjects, criticising his first productions. Burns says, "Never did a heart pant more ardently than mine to be distinguished." He thus divined what he did not learn, rose of himself to the level of the most highly cultivated; in a while, at Edinburgh, he was to read through and through respected doctors, Blair himself; he was to see that Blair had attainments, but no depth. At this time he studied minutely and lovingly the old Scotch ballads; and by night in his cold little room, by day whilst whistling at the plough, he invented forms and ideas. We must think of this in order to measure his efforts, to understand his miseries and his revolt. We must think that the man in whom these great ideas are stirring, threshed the corn, cleaned his cows; went out to dig peats, waded in the muddy snow, and dreaded to come home and find the bailiffs prepared to carry him off to prison. We must think also, that with the ideas of a thinker he had the delicacies and reveries of a poet. Once having cast his eyes on an engraving representing a dead soldier, and his wife beside him, his child and dog lying in the snow, suddenly, involuntarily, he burst into tears. He writes:

"There is scarcely any earthly object gives me more— I do not know if I should call it pleasure— but something which exalts me, something which enraptures me— than to walk in the sheltered side of a wood, or high plantation, in a cloudy winter day, and hear the stormy wind howling among the trees and raving over the plain.[68]... I listened to the birds and frequently turned out of my path, lest I should disturb their little songs or frighten them to another station."

The slavery of mechanical toil and perpetual economy crushed this swarm of grand or graceful dreams as soon as they began to soar. Burns was moreover proud, so proud, that afterwards in the world, amongst the great, "an honest contempt for whatever bore the appearance of meanness and servility" made him "fall into the opposite error of hardness of manner." He had also the consciousness of his own merits. "*Pauvre inconnu* as I then was, I had pretty nearly as high an opinion of myself and of my works as I have at this moment, when the public has decided in their favor."[69] Who can wonder that we find at every step in his poems the bitter protests of an oppressed and rebellious plebeian?

We find such recriminations against all society, against State and Church. Burns has a harsh tone, often the very phrases of Rousseau, and wished to be a "vigorous savage," quit civilized life, the dependence and humiliations which it imposes on the wretched.

"It is mortifying to see a fellow, whose abilities would scarcely have made an eight-penny tailor, and whose heart is not worth three farthings, meet with attention and notice that are withheld from the son of genius and poverty."[70] It is hard to

> "See yonder poor, o'erlabour'd wight,
> So abject, mean, and vile,
> Who begs a brother of the earth
> To give him leave to toil;
> And see his lordly fellow-worm
> The poor petition spurn,
> Unmindful, though a weeping wife
> And helpless offspring mourn."[71]

Burns says also:

> "While winds frae off Ben-Lomond blaw,
> And bar the doors wi' driving snaw,...
> I grudge a wee the great folks' gift,
> That live so bien an' snug:
> I tent less, and want less
> Their roomy fire-side;
> But hanker and canker
> To see their cursed pride.
>
> "It's hardly in a body's power
> To keep, at times, frae being sour,
> To see how things are shar'd;
> How best o' chiels are whiles in want,
> While coofs on countless thousands rant,
> And ken na how to wair't."[72]

But "a man's a man for a' that," and the peasant is as good as the lord. There are men noble by nature, and they alone are noble; the coat is the business of the tailor, titles a matter for the Herald's office. "The rank is but the guinea's stamp, the man's the gowd for a' that."

Against men who reverse this natural equality Burns is pitiless; the least thing puts him out of temper. Read his "Address of Beelzebub, to the Right Honourable the Earl of Breadalbane, President of the Right Honourable and Honourable the Highland Society, which met on the 23d of May last at the Shakespeare, Covent Garden, to concert ways and means to frustrate the designs of five hundred Highlanders, who, as the society were informed by Mr. Mackenzie of Applecross, were so audacious as to attempt an escape from their lawful lords and masters, whose property they were, by emigrating from the lands of Mr. M'Donald of Glengarry to the wilds of Canada, in search of that fantastic thing— liberty!" Rarely was an insult more prolonged and more biting, and the threat is not far behind. He warns Scotch members like a revolutionist, to withdraw "that curst restriction on aquavitæ, get auld Scotland back her kettle":

> "An', Lord, if ance they pit her till't,
> Her tartan petticoat she'll kilt,
> An' durk an' pistol at her belt,
> She'll tak the streets,
> An' rin her whittle to the hilt
> I' the first she meets!"[73]

In vain he writes, that

BOOK IV– MODERN LIFE

> "In politics if thou wouldst mix
> And mean thy fortunes be;
> Bear this in mind, be deaf and blind,
> Let great folks hear and see."[74]

Not alone did he see and hear, but he also spoke, and that aloud. He congratulates the French, on having repulsed conservative Europe, in arms against them. He celebrates the Tree of Liberty, planted "where ance the Bastile stood":

> "Upo' this tree there grows sic fruit,
> Its virtues a' can tell, man;
> It raises man aboon the brute,
> It makes him ken himsel', man.
> Gif ance the peasant taste a bit,
> He's greater than a Lord, man....
> King Loui' thought to cut it down,
> When it was unco sma', man.
> For this the watchman cracked his crown.
> Cut off his head and a', man."[75]

A strange gayety, savage and nervous, and which, in better style, resembles that of the *Ça ira.*

Burns is hardly more tender to the church. At that time the strait puritanical garment began to give way. Already the learned world of Edinburgh had Frenchified, widened, adapted it to the fashions of society, decked it with ornaments, not very brilliant, it is true, but select. In the lower strata of society dogma became less rigid, and approached by degrees the looseness of Arminius and Socinus. John Goldie, a merchant, had quite recently discussed the authority of Scripture.[76] John Taylor had denied original sin. Burns's father, pious as he was, inclined to liberal and humane doctrines, and detracted from the province of faith to add to that of reason. Burns, after his wont, pushed things to an extreme, thought himself a deist, saw in the Saviour only an inspired man, reduced religion to an inner and poetic sentiment, and attacked with his railleries the paid and patented orthodox people. Since Voltaire, no literary man in religious matters was more bitter or more jocose. According to him, ministers are shopkeepers trying to cheat each other out of their customers, decrying at the top of their voice the shop next door, puffing their drugs in numberless advertisements, and here and there setting up fairs to push the trade. These "holy fairs" are gatherings of the pious, where the sacrament is administered. One after another the clergymen preach and thunder, in particular a Rev. Mr. Moodie, who raves and fumes to throw light on points of faith— a terrible figure:

"Should Hornie, as in ancient days,
'Mong sons o' God present him,
The vera sight o' Moodie's face
To's ain het hame had sent him
Wi' fright that day.

"Hear how he clears the points o' faith
Wi' rattlin' an' wi' thumpin'!
Now meekly calm, now wild in wrath,
He's stampin' an' he's jumpin'!
His lengthen'd chin, his turn'd-up snout,
His eldritch squeel and gestures,
Oh! how they fire the heart devout.
Like cantharidian plasters,
On sic a day!"[77]

The minister grows hoarse; now "Smith opens out his cauld harangues," then two more ministers speak. At last the audience rest, "the Change-house fills," and people begin to eat; each brings cakes and cheese from his bag; the young folks have their arms round their lasses' waists. That was an attitude to listen in! There is a great noise in the inn; the cans rattle on the board; whiskey flows, and provides arguments to the tipplers commenting on the sermons. They demolish carnal reason, and exalt free faith. Arguments and stamping, shouts of sellers and drinkers, all mingle together. It is a "holy fair":

"But now the Lord's ain trumpet touts,
Till a' the hills are rairin',
An' echoes back return the shouts;
Black Russell is na sparin';
His piercing words, like Highlan' swords,
Divide the joints and marrow.
His talk o' hell, where devils dwell,
Our vera sauls does harrow
Wi' fright that day.

"A vast unbottom'd boundless pit,
Fill'd fu' o' lowin' brunstane.
Wha's raging flame, an scorchin' heat,
Wad melt the hardest whunstane.
The half-asleep start up wi' fear,
An' think they hear it roarin',
When presently it does appear
'Twas but some neebor snorin'

Asleep that day....

> "How monie hearts this day converts
> O' sinners and o' lasses!
> Their hearts o' stane, gin night, are gane,
> As saft as ony flesh is.
> There's some are fou o' love divine,
> There's some are fou o' brandy."[78]
> Etc., etc.

The young men meet the girls, and the devil does a better business than God. A fine ceremony and morality! Let us cherish it carefully, and our wise theology too, which damns men.

As for that poor dog common-sense, which bites so hard, let us send him across seas; let him go "and bark in France." For where shall we find better men than our "unco guid"— Holy Willie for instance? He feels himself predestinated, full of never-failing grace; therefore all who resist him resist God, and are fit only to be punished; may He "blast their name, who bring thy elders to disgrace, and public shame."[79] Burns says also:

> "An honest man may like a glass,
> An honest man may like a lass,
> But mean revenge an' malice fause
> He'll still disdain;
> And then cry zeal for gospel laws
> Like some we ken....
> ... I rather would be
> An atheist clean,
> Than under gospel colours hid be
> Just for a screen."[80]

There is a beauty, an honesty, a happiness outside the conventionalities and hypocrisy, beyond correct preachings and proper drawing-rooms, unconnected with gentlemen in white ties and reverends in new bands.

In 1785 Burns wrote his masterpiece, the "Jolly Beggars," like the "Gueux" of Béranger; but how much more picturesque, varied, and powerful! It is the end of autumn, the gray leaves float on the gusts of the wind; a joyous band of vagabonds, happy devils, come for a junketing at the change-house of Poosie Nansie:

> "Wi' quaffing and laughing
> They ranted and they sang;

Wi' jumping and thumping
The very girdle rang."

First, by the fire, in old red rags, is a soldier, and his old woman is with him; the jolly old girl has drunk freely; he kisses her, and she again pokes out her greedy lips; the coarse loud kisses smack like "a cadger's whip. Then staggering and swaggering, he roar'd this ditty up:"

> "I lastly was with Curtis, among the floating batt'ries,
> And there I left for witness an arm and a limb;
> Yet let my country need me, with Elliot to head me,
> I'd clatter on my stumps at the sound of a drum....
> He ended; and the kebars sheuk,
> Aboon the chorus' roar;
> While frighted rattoons backward leuk,
> And seek the benmost bore."

Now it is the "doxy's" turn:

> "I once was a maid, tho' I cannot tell when,
> And still my delight is in proper young men....
> Some one of a troop of dragoons was my daddie,
> No wonder I'm fond of a sodger laddie.
> The first of my loves was a swaggering blade,
> To rattle the thundering drum was his trade....
> The sword I forsook for the sake of the church....
> Full soon I grew sick of my sanctified sot,
> The regiment at large for a husband I got,
> From the gilded spontoon to the fife I was ready,
> I ask no more but a sodger laddie.
> But the peace it reduc'd me to beg in despair,
> Till I met my old boy at a Cunningham fair;
> His rags regimental they flutter'd so gaudy,
> My heart it rejoic'd at a sodger laddie....
> But whilst with both hands I can hold the glass steady,
> Here's to thee, my hero, my sodger laddie."

This is certainly a free and easy style, and the poet is not mealy mouthed. His other characters arc in the same taste, a Merry Andrew, a raucle carlin (a stout beldame), "a pigmy-scraper wi' his fiddle," a travelling tinker— all in rags, brawlers and gypsies, who fight, bang, and kiss each other, and make the glasses ring with the noise of their good humor:

BOOK IV— MODERN LIFE

> "They toomed their pocks, and pawned their duds,
> They scarcely left to co'er their fuds,
> To quench their lowin' drouth."

And their chorus rolls about like thunder, shaking the rafters and walls.

> "A fig for those by law protected!
> Liberty's a glorious feast!
> Courts for cowards were erected,
> Churches built to please the priest!
>
> "What is title? What is treasure?
> What is reputation's care?
> If we lead a life of pleasure,
> 'Tis no matter how or where!
>
> "With the ready trick and fable,
> Round we wander all the day;
> And at night, in barn or stable,
> Hug our doxies on the hay.
>
> "Life is all a variorum,
> We regard not how it goes;
> Let them cant about decorum,
> Who have characters to lose.
>
> "Here's to budgets, bags and wallets!
> Here's to all the wandering train!
> Here's our ragged brats and callets!
> One and all cry out— Amen."

Has any man better spoken the language of rebels and levellers? There is here, however, something else than the instinct of destruction and an appeal to the senses; there is hatred of cant and return to nature. Burns sings:

> "Morality, thou deadly bane,
> Thy tens o' thousands thou hast slain;
> Vain is his hope, whose stay and trust is
> In moral mercy, truth and justice!"[81]

Mercy! this grand word renews all. Now, as formerly, eighteen centuries ago, men rose above legal formulas and prescriptions; now, as formerly, under Vergil and Marcus Aurelius, refined sensibility and wide sympathies embraced beings who seemed forever out of the pale of society and law. Burns pities, and that sincerely, a wounded hare, a mouse whose nest was upturned by his plough, a mountain daisy. Is there such a very great difference between man, beast, or plant? A mouse stores up, calculates, suffers like a man:

> "I doubt na, whiles, but thou may thieve;
> What then? poor beastie, thou maun live."

We even no longer wish to curse the fallen angels, the grand malefactors, Satan and his troop. Like the "randie, gangrel bodies, who in Poosie Nancy's held the splore," they have their good points, and perhaps after all are not so bad as people say:

> "Hear me, auld Hangie, for a wee,
> An' let poor damned bodies be;
> I'm sure sma' pleasure it can gie,
> E'n to a deil,
> To skelp an' scaud poor dogs like me,
> An' hear us squeel!...
>
> "Then you, ye auld, snic-drawing dog!
> Ye came to Paradise incog.,
> An' played on man a cursed brogue,
> (Black be your fa'!)
> An' gied the infant warld a shog,
> 'Maist ruin'd a'....
>
> "But, fare you weel, auld Nickie-ben!
> O wad ye tak a thought an' men'!
> Ye aiblins might— I dinna ken—
> Still hae a stake—
> I'm wae to think upo' yon den,
> Ev'n for your sake."[82]

We see that he speaks to the devil as to an unfortunate comrade, a disagreeable fellow, but fallen into trouble. Let us take another step, and we will see in a contemporary, Goethe, that Mephistopheles himself is not overmuch damned; his god, the modern god, tolerates him and tells him he has never hated such as he. For wide conciliating nature assembles in her company, on equal terms, the ministers of destruction and life. In this deep change the ideal changes; citizen and orderly life, strict Puritan duty, do not exhaust all the powers of man. Burns cries out in favor of instinct and enjoyment, so as to seem epicurean. He has genuine gayety, a glow of jocularity; laughter commends itself to him; he praises it as well as the good suppers of good comrades, where wine is plentiful, pleasantry abounds, ideas pour forth, poetry sparkles, and causes a carnival of beautiful figures and good-humored people to move about in the human brain.

He always was in love.[83] He made love the great end of existence, to such a degree that at the club which he founded with the young men of Tarbolton, every member was obliged "to be the declared lover of one or more fair ones." From the age of fifteen this was his main business. He had for companion in his harvest toil a sweet and lovable girl, a year younger than himself: "In short, she, altogether unwittingly to herself, initiated me in that delicious passion, which, in spite of acid disappointment, gin-horse prudence, and book-worm philosophy, I hold to be the first of human joys, our dearest blessing here below."[84] He sat beside her with a joy which he did not understand, to "pick out from her little hand the cruel nettle-stings and thistles." He had many other less innocent fancies; it seems to me that by his very nature he was in love with all women: as soon as he saw a pretty one, he grew lively; his commonplace-book and his songs show that he set off in pursuit after every butterfly, golden or not, which seemed about to settle. Moreover, he did not confine himself to Platonic reveries; he was as free of action as of words; broad jests crop up freely in his verses. He calls himself an unregenerate heathen, and he is right. He has even written obscene verses; and Lord Byron refers to a quantity of his letters, of course unpublished, than which worse could not be imagined:[85] it was the excess of the sap which overflowed in him, and soiled the bark. Doubtless he did not boast about these excesses, he rather repented of them; but as to the uprising and blooming of the free poetic life in the open air, he found no fault with it. He thought that love, with the charming dreams it brings, poetry, pleasure, and the rest, are beautiful things, suitable to human instincts, and therefore to the designs of God. In short, in contrast with morose Puritanism, he approved joy and spoke well of happiness.[86]

Not that he was a mere epicurean; on the contrary, he could be religious. When, after the death of his father, he prayed aloud in the evening, he drew tears from those present; and his "Cottar's Saturday Night" is the most heartfelt of virtuous idyls. I even believe he was fundamentally religious. He advised his "pupil as he tenders his own peace, to keep up a regular warm intercourse with the Deity." What he made fun of was official worship; but as for religion, the language of the soul, he was greatly attached to it. Often before Dugald Stewart at Edinburgh, he disapproved of the sceptical jokes which he heard at the supper table. He thought he had "every evidence for the reality of a life beyond the stinted bourne of our present existence"; and many a time, side by side with a jocose satire, we find in his writings stanzas full of humble repentance, confiding fervor, or Christian resignation. These, if you will, are a poet's contradictions, but they are also a poet's divinations;

under these apparent variations there rises a new ideal; old narrow moralities are to give place to the wide sympathy of the modern man, who loves the beautiful wherever it meets him, and who, refusing to mutilate human nature, is at once Pagan and Christian.

This originality and divining instinct exist in his style as in his ideas. The specialty of the age in which we live, and which he inaugurated, is to blot out rigid distinctions of class, catechism, and style; academic, moral, or social conventions are falling away, and we claim in society a mastery for individual merit, in morality for inborn generosity, in literature for genuine feeling. Burns was the first to enter on this track, and he often pursues it to the end. When he wrote verses, it was not on calculation or in obedience to fashion: "My passions, when once lighted up, raged like so many devils, till they got vent in rhyme; and then the conning over my verses, like a spell, soothed all into quiet."[87] He hummed them to old Scotch airs which he passionately loved, as he drove his plough, and which, he says, as soon as he sang them, brought ideas and rhymes to his lips. That, indeed, was natural poetry; not forced in a hot-house, but born of the soil between the furrows, side by side with music, amidst the gloom and beauty of the climate, like the violet heather of the moors and the hillside. We can understand that it gave vigor to his tongue. For the first time this man spoke as men speak, or rather as they think, without premeditation, with a mixture of all styles, familiar and terrible, hiding an emotion under a joke, tender and jeering in the same place, apt to place side by side tap-room trivialities and the high language of poetry,[88] so indifferent was he to rules, content to exhibit his feeling as it came to him, and as he felt it. At last, after so many years, we escape from measured declamation, we hear a man's voice! and what is better still, we forget the voice in the emotion which it expresses, we feel this emotion reflected in ourselves, we enter into relations with a soul. Then form seems to fade away and disappear: I think that this is the great feature of modern poetry; seven or eight times has Burns reached it.

He has done more; he has made his way, as we say nowadays. On the publication of his first volume he became suddenly famous. Coming to Edinburgh, he was feasted, caressed, admitted on a footing of equality in the best drawing-rooms, amongst the great and the learned, loved of a woman who was almost a lady. For one season he was sought after, and he behaved worthily amidst these rich and noble people. He was respected, and even loved. A subscription brought him a second edition and five hundred pounds. He also at last had won his position, like the great French plebeians, amongst whom Rousseau was the first. Unfortunately, he brought thither, like them, the vices of his condition and of his genius. A man does not rise with impunity, nor, above all, desire to rise with impunity: we also have our vices, and suffering vanity is the first of them. "Never did a heart pant more ardently than mine to be distinguished," said Burns. This grievous pride marred his talent, and threw him into follies. He labored to attain a fine epistolary style, and brought ridicule on himself by imitating in his letters the men of the academy and the court. He wrote to his lady-loves with choice phrases, full of periods as pedantic as those of Dr. Johnson. Certainly we dare hardly quote them, the emphasis is so grotesque.[89] At other times he committed to his commonplace-book literary expressions that occurred to him, and six months afterwards sent them to his correspondents as extemporary effusions and natural improvisations. Even in his verses, often enough, he fell into a grand conventional style;[90] brought into play sighs, ardors, flames, even the big classical and mythological machinery. Béranger, who thought or called himself the poet of the people, did the same. A plebeian must have much courage to venture on always remaining himself, and never slipping on the court dress. Thus Burns, a Scottish villager, avoided, in speaking, all Scotch village expressions: he was pleased to show himself as well-bred as fashionable folks. It was forcibly and by surprise that his genius drew him away from the proprieties: twice out of three times his feeling was marred by his pretentiousness.

His success lasted one winter, after which the wide incurable wound of plebeianism made itself felt— I mean that he was obliged to work for his living. With the money gained by the second edition of his poems he took a little farm. It was a bad bargain; and, moreover, we can imagine that he had not the money-grubbing character necessary. He says: "I might write you on farming, on building, on marketing; but my poor distracted mind is so torn, so jaded, so racked, and bedeviled with the task of the superlatively damned obligation to make one guinea do the business of three, that I detest, abhor, and swoon at the very word business." Soon he left his farm, with empty pockets, to fill at Dumfries the small post of exciseman, which was worth, in all, £90 a year. In this fine employment he branded leather, gauged casks, tested the make of candles, issued licenses for the transit of spirits. From his dunghills he passed to office work and grocery: what a life for such a man! He would have been unhappy, even if independent and rich. These great innovators, these poets, are all alike. What makes them poets is the violent afflux of sensations. They have a nervous mechanism more sensitive than ours; the objects which leave us cool, transport them suddenly beyond themselves. At the least shock their brain is set going, after which they once more fall flat, loathe existence, sit morose amidst the memories of their faults and their lost pleasures. Burns said: "My worst enemy is *moi-même*.... There are just two creatures I would envy: a horse in his wild state traversing the forests of Asia, or an oyster on some of the desert shores of Europe. The one has not a wish without enjoyment, the other has neither wish nor fear." He was always in extremes, at the height of exaltation or in the depth of depression; in the morning, ready to weep; in the evening at table or under the table; enamored of Jean Armour, then on her refusal engaged to another, then returning to Jean, then quitting her, then taking her back, amidst much scandal, many blots on his character, still more disgust. In such heads ideas are like cannon balls: the man, hurled onward, bursts through everything, shatters himself, begins again the next day, but in a contrary direction, and ends by finding nothing left in him, but ruins within and without. Burns had never been prudent, and was so less than ever, after his success at Edinburgh. He had enjoyed too much; he henceforth felt too acutely the painful sting of modern man, namely the disproportion between the desire for certain things and the power of obtaining them. Debauch had all but spoiled his fine imagination, which had before been "the chief source of his happiness"; and he confessed that, instead of tender reveries, he had now nothing but sensual desires. He had been kept drinking till six in the morning; he was very often drunk at Dumfries, not that the whiskey was very good, but it makes thoughts to whirl about in the head; and hence poets, like the poor, are fond of it. Once at Mr. Riddell's he made himself so tipsy that he insulted the lady of the house; next day he sent her an apology which was not accepted, and, out of spite, wrote rhymes against her: a lamentable excess, betraying an unseated mind. At thirty-seven he was worn out. One night, having drunk too much, he sat down and went to sleep in the street. It was January, and he caught rheumatic fever. His family wanted to call in a doctor. "What business has a physician to waste his time on me?" he said; "I am a poor pigeon not worth plucking." He was horribly thin, could not sleep, and could not stand on his legs. "As to my individual self, I am tranquil. But Burns' poor widow and half a dozen of his dear little ones, there I am as weak as a woman's tear." He was even afraid he should not die in peace, and had the bitterness of being obliged to beg. Here is a letter he wrote to a friend: "A rascal of a haberdasher, taking into his head that I am dying, has commenced a process against me, and will infallibly put my emaciated body into jail. Will you be so good as to accommodate me, and that by return of post, with ten pounds? O James! did you know the pride of my heart, you would feel doubly for me! Alas, I am not used to beg!"[91] He died a few days afterwards, at thirty-eight. His wife was lying-in of her fifth child at the time of her husband's funeral.

Section III.—Conservative Rule in England.—Cowper's Poetry

A sad life, most often the life of the men in advance of their age; it is not wholesome to go too quick. Burns was so much in advance that it took forty years to catch him. At this time in England the conservatives and the believers took the lead before sceptics and revolutionists. The constitution was liberal, and seemed to be a guarantee of rights; the church was popular, and seemed to be the support of morality. Practical capacity and speculative incapacity turned the mind aside from the propounded innovations, and bound them down to the established order. The people found themselves well off in their great feudal house, widened and accommodated to modern needs; they thought it beautiful, they were proud of it; and national instinct, like public opinion, declared against the innovators who would throw it down to build it up again. Suddenly a violent shock changed this instinct into a passion, and this opinion into fanaticism. The French Revolution, at first admired as a sister, had shown itself a fury and a monster. Pitt declared in Parliament, "that one of the leading features of this (French) Government was the extinction of religion and the destruction of property."[92] Amidst universal applause, the whole thinking and influential class rose to stamp out this party of robbers, united brigands, atheists on principle; Jacobinism, sprung from blood to sit in purple, was persecuted even in its child and champion, "Buonaparte, who is now the sole organ of all that was formerly dangerous and pestiferous in the revolution."[93] Under this national rage liberal ideas dwindled; the most illustrious friends of Fox— Burke, Windham, Spencer— abandoned him: out of a hundred and sixty partisans in the House of Commons, only fifty remained to him. The great Whig party seemed to be disappearing; and in 1799, the strongest minority that could be collected against the Government was twenty-nine. Yet English Jacobinism was taken by the throat and held down:

"The Habeas Corpus Act was repeatedly suspended.... Writers who propounded doctrines adverse to monarchy and aristocracy, were proscribed and punished without mercy. It was hardly safe for a republican to avow his political creed over his beefsteak and his bottle of port at a chophouse.... Men of cultivated mind and polished manners were (in Scotland), for offences which at Westminster would have been treated as mere misdemeanours, sent to herd with felons at Botany Bay."[94]

But the intolerance of the nation aggravated that of the Government. If anyone had dared to avow democratic sentiments, he would have been insulted. The papers represented the innovators as wretches and public enemies. The mob in Birmingham burned the houses of Priestley and the Unitarians. And in the end Priestley was obliged to leave England.

New theories could not arise in this society armed against new theories. Yet the revolution made its entrance; it entered disguised, and through an indirect way, so as not to be recognized. It was not social ideas, as in France, that were transformed, nor philosophical ideas as in Germany, but literary ideas; the great rising tide of the modern mind, which elsewhere overturned the whole edifice of human conditions and speculations, succeeded here only at first in changing style and taste. It was a slight change, at least apparently, but on the whole of equal value with the others; for this renovation in the manner of writing is a renovation in the manner of thinking: the one led to all the rest, as a central pivot being set in motion causes all the indented wheels to move also.

Wherein consists this reform of style? Before defining it, I prefer to exhibit it; and for that purpose, we must study the character and life of a man who was the first to use it, without any system— William Cowper: for his talent is but the picture of his character, and his poems but the echo of his life. He was a delicate, timid child, of a tremulous sensibility, passionately tender, who, having lost his mother at six, was almost at once subjected to the fagging and brutality of a public school. These, in England, are peculiar: a boy of about fifteen singled him out as a proper object upon whom he might practise the cruelty of his temper: and the poor little fellow, ceaselessly ill-treated, "conceived," he says, "such a dread of his (tormentor's) figure,... that I well remember being afraid to lift my eyes upon him higher than his knees; and that I knew him better by his shoe-buckles than by any other part of his dress."[95] At the age of nine melancholy seized him, not the sweet reverie which we call by that name, but the profound dejection, gloomy and continual despair, the horrible malady of the nerves and the soul, which leads to suicide, Puritanism, and madness. "Day and night I was upon the rack, lying down in horror, and rising up in despair."[96]

The evil changed form, diminished, but did not leave him. As he had only a small fortune, though born of a high family, he accepted, without reflection, the offer of his uncle, who wished to give him a place as clerk of the journals of the House of Lords; but he had to undergo an examination, and his nerves were unstrung at the very idea of having to speak in public. For six months he tried to prepare himself; but he read without understanding. His continual misery brought on at last a nervous fever. Cowper writes of himself: "The feelings of a man when he arrives at the place of execution, are probably much like mine, every time I set my foot in the office, which was every day, for more than a half year together.[97] In this situation, such a fit of passion has sometimes seized me, when alone in my chambers, that I have cried out aloud, and cursed the hour of my birth; lifting up my eyes to heaven not as a suppliant, but in the hellish spirit of rancorous reproach and blasphemy against my Maker."[98] The day of examination came on: he hoped he was going mad, so that he might escape from it; and as his reason held out, he thought even of "self-murder." At last, "in a horrible dismay of soul," insanity came, and he was placed in an asylum, whilst "his conscience was scaring him, and the avenger of blood pursuing him"[99] to the extent even of thinking himself damned, like Bunyan and the first Puritans. After several months his reason returned, but it bore traces of the strange lands where it had journeyed alone. He remained sad, like a man who thought himself in disfavor with God, and felt himself incapable of an active life. However, a clergyman, Mr. Unwin, and his wife, very pious and very regular people, had taken charge of him. He tried to busy himself mechanically, for instance, in making rabbit-hutches, in gardening, and in taming hares. He employed the rest of the day like a Methodist, in reading Scripture or sermons, in singing hymns with his friends, and speaking of spiritual matters. This way of Irving, the wholesome country air, the maternal tenderness of Mrs. Unwin and Lady Austen, brought him a few gleams of light. They loved him so generously, and he was so lovable! Affectionate, full of freedom and innocent raillery, with a natural and charming imagination, a graceful fancy, and exquisite delicacy, and so unhappy! He was one of those to whom women devote themselves, whom they love maternally, first from compassion, then by attraction, because they find in them alone the consideration, the minute and tender attentions, the delicate observances which men's rude nature cannot give them, and which their more sensitive nature nevertheless craves. These sweet moments, however, did not last. He says: "My mind has always a melancholy cast, and is like some pools I have seen, which, though filled with a black and putrid water, will nevertheless in a bright day reflect the sunbeams from their surface." He smiled as well as he could, but with effort; it was the smile of a sick man who knows himself incurable, and tries to forget it for an instant, at least to make others forget it: "Indeed, I wonder that a sportive thought should ever knock at the door of my intellects, and still more that it should gain admittance. It is as if harlequin should intrude himself into the gloomy chamber where a corpse is deposited in state. His antic gesticulations would be unseasonable at any rate, but more specially so if they should distort the features of the mournful attendants into laughter. But the mind, long wearied with the sameness of a dull, dreary prospect, will gladly fix his eyes on anything that may make a little variety in its contemplations, though it were but a kitten playing with her tail."[100] In reality, he had too delicate and too pure a heart: pious, irreproachable, austere, he thought himself unworthy of going to church, or even of praying to God. He says also: "As for happiness, he that once had communion with his Maker must be more frantic than ever I was yet, if he can dream of finding it at a distance from him."[101] And elsewhere: "The heart of a Christian, mourning yet rejoicing, (is) pierced with thorns, yet wreathed about with roses. I have the thorn without the rose. My brier is a wintry one; the flowers are withered, but the thorn remains." On his death-bed, when the clergyman told him to confide in the love of the Redeemer, who desired to save all men, he uttered a passionate cry, begging him not to give him such consolations. He thought himself lost, and had thought so all his life. One by one, under this terror all his faculties gave way. Poor charming soul, perishing like a frail flower transplanted from a warm land to the snow: the world's temperature was too rough for it; and the moral law, which should have supported it, tore it with its thorns.

Such a man does not write for the pleasure of making a noise. He made verses as he painted or worked at his bench to occupy himself, to distract his mind. His soul was too full; he need not go far for subjects. Picture this pensive figure, silently-wandering and gazing along the banks of the Ouse. He gazes and dreams. A buxom peasant girl, with a basket on her arm; a distant cart slowly rumbling on behind horses in a sweat; a sparkling spring, which polishes the blue pebbles— this is enough to fill him with sensations and thoughts. He returned, sat in his little summer-house, as large as a sedan-chair, the window of which opened out upon a neighbor's orchard, and the door on a garden full of pinks, roses, and honeysuckle. In this nest he labored. In the evening, beside his friend, whose needles were working for him, he read, or listened to the drowsy sounds without. Rhymes are born in such a life as this. It sufficed for him, and for their birth. He did not need a more violent career: less harmonious or monotonous, it would have upset him; impressions small to us were great to him; and in a room, a garden, he found a world. In his eyes the smallest objects were poetical. It is evening; winter; the postman comes:

> "The herald of a noisy world,
> With spatter'd boots, strapp'd waist, and frozen locks;
> News from all nations lumbering at his back.
> True to his charge, the close-packed load behind,
> Yet careless what he brings, his one concern
> Is to conduct it to the destined inn;
> And, having dropped the expected bag, pass on.
> He whistles as he goes, light-hearted wretch,
> Cold and yet cheerful: messenger of grief
> Perhaps to thousands, and of joy to some."[102]

At last we have the precious "close-packed load"; we open it; we wish to hear the many noisy voices it brings from London and the universe:

> "Now stir the fire, and close the shutters fast,
> Let fall the curtains, wheel the sofa round,
> And while the bubbling and loud-hissing urn
> Throws up a steamy column, and the cups,
> That cheer but not inebriate, wait on each,
> So let us welcome peaceful evening in."[103]

Then he unfolds the whole contents of the newspaper— politics, news, even advertisements— not as a mere realist, like so many writers of to-day, but as a poet; that is, as a man who discovers a beauty and harmony in the coals of a sparkling fire, or the movement of fingers over a piece of wool-work; for such is the poet's strange distinction. Objects not only spring up in his mind more powerful and more precise than they were of themselves, and before entering there; but also, once conceived, they are purified, ennobled, colored, like gross vapors, which, being transfigured by distance and light, change into silky clouds, lined with purple and gold. For him there is a charm in the rolling folds of the vapor sent up by the tea-urn, sweetness in the concord of guests assembled around the same table in the same house. This one expression, "News from India," causes him to see India itself, "with her plumed and jeweled turban."[104] The mere notion of "excise" sets before his eyes "ten thousand casks, forever dribbling out their base contents, touched by the Midas finger of the State, (which) bleed gold for ministers to sport away."[105] Strictly speaking, nature is to him like a gallery of splendid and various pictures, which to us ordinary folk are always covered up with cloths. At most, now and then, a rent suffers us to imagine the beauties hid behind the uninteresting curtains; but the poet raises these curtains, one and all, and sees a picture where we see but a covering. Such is the new truth Cowper's poems brought to light. We know from him that we need no longer go to Greece, Rome, to the palaces, heroes, and academicians, in search of poetic objects. They are quite near us. If we see them not, it is because we do not know how to look for them; the fault is in our eyes, not in the things. We may find poetry, if we wish, at our fireside, and amongst the beds of our kitchen-garden.[106]

Is the kitchen-garden indeed poetical? To-day, perhaps; but to-morrow, if my imagination is barren, I shall see there nothing but carrots and other kitchen stuff. It is my feelings which are poetical, which I must respect, as the most precious flower of beauty. Hence a new style. We need no longer, after the old oratorical fashion, box up a subject in a regular plan, divide it into symmetrical portions, arrange ideas into files, like the pieces on a draught-board. Cowper takes the first subject that comes to hand— one which Lady Austen gave him at haphazard— the "Sofa," and speaks about it for a couple of pages; then he goes whither the bent of his mind leads him, describing a winter evening, a number of interiors and landscapes, mingling here and there all kinds of moral reflections, stories, dissertations, opinions, confidences, like a man who thinks aloud before the most intimate and beloved of his friends. Let us look at his great poem, the "Task. The best didactic poems," says Southey, "when compared with the 'Task,' are like formal gardens in comparison with woodland scenery." If we enter into details, the contrast is greater still. He does not seem to dream that he is being listened to; he only speaks to himself. He does not dwell on his ideas, as the classical writers do, to set them in relief, and make them stand out by repetitions and antitheses; he marks his sensation, and that is all. We follow this sensation in him as it gradually springs up; we see it rising from a former one, swelling, falling, remounting, as we see vapor issuing from a spring, and insensibly rising, unrolling, and developing its shifting forms. Thought, which in others was congealed and rigid, becomes here mobile and fluent; the rectilinear verse grows flexible; the noble vocabulary widens its scope to let in vulgar words of conversation and life. At length poetry has again become lifelike; we no longer listen to words, but we feel emotions; it is no longer an author, but a man who speaks. His whole life is there, perfect, beneath its black lines, without falsehood or concoction; his whole effort is bent on removing falsehood and concoction. When he describes his little river, his dear Ouse, "slow winding through a level plain of spacious meads, with cattle sprinkled o'er,"[107] he sees it with his inner eye; and each word, caesura, sound, answers to a change of that inner vision. It is so in all his verses; they are full of personal emotions, genuinely felt, never altered or disguised; on the contrary, fully expressed, with their transient shades and fluctuations; in a word, as they are, that is, in the process of production and destruction, not all complete, motionless, and fixed, as the old style represented them. Herein consists the great revolution of the modern style. The mind, outstripping the known rules of rhetoric and eloquence, penetrates into profound psychology, and no longer employs words except to mark emotions.

Section IV.—The Romantic School

Now[108] appeared the English romantic school, closely resembling the French in its doctrines, origin, and alliances, in the truths which it discovered, the exaggerations it committed, and the scandal it excited. The followers of that school formed a sect, a sect of "dissenters in poetry," who spoke out aloud, kept themselves close together, and repelled settled minds by the audacity and novelty of their theories. For their foundation were attributed to them the anti-social principles and the sickly sensibility of Rousseau; in short, a sterile and misanthropical dissatisfaction with the present institutions of society. Southey, one of their leaders, began by being a Socinian and Jacobin; and one of his first poems, "Wat Tyler," cited the glory of the past Jacquerie in support of the present revolution. Another, Coleridge, a poor fellow, who had served as a dragoon, his brain stuffed with incoherent reading and humanitarian dreams, thought of founding in America a communist republic, purged of kings and priests; then, having turned Unitarian, steeped himself at Göttingen in heretical and mystical theories on the Logos and the absolute. Wordsworth himself, the third and most moderate, had begun with enthusiastic verses against kings:

>"Great God,... grant that every sceptred child of clay,
>Who cries presumptuous, 'Here the flood shall stay,'
>May in its progress see thy guiding hand,
>And cease the acknowledged purpose to withstand;
>Or, swept in anger from the insulted shore,
>Sink with his servile bands, to rise no more!"[109]

But these rages and aspirations did not last long; and at the end of a few years, the three, brought back into the pale of Church and State, became, Coleridge, a Pittite journalist, Wordsworth, a distributor of stamps, and Southey, poet-laureate; all zealous converts, decided Anglicans, and intolerant Conservatives. In point of taste, however, they had advanced, not retired.

BOOK IV— MODERN LIFE

They had violently broken with tradition, and leaped over all classical culture to take their models from the Renaissance and the Middle Ages. One of their friends, Charles Lamb, like Saint-Beuve, had discovered and restored the sixteenth century. The most unpolished dramatists, like Marlowe, seemed to these men admirable; and they sought in the collections of Percy and Warton, in the old national ballads and ancient poetry of foreign lands, the fresh and primitive accent which had been wanting in classical literature, and whose presence seemed to them to be a sign of truth and beauty. Above every other reform, they labored to destroy the grand aristocratical and oratorical style, such as it sprang from methodical analyses and court polish. They proposed to adapt to poetry the ordinary language of conversation, such as is spoken in the middle and lower classes, and to replace studied phrases and a lofty vocabulary by natural tones and plebeian words. In place of the classical mould, they tried stanzas, sonnets, ballads, blank verse, with the roughness and subdivisions of the primitive poets. They adopted or arranged the metres and diction of the thirteenth and sixteenth centuries. Charles Lamb wrote an archaic tragedy, "John Woodvil," which we might fancy to have been written during Elizabeth's reign. Others, like Southey, and Coleridge, in particular, manufactured totally new rhythms, as happy at times, and at times also as unfortunate, as those of Victor Hugo: for instance, a verse in which accents, and not syllables, were counted;[110] a singular medley of confused attempts, manifest abortions, and original inventions. The plebeian having doffed the aristocratical costume, sought another; borrowed one piece of his dress from the knights or the barbarians, another from peasants or journalists, not too critical of incongruities, pretentious and satisfied with his motley and badly sewn cloak, till at last, after many attempts and many rents, he ended by knowing himself, and selecting the dress that fitted him.

In this confusion of labors two great ideas stand out: the first producing historical poetry, the second philosophical; the one especially manifest in Southey and Walter Scott, the other in Wordsworth and Shelley; both European, and displayed with equal brilliancy in France by Hugo, Lamartine, and Musset; with greater brilliancy in Germany by Goethe, Schiller, Rückert, and Heine; both so profound, that none of their representatives, except Goethe, divined their scope; and hardly now, after more than half a century, can we define their nature, so as to forecast their results.

The first consists in saying, or rather foreboding, that our ideal is not the ideal; it is only one ideal, but there are others. The barbarian, the feudal man, the cavalier of the Renaissance, the Mussulman, the Indian, each age and each race has conceived its beauty, which was a beauty. Let us enjoy it, and for this purpose put ourselves entirely in the place of the discoverers; for it will not suffice to depict, as the previous novelists and dramatists have done, modern and national manners under old and foreign names; let us paint the sentiments of other ages and other races with their own features, however different these features may be from our own, and however unpleasing to our taste. Let us show our hero as he was, grotesque or not, with his true costume and speech: let him be fierce and superstitious if he was so; let us dash the barbarian with blood, and load the Covenanter with his bundle of biblical texts. Then one by one on the literary stage men saw the vanished or distant civilizations return; first the Middle Age and the Renaissance; then Arabia, Hindostan, and Persia; then the classical age, and the eighteenth century itself; and the historic taste becomes so eager, that from literature the contagion spread to other arts. The theatre changed its conventional costumes and decorations into true ones. Architecture built Roman villas in our northern climates, and feudal towers amidst our modern security. Painters travelled to imitate local coloring, and studied to reproduce moral coloring. Every man became a tourist and an archæologist; the human mind quitting its individual sentiments to adopt all sentiments really felt, and finally all possible sentiments, found its pattern in the great Goethe, who by his "Tasso, Iphigenia, Divan," his second part of "Faust," became a citizen of all nations and a contemporary of all ages, seemed to live at pleasure at every point of time and place, and gave an idea of universal mind. Yet this literature, as it approached perfection, approached its limit, and was only developed in order to die. Men did comprehend at last that attempted resurrections are always incomplete, that every imitation is only an imitation, that the modern accent infallibly penetrates the words which we place in the mouths of ancient characters, that every picture of manners must be indigenous and contemporaneous, and that archaic literature is essentially untrue. People saw at last that it is in the writers of the past that we must seek the portraiture of the past; that there are no Greek tragedies but the Greek tragedies; that the concocted novel must give place to authentic memoirs, as the fabricated ballad to the spontaneous; in other words, that historical literature must vanish and become transformed into criticism and history, that is, into exposition and commentary of documents.

How shall we select in this multitude of travellers and historians, disguised as poets? They abound like swarms of insects, hatched on a summer's day amidst a rank vegetation; they buzz and glitter, and the mind is lost in their sparkle and hum. Which shall I quote? Thomas Moore, the gayest and most French of all, a witty railer,[111] too graceful and *recherché*, writing descriptive odes on the Bermudas, sentimental Irish melodies, a poetic Egyptian tale,[112] a romantic poem on Persia and India;[113] Lamb, a restorer of the old drama; Coleridge, a thinker and dreamer, a poet and critic, who in "Christabel" and the "Ancient Mariner" reopened the vein of the supernatural and the fantastic; Campbell, who, having begun with a didactic poem on the "Pleasures of Hope," entered the new school without giving up his noble and half-classical style, and wrote American and Celtic poems, only slightly Celtic and American; in the first rank, Southey, a clever man, who, after several mistakes in his youth, became the professed defender of aristocracy and cant, an indefatigable reader, an inexhaustible writer, crammed with erudition, gifted in imagination, famed like Victor Hugo for the freshness of his innovations, the combative tone of his prefaces, the splendors of his picturesque curiosity, having spanned the universe and all history with his poetic shows, and embraced in the endless web of his verse, Joan of Arc, Wat Tyler, Roderick the Goth, Madoc, Thalaba, Kehama, Celtic and Mexican traditions, Arabic and Indian legends, successively a Catholic, a Mussulman, a Brahmin, but only in verse; in reality, a prudent and respectable Protestant. The above-mentioned authors have to be taken as examples merely— there are dozens behind; and I think that, of all fine visible or imaginable sceneries, of all great real or legendary events, at all times, in the four quarters of the world, not one has escaped them. The diorama they show us is very brilliant; unfortunately we perceive that it is manufactured. If we would have its fellow picture, let us imagine ourselves at the opera. The decorations are splendid, we see them coming down from above, that is, from the ceiling, thrice in an act; lofty Gothic cathedrals, whose rose-windows glow in the rays of the setting sun, whilst processions wind round the pillars, and the lights flicker over the elaborate copes and the gold embroidery of the priestly vestments; mosques and minarets, moving caravans creeping afar over the yellow sand, whose lances and canopies, ranged in line, fringe the immaculate whiteness of the horizon; Indian paradises, where the heaped roses swarm in myriads, where fountains mingle their plumes of pearls, where the lotus spreads its large leaves, where thorny plants raise their many thousand purple calices around the apes and crocodiles which are worshipped as divinities, and crawl in the thickets. Meantime the dancing-girls lay their hands on their heart with deep and delicate emotion, the tenors sing that they are ready to die, tyrants roll forth their deep bass voice, the orchestra struggles hard, accompanying the variations of sentiment with the gentle sounds of flutes, the lugubrious clamors of the trombones, the angelic melodies of the harps; till at last, when the heroine sets her foot on the throat of the traitor, it breaks out triumphantly with its thousand vibrant voices harmonized into a single strain. A fine spectacle! we depart mazed, deafened; the senses give way under this inundation of splendors; but as we return home, we ask ourselves what we have learnt, felt— whether we have, in truth, felt anything. After all, there is little here but decoration and scenery; the sentiments are factitious; they are operatic sentiments: the authors are only clever men, libretti-makers, manufacturers of painted canvas; they have talent without genius; they draw their ideas not from the heart, but from the head. Such is the impression left by "Lalla Rookh, Thalaba, Roderick the last of the Goths, The Curse of Kehama," and the rest of these poems. They are great decorative machines suited to the fashion. The mark of genius is the discovery of some wide unexplored region in human nature, and this mark fails them; they prove only much cleverness and knowledge. After all, I prefer to see the East in Orientals

HISTORY OF ENGLISH LITERATURE

from the East, rather than in Orientals in England; in Vyasa or Firdousi, rather than in Southey[114] and Moore. These poems may be descriptive or historical; they are less so than the texts, notes, emendations, and justifications which their authors carefully print at the foot of the page.

Beyond all general causes which have fettered this literature, there is a national one: the mind of these men is not sufficiently flexible, and too moral. Their imitation is only literal. They know past times and distant lands only as antiquaries and travellers. When they mention a custom, they put their authorities in a foot-note; they do not present themselves before the public without testimonials; they establish by weighty certificates that they have not committed an error in topography or costume. Moore, like Southey, named his authorities; Sir John Malcolm, Sir William Ouseley, Mr. Cary, and others, who returned from the East, and had lived there, state that his descriptions are wonderfully faithful, that they thought that Moore had travelled in the East. In this respect their minuteness is ridiculous;[115] and their notes, lavished without stint, show that their matter-of-fact public required to ascertain whether their poetical commodities were genuine produce. But that broader truth, which lies in penetrating into the feelings of characters, escaped them; these feelings are too strange and immoral. When Moore tried to translate and recast Anacreon, he was told that his poetry was fit for "the stews."[116] To write an Indian poem, we must be pantheistical at heart, a little mad, and pretty generally visionary; to write a Greek poem, we must be polytheistic at heart, fundamentally pagan, and a naturalist by profession. This is the reason that Heine spoke so fitly of India, and Goethe of Greece. A genuine historian is not sure that his own civilization is perfect, and lives as gladly out of his country as in it. Judge whether Englishmen can succeed in this style. In their eyes there is only one rational civilization, which is their own; every other morality is inferior, every other religion is extravagant. With such narrowness, how can they reproduce these other moralities and religions? Sympathy alone can restore extinguished or foreign manners, and sympathy here is forbidden. Under this narrow rule, historical poetry, which itself is hardly likely to live, languishes as though suffocated under a leaden cover.

One of them, a novelist, critic, historian, and poet, the favorite of his age, read over the whole of Europe, was compared and almost equalled to Shakespeare, had more popularity than Voltaire, made dressmakers and duchesses weep, and earned about two hundred thousand pounds. Murray, the publisher, wrote to him: "I believe I might swear that I never experienced such unmixed pleasure as the reading of this exquisite work (first series of 'Tales of my Landlord' has afforded me....) Lord Holland said, when I asked his opinion: 'Opinion! we did not one of us go to bed last night— nothing slept but my gout.'"[117] In France, fourteen hundred thousand volumes of these novels were sold, and they continue to sell. The author, born in

BOOK IV— MODERN LIFE

Edinburgh, was the son of a writer to the signet, learned in feudal law and ecclesiastical history, himself an advocate, a sheriff, and always fond of antiquities, especially national antiquities; so that by his family, education, by his own instincts, he found the materials for his works and the stimulus for his talent. His past recollections were impressed on him at the age of three, in a farm-house, where he had been taken to try the effect of bracing air on his little shrunken leg. He was wrapped naked in the warm skin of a sheep just killed, and he crept about in this attire, which passed for a specific. He continued to limp, and became a reader. From his infancy he listened to the stories which he afterwards gave to the public— that of the battle of Culloden, of the cruelties practised on the Highlanders, the wars and sufferings of the Covenanters. At three he used to sing out the ballad of Hardyknute so loudly that he prevented the village minister, a man gifted with a very fine voice, from being heard, and even from hearing himself. As soon as he had heard "a Border-raid ballad," he knew it by heart. But in other things he was indolent, studied by fits and starts, and did not readily learn dry, hard facts; yet for poetry, old songs, and ballads, the flow of his genius was precocious, swift, and invincible. The day on which he first opened, "under a platanus tree," the volumes in which Percy had collected the fragments of ancient poetry, he forgot dinner, "notwithstanding the sharp appetite of thirteen," and thenceforth he overwhelmed with these old rhymes not only his schoolfellows, but everyone else who would listen to him. After he had become a clerk to his father, he crammed into his desk all the works of imagination which he could find. "The whole Jemmy and Jenny Jessamy tribe I abhorred," he said, "and it required the art of Burney, or the feeling of Mackenzie, to fix my attention upon a domestic tale. But all that was adventurous and romantic,... that touched upon knight-errantry, I devoured."[118] Having fallen ill, he was kept a long time in bed, forbidden to speak, with no other pleasure than to read the poets, novelists, historians, and geographers, illustrating the battle-descriptions by setting in line and disposing little pebbles, which represented the soldiers. Once cured, and able to walk well, he turned his walks to the same purpose, and developed a passion for the country, especially the historical regions. He said:

"But show me an old castle or a field of battle, and I was at home at once, filled it with its combatants in their proper costume, and overwhelmed my hearers by the enthusiasm of my description. In crossing Magus Moor, near St. Andrews, the spirit moved me to give a picture of the assassination of the Archbishop of St. Andrews to some fellow-travellers with whom I was accidentally associated, and one of them, though well acquainted with the story, protested my narrative had frightened away his night's sleep."[119]

Amidst other excursions, in search after knowledge, he travelled once every year during seven years in the wild district of Liddesdale, exploring every stream and every ruin, sleeping in the shepherds' huts, gleaning legends and ballads. We can judge from this of his antiquarian tastes and habits. He read provincial charters, the wretched Middle Age Latin verses, the parish registers, even contracts and wills. The first time he was able to lay his hand on one of the great "old Border war-horns," he blew it all along his route. Rusty mail and dirty parchment attracted him, filled his head with recollections and poetry. In truth, he had a feudal mind, and always wished to be the founder of a distinct branch of an historical family. Literary glory was only secondary; his talent was to him only as an instrument. He spent the vast sums which his prose and verse had won, in building a castle in imitation of the ancient knights, "with a tall tower at either end,... sundry zigzagged gables,... a myriad of indentations and parapets, and machicollated eaves; most fantastic waterspouts; labelled windows, not a few of them painted glass;... stones carved with heraldries innumerable";[120] apartments filled with sideboards and carved chests, adorned with "cuirasses, helmets, swords of every order, from the claymore and rapier to some German executioner's swords." For long years he held open house there, so to speak, and did to every stranger the "honours of Scotland," trying to revive the old feudal life, with all its customs and its display; dispensing liberal and joyous hospitality to all comers, above all to relatives, friends, and neighbors; singing ballads and sounding pibrochs amidst the clinking of glasses; holding gay hunting-parties, where the yeomen and gentlemen rode side by side; and encouraging lively dances, where the lord was not ashamed to give his hand to the miller's daughter. He himself, frank of speech, happy, amidst his forty guests, kept up the conversation with a profusion of stories, lavished from his vast memory and imagination, conducted his guests over his domain, extended at large cost, amidst new plantations whose future shade was to shelter his posterity; and he thought with a poet's smile of the distant generations who would acknowledge for their ancestor Sir Walter Scott, first baronet of Abbotsford.

"The Lady of the Lake, Marmion, The Lord of the Isles, The Fair Maid of Perth, Old Mortality, Ivanhoe, Quentin Durward," who does not know these names by heart? From Walter Scott we learned history. And yet is this history? All these pictures of a distant age are false. Costumes, scenery, externals alone are exact; actions, speech, sentiments, all the rest is civilized, embellished, arranged in modern guise. We might suspect it when looking at the character and life of the author; for what does he desire, and what do the guests, eager to hear him, demand? Is he a lover of truth as it is, foul and fierce; an inquisitive explorer, indifferent to contemporary applause, bent alone on defining the transformations of living nature? By no means. He is in history, as he is at Abbotsford, bent on arranging points of view and Gothic halls. The moon will come in well there between the towers; here is a nicely placed breastplate, the ray of light which it throws back is pleasant to see on these old hangings; suppose we took out the feudal garments from the wardrobe and invited the guests to a masquerade? The entertainment would be a fine one, in accordance with their reminiscences and their aristocratic principles. English lords, fresh from a bitter war against French democracy, ought to enter zealously into this commemoration of their ancestors. Moreover, there are ladies and young girls, and we must arrange the show, so as not to shock their severe morality and their delicate feelings, make them weep becomingly; not put on the stage over-strong passions, which they would not understand; on the contrary, select heroines to resemble them, always touching, but above all correct; young gentlemen, Evandale, Morton, Ivanhoe, irreproachably brought up, tender and grave, even slightly melancholic (it is the latest fashion), and worthy to lead them to the altar. Is there a man more suited than the author to compose such a spectacle? He is a good Protestant, a good husband, a good father, very moral, so decided a Tory that he carries off as a relic a glass from which the king has just drunk. In addition, he has neither talent nor leisure to reach the depths of his characters. He devotes himself to the exterior; he sees and describes forms and externals much more at length than inward feelings. Again, he treats his mind like a coal-mine, serviceable for quick working, and for the greatest possible gain: a volume in a month, sometimes in a fortnight even, and this volume is worth one thousand pounds. How should he discover, or how dare exhibit, the structure of barbarous souls? This structure is too difficult to discover, and too little pleasing to show. Every two centuries, amongst men, the proportion of images and ideas, the mainspring of passions, the degree of reflection, the species of inclinations, change. Who, without a long preliminary training, now understands and relishes Dante, Rabelais, and Rubens? And how, for instance, could these great Catholic and mystical dreams, these vast temerities, or these impurities of carnal art, find entrance into the head of this gentlemanly citizen? Walter Scott pauses on the threshold of the soul, and in the vestibule of history, selects in the Renaissance and the Middle Ages only the fit and agreeable, blots out plain-spoken words, licentious sensuality, bestial ferocity. After all, his characters, to whatever age he transports them, are his neighbors, "cannie" farmers, vain lairds, gloved gentlemen, young marriageable ladies, all more or less commonplace, that is, steady; by their education and character at a great distance from the voluptuous fools of the Restoration, or the heroic brutes and fierce beasts of the Middle Ages. As he has the greatest supply of rich costumes, and the most inexhaustible talent for scenic effect, he makes all his people get on very pleasantly, and composes tales which, in truth, have only the merit of fashion, though that fashion may last a hundred years yet.

That which he himself acted lasted for a shorter time. To sustain his princely hospitality and his feudal magnificence, he went into partnership with his printers; lord of the manor in public and merchant in private, he gave them his signature, without keeping a check over the use they made of it.[121] Bankruptcy followed; at the age of fifty-five he was ruined, and one hundred and seventeen thousand pounds in debt. With admirable courage and uprightness he refused all favor, accepting nothing but time, set to work on the very day, wrote untiringly, in four years paid seventy thousand pounds, exhausted his brain so as to become paralytic, and to perish in the attempt. Neither in his conduct nor his literature did his feudal tastes succeed, and his manorial splendor was as fragile as his Gothic imaginations. He had relied on imitation, and we live by truth only; his glory is to be found elsewhere; there was something solid in his mind as well as in his writings. Beneath the lover of the Middle Ages we find, first the "pawky" Scotchman, an attentive observer, whose sharpness became more intense by his familiarity with law; a good-natured man, easy and cheerful, as beseems the national character, so different from the English. One of his walking companions (Shortreed) said: "Eh me, sic an endless fund o' humour and drollery as he had wi' him! Never ten yards but we were either laughing or roaring and singing. Wherever we stopped, how brawlie he suited himsel' to everybody! He aye did as the lave did; never made himsel' the great man, or took ony airs in the company."[122] Grown older and graver, he was none the less amiable, the most agreeable of hosts, so that one of his guests, a farmer, I think, said to his wife, when home, after having been at Abbotsford, "Ailie, my woman, I'm ready for my bed.... I wish I could sleep for a towmont, for there's only ae thing in this warld worth living for, and that's the Abbotsford hunt!"[123]

In addition to a mind of this kind, he had all-discerning eyes, an all-retentive memory, a ceaseless studiousness which comprehended the whole of Scotland, and all classes of people; and we see his true talent arise, so agreeable, so abundant and so easy, made up of minute observation and gentle raillery, recalling at once Teniers and Addison. Doubtless he wrote badly, at times in the worst possible manner:[124] it is clear that he dictated, hardly reread his writing, and readily fell into a pasty and emphatic style— a style very common in the present times, and which we read day after day in the prospectuses and newspapers. What is worse, he is terribly long and diffuse; his conversations and descriptions are interminable; he is determined, at all events, to fill three volumes. But he has given to Scotland a citizenship of literature— I mean to the whole of Scotland: scenery, monuments, houses, cottages, characters of every age and condition, from the baron to the fisherman, from the advocate to the beggar, from the lady to the fishwife. When we mention merely his name they crowd forward; who does not see them coming from every niche of memory? The Baron of Bradwardine, Dominie Sampson, Meg Merrilies, the Antiquary, Edie Ochiltree, Jeanie Deans and her father— innkeepers, shopkeepers, old wives, an entire people. What Scotch features are absent? Saving, patient, "cannie," and of course "pawky"; the poverty of the soil and the difficulty of existence has compelled them to be so: this is the specialty of the race. The same tenacity which they introduced into every-day affairs they have introduced into mental concerns— studious readers and perusers of antiquities and controversies, poets also; legends spring up readily in a romantic land, amidst time-honored wars and brigandism. In a land thus prepared, and in this gloomy clime, Presbyterianism sunk its sharp roots. Such was the real and modern world, lit up by the far-setting sun of chivalry, as Sir Walter Scott found it; like a painter who, passing from great show-pictures, finds interest and beauty in the ordinary houses of a paltry provincial town, or in a farm surrounded by beds of beet-roots and turnips. A continuous archness throws its smile over these interior and *genre* pictures, so local and minute, and which, like the Flemish, indicate the rise of well-to-do citizens. Most of these good folk are comic. Our author makes fun of them, brings out their little deceits, parsimony, fooleries, vulgarity, and the hundred thousand ridiculous habits people always contract in a narrow sphere of life. A barber, in "The Antiquary," moves heaven and earth about his wigs; if the French Revolution takes root everywhere, it was because the magistrates gave up this ornament. He cries out in a lamentable voice: "Haud a care, haud a care, Monkbarns! God's sake, haud a care!— Sir Arthur's drowned already, and an ye fa' over the cleugh too, there will be but ae wig left in the parish, and that's the minister's."[125] Mark how the author smiles, and without malice: the barber's candid selfishness is the effect of the man's calling, and does not repel us. Walter Scott is never bitter; he loves men from the bottom of his heart, excuses or tolerates them; does not chastise vices, but unmasks them, and that not rudely. His greatest pleasure is to pursue at length, not indeed a vice, but a hobby; the mania for odds and ends in an antiquary, the archaeological vanity of the Baron of Bradwardine, the aristocratic drivel of the Dowager Lady Bellenden— that is, the amusing exaggeration of an allowable taste; and this without anger, because, on the whole, these ridiculous people are estimable, and even generous. Even in rogues like Dirk Hatteraick, in cut-throats like Bothwell, he allows some goodness. In no one, not even in Major Dalgetty, a professional murderer, a result of the thirty years' war, is the odious unveiled by the ridiculous. In this critical refinement and this benevolent philosophy, he resembles Addison.

He resembles him again by the purity and endurance of his moral principles. His amanuensis, Mr. Laidlaw, told him that he was doing great good by his attractive and noble tales, and that young people would no longer wish to look in the literary rubbish of the circulating libraries. When Walter Scott heard this, his eyes filled with tears: "On his deathbed he said to his son-in-law: 'Lockhart, I have but a minute to speak to you. My dear, be a good man— be virtuous, be religious— be a good man. Nothing else will give you any comfort when you come to lie here.'"[126] This was almost his last word. By this fundamental honesty, and this broad humanity, he was the Homer of modern citizen life. Around and after him, the novel of manners, separated from the historical romance, has produced a whole literature, and preserved the character which he stamped upon it. Miss Austen, Miss Brontë, Mrs. Gaskell, George Eliot, Bulwer, Thackeray, Dickens, and many others, paint, especially or entirely in his style, contemporary life, as it is, unembellished, in all ranks, often amongst the people, more frequently still amongst the middle class. And the causes which made the historical novel come to naught, in Scott and others, made the novel of manners, by the same authors, succeed. These men were too minute copyists and too decided moralists, incapable of the great divinations and the wide sympathies which unlock the door of history; their imagination was too literal, and their judgment too unwavering. It is precisely by these faculties that they created a new species of novel, which multiplies to this day in thousands of offshoots, with such abundance, that men of talent in this branch of literature may be counted by hundreds, and that we can only compare them, for their original and national spirit, to the great age of Dutch painting. Realistic and moral, these are their two features. They are far removed from the great imagination which creates and transforms, as it appeared in the Renaissance or in the seventeenth century, in the heroic or noble ages. They renounce free invention; they narrow themselves to scrupulous exactness; they paint with infinite detail costumes and places, changing nothing; they mark little shades of language; they are not disgusted by vulgarities or platitudes. Their information is authentic and precise. In short, they write like citizens for fellow-citizens, that is, for well-ordered people, members of a profession, whose imagination does not soar high, and sees things through a magnifying glass, unable to relish anything in the way of a picture except interiors and make-believes. Ask a cook which picture she prefers in the museum, and she will point to a kitchen, in which the stewpans are so well painted that a man is tempted to put soup and bread in them. Yet beyond this inclination, which is now European, Englishmen have a special craving, which with them is national and dates from the preceding century; they desire that the novel, like all other things, should contribute to their great work— the amelioration of man and society. They ask from it the glorification of virtue, and the chastisement of vice. They send it into all the corners of civil society, and all the events of private history, in search of examples and expedients, to learn thence the means of remedying abuses, succoring miseries, avoiding temptations. They make of it an instrument of inquiry, education, and morality. A singular work, which has not its equal in all history, because in all history there has been no society like it, and which— of moderate attraction for lovers of the beautiful, admirable to lovers of the useful— offers, in the countless variety of its painting, and the invariable stability of its spirit, the picture of the only democracy which knows how to restrain, govern, and reform itself.

Section V.—Philosophy Enters into Literature.—Wordsworth.—Shelley

Side by side with this development there was another, and with history philosophy entered into literature, in order to widen and modify it. It was manifest throughout, on the threshold as in the centre. On the threshold it had planted aesthetics: every poet, becoming theoretic, defined before producing the beautiful, laid down principles in his preface and originated only after a preconceived system. But the ascendancy of metaphysics was much more visible yet in the middle of the work than on its threshold; for not only did it prescribe the form of poetry, but it furnished it with its elements. What is man, and what has he come into the world to do? What is this far-off greatness to which he aspires? Is there a haven which he may reach, and a hidden hand to conduct him thither? These are the questions which poets, transformed into thinkers, agreed to agitate; and Goethe, here as elsewhere the father and promoter of all lofty modern ideas, at once sceptical, pantheistic, and mystic, wrote in "Faust" the epic of the age and the history of the human mind. Need I say that in Schiller, Heine, Beethoven, Victor Hugo, Lamartine, and de Musset, the poet, in his individual person, always speaks the words of the universal man? The characters which they have created, from Faust to Ruy Blas, only served them to exhibit some grand metaphysical and social idea; and twenty times this too great idea, bursting its narrow envelope, broke out beyond all human likelihood and all poetic form, to display itself to the eyes of the spectators. Such was the domination of the philosophical spirit, that, after doing violence to literature, or rendering it rigid, it imposed on music humanitarian ideas, inflicted on painting symbolical designs, penetrated current speech, and marred style by an overflow of abstractions and formulas, from which all our efforts now fail to liberate us. As an overstrong child, which at its birth injures its mother, so it has contorted the noble forms which had endeavored to contain it, and dragged literature through an agony of struggles and sufferings.

This philosophical spirit was not born in England, and from Germany to England the passage was very long. For a considerable time it appeared dangerous or ridiculous. One of the reviews stated even, that Germany was a large country peopled by hussars and classical scholars; that if folks go there, they will see at Heidelberg a very large tun, and could feast on excellent Rhine wine and Westphalian ham, but that their authors were, very heavy and awkward, and that a sentimental German resembles a tall and stout butcher crying over a killed calf. If at length German literature found entrance, first by the attraction of extravagant dramas and fantastic ballads, then by the sympathy of the two nations, which, allied against French policy and civilization, acknowledged their cousinship in speech, religion, and blood, German metaphysics did not enter, unable to overturn the barrier which a positive mind and a national religion opposed to it. It tried to pass, with Coleridge for instance, a philosophical theologian and dreamy poet, who toiled to widen conventional dogma, and who, at the close of his life, having become a sort of oracle, endeavored, in the pale of the Church, to unfold and unveil before a few faithful disciples the Christianity of the future. It did not make head; the English mind was too positive, the theologians too enslaved. It was constrained to transform itself and become Anglican, or to deform itself and become revolutionary; and to produce a Wordsworth, a Byron, a Shelley, instead of a Schiller and Goethe.

The first, Wordsworth, a new Cowper, with less talent and more ideas than the other, was essentially a man of inner feelings, that is, engrossed by the concerns of the soul. Such men ask what they have come to do in this world, and why life has been given to them; if they are right or wrong, and if the secret movements of their heart are conformable to the supreme law, without taking into account the visible causes of their conduct. Such, for men of this kind, is the master conception which renders them serious, meditative, and as a rule gloomy.[127] They live with eyes turned inwards, not to mark and classify their ideas, like physiologists, but as moralists, to approve or blame their feelings. Thus understood, life becomes a grave business, of uncertain issue, on which we must incessantly and scrupulously reflect. Thus understood, the world changes its aspect; it is no longer a machine of wheels working into each other, as the philosopher says, nor a splendid blooming plant, as the artist feels— it is the work of a moral being, displayed as a spectacle to moral beings.

Figure such a man facing life and the world; he sees them, and takes part in it, apparently like anyone else; but how different is he in reality! His great thought pursues him; and when he beholds a tree, it is to meditate on human destiny. He finds or lends a sense to the least objects: a soldier marching to the sound of the drum makes him reflect on heroic sacrifice, the support of societies; a train of clouds lying heavily on the verge of a gloomy sky, endues him with that melancholy calm, so suited to nourish moral life. There is nothing which does not recall him to his duty and admonish him of his origin. Near or far, like a great mountain in a landscape, his philosophy will appear behind all his ideas and images. If he is restless, impassioned, sick with scruples, it will appear to him amidst storm and lightning, as it did to the genuine Puritans, to Cowper, Pascal, Carlyle. It will appear to him in a grayish kind of fog, imposing and calm, if he enjoys, like Wordsworth, a calm mind and a quiet life. Wordsworth was a wise and happy man, a thinker and a dreamer, who read and walked. He was from the first in tolerably easy circumstances, and had a small fortune. Happily married, amidst the favors of government and the respect of the public, he lived peacefully on the margin of a beautiful lake, in sight of noble mountains, in the pleasant retirement of an elegant house, amidst the admiration and attentions of distinguished and chosen friends, engrossed by contemplations which no storm came to distract, and by poetry which was produced without any hinderance. In this deep calm he listens to his own thoughts; the peace was so great, within him and around him, that he could perceive the imperceptible. "To me, the meanest flower that blows, can give Thoughts that do often lie too deep for tears." He saw a grandeur, a beauty, a teaching in the trivial events which weave the woof of our most commonplace days. He needed not, for the sake of emotion, either splendid sights or unusual actions. The dazzling glare of lamps, the pomp of the theatre, would have shocked him; his eyes were too delicate, accustomed to quiet and uniform tints. He was a poet of the twilight. Moral existence is commonplace existence, such was his object— the object of his choice. His paintings are cameos with a gray ground, which have a meaning; designedly he suppresses all which might please the senses, in order to speak solely to the heart.

Out of this character sprang a theory— his theory of art, altogether spiritualistic, which, after repelling classical habits, ended by rallying Protestant sympathies, and won for him as many partisans as it had raised enemies.[128] Since the only important thing is moral life, let us devote ourselves solely to nourishing it. The reader must be moved, genuinely, with profit to his soul; the rest is indifferent: let us, then, show him objects moving in themselves, without dreaming of clothing them in a beautiful style. Let us strip ourselves of conventional language and poetic diction. Let us neglect noble words, scholastic and courtly epithets, and all the pomp of factitious splendor, which the classical writers thought themselves bound to assume, and justified in imposing. In poetry, as elsewhere, the grand question is, not ornament, but truth. Let us leave show, and seek effect. Let us speak in a bare style, as like as possible to prose, to ordinary conversation, even to rustic conversation, and let us choose our subjects at hand, in humble life. Let us take for our characters an idiot boy, a shivering old peasant woman, a hawker, a servant stopping in the street. It is the truth of sentiment, not the dignity of the folks, which makes the beauty of a subject; it is the truth of sentiment, not dignity of the words, which makes the beauty of poetry. What matters that it is a villager who weeps, if these tears enable me to see the maternal sentiment? What matters that my verse is a line of rhymed prose, if this line displays a noble emotion? Men read that they may carry away emotion, not phrases; they come to us to look for moral culture, not pretty ways of speaking. And thereupon Wordsworth classifying his poems according to the different faculties of men and the different ages of life, undertakes to lead us through all compartments and degrees of inner education, to the convictions and sentiments which he has himself attained.

All this is very well, but on condition that the reader is in Wordsworth's position; that is, essentially a philosophical moralist, and an excessively sensitive man. When I shall have emptied my head of all worldly thoughts, and looked up at the clouds for ten years to refine my soul, I shall love this poetry. Meanwhile the web of imperceptible threads by which Wordsworth endeavors to bind together all sentiments and embrace all nature, breaks in my fingers; it is too fragile; it is a woof of woven spider-web, spun by a metaphysical imagination, and tearing as soon as a hand of flesh and blood tries to touch it. Half of his pieces are childish, almost foolish;[129] dull events described in a dull style, one platitude after another, and that on principle. All the poets in the world would not reconcile us to so much tedium. Certainly a cat playing with three dry leaves may furnish a philosophical reflection, and figure forth a wise man sporting with the fallen leaves of life; but eighty lines on such a subject make us yawn— much worse, smile. At this rate we will find a lesson in an old tooth-brush, which still continues in use. Doubtless, also, the ways of Providence are not to be fathomed, and a selfish and brutal artisan like Peter Bell may be converted by the beautiful conduct of an ass full of fidelity and unselfishness; but this sentimental prettiness quickly grows insipid, and the style, by its factitious simplicity, renders it still more insipid. We are not over-pleased to see a grave man seriously imitate the language of nurses, and we murmur to ourselves that, with so many emotions, he must wet so many handkerchiefs. We will acknowledge, if you like, that your sentiments are interesting; yet there is no need to trot them all out before us.

We imagine we hear him say: "Yesterday I read Walton's 'Complete Angler'; let us write a sonnet about it. On Easter Sunday I was in a valley in Westmoreland; another sonnet. Two days ago I put too many questions to my little boy and caused him to tell a lie; a poem. I am going to travel on the Continent and through Scotland; poems about all the incidents, monuments, adventures of the journey."

You must consider your emotions very precious, that you put them all under glass! There are only three or four events in each of our lives worthy of being related; our powerful sensations deserve to be exhibited, because they recapitulate our whole existence; but not the little effects of the little agitations which pass through us, and the imperceptible oscillations of our every-day condition. Else I might end by explaining in rhyme that yesterday my dog broke his leg, and that this morning my wife put on her stockings inside out. The specialty of the artist is to cast great ideas in moulds as great; Wordsworth's moulds are of bad common clay, cracked, unable to hold the noble metal which they ought to contain.

But the metal is really noble: and besides several very beautiful sonnets, there is now and then a work, amongst others his largest, "The Excursion," in which we forget the poverty of the getting up to admire the purity and elevation of the thought. In truth, the author hardly puts himself to the trouble of imagining; he walks along and converses with a pious Scotch peddler; this is the whole of the story. The poets of this school always walk, look at nature and think of human destiny; it is their permanent attitude. He converses, then, with the peddler, a meditative character, who has been educated by a long experience of men and things, who speaks very well (too welll!) of the soul and of God, and relates to him the history of a good woman who died of grief in her cottage; then he meets a solitary, a sort of sceptical Hamlet— morose, made gloomy by the death of his family, and the disappointments suffered during his long journeyings; then a clergyman, who took them to the village churchyard, and described to them the life of several interesting people who are buried there. Observe that, just in proportion as reflections and moral discussions arise, and as scenery and moral descriptions spread before us in hundreds, so also dissertations entwine their long thorny hedgerows, and metaphysical thistles multiply in every corner. In short, the poem is as grave and dull as a sermon. And yet, in spite of this ecclesiastical air and the tirades against Voltaire and his age,[130] we feel ourselves impressed as by a discourse of Théodore Jouffroy. After all, Wordsworth is convinced; he has spent his life meditating on these kind of ideas, they are the poetry of his religion, race, climate; he is imbued with them; his pictures, stories, interpretations of visible nature and human life tend only to put the mind in a grave disposition which is proper to the inner man. I enter here as in the valley of Port Royal: a solitary nook, stagnant waters, gloomy woods, ruins, gravestones, and above all the idea of responsible man and the obscure beyond, to which we involuntarily move. I forget the careless French fashions, the custom of not disturbing the even tenor of life. There is an imposing seriousness, an austere beauty in this sincere reflection; we begin to feel respect, we stop and are moved. This book is like a Protestant temple, august, though bare and monotonous. The poet sets forth the great interests of the soul:

> "On Man, on Nature, and on Human Life,
> Musing in solitude, I oft perceive
> Fair trains of imagery before me rise,
> Accompanied by feelings of delight
> Pure, or with no unpleasing sadness mixed;
> And I am conscious of affecting thoughts
> And dear remembrances, whose presence soothes
> Or elevates the Mind, intent to weigh
> The good and evil of our mortal state.
> — To these emotions, whencesoe'er they come,
> Whether from breath of outward circumstance,
> Or from the Soul— an impulse to herself,—
> I would give utterance in numerous verse.
> Of Truth, of Grandeur, Beauty, Love, and Hope,
> And melancholy Fear subdued by Faith;
> Of blessed consolations in distress;
> Of moral strength, and intellectual Power;
> Of joy in widest commonalty spread;

> Of the individual Mind that keeps her own
> Inviolate retirement, subject there
> To Conscience only, and the law supreme
> Of that Intelligence which governs all—
> I sing."[131]

This intelligence, the only holy part of man, is holy in all stages; for this, Wordsworth selects as his characters a peddler, a parson, villagers; in his eyes rank, education, habits, all the worldly envelope of a man, is without interest; what constitutes our worth is the integrity of our conscience; science itself is only profound when it penetrates moral life; for this life fails nowhere;

> "To every Form of being is assigned...
> An active principle:— howe'er removed
> From sense and observation, it subsists
> In all things, in all natures; in the stars
> Of azure heaven, the unenduring clouds,
> In flow'r and tree, in every pebbly stone
> That paves the brooks, the stationary rocks,
> The moving waters, and the invisible air.
> Whate'er exists hath properties that spread
> Beyond itself, communicating good,
> A simple blessing, or with evil mixed;
> Spirit that knows no insulated spot,
> No chasm, no solitude; from link to link
> It circulates, the Soul of all the worlds."[132]

Reject, then, with disdain this arid science:

> "Where Knowledge, ill begun in cold remarks
> On outward things, with formal inference ends;
> Or, if the mind turn inward, she recoils,
> At once— or not recoiling, is perplexed— [133]
> Lost in a gloom of uninspired research....
> Viewing all objects unremittingly
> In disconnexion dead and spiritless;
> And still dividing, and dividing still,
> Breaks down all grandeur."[134]

Beyond the vanities of science and the pride of the world, there is the soul, whereby all are equal, and the broad and inner Christian life opens at once its gates to all who would enter:

> "The sun is fixed,
> And the infinite magnificence of heaven
> Fixed within reach of every human eye.
> The sleepless Ocean murmurs for all ears,
> The vernal field infuses fresh delight
> Into all hearts....
> The primal duties shine aloft like stars,
> The charities that soothe and heal and bless
> Are scattered at the feet of man— like flowers."

So, at the end of all agitation and all search appears the great truth, which is the abstract of the rest:

> "Life, I repeat, is energy of love
> Divine or human; exercised in pain,
> In strife and tribulation; and ordained,
> If so approved and sanctified, to pass
> Through shades and silent rest to endless joy."[135]

The verses sustain these serious thoughts by their grave harmony, as a motet accompanies meditation or prayer. They resemble the grand and monotonous music of the organ, which in the eventide, at the close of the service, rolls slowly in the twilight of arches and pillars.

When a certain phase of human intelligence comes to light, it does so from all sides; there is no part where it does not appear, no instinct which it does not renew. It enters simultaneously the two opposite camps, and seems to undo with one hand what it has made with the other. If it is, as it was formerly, the oratorical style, we find it at the same time in the service of cynical misanthropy, and in that of decorous humanity, in Swift and in Addison. If it is, as now, the philosophical spirit, it produces at once conservative harangues and socialistic utopias, Wordsworth and Shelley.[136] The latter, one of the greatest poets of the age, son of a rich baronet, beautiful as an angel, of extraordinary precocity, gentle, generous, tender, overflowing with all the gifts of heart, mind, birth, and fortune, marred his life, as it were, wantonly, by allowing his conduct to be guided by an enthusiastic imagination which he should have kept for his verses. From his birth he had "the vision" of sublime beauty and happiness; and the contemplation of an ideal world set him in arms against the real. Having refused at Eton to be a fag of the big boys, he was treated by boys and masters with a revolting cruelty; suffered himself to be made a martyr, refused to obey, and, falling back into forbidden studies, began to form the most immoderate and most poetical dreams. He judged society by the oppression which he underwent, and man by the generosity which he felt in himself; thought that man was good, and society bad, and that it was only necessary to suppress established institutions to make earth "a paradise." He became a republican, a communist, preached fraternity, love, even abstinence from flesh, and as a means the abolition of kings, priests, and God.[137] We can fancy the indignation which such ideas roused in a society so obstinately attached to established order— so intolerant, in which, above the conservative and religious instincts, Cant spoke like a master. Shelley was expelled from the university; his father refused to see him; the Lord Chancellor, by a decree took from him, as being unworthy, the custody of his two children; finally, he was obliged to quit England. I forgot to say that at eighteen he married a young girl of inferior rank, that they separated, that she committed suicide, that he undermined his health by his excitement and suffering,[138] and that to the end of his life he was nervous or ill. Is not this the life of a genuine poet? Eyes fixed on the splendid apparitions with which he peopled space, he went through the world not seeing the highroad, stumbling over the stones of the roadside. He possessed not that knowledge of life which most poets share in common with novelists. Seldom has a mind been seen in which thought soared in loftier regions, and more removed from actual things. When he tried to create characters and events— in "Queen Mab," in "Alastor," in "The Revolt of Islam," in "Prometheus"— he only produced unsubstantial phantoms. Once only, in the "Cenci," did he inspire a living figure (Beatrice) worthy of Webster or old Ford; but in some sort this was in spite of himself, and because in it the sentiments were so unheard of and so strained that they suited superhuman conceptions. Elsewhere his world is throughout beyond our own. The laws of life are suspended or transformed. We move in Shelley's world between heaven and earth, in abstraction, dreamland, symbolism: the beings float in it like those fantastic figures which we see in the clouds, and which alternately undulate and change form capriciously, in their robes of snow and gold.

For souls thus constituted, the great consolation is nature. They are too finely sensitive to find amusement in the spectacle and picture of human passions. Shelley instinctively avoided that spectacle; the sight reopened his own wounds. He was happier in the woods, at the sea-side, in contemplation of grand landscapes. The rocks, clouds, and meadows, which to ordinary eyes seem dull and insensible, are, to a wide sympathy, living and divine existences, which are an agreeable change from men. No virgin smile is so charming as that of the dawn, nor any joy more triumphant than that of the ocean when its waves swell and shimmer, as far as the eye can reach, under the lavish splendor of heaven. At this sight the heart rises unwittingly to the sentiment of ancient legends, and the poet perceives in the inexhaustible bloom of things the peaceful soul of the great mother by whom everything grows and is supported. Shelley spent most of his life in the open air, especially in his boat; first on the Thames, then on the Lake of Geneva, then on the Arno, and in the Italian waters. He loved desert and solitary places, where man

BOOK IV— MODERN LIFE

enjoys the pleasure of believing infinite what he sees, infinite as his soul. And such was this wide ocean, and this shore more barren than its waves. This love was a deep Teutonic instinct, which, allied to pagan emotions, produced his poetry, pantheistic and yet full of thought, almost Greek and yet English, in which fancy plays like a foolish, dreamy child, with the splendid skein of forms and colors. A cloud, a plant, a sunrise— these are his characters: they were those of the primitive poets, when they took the lightning for a bird of fire, and the clouds for the flocks of heaven. But what a secret ardor beyond these splendid images, and how we feel the heat of the furnace beyond the colored phantoms, which it sets afloat over the horizon![139] Has anyone since Shakespeare and Spenser lighted on such tender and such grand ecstasies? Has anyone painted so magnificently the cloud which watches by night in the sky, enveloping in its net the swarm of golden bees, the stars:

> "The sanguine sunrise, with his meteor eyes,
> And his burning plumes outspread,
> Leaps on the back of my sailing rack,
> When the morning star shines dead...[140]
> That orbed maiden with white fire laden,
> Whom mortals call the moon,
> Glides glimmering o'er my fleece-like floor,
> By the midnight breezes strewn."[141]

Read again those verses on the garden, in which the sensitive plant dreams. Alas! they are the dreams of the poet; and the happy visions which floated in his virgin heart up to the moment when it opened out and withered. I will pause in time; I will not proceed, as he did, beyond the recollections of his springtime:

> "The snowdrop, and then the violet,
> Arose from the ground with warm rain wet,
> And their breath was mixed with fresh odor, sent
> From the turf, like the voice and the instrument.
>
> "Then the pied wind-flowers and the tulip tall,
> And narcissi, the fairest among them all,
> Who gaze on their eyes in the stream's recess,
> Till they die of their own dear loveliness.
>
> "And the Naiad-like lily of the vale,
> Whom youth makes so fair and passion so pale,
> That the light of its tremulous bells is seen
> Through their pavilions of tender green;

"And the hyacinth purple, and white, and blue,
Which flung from its bells a sweet peal anew
Of music so delicate, soft, and intense,
It was felt like an odor within the sense;

"And the rose like a nymph to the bath addrest,
Which unveiled the depth of her glowing breast,
Till, fold after fold, to the fainting air
The soul of her beauty and love lay bare;

"And the wand-like lily, which lifted up,
As a Mænad, its moonlight-colored cup,
Till the fiery star, which is its eye,
Gazed through the clear dew on the tender sky...

"And on the stream whose inconstant bosom
Was prankt, under boughs of embowering blossom,
With golden and green light, slanting through
Their heaven of many a tangled hue,

"Broad water-lilies lay tremulously,
And starry river-buds glimmered by,
And round them the soft stream did glide and dance
With a motion of sweet sound and radiance.

"And the sinuous paths of lawn and of moss,
Which led through the garden along and across,
Some open at once to the sun and the breeze,
Some lost among bowers of blossoming trees,

"Were all paved with daisies and delicate bells,
As fair as the fabulous asphodels,
And flowerets which drooping as day drooped too,
Fell into pavilions, white, purple, and blue,
To roof the glow-worm from the evening dew."[142]

Everything lives here, everything breathes and yearns for something. This poem, the story of a plant, is also the story of a soul— Shelley's soul, the sensitive. Is it not natural to confound them? Is there not a community of nature amongst all the dwellers in this world? Verily there is a soul in everything; in the universe is a soul; be the existence what it will, uncultured or rational, defined or vague, ever beyond its sensible form shines a secret essence and something divine, which we catch sight of by sublime illuminations, never reaching or penetrating it. It is this presentiment and yearning which sustains all modern poetry— now in Christian meditations, as with Campbell and Wordsworth, now in pagan visions, as with Keats and Shelley. They hear the great heart of nature beat; they wish to reach it; they try all spiritual and sensible approaches, through Judea and through Greece, by consecrated doctrines and by proscribed dogmas. In this splendid and fruitless effort the greatest become exhausted and die. Their poetry, which they drag with them over these sublime tracks, is torn to pieces. One alone, Byron, attains the summit; and of all these grand poetic draperies, which float like banners, and seem to summon men to the conquest of supreme truth, we see now but tatters scattered by the wayside.

Yet these men did their work. Under their multiplied efforts, and by their unconscious working together, the idea of the beautiful is changed, and other ideas change by contagion. Conservatives contribute to it as well as revolutionaries, and the new spirit breathes through the poems which bless and those which curse Church and State. We learn from Wordsworth and Byron, by profound Protestantism[143] and confirmed scepticism, that in this sacred cant-defended establishment there is matter for reform or for revolt; that we may discover moral merits other than those which the law tickets and opinion accepts; that beyond conventional confessions there are truths; that beyond respected social conditions there are grandeurs; that beyond regular positions there are virtues; that greatness is in the heart and the genius; and all the rest, actions and beliefs, are subaltern. We have just seen that beyond literary conventionalities there is a poetry, and consequently we are disposed to feel that beyond religious dogmas there may be a faith, and beyond social institutions a justice. The old edifice totters, and the Revolution enters, not by a sudden inundation, as in France, but by slow infiltration. The wall built up against it by public intolerance cracks and opens: the war waged against Jacobinism, republican and imperial, ends in victory; and henceforth we may regard opposing ideas, not as opposing enemies, but as ideas. We regard them, and, accommodating them to the different countries, we import them. Roman Catholics are enfranchised, rotten boroughs abolished, the electoral franchise lowered; unjust taxes, which kept up the price of corn, are repealed; ecclesiastical tithes changed into rent-charges; the terrible laws protecting property are modified, the assessment of taxes brought more and more on the rich classes; old institutions, formerly established for the advantage of a race, and in this race of a class, are only maintained when for the advantage of all classes; privileges become functions; and in this triumph of the middle class, which shapes opinion and assumes the ascendancy, the aristocracy, passing from sinecures to services, seems now legitimate only as a national nursery, kept up to furnish public men. At the same time narrow orthodoxy is enlarged. Zoology, astronomy, geology, botany, anthropology, all the sciences of observation, so much cultivated and so popular, forcibly introduce their dissolvent discoveries. Criticism comes in from Germany, rehandles the Bible, rewrites the history of dogma, attacks dogma itself. Meanwhile, poor Scottish philosophy is dried up. Amidst the agitations of sects, endeavoring to transform each other, and rising Unitarianism, we hear at the gates of the sacred ark the continental philosophy roaring like a tide. Now already it has reached literature: for fifty years all great writers have plunged into it— Sydney Smith, by his sarcasms against the numbness of the clergy, and the oppression of the Catholics; Arnold, by his protests against the religious monopoly of the clergy, and the ecclesiastical monopoly of the Anglicans; Macaulay, by his history and panegyric of the liberal revolution; Thackeray, by attacking the nobles, in the interests of the middle class; Dickens, by attacking dignitaries and wealthy men, in the interests of the lowly and poor; Currer Bell and Mrs. Browning, by defending the initiative and independence of women; Stanley and Jowett, by introducing the German exegesis, and by giving precision to biblical criticism; Carlyle, by importing German metaphysics in an English form; Stuart Mill, by importing French positivism in an English form; Tennyson himself, by extending over the beauties of all lands and all ages the protection of his amiable dilettantism and his poetical sympathies— each according to his power and his difference of position; all retained within reach of the shore by their practical prejudices, all strengthened against falling by their moral prejudices; all bent, some with more of eagerness, others with more of distrust, in welcoming or giving entrance to the growing tide of modern democracy and philosophy in State and Church, without doing damage, and gradually, so as to destroy nothing, and to make everything bear fruit.

---

[60]See Alison, "History of Europe"; Porter, "Progress of the Nation."

[61]In the "Fourth Estate," by F. Knight Hunt, 2 vols. 1840, it is said (I. 175) that the first daily and morning paper, "The Daily Courant," appeared in 1709.— Tr.

[62]To realize the contrast, compare Gil Blas and Ruy Blas, Marivaux's Paysan Parvenu and Stendhal's Julien Sorel (in "Rouge et Noir").

[63]The disciple of Faust.

[64]Goethe's "Faust," sc. 1.

[65]Most of these details are taken from the "Life and Works of Burns," by R. Chambers, 1851, 4 vols.

[66]Ibid. I. 14.

[67]My great constituent elements are pride and passion.

[68]Extract from Burns's commonplace-book; Chambers's "Life," I. 79.

[69]Ibid. I. 231. Burns had a right to think so; when he arrived at night in an inn, the very servants woke their fellow-laborers to come and hear him talk.

[70]Ibid. II. 68.

[71]"Man was made to Mourn," a dirge.
[72]"First Epistle to Davie, a brother poet."
[73]"Earnest Cry and Prayer to the Scotch Representatives."
[74]"The Creed of Poverty;" Chambers's "Life," IV. 86.
[75]"The Tree of Liberty."
[76]1780.
[77]"The Holy Fair."
[78]"The Holy Fair."
[79]"Holy Willie's Prayer."
[80]"Epistle to the Rev. John M'math."
[81]"A Dedication to Gavin Hamilton."
[82]"Address to the Deil."
[83]He himself says: "I have been all along a miserable dupe to Love." His brother Gilbert said: "He was constantly the victim of some fair enslaver."
[84]Chambers's "Life of Burns," I. 12.
[85]Byron's Works, ed. Moore, 17 vols, II. 302, "Journal," Dec. 13, 1813.
[86]See a passage from Burns's commonplace-book in Chambers's "Life of Burns," I. 93.
[87]Chambers's "Life," I. 38.
[88]See "Tam o' Shanter. Address to the Deil, The Jolly Beggars, A Man's a Man for a' that, Green Grow the Rashes," etc.
[89]"O Clarinda, shall we not meet in a state, some yet unknown state of being, where the lavish hand of plenty shall minister to the highest wish of benevolence, and where the chill north-wind of prudence shall never blow over the flowery fields of enjoyment?"
[90]"Epistle to James Smith:"
"O Life, how pleasant is thy morning,
Young Fancy's rays the hills
adorning, Cold-pausing Caution's lesson
spurning!"
[91]Chambers's "Life"; Letter to Mr. Js. Burnes, IV. 205.
[92]"The Speeches of William Pitt," 2d ed. 3 vols. 1808, II. 17, Jan. 21, 1794.
[93]"The Speeches of William Pitt," III. 152, Feb. 17, 1800.
[94]Macaulay's Works, VII.; "Life of William Pitt," 396.
[95]"The Works of W. Cowper," ed. Southey, 8 vols. 1843.
[96]Ibid. I. 18.
[97]Ibid. 79.
[98]Ibid. 81.
[99]"The Works of W. Cowper," I. 97.
[100]"The Works of W. Cowper," ed. Southey; Letter to the Rev. John Newton, July 12, 1780.
[101]Ibid. Letter to Rev. J. Newton, August 5, 1786.

[102]"The Task," IV; The Winter Evening.
[103]Ibid.
[104]Ibid.
[105]"The Task," IV; The Winter Evening.
[106]Crabbe may also be considered one of the masters and renovators of poetry, but his style is too classical, and he has been rightly nicknamed "a Pope in worsted stockings."
[107]"The Task," I; The Sofa.
[108]1793-1794.
[109]Wordsworth's Works, new edition, 1870, 6 vols.; "Descriptive Sketches during a Pedestrian Tour," I. 42.
[110]In English poetry as since modified, no one dreams of limiting the number of syllables, even in blank verse.— Tr.
[111]See "The Fudge Family."
[112]"The Epicurean."
[113]"Lalla Rookh."
[114]See also "The History of the Caliph Vathek," a fantastic but powerfully written tale, by W. Beckford, published first in French in 1784.
[115]See the notes of Southey, worse than those of Chateaubriand in the "Martyrs."
[116]"Edinburgh Review."
[117]Lockhart, "Life of Sir Walter Scott," 10 vols. 2d ed. 1839, II. ch. XXXVII. p. 170.
[118]Lockhart's "Life of Sir Walter Scott;" Autobiography, I. 62.
[119]Lockhart's "Life of Sir Walter Scott," Autobiography, I. 72.
[120]Ibid, VII; Abbotsford in 1825.
[121]If Constable's "Memorials" (3 vols. 1873) had been published when M. Taine wrote this portion of his work he perhaps would have seen reason to alter this opinion, because it is clear that, so far from Sir Walter's printer and publisher ruining him, they, if not ruined by Sir Walter, were only equal sharers with him in the imprudences that led to the disaster.— Tr.
[122]Lockhart's "Life," I. ch. VII. 269.
[123]Ibid. VI. ch. XLIX. 252.
[124]See the opening of "Ivanhoe": "Such being our chief scene, the date of our story refers to a period towards the end of the reign of Richard I., when his return from his long captivity had become an event rather wished than hoped for by his despairing subjects, who were in the meantime subjected to every species of subordinate oppression." It is impossible to write in a heavier style.
[125]Sir Walter Scott's Works, 48 vols., 1829; "The Antiquary," ch. VIII.
[126]Lockhart's "Life," X. 217.
[127]The Jansenists, the Puritans, and the Methodists are the extremes of this class.

[128] See the preface of his second edition of "Lyrical Ballads."

[129] "Feter Bell, The White Doe, The Kitten and Falling Leaves," etc.

[130] "This dull product of a scoffer's pen
Impure conceits discharging from a
heart
Hardened by impious pride!"
— Wordsworth's Works, 7 vols. 1849; "The Excursion," book 2; "The Solitary."

[131] Wordsworth's Works, 7 vols. 1849, VII; "The Excursion," Preface, 11.

[132] Wordsworth's Works, 7 vols. 1849, VII. book 9; "Discourse of the Wanderer," opening verses, 315.

[133] Ibid. VII; "The Excursion," book 4; "Despondency Corrected," 137.

[134] Ibid, VII; "The Excursion," book 4; "Despondency Corrected," 149.

[135] Ibid, last lines of book 5, "The Pastor," 20.

[136] See also the novels of Godwin, "Caleb Williams" and others.

[137] "Queen Mab," and notes. At Oxford Shelley issued a kind of thesis, calling it "On the Necessity of Atheism."

[138] Some time before his death, when he was twenty-nine, he said, "If I die now, I shall have lived as long as my father."

[139] See in Shelley's Works, 1853, "The Witch of Atlas, The Cloud, To a Sky-lark," the end of "The Revolt of Islam, Alastor," and the whole of "Prometheus."

[140] "The Cloud," c. III. 502.

[141] Ibid. c. IV. 503.

[142] Shelley's Works, 1853, "The Sensitive Plant," 490.

[143] "Our life is turned out of her course, whenever man is made an offering, a sacrifice, a tool, or implement, a passive thing employed as a brute mean."— Wordsworth, "The Excursion."

Chapter Second. Lord Byron

Section I.—His Life and Character

I have reserved for the last the greatest and most English of these literary men; he is so great and so English that from him alone we shall learn more truths of his country and of his age than from all the rest put together. His ideas were proscribed during his life; it has been attempted to depreciate his genius since his death. Even at the present day English critics are hardly just to him. He fought all his life against the society from which he was descended; and during his life, as after his death, he suffered the penalty of the resentment which he provoked, and the dislike to which he gave rise. A foreign critic may be more impartial, and freely praise the powerful hand whose blows he has not felt.

If ever there was a violent and madly sensitive soul, but incapable of shaking off its bonds; ever agitated, but yet shut in; predisposed to poetry by its innate fire, but limited by its natural barriers to a single kind of poetry— it was Byron's.

This promptitude to extreme emotions was with him a family legacy, and the result of education. His great-uncle, a sort of raving and misanthropical maniac, had slain in a tavern brawl, by candle-light, Mr. Chaworth, his relative, and had been tried before the House of Lords. His father, a brutal roisterer, had eloped with the wife of Lord Carmarthen, ruined and ill-treated Miss Gordon, his second wife; and, after living like a madman and a scoundrel, had gone with the remains of his wife's family property, to die abroad. His mother, in her moments of fury, would tear her dresses and her bonnets to pieces. When her wretched husband died she almost lost her reason, and her cries were heard in the street. It would take a long story to tell what a childhood Byron passed under the care of "this lioness"; in what torrents of insults, interspersed with softer moods, he himself lived, just as passionate and more bitter. His mother ran after him, called him a "lame brat," shouted at him, and threw fire-shovel and tongs at his head. He held his tongue, bowed, and none the less felt the outrage. One day, when he was "in one of his silent rages," they had to take out of his hand a knife which he had taken from the table, and which he was already raising to his throat. Another time the quarrel was so terrible that son and mother, each privately, went to "the apothecary's, inquiring anxiously whether the other had been to purchase poison, and cautioning the vendor of drugs not to attend to such an application, if made."[144] When he went to school, "his friendships were passions." Many years after he left Harrow, he never heard the name of Lord Clare, one of his old schoolfellows, pronounced, without "a beating of the heart."[145] A score of times he got himself into trouble for his friends, offering them his time, his pen, his purse. One day, at Harrow, a big boy claimed the right to fag his

BOOK IV– MODERN LIFE

friend, little Peel, and finding him refractory, gave him a beating on the inner fleshy side of his arm, which he had twisted round to render the pain more acute. Byron, too small to fight the rascal, came up to him, "blushing with rage," tears in his eyes, and asked with a trembling voice how many stripes he meant to inflict. "Why," returned the executioner, "you little rascal, what is that to you? Because, if you please," said Byron, holding out his arm, "I would take half."[146] He never met with objects of distress without affording them succor.[147] In his latter days, in Italy, he gave away a thousand pounds out of every four thousand he spent. The upwellings of this heart were too copious, and flooded forth good and evil impetuously, and at the least collision. Like Dante, in his early youth, Byron, at the age of eight, fell in love with a child named Mary Duff.

> "How very odd that I should have been so utterly, devotedly fond of that girl, at an age when I could neither feel passion, nor know the meaning of the word!... I recollect all our caresses,... my restlessness, my sleeplessness. My misery, my love for that girl were so violent, that I sometimes doubt if I have ever been really attached since. When I heard of her being married,... it nearly threw me into convulsions."[148]

At twelve years he fell in love with his cousin, Margaret Parker:

> "My passion had its usual effects upon me. I could not sleep— I could not eat— I could not rest; and although I had reason to know that she loved me, it was the texture of my life to think of the time which must elapse before we could meet again, being usually about twelve hours of separation. But I was a fool then, and am not much wiser now."[149]

He never was wiser, read hard at school; took too much exercise; later on, at Cambridge, Newstead, and London, he changed night into day, rushed into debauchery, kept long fasts, led an unwholesome way of living, and engaged in the extreme of every taste and every excess. As he was a dandy, and one of the most brilliant, he nearly let himself die of hunger for fear of becoming fat, then drank and ate greedily during his nights of recklessness. Moore said:
"Lord Byron, for the last two days, had done nothing towards sustenance beyond eating a few biscuits and (to appease appetite) chewing mastic.... He confined himself to lobsters, and of these finished two or three to his own share,— interposing, sometimes, a small liqueur-glass of strong white brandy, sometimes a tumbler of very hot water, and then pure brandy again, to the amount of near half a dozen small glasses of the latter.... After this we had

claret, of which having despatched two bottles between us, at about four o'clock in the morning we parted."[150]

Another day we find in Byron's journal the following words:

"Yesterday, dined *tête-à-tête* at the 'Cocoa' with Scrope Davies— sat from six till midnight— drank between us one bottle of champagne and six of claret, neither of which wines ever affect me."[151]

Later, at Venice:

"I have hardly had a wink of sleep this week past. I have had some curious masking adventures this carnival.... I will work the mine of my youth to the last vein of the ore, and then— good night. I have lived, and am content."[152]

At this rate the organs wear out, and intervals of temperance are not sufficient to repair them. The stomach does not continue to act, the nerves get out of order, and the soul undermines the body, and the body the soul.

"I always wake in actual despair and despondency, in all respects, even of that which pleased me over-night. In England, five years ago, I had the same kind of hypochondria, but accompanied with so violent a thirst that I have drank as many as fifteen bottles of soda-water in one night after going to bed, and been still thirsty,... striking off the necks of bottles from mere thirsty impatience."[153]

Much less is necessary to ruin mind and body wholly. Thus these vehement minds live, ever driven and broken by their own energy, like a cannon ball, which, when fired, turns and spins round quickly, but at the smallest obstacle leaps up, rebounds, destroys everything, and ends by burying itself in the earth. Beyle, a most shrewd observer, who lived with Byron for several weeks, says that on certain days he was mad; at other times, in presence of beautiful things, he became sublime. Though reserved and proud, music made him weep. The rest of his time, petty English passions, pride of rank, for instance, a vain dandyism, unhinged him: he spoke of Brummel with a shudder of jealousy and admiration. But small or great, the passion of the hour swept down upon his mind like a tempest, roused him, transported him either into imprudence or genius. Byron's own journal, his familiar letters, all his unstudied prose, is, as it were, trembling with wit, anger, enthusiasm; the smallest words breathe sensitiveness; since Saint Simon we have not seen more lifelike confidences. All styles appear dull, and all souls sluggish by the side of his.

In this splendid rush of unbridled and disbanded faculties, which leaped up at random, and seemed to drive him without option to the four quarters of the globe, one took the reins, and cast him on the wall against which he was broken.

"Sir Walter Scott describes Lord Byron as being a man of real goodness of heart, and the kindest and best feelings, miserably thrown away by his foolish contempt of public opinion. Instead of being warned or checked by public opposition, it roused him to go on in a worse strain, as if he said, 'Ay, you don't like it; well, you shall have something worse for your pains.'"[154]

This rebellious instinct is inherent in the race; there was a whole cluster of wild passions, born of the climate,[155] which nourished him: a gloomy humor, violent imagination, indomitable pride, a relish for danger, a craving for strife, that inner exaltation, only satiated by destruction, and that sombre madness which urged forward the Scandinavian Berserkirs, when, in an open bark, beneath a sky cloven with lightning, they abandoned themselves to the tempest, whose fury they had breathed. This instinct is in the blood: people are born so, as they are born lions or bull-dogs.[156] Byron was still a little boy in petticoats when his nurse scolded him roughly for having soiled or torn a new frock which he had just put on. He got into one of his silent rages, seized the garment with his hands, rent it from top to bottom, and stood erect, motionless, and gloomy before the storming nurse, so as to set more effectually her wrath at defiance. His pride mastered him. When at ten he inherited the title of lord, and his name was first called at school, preceded by the title dominas, he could not answer the customary *adsum*, stood silent amidst the general stare of his school-fellows, and at last burst into tears. Another time, at Harrow, in a dispute which was dividing the school, a boy said, "Byron won't join us, for he never likes to be second anywhere." He was offered the command, and then only would he condescend to take part with them. Never to submit to a master; to rise with his whole soul against every semblance of encroachment or rule; to keep his person intact and inviolate at all cost, and to the end against all; to dare everything rather than give any sign of submission,— such was his character. This is why he was disposed to undergo anything rather than give signs of weakness. At ten he was a stoic from pride. His foot was painfully stretched in a wooden contrivance whilst he was taking his Latin lesson, and his master pitied him, saying "he must be suffering. Never mind, Mr. Rogers," he said, "you shall not see any signs of it in me."[157] Such as he was as a child, he continued as a man. In mind and body he strove, or prepared himself for strife. Every day, for hours at a time, he boxed, fired pistols, practised sword-exercise, ran and leaped, rode, overcame obstacles. These were the exploits of his hands and muscles; but he needed others. For lack of enemies he found fault with society, and made war upon it. We know to what excesses the dominant opinions then ran. England was at the height of the war with France, and thought it was fighting for morality and liberty. In English eyes, at this time, Church and State were holy things: anyone who touched them became a public enemy. In this fit of natural passion and Protestant severity, whosoever publicly avowed liberal ideas and manners seemed an incendiary, and stirred up against himself the instincts of property, the doctrines of moralists, the interests of politicians, and the prejudices of the people. Byron chose this moment to praise Voltaire and Rousseau, to admire Napoleon, to avow himself a sceptic, to plead for nature and pleasure against cant and regularity, to say that high English society, debauched and hypocritical, made phrases and killed men, to preserve its sinecures and rotten boroughs. As though political hatred was not enough, he contracted, in addition, literary animosities, attacked the whole body of critics,[158] ran down the new poetry, declared that the most celebrated were "Claudians," men of the later empire, raged against the Lake school, and in consequence had in Southey a bitter and unwearied enemy. Thus provided with enemies, he laid himself open to attack on all sides. He decried himself through his hatred of cant, his bravado, his boasting about his vices. He depicted himself in his heroes, but for the worse; in such a way that no man could fail to recognize him, and think him much worse than he was. Walter Scott wrote, immediately after seeing "Childe Harold":

"'Childe Harold' is, I think, a very clever poem, but gives no good symptom of the writer's heart or morals... Vice ought to be a little more modest, and it must require impudence almost equal to the noble Lord's other powers, to claim sympathy gravely for the ennui arising from his being tired of his wassailers and his paramours. There is a monstrous deal of conceit in it, too, for it is informing the inferior part of the world that their little old-fashioned scruples of limitation are not worthy of his regard."[159]

"My noble friend is something like my old peacock, who chooses to bivouac apart from his lady, and sit below my bedroom window, to keep me awake with his screeching lamentation. Only, I own he is not equal in melody to Lord Byron."[160]

Such were the sentiments which he called forth in all respectable classes. He was pleased thereat, and did worse— giving out that in his adventures in the East he had dared a good many things; and he was not indignant when identified with his heroes. He said he should like to feel for once the sensations of a man who had committed a murder. Another time he wrote in his diary:

"Hobhouse told me an odd report— that I am the actual Conrad, the veritable Corsair, and that part of my travels are supposed to have passed in privacy. Um! people sometimes hit near the truth, but never the whole truth. He don't know what I was about the year after he left the Levant; nor does anyone— nor— nor— nor— however, it is a lie— 'but I doubt the equivocation of the fiend that lies like truth.'"[161]

These dangerous words were turned against him like a dagger; but he loved danger, mortal danger, and was only at ease when he saw the points of all angers bristling against him. Alone against all, against an armed society; erect, invincible, even against common-sense, even against conscience— it was then he felt in all his strained nerves the great and terrible sensation, to which his whole being involuntarily inclined.

A last imprudence brought down the attack. As long as he was an unmarried man, his excesses might be excused by the overstrong passions of a temperament which often causes youth in England to revolt against good taste and rule; but marriage settles them, and it was marriage which in him completed his unsettling. He found that his wife was a kind of paragon of virtue, known as such, "a creature of rule," correct and without feelings, incapable of committing a fault herself, and of forgiving. His servant Fletcher observed, "It is very odd, but I never yet knew a lady that could not manage my Lord *except* my Lady."[162] Lady Byron thought her husband mad, and had him examined by physicians. Having learned that he was in his right mind, she left him, returned to her father, and refused ever to see him again. Thereupon he passed for a monster. The papers covered him with obloquy; his friends induced him not to go to a theatre or to Parliament, fearing that he would be hooted or insulted. The rage and pangs which so violent a soul, precociously accustomed to brilliant glory felt in this universal storm of outrage, can only be learned from his verses. He grew stubborn, went to Venice, and steeped himself in the voluptuous Italian life, even in low debauchery, the better to insult the Puritan prudery which had condemned him, and left it only through an offence still more blamed, his public intimacy with the young Countess Guiccioli. Meanwhile he showed himself as bitterly republican in politics as in morality. He wrote in 1813: "I have simplified my politics into an utter detestation of all existing governments." This time, at Ravenna, his house was the centre and storehouse of conspirators, and he generously and imprudently prepared to take arms with them, to strike for the deliverance of Italy:

"They meant to insurrect here, and are to honour me with a call thereupon. I shall not fall back; though I don't think them in force and heart sufficient to make much of it. But, *onward*.... What signifies *self*?... It is not one man nor a million, but the *spirit* of liberty which must be spread.... The mere selfish calculation ought never to be made on such occasions; and, at present, it shall not be computed by me.... I should almost regret that my own affairs went well, when those of nations are in peril."[163]

In the meantime he had quarrels with the police: his house was watched, he was threatened with assassination, and yet he rode out daily, and went into the neighboring pine-forest to practise pistol-shooting. These are the sentiments of a man standing at the muzzle of a loaded cannon, waiting for it to go off. The emotion is great, nay, heroic, but it is not agreeable; and certainly, even at this season of great emotion, he was unhappy. Nothing is more likely to poison happiness than a combative spirit. He writes:

"What is the reason that I have been, all my lifetime, more or less *ennuyé?*... I do not know how to answer this, but presume that it is constitutional,— as well as the waking in low spirits, which I have invariably done for many years. Temperance and exercise, which I have practised at times, and for a long time together vigorously and violently, made little or no difference. Violent passions did: when under their immediate influence— it is odd, but— I was in agitated, but *not* in depressed spirits.... Wine and spirits make me sullen and savage to ferocity— silent, however, and retiring, and not quarrelsome, if not spoken to. Swimming also raises my spirits; but in general they are low, and get daily lower. That is *hopeless*; for I do not think I am so much *ennuyé* as I was at nineteen. The proof is, that then I must game, or drink, or be in motion of some kind, or I was miserable."[164]

"What I feel most growing upon me are laziness, and a disrelish more powerful than indifference. If I rouse, it is into fury. I presume that I shall end (if not earlier by accident, or some such termination) like Swift, 'dying at top.'[165] Lega (his servant) came in with a letter about a bill unpaid at Venice which I thought paid months ago. I flew into a paroxysm of rage, which almost made me faint. I have always had *une âme*, which not only tormented itself, but everybody else in contact with it, and an *esprit violent*, which has almost left me without any esprit at all."[166]

A horrible foreboding, which haunted him to the end! On his death-bed, in Greece, he refused, I know not why, to be bled, and preferred to die at once. They threatened that the uncontrolled disease might end in madness. He sprang up: "There! you are, I see, a d— d set of butchers! Take away as much blood as you like, but have done with it,"[167] and stretched out his arm. Amidst such wild outbursts and anxieties he passed his life. Anguish endured, danger braved, resistance overcome, grief relished, all the greatness and sadness of the black warlike madness— such are the images which he needs must let pass before him. In default of action he had dreams, and he only betook himself to dreams for want of action. He said, when embarking for Greece, that he had taken poetry for lack of better, and that it was not his fit work. "What is a poet? what is he worth? what does he do? He is a babbler." He augured ill of the poetry of his age, even of his own; saying that, if he lived ten years more, they should see something else from him than verses. In reality, he would have been more at home as a sea-king, or a captain of a band of troopers during the Middle Ages. Except two or three gleams of Italian sunshine, his poetry and life, are those of a Scald transplanted into modern life, who in this over-well-regulated world did not find his vocation.

Section II.—The Style of Byron's Poetry

Byron was a poet, but in his own way— a strange way, like that in which he lived. There were internal tempests within him, avalanches of ideas, which found issue only in writing. He wrote: "I have written from the fulness of my mind, from passion, from impulse, from many motives, but not 'for their sweet voices.' To withdraw myself from myself has ever been my sole, my entire, my sincere motive in scribbling at all— and publishing also the continuance of the same object, by the action it affords to the mind, which else recoils upon itself." He wrote almost always with astonishing rapidity, "The Corsair" in ten days, "The Bride of Abydos" in four days. While it was printing he added and corrected, but without recasting: "I told you before that I can never recast anything. I am like the tiger. If I miss the first spring, I go grumbling back to my jungle again; but if I do it, it is crushing."[168] Doubtless he sprang, but he had a chain: never, in the freest flight of his thoughts, did he liberate himself from himself. He dreams of himself, and sees himself throughout. It is a boiling torrent, but hedged in with rocks. No such great poet has had so narrow an imagination; he could not metamorphose himself into another. They are his own sorrows, his own revolts, his own travels, which, hardly transformed and modified, he introduces into his verses. He does not invent, he observes; he does not create, he transcribes. His copy is darkly exaggerated, but it is a copy. "I could not write upon anything," says he, "without some personal experience and foundation." We will find in his letters and note-books, almost feature for feature, the most striking of his descriptions. The capture of Ismail, the shipwreck of Don Juan, are, almost word for word, like two accounts of it in prose. If none but cockneys could attribute to him the crimes of his heroes, none but blind men could fail to see in him the sentiments of his characters. This is so true that he has not created more than one. Childe Harold, Lara, the Giaour, the Corsair, Manfred, Sardanapalus, Cain, Tasso, Dante, and the rest, are always the same— one man represented under various costumes, in several lands, with different expressions; but just as painters do, when, by change of garments, decorations, and attitudes, they draw fifty portraits from the same model. He meditated too much upon himself to be enamored of anything else. The habitual sternness of his will prevented his mind from being flexible; his force, always concentrated for effort and bent upon strife, shut him up in self-contemplation, and reduced him never to make a poem, save of his own heart.

What style would he adopt? With these concentrated and tragic sentiments he had a classical mind. By the strangest mixture, the books which he preferred were at once the most violent or the most proper, the Bible above all: "I am a great reader and admirer of those books (the Bible), and had read them through and through before I was eight years old; that is to say, the Old Testament, for the New struck me as a task, but the other as a pleasure."[169] Observe this word: he did not relish the tender, and self-denying mysticism of the gospel, but the cruel sternness and lyrical outcries of the old Hebrews. Next to the Bible he loved Pope, the most correct and formal of men:

"As to Pope, I have always regarded him as the greatest name in our poetry. Depend upon it, the rest are barbarians. He is a Greek Temple, with a Gothic Cathedral on one hand, and a Turkish Mosque and all sorts of fantastic pagodas and conventicles about him. You may call Shakspeare and Milton pyramids, but I prefer the Temple of Theseus or the Parthenon to a mountain of burnt brickwork.... The grand distinction of the under-forms of the new school of poets is their vulgarity. By this I do not mean they are coarse, but shabby-genteel."[170]

And he presently wrote two letters with incomparable vivacity and spirit to defend Pope against the scorn of modern writers. These writers, according to him, have spoiled the public taste. The only ones who were worth anything— Crabbe, Campbell, Rogers— imitate the style of Pope. A few others had talent; but, take them all together, those who had come last had perverted literature: they did not know their own language; their expressions are only approximate, above or below the true tone, forced or dull. He ranges himself amongst the corrupters,[171] and we soon see that this theory is not an invention, springing from bad temper and polemics; he returns to it. In his two first attempts— "Hours of Idleness, English Bards and Scotch Reviewers"— he tried to follow it up. Later, and in almost all his works, we find its effect. He recommends and practises the rule of unity in tragedy. He loves oratorical form, symmetrical phrase, condensed style. He likes to plead his passions. Sheridan tried to induce Byron to devote himself to eloquence; and the vigor, piercing logic, wonderful vivacity, close argument of his prose, prove that he would have taken the first rank amongst pamphleteers.[172] If he attains to it amongst the poets, it is partly due to his classical system. This oratorical form, in which Pope compresses his thought like La Bruyère, magnifies the force and swing of vehement ideas; like a narrow and straight canal, it collects and dashes them in their right direction; there is then nothing which their impetus does not carry away; and it is thus Lord Byron from the first, in the face of hostile criticisms, and over jealous reputations, has made his way to the public.[173]

Thus "Childe Harold" made its way. At the first onset every man who read it was agitated. It was more than an author who spoke; it was a man. In spite of his denial, the author was identified with his hero: he calumniated himself, but still it was himself whom he portrayed. He was recognized in that young voluptuous and disgusted man, ready to weep amidst his orgies, who

> "Sore sick at heart,
> And from his fellow bacchanals would flee;
> 'Tis said, at times the sullen tear would start,
> But pride congeal'd the drop within his ee:
> Apart he stalk'd in joyless reverie,
> And from his native land resolved to go,
> And visit scorching climes beyond the sea;
> With pleasure drugg'd, he almost long'd for woe."[174]

Fleeing from his native land, he carried, amongst the splendors and cheerfulness of the south, his unwearying persecutor, "demon thought," implacable behind him. The scenery was recognized: it had been copied on the spot. And what was the whole book but a diary of travel? He said in it what he had seen and thought. What poetic fiction is so valuable as genuine sensation? What is more penetrating than confidence, voluntary or involuntary? Truly, every word here expressed an emotion of eye or heart:

> "The tender azure of the unruffled deep....
> The mountain-moss by scorching skies imbrown'd...
> The orange tints that gild the greenest bough."...[175]

All these beauties, calm or imposing, he had enjoyed, and sometimes suffered through them: and hence we see them through his verse. Whatever he touched, he made palpitate and live, because when he saw it, his heart had beaten and he had lived. He himself, a little later, quitting the mask of Harold, took up the parable in his own name; and who is not touched by an avowal so passionate and complete?

> "Yet must I think less wildly:— I have thought
> Too long and darkly, till my brain became,
> In its own eddy boiling and o'erwrought,
> A whirling gulf of phantasy and flame:
> And thus, untaught in youth my heart to tame,
> My springs of life were poison'd. 'Tis too late!
> Yet am I changed: though still enough the same
> In strength to bear what time can not abate,
> And feed on bitter fruits without accusing Fate....
>
> "But soon he knew himself the most unfit
> Of men to herd with Man; with whom he held
> Little in common; untaught to submit
> His thoughts to others, though his soul was quell'd
> In youth by his own thoughts; still uncompell'd,
> He would not yield dominion of his mind
> To spirits against whom his own rebell'd;
> Proud though in desolation, which could find,
> A life within itself, to breathe without mankind....
>
> "Like the Chaldean, he could watch the stars,
> Till he had peopled them with beings bright
> As their own beams; and earth, and earth-born jars,
> And human frailties, were forgotten quite:
> Could he have kept his spirit to that flight
> He had been happy; but this clay will sink
> In spark immortal, envying it the light

To which it mounts, as if to break the link
That keeps us from yon heaven which woos us to its brink.

"But in Man's dwellings he became a thing
Restless and worn, and stern and wearisome,
Droop'd as a wild-born falcon with clipt wing,
To whom the boundless air alone were home:
Then came his fit again, which to o'ercome,
As eagerly the barr'd-up bird will beat
His breast and beak against his wiry dome
Till the blood tinge his plumage, so the heat
Of his impeded soul would through his bosom eat."[176]

   Such are the sentiments wherewith he surveyed nature and history, not to comprehend them and forget himself before them, but to seek in them and impress upon them the image of his own passions. He does not leave objects to speak of themselves, but forces them to answer him. Amidst their peace, he is only occupied by his own emotion. He attunes them to his soul, and compels them to repeat his own cries. All is inflated here, as in himself; the vast strophe rolls along, carrying in its overflowing bed the flood of vehement ideas; declamation unfolds itself, pompous, and at times artificial (it was his first work), but potent, and so often sublime that the rhetorical rubbish, which he yet preserved, disappeared under the afflux of splendors, with which it is loaded. Wordsworth, Walter Scott, by the side of this prodigality of accumulated splendors, seemed poor and dull: never since Æschylus was seen such a tragic pomp; and men followed with a sort of pang, the train of gigantic figures, whom he brought in mournful ranks before their eyes, from the far past;

"I stood in Venice, on the Bridge of Sighs;
A palace and a prison on each hand:
I saw from out the wave her structures rise
As from the stroke of the enchanter's wand:
A thousand years, their cloudy wings expand
Around me, and a dying Glory smiles
O'er the far times, when many a subject land
Look'd to the winged Lion's marble piles,
Where Venice sate in state, throned on her hundred isles!

"She looks a sea Cybele, fresh from ocean,
Rising with her tiara of proud towers
At airy distance, with majestic motion,
A ruler of the waters and their powers:

BOOK IV— MODERN LIFE

And such she was!— her daughters had their dowers
From spoils of nations, and the exhaustless East
Pour'd in her lap all gems in sparkling showers.
In purple was she robed, and of her feast
Monarchs partook, and deem'd their dignity increased... .[177]

"Lo! Where the Giant on the mountain stands,
His blood-red tresses deep'ning in the sun,
With death-shot glowing in his fiery hands,
And eye that scorcheth all it glares upon;
Restless it rolls, now fix'd and now anon
Flashing afar,— and at his iron feet
Destruction cowers, to mark what deeds are done;
For on this morn three potent nations meet,
To shed before his shrine the blood he deems most sweet.

"By Heaven! It is a splendid sight to see
(For one who hath no friend, no brother there)
Their rival scarfs of mix'' embroidery,
Their various arms that gl'tter in the air!
What gallant war-hounds rouse them from their lair,
And gnash their fangs, loud yelling for the prey!
All join the chase, but few the triumph share;
The Grave shall bear the chiefest prize away,
And Havoc scarce for joy can number their array... .[178]

"What from this barren being do we reap?
Our senses narrow, and our reason frail,
Life short, and truth a gem which loves the deep,
And all things weigh'd in custom's falsest scale;
Opinion an omnipotence, whose veil
Mantles the earth with darkness, until right
And wrong are accidents, and men grow pale
Lest their own judgments should become too bright,
And their free thoughts be crimes, and earth have too much light.

"And thus they plod in sluggish misery,
Rotting from sire to son, and age to age,
Proud of their trampled nature, and so die,
Bequeathing their hereditary rage
To the new race of inborn slaves, who wage
War for their chains, and rather than be free,
Bleed gladiator-like and still engage

> Within the same arena where they see
> Their fellows fall before, like leaves of the same tree."[179]

Has ever style better expressed a soul? It is seen here laboring and expanding. Long and stormily the ideas boiled within this soul like bars of metal heaped in the furnace. They melted there before the strain of the intense heat; they mingled therein their heated mass amidst convulsions and explosions, and then at last the door is opened; a slow stream of fire descends into the trough prepared beforehand, heating the circumambient air, and its glittering hues scorch the eyes which persist in looking upon it.

Section III.—Byron's Short Poems

Description and monologue did not suffice Byron; and he needed, to express his ideal, events and actions. Only events try the force and elasticity of the soul; only actions display and regulate this force and elasticity. Amidst events he sought for the most powerful, amidst actions the strongest; and we see appear successively "The Bride of Abydos, The Giaour, The Corsair, Lara, Parisina, The Siege of Corinth, Mazeppa," and "The Prisoner of Chillon."

I know that these sparkling poems have grown dull in forty years. In their necklace of Oriental pearls have been discovered beads of glass; and Byron, who only half loved them, judged better than his judges. Yet he judged amiss; those which he preferred are the most false. His "Corsair" is marred by classic elegancies: the pirates' song at the beginning is no truer than a chorus at the Italian opera; his scamps propound philosophical antitheses as balanced as those of Pope. A hundred times ambition, glory, envy, despair, and the other abstract personages, whose images in the time of the first Empire the French used to set upon their drawing-room clocks, break in amidst living passions.[180] The noblest passages are disfigured by pedantic apostrophes, and the pretentious poetic diction sets up its threadbare frippery and conventional ornaments.[181] Far worse, he studies effect and follows the fashion. Melodramatic strings pull his characters at the right time, so as to obtain the grimace which shall make his public shudder:

> "Who thundering comes on blackest steed,
> With slacken'd bit and hoof of speed!
> ... Approach, thou craven crouching slave,
> Say, is not this Thermopylæ?"

Wretched mannerisms, emphatic and vulgar, imitated from Lucan and our modern Lucans, but which produce their effect only on a first perusal, and on the common herd of readers. There is an infallible means of attracting a mob, which is, to shout out loud; with shipwrecks, sieges, murders, and combats, we shall always interest them; show them pirates, desperate adventurers— these distorted or raging faces will draw them out of their regular and monotonous existence; they will go to see them as they go to melodramas, and through the same instinct which induces them to read novels in penny numbers. Add, by way of contrast, angelic women, tender and submissive, beautiful as angels. Byron describes all this, and adds to these seductions a bewitching scenery, oriental or picturesque adornments; old Alpine castles, the Mediterranean waves, the setting suns of Greece, the whole in high relief, with marked shadows and brilliant colors. We are all of the people, as regards emotion; and the great lady, like the waiting-woman, sheds tears, without cavilling with the author as to the means he uses.

And yet, after all, there is a great deal of truth in Byron's poems. No; this man is not a mere arranger of effects or an inventor of phrases. He has lived amidst the spectacles he describes; he has experienced the emotions he relates. He has been in the tent of Ali Pacha, and relished the strong savor of ocean adventure and savage manners. He has been a score of times near death— in the Morea, in the anguish and the solitude of fever; at Suli, in a shipwreck; at Malta, in England, and in Italy, in the dangers of a duel, plots of insurrection, commencements of sudden attacks, at sea, in arms, on horseback, having seen assassinations, wounds, agonies close to, him, and that more than once. "I am living here exposed to it (assassination) daily, for I have happened to make a powerful and unprincipled man my enemy; and I never sleep the worse for it, or ride in less solitary places, because precaution is useless, and one thinks of it as of a disease which may or may not strike."[182] He spoke the truth; no one ever held himself more erect and firm in danger. One day, near the Gulf of San Fiorenzo, his yacht was thrown on the coast; the sea was terrific, and the rocks in sight; the passengers kissed their rosaries, or fainted with horror; and the two captains being consulted, declared shipwreck inevitable. "Well," said Lord Byron, "we are all born to die; I shall go with regret, but certainly not with fear." And he took off his clothes, begging the others to do the same, not that they could save themselves amidst such waves; but "it is every man's duty to endeavour to preserve the life God has given him; so I advise you all to strip: swimming, indeed, can be of little use in these billows; but as children, when tired with crying, sink placidly to repose, we, when exhausted with struggling, shall die the easier..." He then sat down, folding his arms, very calm; he even joked with the captain, who was putting his dollars into his waistcoat pocket.... The ship approached the rocks. All this time Byron was not seen to change countenance. A man thus tried and moulded can paint extreme situations and sentiments. After all, they are never painted otherwise than by experience. The most inventive— Dante and Shakespeare— though quite different, yet do the same thing. However high their genius rose, it always had its feet on observation; and their most foolish, as well as their most splendid pictures, never offer to the world more than an image of their age, or of their own heart. At most, they deduce; that is, having derived from two or three features the inward qualities of the man within themselves and of the men around them, they draw thence, by a sudden ratiocination of which they have no consciousness, the varied skein of actions and sentiments. They may be artists, but they are observers. They may invent, but they describe. Their glory does not consist in the display of a phantasmagoria, but in the discovery of a truth. They are the first to enter some unexplored province of humanity, which becomes their domain, and thenceforth supports their name like an appanage. Byron found his domain, which is that of sad and tender sentiments: it is a heath, and full of ruins; but he is at home there, and he is alone.

What an abode! And it is on this desolation that he dwells. He muses on it. See the brothers of Childe Harold pass— the characters who people it. One in his prison, chained up with his two remaining brothers. Their father and three others had perished fighting, or were burnt for their faith. One by one, before the eyes of the eldest, the last two languish and fade: a silent and slow agony amidst the damp darkness into which a beam of the sickly sun pierces through a crevice. After the death of the first, the survivors "begged as a boon" that he shall at least be buried on a spot "whereon the day might shine." The jailers

> "Coldly laugh'd— and laid him there:
> The flat and turfless earth above
> The being we so much did love;
> His empty chain above it leant."[183]

Then the youngest "faded" daily

> "With all the while a cheek whose bloom
> Was as a mockery of the tomb,
> Whose tints as gently sunk away
> As a departing rainbow's ray."[184]

But the pillars to which they are chained are too far apart— the elder cannot approach his dying younger brother; he listens and hears the failing sighs; he cries for succor, and none comes. He bursts his chain with one strong bound: all is over. He takes that cold hand, and then, before the motionless body, his senses are lost, his thoughts arrested; he is like a drowning man, who, after passing through pangs of agony, lets himself sink down like a stone, and no longer feels existence but by a complete petrifaction of horror. Here is another brother of Childe Harold, Mazeppa, bound naked on a wild horse, rushing over the steppes. He writhes, and his swollen limbs, cut by the cords, are bleeding. A whole day the course continues, and behind him the wolves are howling. The night through he hears their long monotonous chase, and at the end his energy fails.

> "... The earth gave way, the skies roll'd round,
> I seem'd to sink upon the ground;
> But err'd, for I was fastly bound.
> My heart turn'd sick, my brain grew sore,
> And throbb'd awhile, then beat no more;
> The skies spun like a mighty wheel;
> I saw the trees like drunkards reel,
> And a slight flash sprang o'er my eyes,
> Which saw no further: he who dies
> Can die no more than then I died....
> I felt the blackness come and go,
> And strove to wake; but could not make
> My senses climb up from below:
> I felt as on a plank at sea,
> When all the waves that dash o'er thee,
> At the same time upheave and whelm,
> And hurl thee towards a desert realm."[185]

THE CASTLE OF CHILLON
Photogravure from an etching.

Shall I enumerate them all? Hugo, Parisina, the Foscari, the Giaour, the Corsair. His hero is always a man striving with the worst anguish, face to face with shipwreck, torture, death— his own painful and prolonged death, the bitter death of his well-beloved, with remorse for his companion, amidst the gloomy prospects of a threatening eternity, with no other support but innate energy and hardened pride. These men have desired too much, too impetuously, with a senseless swing, like a horse which does not feel the bit, and thenceforth their inner doom drives them to the abyss which they see, and cannot escape from. What a night was that of Alp before Corinth! He is a renegade, and comes with the Mussulmans to besiege the Christians, his old friends— Minotti, the father of the girl he loves. Next day he is to lead the assault, and he thinks of his death, which he forebodes, the carnage of his own soldiers, which he is preparing. There is no inner support, but rooted resentment and a firm and stern will. The Mussulmans despise him, the Christians execrate him, and his glory only publishes his treason. Dejected and fevered, he passes through the sleeping camp, and wanders on the shore:

> "'Tis midnight: on the mountains brown
> The cold, round moon shines deeply down;
> Blue roll the waters, blue the sky
> Spreads like an ocean hung on high,
> Bespangled with those isles of light....
> The waves on either shore lay there
> Calm, clear, and azure as the air;
> And scarce their foam the pebbles shook,
> But murmured meekly as the brook.
> The winds were pillow'd on the waves;
> The banners droop'd along their staves....
> And that deep silence was unbroke,
> Save where the watch his signal spoke,
> Save where the steed neighed oft and shrill,...
> And the wide hum of that wild host
> Rustled like leaves from coast to coast...."[186]

How the heart sickens before such spectacles! What a contrast between his agony and the peace of immortal nature! How man stretches then his arms towards ideal beauty, and how impotently they fall back at the contact of our clay and mortality! Alp advances over the sandy shore to the foot of the bastion, exposed to the fire of the sentinels; and he hardly thinks of it:

> "And he saw the lean dogs beneath the wall
> Hold o'er the dead their carnival,
> Gorging and growling o'er carcase and limb;
> They were too busy to bark at him!
> From a Tartar's skull they had stripped the flesh,
> As ye peel the fig when its fruit is fresh;
> And their white tusks crunched o'er the whiter skull,
> As it slipped through their jaws, when their edge grew dull,

As they lazily mumbled the bones of the dead,
When they scarce could rise from the spot where they fed;
So well had they broken a lingering fast
With those who had fallen for that night's repast.
And Alp knew, by the turbans that roll'd on the sand,
The foremost of these were the best of his band:
Crimson and green were the shawls of their wear,
And each scalp had a single long tuft of hair,
All the rest was shaven and bare.
The scalps were in the wild dog's maw,
The hair was tangled round his jaw.
But close by the shore on the edge of the gulf,
There sat a vulture flapping a wolf,
Who had stolen from the hills, but kept away,
Scared by the dogs, from the human prey;
But he seized on his share of a steed that lay,
Pick'd by the birds, on the sands of the bay."[187]

Such is the goal of man; the hot frenzy of life ends here; buried or not, it matters little: vultures or jackals, one gravedigger is as good as another. The storm of his rages and his efforts have but served to cast him to these animals for their food, and to their beaks and jaws he comes only with the sentiment of frustrated hopes and insatiable desires. Could any of us forget the death of Lara after once reading it? Has anyone elsewhere seen, save in Shakespeare, a sadder picture of the destiny of a man vainly rearing against inevitable fate? Though generous, like Macbeth, he has, like Macbeth, dared everything against law and conscience, even against pity and the most ordinary feelings of honor. Crimes committed have forced him into other crimes, and blood poured out has made him glide into a pool of blood. As a corsair, he has slain; as a cut-throat, he assassinates; and his former murders which haunt his dreams come with their bat's-wings beating against the portals of his brain. He does not drive them away, these black visitors; though the mouth remains silent, the pallid brow and strange smile bear witness to their approach. And yet it is a noble spectacle to see man standing with calm countenance even under their touch. The last day comes, and six inches of iron suffice for all this energy and fury. Lara is lying beneath a lime tree, and his wound "is bleeding fast from life away." With each convulsion the stream gushes blacker, then stops; the blood flows now only drop by drop, and his brow is already moist, his eyes dim. The victors arrive— he does not deign to answer them; the priest brings near the absolving cross, "but he look'd upon it with an eye profane." What remains to him of life is for his poor page, the only being who loved him, who has followed him to the end, and who now tries to stanch the blood from his wound:

> "He scarce can speak, but motions him 'tis vain,
> He clasps the hand that pang which would assuage,
> And sadly smiles his thanks to that dark page....
> His dying tones are in that other tongue,
> To which some strange remembrance wildly clung....
> And once, as Kaled's answering accents ceased,
> Rose Lara's hand, and pointed to the East:
> Whether (as then the breaking sun from high
> Roll'd back the clouds) the morrow caught his eye,
> Or that 'twas chance, or some remember'd scene,
> That raised his arm to point where such had been,
> Scarce Kaled seem'd to know, but turn'd away,
> As if his heart abhorr'd that coming day,
> And shrunk his glance before that morning light,
> To look on Lara's brow— where all grew night....
> But from his visage little could we guess,
> So unrepentant, dark, and passionless....
> But gasping heaved the breath that Lara drew,
> And dull the film along his dim eye grew;
> His limbs stretch'd fluttering, and his head droop'd o'er."[188]

All is over, and of this haughty spirit there remains but a poor piece of clay. After all, it is the desirable lot of such hearts; they have spent life amiss, and only rest well in the tomb.

A strange and altogether northern poetry, with its root in the Edda and its flower in Shakespeare, born long ago under an inclement sky, on the shores of a stormy ocean— the work of a too wilful, too strong, too sombre race— and which, after lavishing its images of desolation and heroism, ends by stretching like a black veil over the whole of living nature the dream of universal destruction: this dream is here, as in the Edda, almost equally grand:

> "I had a dream, which was not all a dream.
> The bright sun was extinguish'd, and the stars
> Did wander darkling in the eternal space,
> Rayless, and pathless, and the icy earth
> Swung blind and blackening in the moonless air;
> Morn came and went— and came, and brought no day....
> Forests were set on fire— but hour by hour
> They fell and faded— and the crackling trunks
> Extinguish'd with a crash— and all was black....
> And they did live by watchfires— and the thrones,
> The palaces of crowned kings— the huts,
> The habitations of all things which dwell,

BOOK IV– MODERN LIFE

Were burnt for beacons; cities were consumed,
And men were gathered round their blazing homes
To look once more into each other's face....
The brows of men by the despairing light
Wore an unearthly aspect, as by fits
The flashes fell upon them; some lay down
And hid their eyes and wept; and some did rest
Their chins upon their clenched hands, and smiled;
And others hurried to and fro, and fed
Their funeral piles with fuel, and look'd up
With mad disquietude on the dull sky,
The pall of a past world; and then again
With curses cast them down upon the dust,
And gnash'd their teeth and howl'd: the wild birds shriek'd,
And, terrified, did flutter on the ground,
And flap their useless wings; the wildest brutes
Came tame and tremulous; and vipers crawl'd
And twined themselves among the multitude,
Hissing, but stingless— they were slain for food:
And War, which for a moment was no more,
Did glut himself again; a meal was bought
With blood, and each sate sullenly apart
Gorging himself in gloom: no love was left;
All earth was but one thought— and that was death,
Immediate and inglorious; and the pang
Of famine fed upon all entrails— men
Died, and their bones were tombless as their flesh;
The meagre by the meagre were devour'd,
Even dogs assail'd their masters, all save one.
And he was faithful to a corse, and kept
The birds and beasts and famish'd men at bay,
Till hunger clung them, or the drooping dead
Lured their lank jaws; himself sought out no food,
But with a piteous and perpetual moan,
And a quick desolate cry, licking the hand
Which answer'd not with a caress— he died.
The crowd was famish'd by degrees; but two
Of an enormous city did survive,
And they were enemies: they met beside
The dying embers of an altar-place
Where had been heap'd a mass of holy things
For an unholy usage; they raked up,
And shivering scraped with their cold skeleton hands

> The feeble ashes, and their feeble breath
> Blew for a little life, and made a flame
> Which was a mockery; then they lifted up
> Their eyes as it grew lighter, and beheld
> Each other's aspects— saw, and shriek'd, and died—
> Even of their mutual hideousness they died."[189]

Section IV.—Manfred

Amongst these unrestrained and gloomy poems, which incessantly return and dwell on the same subject, there is one more imposing and lofty than the rest, "Manfred," twin-brother of the greatest poem of the age, Goethe's "Faust." Goethe says of Byron: "This singular intellectual poet has taken my Faustus to himself, and extracted from it the strongest nourishment for his hypochondriac humour. He has made use of the impelling principles in his own way, for his own purposes, so that no one of them remains the same; and it is particularly on this account that I cannot enough admire his genius." The play is indeed original. Byron writes: "His (Goethe's) 'Faust' I never read, for I don't know German, but Matthew Monk Lewis, in 1816, at Coligny, translated most of it to me *vivâ voce*, and I was naturally much struck with it; but it was the 'Steinbach' and the 'Jungfrau' and something else, much more than Faustus, that made me write 'Manfred.'"[190] Goethe adds: "The whole is so completely formed anew, that it would be an interesting task for the critic to point out not only the alterations he (Byron) has made, but their degree of resemblance or dissimilarity to the original." Let us speak of it, then, quite freely: the subject of "Manfred" is the dominant idea of the age, expressed so as to display the contrast of two masters, and of two nations.

What constitutes Goethe's glory is, that in the nineteenth century he did produce an epic poem— I mean a poem in which genuine gods act and speak. This appeared impossible in the nineteenth century, since the special work of our age is the refined consideration of creative ideas, and the suppression of the poetic characters by which other ages have never failed to represent them. Of the two divine families, the Greek and the Christian, neither seemed capable of re-entering the epic world. Classic literature dragged down in its fall the mythological puppets, and the ancient gods slept on their old Olympus, whither history and archaeology alone might go to arouse them. The angels and saints of the Middle Ages, as strange and almost as far from our thoughts, slept on the vellum of their missals and in the niches of their cathedrals; and if a poet, like Chateaubriand, tried to make them enter the modern world,[191] he succeeded only in degrading them, and in making of them vestry decorations and operatic machinery. The mythic credulity disappeared amid the growth of experience, the mystic amid the growth of prosperity. Paganism, at the contact of science, was reduced to the recognition of natural forces; Christianity, at the contact of morality, was reduced to the adoration of the ideal. In order again to deify physical powers, man should have become once more a healthy child, as in Homer's time. In order again to deify spiritual powers, man should have become once more a sickly child as in Dante's time. But he was an adult, and could not ascend again to civilizations or epics, from which the current of his thought and of his life had withdrawn him forever. How was he to be shown his gods, the modern gods? how could he reclothe them in a personal and visible form, since he had toiled to strip them precisely of all personal and sensible form, and had succeeded in this? Instead of rejecting legend, Goethe took it up again. He chose a mediaeval story for his theme. Carefully, scrupulously, he tracked old manners and old beliefs; an alchemist's laboratory, a sorcerer's conjuring-book, coarse villagers, students' or drunkards' gayety, a witches' meeting on the Brocken, a mass in church; we might fancy we saw an engraving of Luther's time, conscientious and minute: nothing is omitted. Heavenly characters appear in consecrated attitudes after the text of Scripture, like the old mysteries: the Lord with his angels, then with the devil, who comes to ask permission to tempt Faust, as formerly he tempted Job; heaven, as St. Francis imagined it and Van Eyck painted it, with anchorites, holy women and doctors— some in a landscape with bluish rocks, others above in the sublime air, hovering in choirs about the Virgin in glory, one tier above another. Goethe affects even to be so orthodox as to write under each her Latin name, and her due niche in the Vulgate.[192] And this very fidelity proclaims him a sceptic. We see that if he resuscitates the ancient world, it is as a historian, not as a believer. He is only a Christian through remembrance and poetic feeling. In him the modern spirit overflows designedly the narrow vessel in which he designedly seems to enclose it. The thinker percolates through the narrator. Every instant a calculated word, which seems involuntary, opens up glimpses of philosophy, beyond the veils of tradition. Who are they, these supernatural personages— this god, this Mephistopheles, these angels? Their substance incessantly dissolves and re-forms, to show or hide alternately the idea which fills it. Are they abstractions or characters? Mephistopheles, a revolutionary and a philosopher, who has read "Candide," and cynically jeers at the Powers— is he anything but "the spirit of negation"?

The angels

> "Rejoice to share
> The wealth exuberant of all that's fair,
> Which lives, and has its being everywhere!
> And the creative essence which surrounds,
> And lives in all, and worketh evermore.
> Encompass... within love's gracious bounds;
> And all the world of things, which flit before

>   The gaze in seeming fitful and obscure.
>   Do... in lasting thoughts embody and secure."[193]

Are these angels, for an instant at least, anything else than the ideal intelligence which comes, through sympathy, to love all, and through ideas, to comprehend all? What shall we say of this Deity, at first biblical and individual, who little by little is unshaped, vanishes and, sinking to the depths, behind the splendors of living nature and mystic reverie, is confused with the inaccessible absolute? Thus is the whole poem unfolded, action and characters, men and gods, antiquity and Middle Ages, aggregate and details, always on the confines of two worlds— one visible and figurative, the other intelligible and formless; one comprehending the moving externals of history or of life, and all that hued and perfumed bloom which nature lavishes on the surface of existence, the other containing the profound generative powers and invisible fixed laws by which all these living beings come to the light of day.[194] At last we see our gods: we no longer parody them, like our ancestors, by idols or persons; we perceive them as they are in themselves, and we have no need, in order to see them, to renounce poetry, nor break with the past We remain on our knees before the shrines where men have, prayed for three thousand years; we do not tear a single rose from the chaplets with which they have crowned their divine Madonnas; we do not extinguish a single candle which they have crowded on the altar steps; we behold with an artist's pleasure the precious shrines where, amidst the wrought candlesticks, the suns of diamonds, the gorgeous copes, they have scattered the purest treasures of their genius and their heart. But our thoughts pierce further than our eyes. For us, at certain moments, these draperies, this marble, all this pomp vacillates; it is no longer aught but beautiful phantoms; it vanishes in the smoke, and we discover through it and behind it the impalpable ideal which has set up these pillars, lighted these roofs, and hovered for centuries over the kneeling multitude.

To understand the legend and also to understand life, is the object of this work, and of the whole work of Goethe. Everything, brutish or rational, vile or sublime, fantastic or tangible, is a group of powers, of which our mind, through study and sympathy, may reproduce in itself the elements and the disposition. Let us reproduce it, and give it in our thought a new existence. Is a gossip like Martha, babbling and foolish— a drunkard like Frosch, brawling and dirty, and the other Dutch boors— unworthy to enter a picture? Even the female apes, and the apes who sit beside the caldron, watching that it does not boil over, with their hoarse cries and disordered fancies, may repay the trouble of art in restoring them. Wherever there is life, even bestial or maniacal, there is beauty. The more we look upon nature, the more we find it divine— divine even in rocks and plants. Consider these forests, they seem motionless; but the leaves breathe, and the sap mounts insensibly through the massive trunks and branches, to the slender shoots, stretched like fingers at the end of the twigs; it fills the swollen ducts, leaks out in living forms, loads the frail aments with fecundating dust, spreads profusely through the fermenting air the vapors and odors: this luminous air, this dome of verdure, this long colonnade of trees, this silent soil, labor and are transformed; they accomplish a work, and the poet's heart has but to listen to them to find a voice for their obscure instincts. They speak in his heart; still better, they sing, and other beings do the same; each, by its distinct melody, short or long, strange or simple, solely adapted to its nature, capable of manifesting it fully, in the same manner as a sound, by its pitch, its height, its force, manifests the inner structure of the body which has produced it. This melody the poet respects; he avoids altering it by confusing its ideas or accent; his whole care is to keep it intact and pure. Thus is his work produced, an echo of universal nature, a vast chorus in which gods, men, past, present, all periods of history, all conditions of life, all orders of existence agree without confusion, and in which the flexible genius of the musician, who is alternately transformed into each one of them in order to interpret and comprehend them, only bears witness to his own thought in giving an insight, beyond this immense harmony, into the group of ideal laws whence it is derived, and the inner reason which sustains it.

Beside this lofty conception, what is the supernatural part of Manfred? Doubtless Byron is moved by the great things of nature; he had just left the Alps; he has seen those glaciers which are like "a frozen hurricane"— those "torrents which roll the sheeted silver's waving column o'er the crag's headlong perpendicular, like the pale courser's tail, as told in the Apocalypse"— but he has brought nothing from them but images. His witch, his spirits, his Arimanes, are but stage gods. He believes in them no more than we do. Genuine gods are created with much greater difficulty; we must believe in them; we must, like Goethe, have assisted long at their birth, like philosophers and scholars; we must have seen of them more than their externals. He who, whilst continuing a poet, becomes a naturalist and geologist, who has followed in the fissures of the rocks the tortuous waters slowly distilled, and driven at length by their own weight to the light, may ask himself, as the Greeks did formerly, when they saw them roll and sparkle in their emerald tints, what these waters might be thinking, whether they thought. What a strange life is theirs, alternately at rest and in violent motion. How far removed from ours! With what effort must we tear ourselves from our worn and complicated passions, to comprehend the youth and divine simplicity of a being without reflection and form! How difficult is such a work for a modern man! How impossible for an Englishman! Shelley, Keats approached it— thanks to the nervous delicacy of their sickly or overflowing imagination; but how partial still was this approach! And how we feel, on reading them, that they would have needed the aid of public culture, and the aptitude of national genius, which Goethe possessed! That which the whole of civilization has alone developed in the Englishman, is energetic will and practical faculties. Here man has braced himself up in his efforts, become concentrated in resistance, fond of action, and hence shut out from pure speculation, from wavering sympathy, and from disinterested art. In him metaphysical liberty has perished under utilitarian preoccupation, and pantheistic reverie under moral prejudices. How would he frame and bend his imagination so as to follow the numberless and fugitive outlines of existences, especially of vague existences? How would he leave his religion so a£ to reproduce indifferently the powers of indifferent nature? And who is further from flexibility and indifference than he? The flowing water, which in Goethe takes the mould of all the contours of the soil, and which we perceive in the sinuous and luminous distance beneath the golden mist which it exhales, was in Byron suddenly frozen into a mass of ice, and makes but a rigid block of crystal. Here, as elsewhere, there is but one character, the same as before. Men, gods, nature, all the changing and multiplex world of Goethe, has vanished. The poet alone subsists, as expressed in his character. Inevitably imprisoned within himself, he could see nothing but himself; if he must come to other existences, it is that they may reply to him; and through this pretended epic he persisted in his eternal monologue.

But how all these powers, assembled in a single being, make him great! Into what mediocrity and platitude sinks the Faust of Goethe, compared to Manfred! As soon as we cease to see humanity in this Faust, what does he become? Is he a hero? A sad hero, who has no other task but to speak, is afraid, studies the shades of his sensations, and walks about! His worst action is to seduce a grisette, and to go and dance by night in bad company— two exploits which many a German student has accomplished. His wilfulness is whim, his ideas are longings and dreams. A poet's soul in a scholar's head, both unfit for action, and not harmonizing well together; discord within, and weakness without; in short, character is wanting: it is German all over. By his side, what a man is Manfred! He is a man; there is no fitter word, or one which could depict him better. He will not, at the sight of a spirit, "quake like a crawling, cowering, timorous worm." He will not regret that "he has neither land, nor pence, nor worldly honours, nor influence." He will not let himself be duped by the devil like a schoolboy, or go and amuse himself like a cockney with the phantasmagoria of the Brocken. He has lived like a feudal chief, not like a scholar who has taken his degree; he has fought, mastered others; he knows how to master himself. If he has studied magic arts, it is not from an alchemist's curiosity, but from a spirit of revolt:

> "From my youth upwards
> My spirit walk'd not with the souls of men,

BOOK IV— MODERN LIFE

Nor look'd upon the earth with human eyes;
The thirst of their ambition was not mine,
The aim of their existence was not mine;
My joys, my griefs, my passions, and my powers
Made me a stranger; though I wore the form,
I had no sympathy with breathing flesh....
My joy was in the Wilderness, to breathe
The difficult air of the iced mountain's top,
Where the birds dare not build, nor insect's wing
Flit o'er the herbless granite, or to plunge
Into the torrent, and to roll along
On the swift whirl of the new breaking wave....
To follow through the night the moving moon,
The stars and their development; or catch
The dazzling lightnings till my eyes grew dim;
Or to look, list'ning, on the scatter'd leaves,
While Autumn winds were at their evening song.
These were my pastimes, and to be alone;
For if the beings, of whom I was one—
Hating to be so— cross'd me in my path,
I felt myself degraded back to them,
And was all clay again....[195]
I could not tame my nature down; for he
Must serve who fain would sway— and soothe— and sue—
And watch all time— and pry into all place—
And be a living lie— who would become
A mighty thing amongst the mean, and such
The mass are; I disdain'd to mingle with
A herd, though to be leader— and of wolves..."[196]

He lives alone, and he cannot live alone. The deep source of love, cut off from its natural issues, then overflows and lays waste the heart which refused to expand. He has loved, too well, one too near to him, his sister it may be; she has died of it, and impotent remorse fills the soul which no human occupation could satisfy:

"... My solitude is solitude no more,
But peopled with the Furies;— I have gnash'd
My teeth in darkness till returning morn,
Then cursed myself till sunset;— I have pray'd
For madness as a blessing— 'tis denied me.
I have affronted death— but in the war
Of elements the waters shrunk from me,

> And fatal things pass'd harmless— the cold hand
> Of an all-pitiless demon held me back,
> Back by a single hair, which would not break.
> In fantasy, imagination, all
> The affluence of my soul.... I plunged deep,
> But, like an ebbing wave, it dashed me back
> Into the gulf of my unfathom'd thought....
> I dwell in my despair,
> And live, and live for ever."[197]

He only wishes to see her once more: to this sole and all-powerful desire flow all the energies of his soul. He calls her up in the midst of spirits; she appears, but answers not. He prays to her— with what cries, what doleful cries of deep anguish! How he loves! With what yearning and effort all his downtrodden and outcrushed tenderness gushes out and escapes at the sight of those well-beloved eyes, which he sees for the last time! With what enthusiasm his convulsive arms are stretched towards that frail form which, shuddering, has quitted the tomb!— towards those cheeks in which the blood, forcibly recalled, plants "a strange hectic— like the unnatural red which Autumn plants upon the perished leaf."

> "... Hear me, hear me—
> Astarte! my beloved! speak to me:
> I have so much endured— so much endure—
> Look on me! the grave hath not changed thee more
> Than I am changed for thee. Thou lovedst me
> Too much as I loved thee: we were not made
> To torture thus each other, though it were
> The deadliest sin to love as we have loved.
> Say that thou loath'st me not— that I do bear
> This punishment for both— that thou wilt be
> One of the blessed— and that I shall die;
> For hitherto all hateful things conspire
> To bind me in existence— in a life
> Which makes me shrink from immortality—
> A future like the past. I cannot rest.
> I know not what I ask, nor what I seek:
> I feel but what thou art— and what I am;
> And I would hear yet once before I perish
> The voice which was my music— Speak to me!
> For I have call'd on thee in the still night,
> Startled the slumbering birds from the hush'd boughs,
> And woke the mountain wolves, and made the caves

BOOK IV— MODERN LIFE

> Acquainted with thy vainly echoed name,
> Which answer'd me— many things answer'd me—
> Spirits and men— but thou wert silent all....
> Speak to me! I have wander'd o'er the earth,
> And never found thy likeness— Speak to me!
> Look on the fiends around— they feel for me:
> I fear them not, and feel for thee alone—
> Speak to me! though it be in wrath;— but say—
> I reck not what— but let me hear thee once—
> This once— once more!"[198]

She speaks. What a sad and doubtful reply! Manfred's limbs are convulsed when she disappears. But an instant after the spirits see that:

> "... He mastereth himself, and makes
> His torture tributary to his will.
> Had he been one of us, he would have made
> An awful spirit."[199]

Will is the unshaken basis of this soul. He did not bend before the chief of the spirits; he stood firm and calm before the infernal throne, whilst all the demons were raging who would tear him to pieces: now he dies, and they assail him, but he still strives and conquers:

> "... Thou hast no power upon me, that I feel;
> Thou never shalt possess me, that I know:
> What I have done is done; I bear within
> A torture which could nothing gain from thine:
> The mind which is immortal makes itself
> Requital for its good or evil thoughts—
> Is its own origin of ill and end—
> And its own place and time— its innate sense,
> When stripp'd of this mortality, derives
> No colour from the fleeting things without;
> But is absorb'd in sufferance or in joy,
> Born from the knowledge of its own desert.
> Thou didst not tempt me, and thou couldst not tempt me;
> I have not been thy dupe, nor am thy prey—
> But was my own destroyer, and will be
> My own hereafter.— Back, ye baffled fiends!
> The hand of death is on me— but not yours!"[200]

This "I," the invincible I, who suffices to himself, on whom nothing has a hold, demons nor men, the sole author of his own good and ill, a sort of suffering or fallen god, but god always, even in its quivering flesh, amidst his soiled and blighted destiny— such is the hero and the work of this mind, and of the men of his race. If Goethe was the poet of the universe, Byron was the poet of the individual; and if in one the German genius found its interpreter, the English genius found its interpreter in the other.

Section V.—What Byron's Contemporaries Thought of Him.—His Morals

We can well imagine that Englishmen clamored at and repudiated the monster. Southey, the poet-laureate, said of him, in good biblical style, that he savored of Moloch and Belial— most of all of Satan; and, with the generosity of a brother poet, called the attention of government to him. We should fill many pages if we were to copy the reproaches of the respectable reviews against these "men of diseased hearts and depraved imaginations, who, forming a system of opinions to suit their own unhappy course of conduct, have rebelled against the holiest ordinances of human society, and, hating that revealed religion which, with all their efforts and bravadoes, they are unable entirely to disbelieve, labour to make others as miserable as themselves, by infecting them with a moral virus that eats into the soul."[201] This sounds like the emphasis of an episcopal charge and scholastic pedantry: in England the press does the duty of the police, and it never did it more violently than at that time. Opinion backed the press. Several times, in Italy, Lord Byron saw gentlemen leave a drawing-room with their wives, when he was announced. Owing to his title and celebrity, the scandal which he caused was more conspicuous than any other: he was a public sinner. One day an obscure parson sent him a prayer which he had found amongst the papers of his wife— a charming and pious lady, recently dead, and who had secretly prayed to God for the conversion of the great sinner. Conservative and Protestant England, after a quarter of a century of moral wars, and two centuries of moral education, carried its severity and rigor to extremes; and Puritan intolerance, like Catholic intolerance previously in Spain, put recusants out of the pale of the law. The proscription of voluptuous or abandoned life, the narrow observation of order and decency, the respect of all police, human and divine; the necessary bows at the mere name of Pitt, of the king, the church, the God of the Bible; the attitude of a gentleman in a white tie, conventional, inflexible, implacable— such were the customs then met with across the Channel, a hundred times more tyrannical than nowadays: at that time, as Stendhal says, a peer at his fireside dared not cross his legs, for fear of its being improper. England held herself stiff, uncomfortably laced in her stays of decorum. Hence arose two sources of misery: a man suffers, and is tempted to throw down the ugly choking apparatus, when he is sure

BOOK IV— MODERN LIFE

that it can be done secretly. On the one side constraint, on the other hypocrisy— these are the two vices of English civilization; and it was these which Byron, with his poet's discernment and his combative instincts, attacked.

He had seen them from the first; true artists are perspicacious: it is in this that they outstrip us; we judge from hearsay and formulas, like cockneys; they, like eccentric beings, from accomplished facts, and things: at twenty-two he perceived the tedium born of constraint desolating all high life:

> "There stands the noble hostess, nor shall sink
> With the three-thousandth curtsy;...
> Saloon, room, hall, o'erflow beyond their brink,
> And long the latest of arrivals halts,
> 'Midst royal dukes and dames condemn'd to climb,
> And gain an inch of staircase at a time."[202]

He wrote also:

> "He (the Count) ought to have been in the country during the hunting season, with 'a select party of distinguished guests,' as the papers term it. He ought to have seen the gentlemen after dinner (on the hunting days), and the soirée ensuing thereupon— and the women looking as if they had hunted, or rather been hunted; and I could have wished that he had been at a dinner in town, which I recollect at Lord C— — 's— small, but select, and composed of the most amusing people. The dessert was hardly on the table, when, out of twelve, I counted five asleep."[203]

As for the morals of the upper classes, this is what he says:

> "Went to my box at Covent Garden to-night.... Casting my eyes round the house, in the next box to me, and the next, and the next, were the most distinguished old and young Babylonians of quality.... It was as if the house had been divided between your public and your understood courtesans;— but the intriguantes much outnumbered the regular mercenaries. Now, where lay the difference between Pauline and her mother,... and Lady— — and daughter? except that the two last may enter Carlton and any other house, and the two first are limited to the Opera and b— house. How I do delight in observing life as it really is!— and myself, after all, the worst of any!"[204]

Decorum and debauchery; moral hypocrites, "*qui mettent leurs vertus en mettant leurs gants blancs*";[205] an oligarchy which, to preserve its places and

- 111 -

its sinecures, ravages Europe, preys on Ireland, and excites the people by making use of the grand words, virtue, Christianity, and liberty: there was truth in all these invectives.[206] It is only thirty years since the ascendancy of the middle class diminished the privileges and corruptions of the great; but at that time hard words could with justice be thrown at their heads. Byron said, quoting from Voltaire:

> "'*La Pudeur s'est enfuie des cœurs, et s'est réfugiée sur les lèvres.*' ... '*Plus les mœurs sont dépravées, plus les expressions deviennent mesurées; on croit regagner en langage ce qu'on a perdu en vertu.*' This is the real fact, as applicable to the degraded and hypocritical mass which leavens the present English generation; and it is the only answer they deserve.... Cant is the crying sin of this double-dealing and false-speaking time of selfish spoilers."[2007]

And then he wrote his masterpiece, "Don Juan."[208]

All here was new, form as well as substance; for he had entered into a new world. The Englishman, the Northman, transplanted amongst southern manners and into Italian life, had become imbued with a new sap, which made him bear new fruit. He had been induced to read[209] the rather free satires of Buratti, and the more than voluptuous sonnets of Baffo. He lived in the happy Venetian society, still exempt from political animosities, where care seemed a folly, where life was looked upon as a carnival, pleasure displayed itself openly, not timid and hypocritical, but loosely arrayed and commended. He amused himself here, impetuously at first, more than sufficient, even more than too much, and almost killed himself by these amusements; but after vulgar gallantries, having felt a feeling of love, he became a *cavalier' servente*, after the fashion of the country where he dwelt, with the consent of the family of the lady, offering his arm, carrying her shawl, a little awkwardly at first, and wonderingly, but on the whole happier than he had ever been, and fanned by a warm breath of pleasure and abandon. He saw in Italy the overthrow of all English morality, conjugal infidelity established as a rule, amorous fidelity raised to a duty: "There is no convincing a woman here that she is in the smallest degree deviating from the rule of right or the fitness of things in having an *amorosa*.[210]... Love (the sentiment of love) is not merely an excuse for it, but makes it an actual virtue, provided it is disinterested, and not a caprice, and is confined to one object."[211] A little later he translated the "Morgante Maggiore" of Pulci, to show "What was permitted in a Catholic country and a bigoted age to a churchman on the score of religion, and to silence those buffoons who accuse me of attacking the Liturgy."[212] He rejoiced in this liberty and this ease, and resolved never to fall again under the pedantic inquisition, which in his country had condemned and damned him past forgiveness. He wrote

BOOK IV— MODERN LIFE

his "Beppo" like an improvisatore, with a charming freedom, a flowing and fantastic lightness of mood, and contrasted in it the recklessness and happiness of Italy with the prejudices and repulsiveness of England:

> "I like... to see the Sun set, sure he'll rise to-morrow,
> Not through a misty morning twinkling weak as
> A drunken man's dead eye in maudlin sorrow,
> But with all Heaven t' himself; that day will break as
> Beauteous as cloudless, nor be forced to borrow
> That sort of farthing candlelight which glimmers
> Where reeking London's smoky caldron simmers.
>
> "I love the language, that soft bastard Latin,
> Which melts like kisses from a female mouth,
> And sounds as if it should be writ on satin,
> With syllables which breathe of the sweet South,
> And gentle liquids gliding all so pat in,
> That not a single accent seems uncouth,
> Like our harsh northern whistling, grunting guttural,
> Which we're obliged to hiss, and spit, and sputter all.
>
> "I like the women too (forgive my folly),
> From the rich peasant cheek of ruddy bronze,
> And large black eyes that flash on you a volley
> Of rays that say a thousand things at once,
> To the high dama's brow, more melancholy,
> But clear, and with a wild and liquid glance,
> Heart on her lips, and soul within her eyes,
> Soft as her clime, and sunny as her skies."[213]

With other manners there existed in Italy another morality; there is one for every age, race, and sky— I mean that the ideal model varies with the circumstances which fashion it. In England the severity of the climate, the warlike energy of the race, and the liberty of the institutions prescribe an active life, severe manners, Puritanic religion, the marriage tie strictly kept, a feeling of duty and self-command. In Italy the beauty of the climate, the innate sense of the beautiful, and the despotism of the government induced an idle life, loose manners, imaginative religion, the culture of the arts, and the search after happiness. Each model has its beauties and its plots— the epicurean artist like the political moralist;[214] each shows by its greatnesses the littlenesses of the other, and, to set in relief the disadvantages of the second, Lord Byron had only to set in relief the seductions of the first.

Thereupon he went in search of a hero, and did not find one, which, in this age of heroes, is "an uncommon want." For lack of a better he chose "our ancient friend Don Juan"— a scandalous choice: what an outcry the English moralists will make! But, to cap the horror, this Don Juan is not wicked, selfish, odious, like his fellows; he does not seduce, he is no corrupter. When an opportunity arises, he lets himself drift; he has a heart and senses, and, under a beautiful sun, they are easily touched: at sixteen a youth cannot help himself, nor at twenty, nor perhaps at thirty. Lay it to the charge of human nature, my dear moralists; it is not I who made it as it is. If you will grumble, address yourselves higher: we are here as painters, not as makers of human puppets, and we do not answer for the inner structure of our dancing-dolls. Our Don Juan is now going about; he goes about in many places, and in all he is young; we will not launch thunderbolts on his head because he is young; that fashion is past: the green devils and their capers only came on the stage in the last act of Mozart's "Don Giovanni." And, moreover, Juan is so amiable! After all, what has he done that others don't do! He has been a lover of Catherine II, but he only followed the lead of the diplomatic corps and the whole Russian army. Let him sow his wild oats; the good grain will spring up in its time. Once in England, he will behave himself decently. I confess that he may even there, when provoked, go a-gleaning in the conjugal gardens of the aristocracy; but in the end he will settle, go and pronounce moral speeches in Parliament, become a member of the Society for the Suppression of Vice. If you wish absolutely to have him punished, we will "make him end in hell, or in an unhappy marriage, not knowing which would be the severest: the Spanish tradition says hell; but it is probably only an allegory of the other state."[215] At all events, married or damned, the good folk at the end of the piece will have the pleasure of knowing that he is burning all alive.

Is not this a singular apology? Does it not aggravate the fault? Let us wait; we know not yet the whole venom of the book: together with Juan there are Donna Julia, Haidée, Gulbeyaz, Dudu, and many more. It is here the diabolical poet digs in his sharpest claw, and he takes care to dig it into our weakest side. What will the clergymen and white-chokered reviewers say? For, to speak the truth, there is no preventing it: we must read on, in spite of ourselves. Twice or three times following we meet here with happiness; and when I say happiness, I mean profound and complete happiness— not mere voluptuousness, not obscene gayety; we are far removed from the nicely-written ribaldry of Dorat, and the unbridled license of Rochester. Beauty is here, southern beauty, resplendent and harmonious, spread over everything, over the luminous sky, the calm scenery, corporal nudity, artlessness of heart. Is there a thing it does not deify? All sentiments are exalted under its hands. What was gross becomes noble; even in the nocturnal adventure in the seraglio, which seems worthy of Faublas, poetry embellishes licentiousness.

BOOK IV— MODERN LIFE

The girls are lying in the large silent apartment, like precious flowers brought from all climates into a conservatory:

> "One with her flush'd cheek laid on her white arm,
> And raven ringlets gather'd in dark crowd
> Above her brow, lay dreaming soft and warm;
> One with her auburn tresses lightly bound,
> And fair brows gently drooping, as the fruit
> Nods from the tree, was slumbering with soft breath,
> And lips apart, which show'd the pearls beneath....
> A fourth as marble, statue-like and still,
> Lay in a breathless, hush'd, and stony sleep;
> White, cold, and pure... a carved lady on a monument."[216]

However, "the fading lamps waned dim and blue"; Dudu is asleep, the innocent girl; and if she has cast a glance on her glass,

> "'Twas like the fawn, which, in the lake display'd,
> Beholds her own shy, shadowy image pass,
> When first she starts, and then returns to peep,
> Admiring this new native of the deep."[217]

What will become now of Puritanic prudery? Can the proprieties prevent beauty from being beautiful? Will you condemn a picture of Titian for its nudity? What gives value to human life, and nobility to human nature, if not the power of attaining delicious and sublime emotions? We have just had one— one worthy of a painter; is it not worth that of an alderman? Shall we refuse to acknowledge the divine because it appears in art and enjoyment, and not only in conscience and action? There is a world beside ours, and a civilization beside ours; our rules are narrow, and our pedantry tyrannic; the human plant can be otherwise developed than in our compartments and under our snows, and the fruits it will then bear will not be less precious. We must confess it, since we relish them when they are offered to us. Who has read the love of Haidée, and has had any other thought than to envy and pity her? She is a wild child who has picked up Juan— another child cast ashore senseless by the waves. She has preserved him, nursed him like a mother, and now she loves him: who can blame her for loving him? Who, in presence of the splendid nature which smiles on and protects them, can imagine for them anything else than the all-powerful feeling which unites them:

> "It was a wild and breaker-beaten coast,
> With cliffs above, and a broad sandy shore,
> Guarded by shoals and rocks as by an host,...

And rarely ceased the haughty billow's roar,
Save on the dead long summer days, which make
The outstretch'd ocean glitter like a lake....
And all was stillness, save the sea-bird's cry,
And dolphin's leap, and little billow crost
By some low rock or shelve, that made it fret
Against the boundary it scarcely wet... .

"And thus they wandered forth, and hand in hand,
Over the shining pebbles and the shells,
Glided along the smooth and harden'd sand,
And in the worn and wild receptacles
Work'd by the storms, yet work'd as it were plann'd,
In hollow halls, with sparry roofs and cells,
They turn'd to rest; and, each clasp'd by an arm,
Yielded to the deep twilight's purple charm.

"They looked up to the sky whose floating glow
Spread like a rosy ocean, vast and bright;
They gazed upon the glittering sea below,
Whence the broad moon rose circling into sight;
They heard the wave's splash and the wind so low,
And saw each other's dark eyes darting light
Into each other— and, beholding this,
Their lips drew nea', and clung into a kiss....

"They were alone, but not alone as they
Who shut in chambers think it loneliness;
The silent ocean, and the starlight bay
The twilight glow, which momently grew less,
The voiceless sand, and dropping caves that lay
Around them, made them to each other press,
As if there were no life beneath the sky
Save theirs, and that their life could never die."[218]

An excellent opportunity to introduce here your formularies and catechisms:

"Haidée spoke not of scruples, ask'd no vows,
Nor offer'd any...
She was all which pure, ignorance allows,
And flew to her young mate like a young bird."[219]

Nature suddenly expands, for she is ripe, like a bud bursting into bloom, nature in her fulness, instinct, and heart:

> "Alas! they were so young, so beautiful,
> So lonely, loving, helpless, and the hour
> Was that in which the heart is always full,
> And, having o'er itself no further power,
> Prompts deeds eternity cannot annul...."[220]

O admirable moralists, you stand before these two flowers like patented gardeners, holding in your hands a model of the bloom sanctioned by your society of horticulture, proving that the model has not been followed, and deciding that the two weeds must be cast into the fire, which you keep burning to consume irregular growths. You have judged well, and you know your art.

Besides British cant, there is universal hypocrisy; besides English pedantry, Byron wars against human roguery. Here is the general aim of the poem, and to this his character and genius tended. His great and gloomy dreams of juvenile imagination have vanished; experience has come; he knows man now; and what is man once known? does the sublime abound in him? Do we think that the grand sentiments— those of Childe Harold, for instance— are the ordinary course of life?[221] The truth is, that man employs most of his time in sleeping, dining, yawning, working like a horse, amusing himself like an ape. According to Byron, he is an animal; except for a few minutes, his nerves, his blood, his instincts lead him. Routine works over it all, necessity whips him on, the animal advances. As the animal is proud, and moreover imaginative, it pretends to be marching for its own pleasure, that there is no whip, that at all events this whip rarely touches its flanks, that at least its stoic back can make-believe that it does not feel it. It thinks that it is decked with the most splendid trappings, and thus struts on with measured steps, fancying that it carries relics and treads on carpets and flowers, whilst in reality it tramples in the mud, and carries with it the stains and bad smells of every dunghill. What a pastime to touch its mangy back, to set before its eyes the sacks full of flour which it carries, and the goad which makes it go![222] What a pretty farce! It is the eternal farce; and not a sentiment thereof but provides him with an act: love in the first place. Certainly Donna Julia is very lovable, and Byron loves her; but she comes out of his hands, as rumpled as any other woman. She is virtuous, of course; and what is better still, she desires to be so. She plies herself, in connection with Don Juan, with the finest arguments; what a fine thing are arguments, and how suited they are to check passion! Nothing can be more solid than a firm purpose, propped up by logic, resting on the fear of the world, the thought of God, the recollection of duty; nothing can prevail against it except a *tête-à-tête* in June, on a moonlight evening. At last the deed is done, and the poor timid lady is surprised by her outraged husband; in what a situation! Let us look again at the book. Of course she will be speechless, ashamed and full of tears, and the moral reader duly reckons on her remorse. My dear reader, you have not reckoned on impulse and nerves. To-morrow she will feel shame; the business is now to overwhelm the husband, to deafen him, to confound him, to save Juan, to save herself, to fight. The war once begun, is waged with all kinds of weapons, and chiefly with audacity and insults. The only idea is the present need, and this absorbs all others; it is in this that woman is a woman. This Julia cries lustily. It is a regular storm: hard words and recriminations, mockery and challenges, fainting and tears. In a quarter of an hour she has gained twenty years' experience. You did not know, nor she either, what an actress can emerge, all on a sudden, unforeseen, out of a simple woman. Do you know what can emerge from yourself? You think yourself rational, humane; I admit it for to-day; you have dined, and you are comfortable in a pleasant room. Your human mechanism works without getting into disorder, because the wheels are oiled and well regulated; but place it in a shipwreck, a battle, let the failing or the plethora of blood for an instant derange the chief pieces, and we shall see you howling or drivelling like a madman or an idiot. Civilization, education, reason, health, cloak us in their smooth and polished cases; let us tear them away one by one, or all together, and we laugh to see the brute, who is lying at the bottom. Here is our friend Juan reading Julia's last letter, and swearing in a transport never to forget the beautiful eyes which he caused to weep so much. Was ever feeling more tender or sincere? But unfortunately Juan is at sea, and sickness sets in. He cries out:

> "Sooner shall earth resolve itself to sea,
> Than I resign thine image, oh, my fair!...
> (Here the ship gave a lurch, and he grew sea-sick.)...
> Sooner shall heaven kiss earth— (here he fell sicker.)
> Oh, Julia! what is every other woe?
> (For God's sake let me have a glass of liquor;
> Pedro, Battista, help me down below.)
> Julia, my love!— (You rascal, Pedro, quicker)—
> Oh, Julia!— (this curst vessel pitches so)
> Beloved Julia, hear me still beseeching!
> (Here he grew inarticulate with retching.)...
> Love's a capricious power...
> Against all noble maladies he's bold,
> But vulgar illnesses don't like to meet;...
> Shrinks from the application of hot towels,
> And purgatives are dangerous to his reign,
> Sea-sickness death."[223]

Many other things cause the death of Love:

> "'Tis melancholy, and a fearful sign
> Of human frailty, folly, also crime,
> That love and marriage rarely can combine.
> Although they both are born in the same clime;
> Marriage from love, like vinegar from wine—
> A sad, sour, sober beverage.[224]...
> An honest gentleman, at his return,
> May not have the good fortune of Ulysses;...
> The odds are that he finds a handsome urn
> To his memory— and two or three young misses
> Born to some friend, who holds his wife and riches—
> And that his Argus bites him by— the breeches."[225]

These are the words of a sceptic, even of a cynic. Sceptic and cynic, it is in this he ends. Sceptic through misanthropy, cynic through bravado, a sad and combative humor always impels him; southern voluptuousness has not conquered him; he is only an epicurean through contradiction and for a moment:

> "Let us have wine and women, mirth and laughter,
> Sermons and soda-water the day after.
> Man, being reasonable, must get drunk;
> The best of life is but intoxication."[226]

We see clearly that he is always the same, going to extremes and unhappy, bent on destroying himself. His "Don Juan," also, is a debauchery; in it he diverts himself outrageously at the expense of all respectable things, as a bull in a china shop. He is always violent, and often ferocious; a sombre imagination intersperses his love stories with horrors leisurely enjoyed, the despair and famine of shipwrecked men, and the emaciation of the raging skeletons feeding on each other. He laughs at it horribly, like Swift; he jests over it like Voltaire:

> "And next they thought upon the master's mate,
> As fattest; but he saved himself, because,
> Besides being much averse from such a fate,
> There were some other reasons: the first was,
> He had been rather indisposed of late;
> And that which chiefly proved his saving clause,
> Was a small present made to him at Cadiz,
> By general subscription of the ladies."[227]

With his specimens in hand,[228] Byron follows with a surgeon's exactness all the stages of death, gorging, rage, madness, howling, exhaustion, stupor; he wishes to touch and exhibit the naked and ascertained truth, the last grotesque and hideous element of humanity. Let us read again the assault on Ismail— the grape-shot and the bayonet, the street massacres, the corpses used as fascines, and the thirty-eight thousand slaughtered Turks. There is blood enough to satiate a tiger, and this blood flows amidst an accompaniment of jests; it is in order to rail at war, and the butcheries dignified with the name of exploits. In this pitiless and universal demolition of all human vanities, what remains? What do we know except that life is a "scene of all-confess'd inanity," and that men are,

> "Dogs, or men!— for I flatter you in saying
> That ye are dogs— your betters far— ye may
> Read, or read not, what I am now essaying
> To show ye what ye are in every way?"[229]

What does he find in science but deficiencies, and in religion but mummeries?[230] Does he so much as preserve poetry? Of the divine mantle, the last garment which a poet respects, he makes a rag to trample upon, to wring, to make holes in, out of sheer wantonness. At the most touching moment of Haidée's love he vents a buffoonery. He concludes an ode with caricatures. He is Faust in the first verse, and Mephistopheles in the second. He employs, in the midst of tenderness or of murder, penny-print witticisms, trivialities, gossip, with a pamphleteer's vilification and a buffoon's whimsicalities. He lays bare the poetic method, asks himself where he has got to, counts the stanzas already done, jokes the Muse, Pegasus, and the whole epic stud, as though he wouldn't give twopence for them. Again, what remains? Himself, he alone, standing amidst all this ruin. It is he who speaks here; his characters are but screens; half the time even he pushes them aside, to occupy the stage. He lavishes upon us his opinions, recollections, anger, tastes; his poem is a conversation, a confidence, with the ups and downs, the rudeness and freedom of a conversation and a confidence, almost like the holographic journal, in which, by night, at his writing-table, he opened his heart and discharged his feelings. Never was seen in such a clear glass the birth of lively thought, the tumult of great genius, the inner life of a genuine poet, always impassioned, inexhaustibly fertile and creative, in whom suddenly, successively, finished and adorned, bloomed all human emotions and ideas— sad, gay, lofty, low, hustling one another, mutually impeding one another like swarms of insects who go humming and feeding on flowers and in the mud. He may say what he likes; willingly or unwillingly we listen to him; let him leap from sublime to burlesque, we leap with him. He has so much wit, so fresh a wit, so sudden, so biting, such a prodigality of knowledge, ideas, images picked up from the four corners of the horizon, in heaps and masses, that we are captivated, transported beyond all limits; we cannot dream of resisting. Too vigorous, and hence unbridled— that is the word which ever recurs when we speak of Byron; too vigorous against others and himself, and so unbridled, that after spending his life in setting the world at defiance, and his poetry in depicting revolt, he can only find the fulfilment of his talent and the satisfaction of his heart, in a poem waging war on all human and poetic conventions. When a man lives in such a manner he must be great, but he becomes also morbid. There is a malady of heart and mind in the style of "Don Juan," as in Swift. When a man jests amidst his tears, it is because he has a poisoned imagination. This kind of laughter is a spasm, and we see in one man a hardening of the heart, or madness; in another, excitement or disgust. Byron was exhausted, at least the poet was exhausted in him. The last cantos of "Don Juan" drag: the gayety became forced, the escapades became digressions; the reader began to be bored. A new kind of poetry, which he had attempted, had given way in his hands; in the drama he only attained to powerful declamation, his characters had no life; when he forsook poetry, poetry forsook him; he went to Greece in search of action, and only found death.

Section VI.—The Malady of the Age

So lived and so died this unhappy great man; the malady of the age had no more distinguished prey. Around him, like a hecatomb, lie the others, wounded also by the greatness of their faculties and their immoderate desires— some ending in stupor or drunkenness, others worn out by pleasure or work: these driven to madness or suicide; those beaten down by impotence, or lying on a sick-bed; all agitated by their too acute or aching nerves; the strongest carrying their bleeding wound to old age, the happiest, having suffered as much as the rest, and preserving their scars, though healed. The concert of their lamentations has filled their century, and we stood around them, hearing in our hearts the low echo of their cries. We were sad like them, and like them inclined to revolt. The reign of democracy excited our ambitions without satisfying them; the proclamation of philosophy kindled our curiosity without satisfying it. In this wide-open career, the plebeian suffered for his mediocrity, and the sceptic for his doubt. The plebeian, like the sceptic, attacked by a precocious melancholy, and withered by a premature experience, abandoned his sympathies and his conduct to the poets, who declared happiness impossible, truth unattainable, society ill-arranged, man abortive or marred. From this unison of voices an idea arose, the centre of the literature, the arts, the religion of the age, to-wit, that here is a monstrous disproportion between the different parts of our social structure, and that human destiny is vitiated by this disagreement.

What advice have they given us to cure this? They were great; were they wise? "Let deep and strong sensations rain upon you; if the human mechanism breaks, so much the worse! Cultivate your garden, bury yourself in a little circle, re-enter the flock, be a beast of burden. Turn believer again, take holy water, abandon your mind to dogmas, and your conduct to manuals of devotion. Make your way; aspire to power, honours, wealth." Such are the various replies of artists and citizens, Christians and men of the world. Are they replies? And what do they propose but to satiate one's self, to become stupid, to turn aside, to forget? There is another and a deeper answer which Goethe was the first to give, the truth of which we begin to conceive, in which issue all the labor and experience of the age, and which may perhaps be the subject-matter of future literature: "Try to understand yourself, and things in general." A strange reply, which seems hardly new, whose scope we shall only hereafter discover. For a long time yet men will feel their sympathies thrill at the sound of the sobs of their great poets. For a long time they will rage against a destiny which opens to their aspirations the career of limitless space, to shatter them, within two steps of the goal, against a wretched post which they had not seen. For a long time they will bear like fetters the necessities which they ought to have embraced as laws. Our generation, like the preceding, has been tainted by the malady of the age, and will never more than half get rid of it. We shall arrive at truth, not at tranquillity. All we can heal at present is our intellect; we have no hold upon our feelings. But we have a right to conceive for others the hopes which we no longer entertain for ourselves, and to prepare for our descendants the happiness which we shall never enjoy. Brought up in a more wholesome air, they will have, mayhap, a wholesomer heart. The reformation of ideas ends by reforming the rest, and the light of the mind produces serenity of heart. Hitherto, in our judgments on men, we have taken for our masters the oracles and poets, and like them we have received for undoubted truths the noble dreams of our imagination and the imperious suggestions of our heart. We have bound ourselves to the partiality of religious divinations, and the inexactness of literary divinations, and we have shaped our doctrines according to our instincts and our vexations. Science at last approaches, and approaches man; it has gone beyond the visible and palpable world of stars, stones, plants, amongst which man disdainfully confined her. It reaches the heart provided with exact and penetrating implements, whose justness has been proved, and their reach measured by three hundred years of experience. Thought, with its development and rank, its structure and relations, its deep material roots, its infinite growth through history, its lofty bloom at the summit of things, becomes the object of science— an object which, sixty years ago, it foresaw in Germany, and which, slowly and surely probed, by the same methods as the physical world, will be transformed before our eyes, as the physical world has been transformed. It is already being transformed, and we have left behind us the light in which Byron and the French poets had considered it. No, man is not an abortion or a monster; no, the business of poetry is not to disgust or defame him. He is in his place, and completes a chain. Let us watch him grow and increase, and we shall cease to rail at or curse him. He, like everything else, is a product, and as such it is right he should be what he is. His innate imperfection is in order, like the constant abortion of a stamen in a plant, like the fundamental irregularity of four facets in a crystal. What we took for a deformity, is a form; what seemed to us the subversion of a law, is the accomplishment of a law. Human reason and virtue have for their foundation instincts and animal images, as living forms have for their instruments physical laws, as organic matters have for their elements mineral substances. What wonder if virtue or human reason, like living form or organic matter, sometimes fails or decomposes, since like them, and like every superior and complex existence, they have for support and control inferior and simple forces, which, according to circumstances, now maintain it by their harmony, now mar it by their discord? What wonder if the elements of existence, like those of quantity, receive, from their very nature, the immutable laws which constrain and reduce them to a certain species and order of formation? Who will rise up against geometry? Who, especially, will rise up against a living geometry? Who will not, on the contrary, feel moved with admiration at the sight of those grand powers which, situated at the heart of things, incessantly urge the blood through the limbs of the old world, disperse it quickly in the infinite network of arteries, and spread over the whole surface the eternal flower of youth and beauty? Who, finally, will not feel himself ennobled, when he finds that this pile of laws results in a regular series of forms, that matter has thought for its goal, that nature ends in reason, and that this ideal to which, amidst so many errors, all the aspirations of men cling, is also the end to which aim, amidst so many obstacles, all the forces of the universe? In this employment of science, and in this conception of things, there is a new art, a new morality, a new polity, a new religion, and it is in the present time our task to try and discover them.

---

[144]Byron's Works, ed. Moore, 17 vols. 1832; "Life," I. 102.
[145]Ibid. 63.
[146]Ibid. 69.
[147]Ibid. 137.
[148]Ibid. 26.
[149]Byron's Works, "Life," I. 53.
[150]Ibid. III. 83.
[151]Ibid. III. 20, March 28, 1814.
[152]Ibid. IV. 81; Letter to Moore, Feb. 12, 1818.
[153]Byron's Works, "Life," V. 96, Feb. 2, 1821.
[154]Lockhart's "Life of Sir Walter Scott," VII. 323.

[155]"If I was born, as the nurses say, with a 'silver spoon in my mouth,' it has stuck in my throat, and spoiled my palate, so that nothing put into it is swallowed with much relish— unless it be cayenne.... I see no such horror in a dreamless sleep, and I have no conception of any existence which duration would not make tiresome."

[156]"I like Junius: he was a good hater. I don't understand yielding sensitiveness. What I feel is an immense rage for forty-eight hours."

[157]Byron's Works, "Life," I. 41.

[158]In "English Bards and Scotch Reviewers."

[159]Lockhart's "Life of Sir Walter Scott," III. 389.

[160]Ibid. V. 141.

[161]Moore's "Life of Byron," III. 12, March 10, Thor's day. The last part of the sentence is a quotation from "Macbeth," V. 5.

[162]Ibid. IV. 169, note.

[163]Moore, Byron's Works; "Life," V. 67, Jan. 9, 1821.

[164]Ibid. V. 60, Jan. 6, 1821.

[165]Moore, Byron's Works; "Life," V. 97, February 2, 1821.

[166]Ibid. 95.

[167]Ibid. VI. 206.

[168]Moore, Byron's Works; "Life," V. 33, Ravenna, Nov. 18, 1820.

[169]Moore, Byron's Works; "Life," V. 265.

[170]Ibid. V. 150, Ravenna, May 3, 1821.

[171]"All the styles of the day are bombastic. I don't except my own; no one has done more through negligence to corrupt the language."

[172]See his "English Bards and Scotch Reviewers."

[173]Thirty thousand copies of "The Corsair" were sold in one day.

[174]Byron's Works, VIII; "Childe Harold's Pilgrimage," c. I. 6.

[175]"Childe Harold's Pilgrimage," c. I. 19.

[176]"Childe Harold's Pilgrimage," c. III. 7-15.

[177]"Childe Harold's Pilgrimage," c. IV. 1 and 2.

[178]"Childe Harold's Pilgrimage," c. I. 39 and 40.

[179]Ibid. c. IV. 93 and 94.

[180]For example, "as weeping Beauty's cheek at Sorrow's tale."

[181]Here are verses like Pope, very beautiful and false:
"And havock loath so much the waste of time,
She scarce had left an uncommitted crime,
One hour beheld him since the tide he stemm'd,
Disguised, discover'd, conquering, ta'en condemn'd,
A chief on land, an outlaw on the

deep,
Destroying, saving, prison'd, and
asleep!"

[182]Moore's "Life," IV. 345.
[183]Byron's Works, X., "The Prisoner of Chillon," c. VII. 234.
[184]Byron's Works, X., "The Prisoner of Chillon," c. VIII. 236.
[185]Ibid, XI., "Mazeppa," c. XIII. 167.
[186]Byron's Works, X., "The Siege of Corinth," c. XI. 116.
[187]Byron's Works, X., "The Siege of Corinth," c. XVI. 123.
[188]Byron's Works, X; "Lara," c. 2, st. 17-20, 60.
[189]Byron's Works, X; "Darkness," 283.
[190]Byron's Works, IV. 320; Letter to Mr. Murray, Ravenna, June 7, 1820.
[191]The angel of holy loves, the angel of the ocean, the choirs of happy spirits. See this at length in the "Martyrs."
[192]"Magna peccatrix." S. Lucæ. VII. 36: "Mulier Samaritana." S. Johannis, IV; "Maria Ægyptiaca" (Acta Sanctorum), etc.
[193]Goethe's "Faust," translated by Theodore Martin. Prologue in Heaven.
[194]Goethe sings:
"Wer ruft das Einzelne zur allgemeinen Weihe
Wo es in herrlichen Accorden schlägt?"

[195]Byron's Works, XI; "Manfred," II. 2, 32.
[196]Ibid.; "Manfred," III. 1, 56.
[197]Ibid.; "Manfred," II. 2, 35.
[198]Byron's Works, XI; "Manfred," II. 4, 47.
[199]Byron's Works, XI; "Manfred," II. 4, 49.
[200]Ibid. III. 4. 70.
[201]Southey, Preface to "A Vision of Judgment."
[202]Byron's Works, XVII; "Don Juan," c. 11, st. LXVII.
[203]Ibid. VI. 18; Letter 512, April 5, 1823.
[204]Ibid. II. 303; Journal, December 17, 1813.
[205]Alfred de Musset.
[206]See his terrible satirical poem, "The Vision of Judgment," against Southey, George IV, and official pomp.
[207]Byron's Works, XVI. 131; Preface to "Don Juan," cantos VI., VII., and VIII.
[208]"Don Juan" is a satire on the abuses in the present state of society, and not a eulogy of vice.
[209]Stendhal, "Mémoires sur Lord Byron."
[210]Byron's Works, III. 333; Letter to Murray, Venice, January 2, 1817.
[211]Ibid. III. 363; Letter to Moore, Venice, March 25, 1817.
[212]Byron's Works, IV. 279; Letter to Murray. Ravenna, February 7, 1820.
[213]Ibid. XI; "Beppo," c. XLIII-XLV. 121.

HISTORY OF ENGLISH LITERATURE

[214]See Stendhal, "Vie de Giacomo Rossini," and Dean Stanley's "Life of Dr. Arnold." The contrast is complete. See also Mme. de Staël's "Corinne," where this opposition is very clearly grasped.

[215]Byron's Works, V. 127; Letter to Mr. Murray, Ravenna, February 16, 1821.

[216]Ibid. XVI; "Don Juan," c. VI. st. LXVI-LXVIII.

[217]Byron's Works, "Don Juan," c. VI. st. LX.

[218]Byron's Works, XV; "Don Juan," c. II. st. CLXXVII-CLXXXVIII.

[219]Ibid, XV; "Don Juan," c. II. st CXC.

[220]Ibid. c. II. st. CXCII.

[221]Byron says (V. October 12, 1820), "Don Juan is too true, and would. I suspect, live longer than Childe Harold. The women hate many things which strip off the tinsel of sentiment."

[222]"Don Juan," c. VII. st. 2. "I hope it is no crime to laugh at all things. For I wish to know what, after all, are all things— but a show?"

[223]Byron's Works, XV; "Don Juan," c. II. st. XIX-XXIII.

[224]Ibid. c. III. st. V.

[225]Ibid. c. III. st. XXIII.

[226]Ibid. c. II. st. CLXXVIII., CLXXIX.

[227]Byron's Works, XV; "Don Juan," c. II. st. LXXXI.

[228]Byron had before him a dozen authentic descriptions.

[229]Byron's Works, XVI; "Don Juan," c. VII. st. 7.

[230]See his "Vision of Judgment."

BOOK IV— MODERN LIFE

CHAPTER THIRD. THE PAST AND PRESENT

PART I.—THE PAST

Section I.—The Saxon Invasion.—The Norman Conquest

Having reached the limits of this long review, we can now survey as a whole the aggregate of English civilization: everything is connected there: a few primitive powers and circumstances have produced the rest, and we have only to pursue their continuous action in order to comprehend the nation and its history, its past and its present. At the beginning and far away in the region of causes, comes the race. A whole people, Angles and Saxons, destroyed, drove away, or enslaved the old inhabitants, wiped out the Roman culture, settled by themselves and unmixed, and, amongst the later Danish pirates, only encountered a new reinforcement of the same blood. This is the primitive stock: from its substance and innate properties is to spring almost the whole future growth. At this time and as they then were, alone in their island, the Angles and Saxons attained a development such as it was, rough, brutal, and yet solid. They ate and drank, built and cleared the land, and in particular, multiplied: the scattered tribes who crossed the sea in leather boats, became a strong compact nation— three hundred thousand families, rich, with store of cattle, abundantly provided with corporal subsistence, partly at rest in the security of social life, with a king, respected and frequent assemblies, good judicial customs: here, amidst the fire and vehemence of barbarian temperament, the old Germanic fidelity held men together, whilst the old Germanic independence held them upright. In all else they barely advanced. A few fragmentary songs, an epic in which still are to be found traces of the warlike excitement of ancient barbarism, gloomy hymns, a harsh and fierce poetry, sometimes sublime and always rude— this is all that remains of them. In six centuries they had scarcely gone one step beyond the manners and sentiments of their uncivilized Germany: Christianity, which obtained a hold on them by the greatness of its biblical tragedies and the troubled sadness of its aspirations, did not bring to them a Latin civilization: this remained outside, hardly accepted by a few great men, deformed, when it did enter, by the difference between the Roman and Saxon genius— always altered and reduced; so much so, that for the men of the Continent these islanders were but illiterate dullards, drunkards, and gluttons; at all events, savage and slow by mood and nature, rebellious against culture, and sluggish in development.

The empire of this world belongs to force. These people were conquered forever and permanently— conquered by Normans; that is, by Frenchmen more clever, more quickly cultivated and organized than they. This is the great event which was to complete their character, decide their history, and stamp upon character and history an impress of the political and practical spirit which separates them from other German nations. Oppressed, enclosed in the unyielding meshes of Norman organization, they were not destroyed although they were conquered, they were on their own soil, each with his friends and in his tithings; they formed a body; they were yet twenty times more numerous than their conquerors. Their situation and their necessities create their habits and their aptitudes. They endure, protest, struggle, resist together and unanimously; strive to-day, to-morrow, daily, not to be slain or plundered, to restore their old laws, to obtain or extort guarantees; and they gradually acquire patience, judgment, all the faculties and inclinations by which liberties are maintained and states are founded. By a singular good fortune, the Norman lords assist them in this; for the king has secured to himself so much, and is so formidable, that, in order to repress the great pillager, the lesser ones are forced to make use of their Saxon subjects, to ally themselves with them, to give them a share in their charters, to become their representatives, to admit them into Parliament, to leave them to labor freely, to grow rich, to acquire pride, strength, authority, to interfere with themselves in public affairs. Thus, then, gradually the English nation, struck down by the Conquest to the ground, as if with a mace, extricates and raises itself; five hundred years and more being occupied in this re-elevation. But during all this time, leisure failed for refined and lofty culture: it was needful to live and defend themselves, to dig the ground, spin wool, practise the bow, attend public meetings, serve on juries, to contribute and argue for common interests: the important and respected man is he who knows how to fight well and to gain much money. It was the energetic and warlike manners which were developed, the active and positive spirit which predominated; learning and elegance were left to the gallicized nobles of the court. When the valiant Saxon townsfolk quitted bow and plough, it was to feast copiously, or to sing the ballad of "Robin Hood." They lived and acted; they did not reflect or write; their national literature was reduced to fragments and rudiments, harpers' songs, tavern epics, a religious poem, a few books on religious reformation. At the same time Norman literature faded; separated from the stem, and on a foreign soil, it languished in imitations; only one great poet, almost French in mind, quite French in style, appeared, and, after him, as before him, we find helpless drivel. For the second time, a civilization of five centuries became sterile in great ideas and works; this still more so than its neighbors, and for a twofold reason— because to the universal impotence of the Middle Ages was added the impoverishment of the Conquest, and because of the two component literatures, one transplanted, became abortive, and the other, mutilated, ceased to expand.

Section II.—Formative Periods

But amongst so many attempts and trials a character was formed, and the rest was to spring from it. The barbarous age established on the soil a German race, phlegmatic and grave, capable of spiritual emotions and moral discipline. The feudal age imposed on this race habits of resistance and association, political and utilitarian prepossessions. Fancy a German from Hamburg or Bremen confined for five hundred years in the iron corselet of William the Conqueror: these two natures, one innate, the other acquired, constitute all the springs of his conduct. So it was in other nations. Like runners drawn up in line at the entrance of the arena, we see at the epoch of the Renaissance the five great peoples of Europe start, though we are unable at first to foresee anything of their career. At first sight it seems as if accidents or circumstances will alone regulate their speed, their fall, and their success. It is not so: from themselves alone their history depends: each nation will be the artisan of its fortune; chance has no influence over events so vast; and it is national tendencies and faculties which, overturning or raising obstacles, will lead them, according to their fate, each one to its goal— some to the extreme of decadence, others to the height of prosperity. After all, man is ever his own master and his own slave. At the outset of every age he in a certain fashion *is*: his body, heart, mind have a distinct structure and disposition: and from this lasting arrangement, which all preceding centuries have contributed to consolidate or construct, spring permanent desires or aptitudes, by which he determines and acts. Thus is formed in him the ideal model, which, whether obscure or distinct, complete or rough-hewn, will henceforth float before his eyes, rally all his aspirations, efforts, forces, and will cause him to aim for centuries at one effect, until at length, renewed by impotence of success, he conceives a new goal, and assumes new energy. The Catholic and enthusiastic Spaniard figures life like the Crusaders, lovers, knights, and abandoning labor, liberty, and science, casts himself, in the wake of the inquisition, and his king, into fanatical war, romanesque slothfulness, superstitious and impassioned obedience, voluntary and incurable ignorance.[231] The theological and feudal German settles in his district docilely and faithfully under his petty chief, through natural patience and hereditary loyalty, engrossed by his wife and household, content to have conquered religious liberty, clogged by the dulness of his temperament in gross physical existence, and in sluggish respect for established order. The Italian, the most richly gifted and precocious of all, but, of all, the most incapable of voluntary discipline and moral austerity, turns towards the fine arts and voluptuousness, declines, deteriorates beneath foreign rule, takes life at its easiest, forgetting to think, and satisfied to enjoy. The sociable and levelling Frenchman rallies round his king, who secures for him public peace, external glory, the splendid display of a sumptuous court, a regular administration, a uniform discipline, a predominating influence in Europe, and universal literature. So, if we look at the Englishman in the sixteenth century, we shall find in him the inclinations and the powers which for three centuries are to govern his culture and shape his constitution. In this European expansion of natural existence and pagan literature we find at first in Shakespeare, Ben Jonson, and the tragic poets, in Spenser, Sidney, and the lyric poets, the national features, all with incomparable depth and splendor, and such as race and history have impressed and implanted in them for a thousand years. Not in vain did invasion settle here so serious a race, capable of reflection. Not in vain did the Conquest turn this race toward warlike life and practical preoccupations. From the first rise of original invention, its work displays the tragic energy, the intense and disorderly passion, the disdain of regularity, the knowledge of the real, the sentiment of inner things, the natural melancholy, the anxious divination of the obscure beyond— all the instincts which, forcing man upon himself, and concentrating him within himself, prepare him for Protestantism and combat. What is this Protestantism which establishes itself? What is this ideal model which it presents; and what original conception is to furnish to this people, its permanent and dominant poem? The harshest and most practical of all— that of the Puritans, which neglecting speculation, falls back upon action, encloses human life in a rigid discipline, imposes on the soul continuous efforts, prescribes to society a cloistral austerity, forbids pleasure, commands action, exacts sacrifice, and forms a moralist, a laborer, a citizen. Thus it is implanted, the great English idea— I mean the conviction that man is before all a free and moral personage, and that, having conceived alone in his conscience and before God the rule of his conduct, he must employ himself entirely in applying it within himself, beyond himself, obstinately, inflexibly, by offering a perpetual resistance to others, and imposing a perpetual restraint upon himself. In vain will this idea at first bring discredit upon itself by its transports and its tyranny; weakened by practice, it will gradually accommodate itself to humanity, and, carried from Puritan fanaticism to laic morality, it will win all public sympathy, because it answers to all the national instincts. In vain it will vanish from high society, under the scorn of the Restoration, and the importation of French culture; it subsists underground. For French culture did not come to a head in England: on this too alien soil it produced only unhealthy, coarse, or imperfect fruit. Refined elegance became low debauchery; hardly expressed doubt became brutal atheism; tragedy failed, and was but declamation; comedy grew shameless, and was but a school of vice; of this literature, there remained only studies of close reasoning and good style; it was driven from the public stage, together with the Stuarts, at the beginning of the eighteenth century; and liberal and moral maxims resumed the ascendancy, which they will not again lose. For, with ideas, events have followed their course: national inclinations have done their work in society as in literature; and the English instincts have transformed the constitution and politics at the same time as the talents and minds. These rich tithings, these valiant yeomen, these rude, well-armed citizens, well-fed, protected by their juries, wont to reckon on themselves, obstinate, combative, sensible, such as the English Middle Ages bequeathed them to modern England, did not object if the king practised his temporary tyranny on the classes above them, and oppressed the nobility with a rigorous despotism, which the recollection of the Civil Wars and the danger of high treason justified. But Henry VIII, and Elizabeth herself were obliged to follow in great interests the current of public opinion: if they were strong, it was because they were popular; the people only supported their designs, and authorized their violences, because they found in them defenders of their religion, and the protectors of their labor.[232] The people themselves became immersed in this religion, and, from under a State-church, attained to personal belief. They grew rich by toil, and under the first Stuart already occupied the highest place in the nation. At this moment everything was decided: whatever happened, they must one day become masters. Social situations create political situations; legal constitutions always accommodate themselves to real things; and acquired preponderance infallibly results in written rights. Men so numerous, so active, so resolute, so capable of keeping themselves, so disposed to educe their opinions from their own reflection, and their subsistence from their own efforts, will under all circumstances seize the guarantees which they need. At the first onset, and in the ardor of primitive faith, they overturn the throne, and the current which bears them is so strong, that, in spite of their excess and their failure, the Revolution is accomplished by the abolition of feudal tenures, and the institution of Habeas Corpus under Charles II; by the universal upheaving of the liberal and Protestant spirit, under James II; by the establishment of the constitution, the act of toleration, the freedom of the press, under William III. From that moment England had found her proper place; her two interior and hereditary forces— moral and religious instinct, practical and political aptitude— had done their work, and were henceforth to build, without impediment or destruction, on the foundation which they had laid.

Section III.—The Broadening of Ideas

Thus was the literature of the eighteenth century born, altogether conservative, useful, moral, and limited. Two powers direct it, one European, the other English: on one side a talent of oratorical analysis and habits of literary dignity, which belong to a classical age; on the other, a taste for application and an energy of precise observation, which are peculiar to the national mind. Hence that excellence and originality of political satire, parliamentary discourse, solid essays, moral novels, and all kinds of literature which demand an attentive good sense, a correct good style, and a talent for advising, convincing, or wounding others. Hence that weakness or impotence of speculative thought, of genuine poetry, of original drama, and of all the kinds which require a grand, free curiosity, or a grand, disinterested imagination. The English did not attain complete elegance, nor superior philosophy; they dulled the French refinements which they copied, and were terrified by the French boldness which they suggested; they remained half cockneys and half barbarians; they only invented insular ideas and English ameliorations, and were confirmed in their respect for their constitution and their tradition. But, at the same time, they cultivated and reformed themselves; their wealth and comfort increased enormously; literature and opinion became severe and even intolerant; their long war against the French Revolution caused their morality to become strict and even immoderate; whilst the invention of machinery developed their comfort and prosperity a hundredfold. A salutary and despotic code of approved maxims, established proprieties, and unassailable beliefs, which fortifies, strengthens, curbs, and employs man usefully and painfully, without permitting him ever to deviate or grow weak; a minute apparatus, and an admirable provision of commodious inventions, associations, institutions, mechanisms, implements, methods, which incessantly co-operate to furnish body and mind with all which they need— such are henceforth the leading and special features of this people. To constrain themselves and to provide for themselves, to govern themselves and nature, to consider life as moralists and economists, like a close garment, in which people must walk becomingly, and like a good garment, the best to be had, to be at once respectable and comfortable: these two words embrace all the mainsprings of English actions. Against this limited good sense, and this pedantic austerity, a revolt broke out. With the universal renewal of thought and imagination, the deep poetic source, which flowed in the sixteenth century, seeks anew an outlet in the nineteenth, and a fresh literature springs up; philosophy and history infiltrate their doctrines into the old establishment; the greatest poet of the time shocks it incessantly with its curses and sarcasms; from all sides, to this day, in science and letters, in practice and theory, in private and in public life, the most powerful minds endeavor to open up a new channel to the stream of continental ideas. But they are patriots as well as innovators, conservative as well as revolutionary; if they touch religion and constitution, manners and doctrines, it is to widen, not to destroy them: England is made; she knows it, and they know it. Such as this country is, based on the whole national history, and on all the national instincts, it is more capable than any other people in Europe of transforming itself without recasting, and of devoting itself to its future without renouncing its past.

Part II.—The Present

Section I.—Effects of the Saxon Invasion and the Norman Conquest

I began to perceive these ideas when I first landed in England, and I was singularly struck how they were corroborated by observation and history; it seemed to me that the present was completing the past, and the past explained the present.

At first the sea troubles and strikes a man with wonder; not in vain is a people insular and maritime, especially with such a sea and such coasts; their painters, not very gifted, perceive, in spite of all, its alarming and gloomy aspect; up to the eighteenth century, amidst the elegance of French culture, and under the joviality of Flemish tradition, we will find in Gainsborough the ineffaceable stamp of this great sentiment. In pleasant moments, in the fine calm summer days, the moist fog stretches over the horizon its pearl-grey veil; the sea has a pale slate color; and the ships, spreading their canvas, advance patiently through the mist. But let us look around, and we will soon see the signs of daily peril. The coast is eaten out, the waves have encroached, the trees have vanished, the earth is softened by incessant showers, the ocean is here, ever intractable and fierce. It growls and bellows eternally, that old hoarse monster; and the barking pack of its waves advances like an endless army, before which all human force must give way. Think of the winter months, the storms, the long hours of the tempest-tossed sailor whirled about blindly by the squalls! Now, and in this fine season, over the whole circle of the horizon, rise the dull, wan clouds, some like the smoke of a coal-fire, some of a frail and dazzling white, so swollen that they seem ready to burst. Their heavy masses creep slowly along; they are gorged, and already here and there on the limitless plain a patch of sky is shrouded in a sudden shower. After an instant, the sea becomes dirty and cadaverous; its waves leap with strange gambols, and their sides take an oily and livid tint. The vast gray dome drowns and hides the whole horizon; the rain falls, close and pitiless. We cannot have an idea of it until we have seen it. When the southern men, the Romans, came here for the first time, they must have thought themselves in the infernal regions. The wide space between earth and sky, and on which our eyes dwell as their domain, suddenly fails; there is no more air, we see but a flowing mist. No more colors or forms. In this yellowish smoke, objects look like fading ghosts; nature seems a bad crayon-drawing, over which a child has awkwardly smeared his sleeve. Here we are at Newhaven, then at London; the sky disgorges rain, the earth returns her mist, the mist floats in the rain; all is swamped: looking round us, we see no reason why it should ever end. Here, truly, is Homer's Cimmerian land: our feet splash, we have no use left for our eyes; we feel all our organs stopped up, becoming rusty by the mounting damp; we think ourselves banished from the breathing world, reduced to the condition of marshy beings dwelling in dirty pools: to live here is not life. We ask ourselves if this vast town is not a cemetery, in which dabble busy and wretched ghosts. Amidst the deluge of moist soot, the muddy stream with its unwearying iron ships, like black insects which take on board and land shades, makes us think of the Styx. As there is no light, they create it. Lately, in a large square in London, in the finest hotel, it was necessary to leave the gas alight for five days running. We become melancholy; we are disgusted with others and with ourselves. What can people do in this sepulchre? To remain at home without working is to gnaw one's vitals, and to prepare one's self for suicide. To go out is to make an effort, to care neither for damp nor cold, to brave discomfort and unpleasant sensations. Such a climate prescribes action, forbids sloth, develops energy, teaches patience. I was looking just now on the steamboat at the sailors at the helm— their tarpaulins, their great steaming boots, their sou'westers, so attentive, so precise in their movements, so grave, so self-contained. I have since seen workmen at their looms— calm, serious, silent, economizing their efforts, and persevering all day, all the year, all their life, in the same regular and monotonous struggle of mind and body: their soul is suited to their climate. Indeed it must be so in order to live: after a week, we feel that here a man must renounce refined and heartfelt enjoyment, the happiness of careless life, complete idleness, the easy and harmonious expansion of artistic and animal nature; that here he must marry, bring up a houseful of children, assume the cares and importance of a family man, grow rich, provide against an evil day, surround himself with comfort, become a Protestant, a manufacturer, a politician; in short, capable of activity and resistance; and in all the ways open to men, endure and strive.

Yet there are charming and touching beauties here— those, to-wit, of a well-watered land. When, on a partly clear day, we take a drive into the country and reach an eminence, our eyes experience a unique sensation, and a pleasure hitherto unknown. In the far distance, wherever we look on the horizon, in the fields, on the hills, spreads the always visible verdure, plants for fodder and food, clover, hops; lovely meadows overflowing with high thick grass; here and there a cluster of lofty trees; pasture lands hemmed in with hedges, in which the heavy cows ruminate in peace. The mist rises insensibly between the trees, and in the distance float luminous vapors. There is nothing sweeter in the world, nor more delicate, than these tints; we might pause for hours together gazing on these pearly clouds, this fine aerial down, this soft transparent gauze which imprisons the rays of the sun, dulls them, and lets them reach the ground only to smile on it and to caress it. On both sides of our carriage pass before our eyes incessantly meadows each more lovely than the last, in which buttercups, meadow-sweet, Easter-daisies, are crowded in succession with their dissolving hues; a sweetness almost painful, a strange charm, breathes from this inexhaustible and transient vegetation. It is too fresh, it cannot last; nothing here is staid, stable and firm, as in the

South; all is fleeting, springing up, or dying away, hovering betwixt tears and joy. The rolling water-drops shine on the leaves like pearls; the round tree-tops, the widespread foliage, whisper in the feeble breeze, and the sound of the falling tears left by the last shower never ceases. How well these plants thrive in the glades, spread out wantonly, ever renewed and watered by the moist air! How the sap mounts in these plants, refreshed and protected against the weather! And how sky and land seem made to guard their tissue and refresh their hues! At the least glimpse of sun they smile with delicious charm; we would call them delicate and timid virgins under a veil about to be raised. Let the sun for an instant emerge, and we will see them grow resplendent as in a ball dress. The light falls in dazzling sheets; the lustrous golden petals shine with a too vivid color; the most splendid embroideries, velvet starred with diamonds, sparkling silk seamed with pearls, are not to be compared to this deep hue; joy overflows like a brimming cup. In the strangeness and the rarity of this spectacle, we understand for the first time the life of a humid land. The water multiplies and softens the living tissues; plants increase, and have no substance; nourishment abounds, and has no savor; moisture fructifies, but the sun does not fertilize. Much grass, much cattle, much meat; large quantities of coarse food: thus an absorbing and phlegmatic temperament is supported; the human growth, like the animal and vegetable, is powerful, but heavy; man is amply but coarsely framed; the machine is solid, but it turns slowly on its hinges, and the hinges generally creak and are rusty. When we look at the people closer, it seems that their various parts are independent, at least that they need time to let sensations pass through them. Their ideas do not at first break out in passions, gestures, actions. As in the Fleming and the German, they dwell first of all in the brain; they expand there, they rest there; man is not shaken by them, he has no difficulty in remaining motionless, he is not wrapped; he can act wisely, uniformly; for his inner motive power is an idea or a watchword, not an emotion or an attraction. He can bear tedium, or rather he does not weary himself; his ordinary course consists of dull sensations, and the insipid monotony of mechanical life has nothing which need repel him. He is accustomed to it, his nature is suited for it. When a man has all his life eaten turnips, he does not wish for oranges. He will readily resign himself to hear fifteen consecutive discourses on the same subject, demanding for twenty years the same reform, compiling statistics, studying moral treatises, keeping Sunday schools, bringing up a dozen children. The piquant, the agreeable, are not a necessity to him. The weakness of his sensitive impulses contributes to the force of his moral impulses. His temperament makes him argumentative; he can get on without policemen; the shocks of man against man do not here end in explosions. He can discuss in the market-place aloud, religion and politics, hold meetings, form associations, rudely attack men in office, say that the Constitution is violated, predict the ruin of the State; there is no objection to this; his nerves are calm; he will argue without cutting throats; he will not raise revolutions; and perhaps he will obtain a reform. Observe the passers-by in the streets; in three hours we will see all the visible features of this temperament: light hair, in children almost white; pale eyes, often blue as Wedgwood-ware, red whiskers, a tall figure, the motions of an automaton; and with these other still more striking features, those which strong food and combative life have added to this temperament. Here the enormous guardsman, with rosy complexion, majestic, slightly bent, who struts along twirling a little cane in his hand, displaying his chest, and showing a clear parting between his pomaded hair; there the over-fed stout man, short, sanguine, like an animal fit for the shambles, with his startled, dazed, yet sluggish air; a little further on the country gentleman, six feet high, stout and tall, like the German who left his forest, with the muzzle and nose of a bulldog, tremendous savage-looking whiskers, rolling eyes, apoplectic face; these are the excesses of coarse blood and food; add to which, even in the women, the white front teeth of a carnivorous animal, and big feet solidly shod, excellent for walking in the mud. Again, look at the young men in a cricket match or picnic party; doubtless mind does not sparkle in their eyes, but life abounds there; there is something of decision and energy in their whole being; healthy and active, ready for motion, for enterprise, these are the words which rise involuntarily to our lips when we speak of them. Many look like fine, slender harriers, sniffing the air, and in full cry. A life passed in gymnastic exercises or in venturesome deeds is honored in England; they must move their body, swim, throw the ball, run in the damp meadow, row, breathe in their boats the briny sea-vapor, feel on their foreheads the raindrops falling from the large oak trees, leap their horses over ditches and gates; the animal instincts are intact. They still relish natural pleasures; precocity has not spoiled them. Nothing can be simpler than the young English girls; amidst many beautiful things, there are few so beautiful in the world; slim, strong, self-assured, so fundamentally honest and loyal, so free from coquetry! A man cannot imagine, if he has not seen it, this freshness and innocence; many of them are flowers, expanded flowers; only a morning rose, with its transient and delicious color, with its petals drenched in dew, can give us an idea of it; it leaves far behind the beauty of the South, and its precise, stable, finished contours, its well-defined outlines; here we perceive fragility, delicacy, the continual budding of life; candid eyes, blue as periwinkles, looking at us without thinking of our look. At the least stirring of the soul, the blood rushes in purple waves into these girls' cheeks, neck, and shoulders; we see emotions pass over these transparent complexions, as the colors change in the meadows; and their modesty is so virginal and sincere, that we are tempted to lower our eyes from respect. And yet, natural and frank as they are, they are not languishing or dreamy; they love and endure exercise like their brothers; with flowing locks, at six years they ride on horseback and take long walks. Active life in this country strengthens the phlegmatic temperament, and the heart is kept more simple whilst the body grows healthier. Another observation: far above all these figures one type stands out, the most truly English, the most striking to a foreigner. Post yourself for an hour, early in the morning, at the terminus of a railway, and observe the men above thirty who come to London on business: the features are drawn, the faces pale, the eyes steady, preoccupied; the mouth open and, as it were, contracted; the man is tired, worn out, and hardened by too much work; he runs without looking round him. His whole existence is directed to a single end; he must incessantly exert himself to the utmost, practise the same exertion, a profitable one; he has become a machine. This is especially visible in workmen; perseverance, obstinacy, resignation, are depicted on their long bony and dull faces. It is still more visible in women of the lower orders: many are thin, consumptive, their eyes hollow, their nose sharp, their skin streaked with red patches; they have suffered too much, have had too many children, have a washed-out, or oppressed, or submissive, or stoically impassive air; we feel that they have endured much, and can endure still more. Even in the middle or upper class this patience and sad hardening are frequent; we think when we see them of those poor beasts of burden, deformed by the harness, which remain motionless under the falling rain without thinking of shelter. Verily the battle of life is harsher and more obstinate here than elsewhere; whoever gives way, falls. Beneath the rigor of climate and competition, amidst the strikes of industry, the weak, the improvident, perish or are degraded; then comes gin and does its work; thence the long files of wretched women who sell themselves by night in the Strand to pay their rent; thence those shameful quarters of London, Liverpool, all the great towns, those spectres in tatters, gloomy or drunk, who crowd the dram-shops, who fill the streets with their dirty linen, and their rags hung out on ropes, who lie on a soot-heap, amidst troops of wan children; horrible shoals, whither descend all whom their wounded, idle, or feeble arms could not keep on the surface of the great stream. The chances of life are tragic here, and the punishment of improvidence cruel. We soon understand why, under this obligation to fight and grow hard, fine sensations disappear; why taste is blunted, how man becomes ungraceful and stiff; how discords, exaggerations, mar the costume and the fashion: why movements and forms become finally energetic and discordant, like the motions of a machine. If the man is German by race, temperament, and mind, he has been compelled in process of time to fortify, alter, altogether turn aside his original nature; he is no longer a primitive animal, but a well-trained animal; his body and mind have been transformed by strong food, by bodily exercise, by austere religion, by public morality, by political strife, by perpetuity of effort; he has become of all men the most capable of acting usefully and powerfully in all directions, the most productive

HISTORY OF ENGLISH LITERATURE

and effectual laborer, as his ox has become the best animal for food, his sheep the best for wool, his horse the best for racing.

Section II.—English Commerce and Industry

Indeed, there is no greater spectacle than his work; in no age or amongst no nation on the earth, I believe, has matter ever been better handled and utilized. If we enter London by water, we see an accumulation of toil and work which has no equal on this planet. Paris, by comparison, is but an elegant city of pleasure; the Seine, with its quays, a pretty serviceable plaything. Here all is vast. I have seen Marseilles, Bordeaux, Amsterdam, but I had no idea of such a mass. From Greenwich to London the two shores are a continuous wharf: merchandise is always being piled up, sacks hoisted, ships moored; ever new warehouses for copper, beer, ropework, tar, chemicals. Docks, timber-yards, calking-basins, and shipbuilders' yards, multiply and encroach on each other. On the left there is the iron framework of a church being finished, to be sent to India. The Thames is a mile broad, and is but a populous street of vessels, a winding workyard. Steamboats, sailing vessels, ascend and descend, come to anchor in groups of two, three, ten, then in long files, then in dense rows; there are five or six thousand of them at anchor. On the right, the docks, like so many intricate, maritime streets, disgorge or store up the vessels. If we get on a height, we see vessels in the distance by hundreds and thousands, fixed as if on the land; their masts in a line, their slender rigging, make a spider-web which girdles the horizon. Yet on the river itself, towards the west, we see an inextricable forest of masts, yards, and cables; the ships are unloading, fastened to one another, mingled with chimneys, amongst the pulleys of the storehouses, cranes, capstans, and all the implements of the vast and ceaseless toil. A foggy smoke, penetrated by the sun, wraps them in its russet veil; it is the heavy and smoky air of a big hot-house; soil and man, light and air, all is transformed by work. If we enter one of these docks, the impression will be yet more overwhelming: each resembles a town; always ships, still more ships, in a line, showing their heads; their wide sides, their copper chests, like monstrous fishes under their breastplate of scales. When we are on the ground, we see that this breastplate is fifty feet high; many ships are of three thousand or four thousand tons. Clippers three hundred feet long are on the point of sailing for Australia, Ceylon, America. A bridge is raised by machinery; it weighs a hundred tons, and only one man is needed to raise it. Here are the wine stores— there are thirty thousand tuns of port in the cellars; here the place for hides, here for tallow, here for ice. The store for groceries extends as far as the eye can see, colossal, sombre as a picture by Rembrandt filled with enormous vats, and crowded with many men, who move about in the flickering shade. The universe tends to this centre. Like a heart, to which blood flows, and from which it pours, money, goods, business arrive hither from the four quarters of the globe, and flow thence to the distant poles. And this circulation seems natural, so well is it conducted. The cranes turn noiselessly; the tuns seem to move of themselves; a little car rolls them at once, and without effort; the bales descend by their own weight on the inclined planes, which lead them to their place. Clerks, without flurry, call out the numbers; men push or pull without confusion, calmly, husbanding their labor; whilst the stolid master, in his black hat, gravely, with spare gestures, and without one word, directs the whole.

Now let us take rail and go to Glasgow, Birmingham, Liverpool, Manchester, to see their industry. As we advance into the coal country, the air is darkened with smoke; the chimneys, high as obelisks, are in hundreds, and cover the plain as far as we can see; many and various rows of lofty buildings, in red monotonous brick, pass before our eyes, like files of economical and busy beehives. The blast-furnaces flame through the smoke; I counted sixteen in one group. The refuse of minerals is heaped up like mountains; the engines run like black ants, with monotonous and violent motion, and suddenly we find ourselves swallowed up in a monstrous town. This manufactory has five thousand hands, one mill three hundred thousand spindles. The Manchester warehouses are Babylonian edifices of six stories high, and wide in proportion. In Liverpool there are five thousand ships along the Mersey, which choke one another up; more wait to enter. The docks are six miles long, and the cotton warehouses on the side extend their vast red rampart out of sight. All things here seem built in unmeasured proportions, and as though by colossal arms. We enter a mill; nothing but iron pillars, as thick as tree-trunks, cylinders as big as a man; locomotive shafts like vast oaks, notching machines which send up iron chips, rollers which bend sheet-iron like paste, flywheels which become invisible by the swiftness of their revolution. Eight workmen, commanded by a kind of peaceful colossus, pushed into and pulled from the fire a tree of red-hot iron as big as my body. Coal has produced all this. England produces twice as much coal as the rest of the world. It has also brick, on account of the great schists, which are close to the surface; it has also estuaries filled by the sea, so as to make natural ports. Liverpool and Manchester, and about ten towns of forty thousand to one hundred thousand souls, are springing up in the basin of Lancashire. If we glance over a geological map we see whole parts shaded with black; they represent the Scotch, the North of England, the Midland, the Welsh, the Irish coal districts. The old antediluvian forests, accumulating here their fuel, have stored up the power which moves matter, and the sea furnishes the true road by which matter can be transported. Man himself, mind and body, seems created to make the most of these advantages. His muscles are firm, and his mind can support tedium. He is less subject to weariness and disgust than other men. He works as well in the tenth hour as in the first. No one handles machines better; he has their regularity and precision. Two workmen in a cotton-mill do the work of three, or even four, French workmen. Let us look now in the statistics how many leagues of stuffs they manufacture every year, how many millions of tons they export and import, how many tens of millions they produce and consume; let us add the industrial or commercial states they have founded, or are founding, in America, China, India, Australia; and then perhaps, reckoning men and money-value— considering that their capital is seven or eight times greater than that of France, that their population has doubled in fifty years, that their colonies, wherever the climate is healthy, are becoming new Englands— we will obtain some notion, very slight, very imperfect, of a work whose magnitude the eyes alone can measure.

There remains yet one of its parts to explore, the cultivation of the land. From the railway carriage we see quite enough to understand it: a field with a hedge, then another field with another hedge, and so on: at times vast squares of turnips; all this well laid out, clean, glossy; no forests, here and there only a cluster of trees. The country is a great kitchen-garden— a manufactory of grass and meat. Nothing is left to nature and chance; all is calculated, regulated, arranged to produce and to bring in profits. If we look at the peasants, we find no genuine peasants; nothing like French peasants— a sort of fellahs, akin to the soil, mistrustful and uncultivated, separated by a gulf from the townsmen. The countryman here is like an artisan; and, in fact, a field is a manufactory, with a farmer for the foreman. Proprietors and farmers lavish their capital like great contractors. They drain the land, and have a rotation of crops; they have produced cattle, the richest in returns of any in the world; they have introduced steam-engines into cultivation, and into the rearing of cattle; they perfect already perfect stables. The greatest of the aristocracy take a pride in it; many country gentlemen have no other occupation. Prince Albert, near Windsor, had a model farm, and this farm brought in money. A few years ago the papers announced that the Queen had discovered a cure for the turkey-disease. Under this universal effort,[233] the products of agriculture have doubled in fifty years. In England, two and a half acres (*hectare*) receive eight or ten times more manure than the same number of French acres; though of inferior quality, the produce is double that of the French. Thirty persons are enough for this work, when in France forty would be required for half thereof. We come upon a farm, even a small one, say of a hundred acres; we find respectable, dignified, well-clad men, who express themselves clearly and sensibly; a large, wholesome, comfortable dwelling— often a little porch, with creepers— a well-kept garden, ornamental trees, the inner walls whitewashed yearly, the floors washed weekly— an almost Dutch cleanliness; therewith plenty of books— travels, treatises on agriculture, a few volumes of religion or history; and above all, the great family Bible. Even in the poorest cottages we find a few objects of comfort and recreation; a large cast-iron stove, a carpet, nearly always paper on the walls, one or two moral tales, and always the Bible. The cottage is clean; the habits are orderly; the plates, with their blue pattern, regularly arranged, look well above the shining dresser; the red floor-tiles have been swept; there are no broken or dirty panes; no doors off hinges, shutters unhung, stagnant pools, straggling dunghills, as amongst the French villagers; the little garden is kept free from weeds; frequently roses and honeysuckle round the door; and on Sunday we can see the father and mother, seated by a well-scrubbed table, with tea, bread and butter, enjoying their *home*, and the order they have established there. In France the peasant on Sunday leaves his hut to visit *his land*: what he aspires to is possession; what Englishmen love is comfort. There is no land in which they demand more in this respect. An Englishman said to me, not very long ago: "Our great vice is the strong desire we feel for all good and comfortable things. We have too many wants, we spend too much. As soon as our peasants have a little money, they buy the best sherry and the best clothes they can get, instead of buying a bit of land."[234]

As we rise to the upper classes, this taste becomes stronger. In the middle ranks a man burdens himself with toil, to give his wife gaudy dresses, and to fill his house with the hundred thousand baubles of quasi-luxury. Higher still, the inventions of comfort are so multiplied that people are bored by them; there are too many newspapers and reviews on the table; too many kinds of carpets, washstands, matches, towels in the dressing-room; their refinement is endless; in thrusting our feet into slippers, we might imagine that twenty generations of inventors were required to bring sole and lining to this degree of perfection. We cannot conceive clubs better furnished with necessaries and superfluities, houses so well arranged and managed, pleasure and abundance so cleverly understood, servants so reliable, respectful, handy. Servants in the last census were "the most numerous class of Her Majesty's subjects"; in England there are five, where in France they have two. When I saw in Hyde Park the rich young ladies, the gentlemen riding or driving, when I thought of their country houses, their dress, their parks and stables, I said to myself that verily this people is constituted after the heart of economists: I mean, that it is the greatest producer and the greatest consumer in the world; that none is more apt at squeezing out and absorbing the quintessence of things; that it has developed its wants at the same time as its resources; and we involuntarily think of those insects which, after their metamorphosis, are suddenly provided with teeth, feelers, unwearying claws, admirable and terrible instruments, fitted to dig, saw, build, do everything, but furnished also with incessant hunger and four stomachs.

Section III.—Agriculture

How is this ant-hill governed? As the train moves on, we perceive, amidst farms and tilled lands, the long wall of a park, the frontage of a castle, more generally of some vast ornate mansion, a sort of country town-house, of inferior architecture, Gothic or Italian pretensions, but surrounded by beautiful lawns, large trees scrupulously preserved. Here lives the rich *bourgeois*; I am wrong, the word is false— I must say *gentleman*: *bourgeois* is a French word, and signifies the lazy *parvenus*, who devote themselves to rest, and take no part in public life; here it is quite different; the hundred or hundred and twenty thousand families, who spend a thousand and more annually, really govern the country. And this is no government imported, implanted artificially and from without; it is a spontaneous and natural government. As soon as men wish to act together, they need leaders; every association, voluntary or not, has one; whatever it be, state, army, ship, or parish, it cannot do without a guide to find the road, to take the lead, call the rest, scold the laggards. In vain we call ourselves independent; as soon as we march in a body, we need a leader; we look right and left, expecting him to show himself. The great thing is to pick him out, to have the best, and not to follow another in his stead; it is a great advantage that there should be one, and that we should acknowledge him. These men, without popular election, or selection from government, find him ready-made and recognized in the large landed proprietor, a man whose family has been long in the county, influential through his connections, dependents, tenantry, interested above all else by his great estates in the affairs of the neighborhood, expert in directing these affairs which his family have managed for three generations, most fitted by education to give good advice, and by his influence to lead the common enterprise to a good result. Indeed, it is thus that things fall out; rich men leave London by hundreds every day to spend a day in the country; there is a meeting on the affairs of the county or of the church; they are magistrates, overseers, presidents of all kinds of societies, and this gratuitously. One has built a bridge at his own expense, another a chapel or a school; many establish public libraries, where books are lent out, with warmed and lighted rooms, in which the villagers in the evening can read the papers, play draughts, chess, and have tea at low charges— in a word, simple amusements which may keep them from the public-house and gin-shop. Many of them give lectures; their sisters or daughters teach in Sunday schools; in fact, they provide for the ignorant and poor, at their own expense, justice, administration, civilization. I know a very rich man who in his Sunday school taught singing to little girls. Lord Palmerston offered his park for archery meetings; the Duke of Marlborough opens his daily to the public, "requesting," this is the word used, "the public not to destroy the grass." A firm and proud sentiment of duty, a genuine public spirit, a noble idea of what a gentleman owes to himself, gives them a moral superiority which sanctions their command; probably from the time of the old Greek cities, no education or condition has been seen in which the innate nobility of man has received a more wholesome or completer development. In short, they are magistrates and patrons from their birth, leaders of the great enterprises in which capital is risked, promoters of all charities, all improvements, all reforms, and with the honors of command they accept its burdens. For observe, in contrast with the aristocracies of other countries, they are are well educated, liberal, and march in the van, not in the rear of public civilization. They are not drawing-room exquisites, like the French marquises of the eighteenth century: an English lord visits his fisheries, studies the system of liquid manures, speaks to the purpose about cheese: and his son is often a better rower, walker, and boxer than the farmers. They are not malcontents, like the French nobility, behind their age, devoted to whist, and regretting the Middle Ages. They have travelled through Europe, and often further; they know languages and literature; their daughters read Schiller, Manzoni, and Lamartine with ease. By means of reviews, newspapers, innumerable volumes of geography, statistics, and travels, they have all the world at their finger-ends. They support and preside over scientific societies; if the free inquirers of Oxford, amidst conventional rigor, have been able to give their explanations of the Bible, it is because they knew themselves to be backed by enlightened laymen of the highest rank. There is also no danger that this aristocracy should become a set; it renews itself; a great physician, a profound lawyer, an illustrious general, become ennobled and found families. When a manufacturer or merchant has gained a large fortune, he first thinks of acquiring an estate; after two or three generations his family has taken root and shares in the government of the country: in this way the best saplings of the great popular forest fill up the aristocratic nursery. Observe, finally, that an aristocracy in England is not an isolated fact. Everywhere there are leaders recognized, respected, followed with confidence and deference, who feel their responsibility, and carry the burden as well as the advantages of the dignity. Such an aristocracy exists in marriage, where the man incontestably rules, followed by his wife to the end of the world, faithfully waited for in the evenings, unshackled in his business, of which he does not speak. There is such in the family, when the father[235] can disinherit his children, and keeps up with them, in the most petty circumstances of daily life, a degree of authority and dignity unknown in France: if in England a son, through ill-health, has been away for some time from his home, he dare not come into the country to see his father without first asking if he may come; a servant to whom I gave my card refused to take it, saying, "Oh! I dare not hand it in now. Master is dining." There is respect in all ranks, in the workshops as well as in the fields, in the army as in the family. Throughout there are inferiors and superiors who feel themselves so; if the mechanism of established power were thrown out of gear, we should behold it reconstructed of itself; below the legal constitution is the social, and human action is forced into a solid mould prepared for it.

It is because this aristocratic network is strong that human action can be free; for local and natural government being rooted throughout, like ivy, by a hundred small, ever-growing fibres, sudden movements, violent as they are, are not capable of pulling it up altogether. In vain men speak, cry out, call meetings, hold processions, form leagues: they will not demolish the state;

they have not to deal with a set of functionaries who have no real hold on the country, and who, like all external applications, can be replaced by another set: the thirty or forty gentlemen of a district, rich, influential, trusted, useful as they are, will become the leaders of the district. "As we see in the papers," says Montesquieu, speaking of England, "that they are playing the devil, we fancy that the people will revolt to-morrow." Not at all, it is their way of speaking; they only talk loudly and rudely. Two days after I arrived in London, I saw advertising men walking with a placard on their backs and their stomachs, bearing these words: "Great usurpation! Outrage of the Lords, in their vote on the budget, against the rights of the people." But then the placard added, "Fellow-countrymen, petition!" Things end thus; they argue freely, and if the reasoning is good it will spread. Another time in Hyde Park, orators were declaiming in the open air against the Lords, who were called rogues. The audience applauded or hissed, as it pleased them. "After all," said an Englishman to me, "this is how we manage our business. With us, when a man has an idea, he writes it; a dozen men think it good, and all contribute money to publish it; this creates a little association, which grows, prints cheap pamphlets, gives lectures, then petitions, calls forth public opinion, and at last takes the matter into Parliament; Parliament refuses or delays it; yet the matter gains weight: the majority of the nation pushes, forces open the doors, and then you'll have a law passed." It is open to everyone to do this; workmen can league against their masters; in fact, their associations embrace all England; at Preston I believe there was once a strike which lasted more than six months. They will sometimes mob, but never revolt; they know political economy by this time, and understand that to do violence to capital is to suppress work. Their chief quality is coolness; here, as elsewhere, temperament has great influence. Anger, blood does not rise at once to their eyes, as in the southern nations; a long interval always separates idea from action, and wise arguments, repeated calculations, occupy the interval. If we go to a meeting, we see men of every condition, ladies who come for the thirtieth time to hear the same speech, full of figures, on education, cotton, wages. They do not seem to be wearied; they can bring argument against argument, be patient, protest gravely, recommence their protest; they are the same people who wait for the train on the platform, without getting crushed, and who play cricket for a couple of hours without raising their voices or quarrelling for an instant. Two coachmen, who run into one another, set themselves free without storming or scolding. Thus their political association endures; they can be free because they have natural leaders and patient nerves. After all, the state is a machine like other machines; let us try to have good wheels, and take care not to break them; Englishmen have the double advantage of possessing very good ones, and of managing them coolly.

Section IV.—English Society.—Philosophy.—Religion

Such is our Englishman, with his laws and his administration. Now that he has private comfort and public security, what will he do, and how will he govern himself in this higher, nobler domain, to which man climbs in order to contemplate beauty and truth? At all events, the arts do not lead him there. That vast London is monumental; but, like the castle of a man who has become rich, everything there is well preserved and costly, but nothing more. Those lofty houses of massive stone, burdened with porches, short columns, Greek decorations, are generally gloomy; the poor columns of the monuments seem washed with ink. On Sunday, in foggy weather, we would think ourselves in a cemetery; the perfect readable names on the houses, in brass letters, are like sepulchral inscriptions. There is nothing beautiful: at most, the varnished middle-class houses, with their patch of green, are pleasant; we feel that they are well kept, commodious, capital for a business man who wants to amuse himself and unbend after a hard day's work. But a finer and higher sentiment could relish nothing here. As to the statues, it is difficult not to laugh at them. We see the Duke of Wellington with a cocked hat and iron plumes; Nelson, with a cable which serves him for a tail, planted on his column, and pierced by a lightning-conductor, like a rat impaled on the end of a pole; or again, the half-dressed Waterloo generals, crowned by Victory. The English, though flesh and bone, seem manufactured out of sheet-iron: how much stiffer will English statues look? They pride themselves on their painting; at least they study it with surprising minuteness, in the Chinese fashion; they can paint a truss of hay so exactly that a botanist will tell the species of every stalk; one artist lived three months under canvas on a heath, so that he might thoroughly know heath. Many are excellent observers, especially of moral expression, and succeed very well in showing the soul in the face; we are instructed by looking at them; we go through a course of psychology with them; they can illustrate a novel; we are touched by the poetic and dreamy meaning of many of their landscapes. But in genuine painting, picturesque painting, they are revolting. I do not think there were ever laid upon canvas such crude colors, such stiff forms, stuffs so much like tin, such glaring contrasts. Fancy an opera with nothing but false notes in it. We may see landscapes painted blood-red, trees which split the canvas, turf which looks like a pot of overturned green, Christs looking as if they were baked and preserved in oil, expressive stags, sentimental dogs, undressed women, to whom we should like forthwith to offer a garment. In music, they import the Italian opera; it is an orange-tree kept up at great cost in the midst of turnips. The arts require idle, delicate minds— not stoics, especially not puritans— easily shocked by dissonance, inclined to visible pleasure, employing their long periods of leisure, their free reveries, in harmoniously arranging, and with no other object but enjoyment, forms, colors, and sounds. I need not say that here the bent of mind is quite the opposite; and we see clearly enough why, amidst these combative politicians, these laborious toilers, these men of energetic action, art can but produce exotic or ill-shaped fruit.

Not so in science; but in science there are two divisions. It may be treated as a business, to glean and verify observations, to combine experiments, to arrange figures, to weigh probabilities to discover facts, partial laws, to possess laboratories, libraries, societies charged with storing and increasing positive knowledge; in all this Englishmen excel. They have even a Lyell, a Darwin, an Owen, able to embrace and renew a science; in the construction of the vast edifice, the industrious masons, masters of the second rank, are not lacking; it is the great architects, the thinkers, the genuine speculative minds, who fail them; philosophy, especially metaphysics, is as little indigenous here as music and painting; they import it, and yet they leave the best part on the road. Carlyle was obliged to transform it into a mystical poetry, humorous and prophetic fancies; Hamilton touched upon it only to declare it chimerical; Stuart Mill and Buckle only seized the most palpable part— a heavy residuum, positivism. It is not in metaphysics that the English mind can find its vent. It is on other objects that the spirit of liberal inquiry— the sublime instincts of the mind, the craving for the universal and the infinite, the desire of ideal and perfect things— will fall back. Let us take the day on which the hush of business leaves a free field for disinterested aspirations. There is no more striking spectacle for a foreigner than Sunday in London. The streets are empty, and the churches full. An Act of Parliament forbids any playing to-day, public or private; the public-houses are not allowed to harbor people during divine service. Moreover, all respectable people are at worship, the seats are full: it is not as in France, where there are none but servants, old women, a few sleepy people, of private means, and a sprinkling of elegant ladies; but in England we see men well dressed, or at least decently clad, and as many gentlemen as ladies in church. Religion does not remain out of the pale, and below the standard of public culture; the young, the learned, the best of the nation, all the upper and middle classes, continue attached to it. The clergyman, even in a village, is not a peasant's son, with not over-much polish, just out of the seminary, shackled in a cloistral education, separated from society by celibacy, half-buried in mediævalism. In England he is a man of the times, often a man of the world, often of good family, with the interests, habits, freedom of other men; keeping sometimes a carriage, several servants, having elegant manners, generally well informed, who has read and still reads. On all these grounds he is able to be in his neighborhood the leader of ideas, as his neighbor the squire is the leader of business. If he does not walk in the same path as the free-thinkers, he is not more than a step or two behind them; a modern man, a Parisian, can talk with him on all lofty themes, and not perceive a gulf between his own mind and the clergyman's. Strictly speaking, he is a layman like ourselves; the only difference is, that he is a superintendent of morality. Even in his externals, except for occasional bands and the perpetual white tie, he is like us; at first sight we would take him for a professor, a magistrate, or a notary; and his sermons agree with his person. He does not anathematize the world; in this his doctrine is modern; he follows the broad path in which the Renaissance and the Reformation impelled religion. When Christianity arose, eighteen centuries ago, it was in the East, in the land of the Essenes and the Therapeutists, amid universal dejection and despair, when the only deliverance seemed a renunciation of the world, an abandonment of civil life, destruction of the natural instincts, and a daily waiting for the kingdom of God. When it rose again, three centuries ago, it was in the West, amongst laborious and half-free peoples, amidst universal restoration and invention, when man, improving his condition, regained confidence in his worldly destiny, and widely expanded his faculties. No wonder if the new Protestantism differs from the ancient Christianity, if it enjoins action instead of preaching asceticism, if it authorizes comforts in place of prescribing mortification, if it honors marriage, work, patriotism, inquiry, science, all natural affections and faculties, in place of praising celibacy, withdrawal from the world, scorn of the age, ecstasy, captivity of mind, and mutilation of the heart. By this infusion of the modern spirit, Christianity has received new blood, and Protestantism now constitutes, with science, the two motive organs, and, as it were, the double heart of European life. For, in accepting the rehabilitation of the world, it has not renounced the purification of man's heart; on the contrary, it is towards this that it has directed its whole effort. It has cut off from religion all the portions which are not this very purification, and, by reducing it, has strengthened it. An institution, like a machine, and like a man, is the more powerful for being more special: a work is done better because it is done singly, and because we concentrate ourselves upon it. By the suppression of legends and religious observances, human thought in its entirety has been concentrated on a single object— moral amelioration. It is of this men speak in the churches, gravely and coldly, with a succession of sensible and solid arguments; how a man ought to reflect on his duties, mark them one by one in his mind, make for himself principles, have a sort of inner code, freely accepted and firmly established, to which he may refer all his actions without bias or hesitation; how these principles may be rooted by practice; how unceasing examination, personal effort, the continual edification of himself by himself ought slowly to confirm our resolution in uprightness. These are the questions which, with a multitude of examples, proofs, appeals to daily experience,[236] are brought forward in all the pulpits, to develop in man a voluntary reformation, a guard and empire over himself, the habit of self-restraint, and a kind of modern stoicism, almost as noble as the ancient. On all hands laymen help in this; and moral warning, given by literature as well as by theology, harmoniously unites society and the clergy. Hardly ever does a book paint a man in a disinterested manner: critics, philosophers, historians, novelists, poets even, give a lesson, maintain a theory, unmask or punish a vice, represent a temptation overcome, relate the history of a character being formed. Their exact and minute description of sentiments ends always in approbation or blame; they are not artists, but moralists: it is only in a Protestant country that we will find a novel entirely occupied in describing the progress of moral sentiment in a child of twelve.[237] All co-operate in this direction in religion, and even in the mystic part of it. Byzantine distinctions and subtleties have been allowed to fall away; Germanic inquisitiveness and speculations have not been introduced; the God of conscience reigns alone; feminine sweetness has been cut off; we do not find the husband of souls, the lovable consoler, whom the author of the "Imitation of Christ" follows even in his tender dreams; something manly breathes from religion in England; we find that the Old Testament, the severe Hebrew Psalms, have left their imprint here. It is no longer an intimate friend to whom a man confides his petty desires, his small troubles, a sort of affectionate and quite human priestly guide; it is no longer a king whose relations and courtiers he tries to gain over, and from whom he looks for favor or place; we see in him only a guardian of duty, and we speak to him of nothing else. What we ask of him is the strength to be virtuous, the inner renewal by which we become capable of always doing good; and such a prayer is in itself a sufficient lever to tear a man from his weaknesses. What we know of the Deity is that he is perfectly righteous; and such a reliance suffices to represent all the events of life as an approach to the reign of righteousness. Strictly speaking, righteousness alone exists; the world is a figure which conceals it, but heart and conscience sustain it, and there is nothing important or true in man but the embrace by which he holds it. So speak the old grave prayers, the severe hymns which are sung in the church, accompanied by the organ. Though a Frenchman, and brought up in a different religion, I listened to them with a sincere admiration and emotion. Serious and grand poems, which, opening a path to the Infinite, let in a ray of light into the limitless darkness, and satisfy the deep poetic instincts, the vague desire of sublimity and melancholy, which this race has manifested from its origin, and which it has preserved to the end.

Section V.—What Forces Have Produced the Present Civilization

As the basis of the present as well as of the past ever reappears an inner and persistent cause, the character of the race; transmission and climate have maintained it; a violent perturbation— the Norman Conquest— warped it; finally, after various oscillations, it was manifested by the conception of a special ideal, which gradually fashioned or produced religion, literature, institutions. Thus fixed and expressed, it was henceforth the mover of the rest; it explains the present, on it depends the future; its force and direction will produce the present and future civilization. Now that great historic violences— I mean the destructions and enslavements of peoples— have become almost impracticable, each nation can develop its life according to its own conception of life; the chances of a war, a discovery, have no hold but on details; national inclinations and aptitudes alone now' show the great features of a national history; when twenty-five millions of men conceive the good and useful after a certain type, they will seek and end by attaining this kind of the good and useful. The Englishman has henceforth his priest, his gentleman, his manufacture, his comfort, and his novel. If we wish to know in what sense this work will alter, we must inquire in what sense the central conception will change. A vast revolution has taken place during the last three centuries in human intelligence— like those regular and vast uprisings which, displacing a continent, displace all the prospects. We know that positive discoveries go on increasing day by day, that they will increase daily more and more, that from object to object they reach the most lofty, that they begin by renewing the science of man, that their useful application and their philosophical consequences are ceaselessly unfolded; in short, that their universal encroachment will at last comprise the whole human mind. From this body of invading truths springs in addition an original conception of the good and the useful, and, moreover, a new idea of church and state, art and industry, philosophy and religion. This has its power, as the old idea had; it is scientific, if the other was national; it is supported on proved facts, if the other was upon established things. Already their opposition is being manifested; already their labors begin; and we may affirm beforehand, that the proximate condition of English civilization will depend upon their divergence or their agreement.

---

[231]See the "Travels of Madame d'Aulnay in Spain," at the end of the seventeenth century. Nothing is more striking than this revolution, if we compare it with the times before Ferdinand the Catholic, namely the reign of Henry IV, the great power of the nobles, and the independence of the towns. Read about this history, Buckle's "History of Civilization," 1867, 3 vols. II. ch. VIII.

[232]Buckle, "History of Civilization," I. ch. VII.

[233]Léonce de Lavergne, "Economie rurale en Angleterre," passim.

[234]De Foe was of the same opinion, and pretended that economy was not an English virtue, and that an Englishman can hardly live with twenty shillings a week, while a Dutchman with the same money becomes wealthy, and leaves his children very well off. An English laborer lives poor and wretchedly with nine shillings a week, whilst a Dutchman lives very comfortably with the same wages.

[235]In familiar language, the father is called in England the "governor"; in France "le banquier."

[236]Let the reader, amongst many others, peruse the sermons of Dr. Arnold, delivered in the school chapel at Rugby.

[237]"The Wide, Wide World," by Elizabeth Wetherell (an American book). See also the novels of Miss Yonge, and chiefly those of George Eliot.

Book V—Modern Authors

Introductory Note

The translator thinks it due to M. Taine to state that the fifth book, on the Modern Authors, was written whilst Dickens, Thackeray, Macaulay, and Mill were still alive. He also gives the original preface of that book:

"This fifth book is the complement to the 'History of English Literature'; it is written on another plan, because the subject is different. The present period is not yet completed, and the ideas which govern it are in process of formation, that is, in the rough. We cannot therefore as yet systematically arrange them. When documents are still mere indications, history is necessarily reduced to 'studies'; knowledge is moulded from life; and our conclusions cannot be other than incomplete, so long as the facts which suggest them are unfinished. Fifty years hence the history of this age may be written; in the meantime we can but sketch it. I have selected from contemporary English writers the most original minds, the most consistent, and the most contrasted; they may be regarded as specimens, representing the common features, the opposing tendencies, and consequently the general direction of the public mind.

"They are only specimens. By the side of Macaulay and Carlyle we have historians like Hallam, Buckle, and Grote; by the side of Dickens, novel-writers like Bulwer, Charlotte Brontë, Mrs. Gaskell, George Eliot, and many more; by the side of Tennyson, poets like Elizabeth Browning; by the side of Stuart Mill, philosophers like Hamilton, Bain, and Herbert Spencer. I pass over the vast number of men of talent who write anonymously in reviews, and who, like soldiers in an army, display at times more clearly than their generals the faculties and inclinations of their time and their country. If we look for the common marks in this multitude of varied minds, we shall, I think, find the two salient features which I have already pointed out. One of these features is proper to English civilization, the other to the civilization of the nineteenth century. The one is national, the other European. On the one hand, special to this people, their literature is an inquiry instituted into humanity, altogether positive, and consequently only partially beautiful or philosophical, but very exact, minute, useful, and moreover very moral; and this to such a degree, that sometimes the generosity or purity of its aspirations raises it to a height which no artist or philosopher has transcended. On the other hand, in common with the various peoples of our age, this literature subordinates dominant creeds and institutions to private inquiry and established science— I mean, to that irresponsible tribunal which is erected in each man's individual conscience, and to that universal authority which the diverse human judgments, mutually rectified, and controlled by practice, borrow from the verifications of experience, and from their own harmony.

"Whatever be the judgment passed on these tendencies and on these doctrines, we cannot, I think, refuse them the merit of spontaneity and originality. They are living and thriving plants. The six writers, described in this volume, have expressed efficacious and complete ideas on God, nature, man, science, religion, art, and morality. To produce such ideas we have in Europe at this day but three nations— England Germany, and France. Those of England will here be found arranged, discussed, and compared with those of the other two thinking countries."

Chapter First. The Novel.—Dickens

Were Dickens dead, his biography might be written.

On the day after the burial of a celebrated man, his friends and enemies apply themselves to the work; his school-fellows relate in the newspapers his boyish pranks; another man recalls exactly, and word for word, the conversations he had with him more than a score of years ago. The lawyer who manages the affairs of the deceased draws up a list of the different offices he has filled, his titles, dates and figures, and reveals to the matter-of-fact readers how the money left has been invested, and how the fortune has been made; the grand-nephews and second cousins publish an account of his acts of humanity, and the catalogue of his domestic virtues. If there is no literary genius in the family, they select an Oxford man, conscientious, learned, who treats the deceased like a Greek author, collects endless documents, overloads them with endless comments, crowns the whole with endless discussions, and comes ten years later, some fine Christmas morning, with his white tie and placid smile, to present to the assembled family three quartos of eight hundred pages each, the easy style of which would send a German from Berlin to sleep. He is embraced by them with tears in their eyes; they make him sit down; he is the chief ornament at their feasts; and his work is sent to the "Edinburgh Review." The latter groans at the sight of the enormous present, and tells off a young and intrepid member of the staff to concoct some kind of a biography from the table of contents. Another advantage of posthumous biographies is, that the dead man is no longer there to refute either biographer or man of learning.

Unfortunately, Dickens is still alive, and refutes the biographies made of him. What is worse, he claims to be his own biographer. His translator in French once asked him for a few particulars of his life; Dickens replied that he kept them for himself. Without doubt, "David Copperfield," his best novel, has much the appearance of a confession;[238] but where does the confession end, and how far does fiction embroider truth? All that is known, or rather all that is told, is that Dickens was born in 1812, that he is the son of a shorthand-writer, that he was at first a shorthand-writer, that he was poor and unfortunate in his youth, that his novels, published in parts, have gained for him a great fortune and an immense reputation. The reader may conjecture the rest; Dickens will tell it him one day, when he writes his memoirs. Meanwhile he closes the door, and leaves outside the too inquisitive folk who go on knocking. He has a right to do so. Though a man may be illustrious, he is not on that account public property; he is not compelled to be confidential; he still belongs to himself; he may reserve of himself what he thinks proper. If we give our works to our readers, we do not give our lives. Let us be satisfied with what Dickens has given us. Forty volumes suffice, and more than suffice, to enable us to know a man well; moreover, they show of him all that is important to know. It is not through the accidental circumstances of his life that he belongs to history, but by his talent; and his talent is in his books. A man's genius is like a clock; it has its mechanism, and amongst its parts a mainspring. Find out this spring, show how it communicates movement to the others, pursue this movement from part to part down to the hands in which it ends. This inner history of genius does not depend upon the outer history of the man; and it is worth more.

PART I.—THE AUTHOR

Section I.—Importance of the Imaginative Faculty

The first question which should be asked in connection with an artist is this: How does he regard objects? With what clearness, what energy, what force? The reply defines his whole work beforehand; for in a writer of novels the imagination is the master faculty; the art of composition, good taste, the feeling of what is true, depend upon it; one degree more of vehemence destroys the style which expresses it, changes the characters which it produces, breaks the plot in which it is enclosed. Consider the imaginative power of Dickens, and you will perceive therein the cause of his faults and his merits, his power and his excess.

Section II.—Boldness of Dickens' Imagination

There is a painter in him, and an English painter. Never surely did a mind figure to itself with more exact detail or greater force all the parts and tints of a picture. Read this description of a storm; the images seem photographed by dazzling flashes of lightning:

"The eye, partaking of the quickness of the flashing light, saw in its every gleam a multitude of objects which it could not see at steady noon in fifty times that period. Bells in steeples, with the rope and wheel that moved them; ragged nests of birds in cornices and nooks; faces full of consternation in the tilted wagons that came tearing past: their frightened teams ringing out a warning which the thunder drowned; harrows and ploughs left out in fields; miles upon miles of hedge-divided country, with the distant fringe of trees as obvious as the scarecrow in the beanfield close at hand; in a trembling, vivid, flickering instant, everything was clear and plain: then came a flush of red into the yellow light; a change to blue; a brightness so intense that there was nothing else but light; and then the deepest and profoundest darkness."[239]

An imagination so lucid and energetic cannot but animate inanimate objects without an effort. It provokes in the mind in which it works extraordinary emotions, and the author pours over the objects which he figures to himself something of the ever-welling passion which overflows in him. Stones for him take a voice, white walls swell out into big phantoms, black wells yawn hideously and mysteriously in the darkness; legions of strange creatures whirl shuddering over the fantastic landscape; blank nature is peopled, inert matter moves. But the images remain clear; in this madness there is nothing vague or disorderly; imaginary objects are designed with outlines as precise and details as numerous as real objects, and the dream is equal to the reality.

There is, amongst others, a description of the night wind, quaint and powerful, which recalls certain pages of "Notre-Dame de Paris." The source of this description, as of all those of Dickens, is pure imagination. He does not, like Walter Scott, describe in order to give his reader a map, and to lay down the locality of his drama. He does not, like Lord Byron, describe from love of magnificent nature, and in order to display a splendid succession of grand pictures. He dreams neither of attaining exactness, nor of selecting beauty. Struck with a certain spectacle, he is transported, and breaks out into unforeseen figures. Now it is the yellow leaves, pursued by the wind, fleeing and jostling, shivering, scared, in a giddy chase, clinging to the furrows, drowned in the ditches, perching on the trees.[240] Here it is the night wind, sweeping round a church, moaning as it tries with an unseen hand the windows and the doors, and seeking out some crevices by which to enter:

"And when it has got in; as one not finding what he seeks, whatever that may be; it wails and howls to issue forth again: and, not content with stalking through the aisles, and gliding round and round the pillars, and tempting the deep organ, soars up to the roof, and strives to rend the rafters: then flings itself despairingly upon the stones below, and passes, muttering, into the vaults. Anon, it comes up stealthily, and creeps along the walls: seeming to read, in whispers, the inscriptions sacred to the dead. At some of these, it breaks out shrilly, as with laughter; and at others, moans and cries as if it were lamenting."[241]

Hitherto you have only recognized the sombre imagination of a man of the north. A little further you perceive the impassioned religion of a revolutionary Protestant, when he speaks to you of "a ghostly sound too, lingering within the altar; where it seems to chaunt, in its wild way, of wrong and murder done, and false Gods worshipped; in defiance of the tables of the law, which look so fair and smooth, but are so flawed and broken. Ugh! Heaven preserve us, sitting snugly round the fire! It has an awful voice, that wind at midnight, singing in a church!" But an instant after, the artist speaks again; he leads you to the belfry, and in the jingle of the accumulated words, communicates to your nerves the sensation of an aerial tempest. The wind whistles, blows, and gambols in the arches: "High up in the steeple, where it is free to come and go through many an airy arch and loop-hole, and to twist and twine itself about the giddy stair, and twirl the groaning weathercock, and make the very tower shake and shiver!"[242] Dickens has seen it all in the old belfry; his thought is a mirror; not the smallest or ugliest detail escapes him.

He has counted "the iron rails ragged with rust"; "the sheets of lead," wrinkled and shrivelled, which crackle and heave beneath the unaccustomed tread; "the shabby nests" which "the birds stuff into corners" of the old oaken joists and beams; the gray dust heaped up; "the speckled spiders, indolent and fat with long security," which, hanging by a thread, "swing idly to and fro in the vibration of the bells," and which "climb up sailor-like in quick-alarm, or drop upon the ground and ply a score of nimble legs to save one life." This picture captivates us. Kept up at such a height, amongst the fleeting clouds which cast their shadows over the town, and the feeble lights scarce distinguished in the mist, we feel a sort of dizziness; and we nearly discover, with Dickens, thought and a soul in the metallic voice of the chimes which inhabit this trembling castle.

He writes a story about them, and it is not the first. Dickens is a poet; he is as much at home in the imaginative world as in the actual. Here the chimes are talking to the old messenger and consoling him. Elsewhere it is the Cricket on the Hearth singing of all domestic joys, and bringing before the eyes of the lonely master the happy evenings, the intimate conversations, the comfort, the quiet cheerfulness which he has enjoyed, and which he has no longer. In another tale it is the history of a sick and precocious child who feels itself dying, and who, sleeping in the arms of its sister, hears the distant song of the murmuring waves which rocked him to sleep. Objects, with Dickens, take their hue from the thoughts of his characters. His imagination is so lively that it carries everything with it in the path which it chooses. If the character is happy, the stones, flowers, and clouds must be happy too; if he is sad, nature must weep with him. Even to the ugly houses in the street, all speak. The style runs through a swarm of visions; it breaks out into the strangest oddities. Here is a young girl, pretty and good, who crosses Fountain Court and the law purlieus in search of her brother. What can be more simple? what even more trivial? Dickens is carried away by it. To entertain her, he summons up birds, trees, houses, the fountain, the offices, law papers, and much besides. It is a folly, and it is all but an enchantment:

"Whether there was life enough left in the slow vegetation of Fountain Court for the smoky shrubs to have any consciousness of the brightest and purest-hearted little woman in the world, is a question for gardeners, and those who are learned in the loves of plants. But that it was a good thing for that same paved yard to have such a delicate little figure flitting through it; that it passed like a smile from the grimy old houses, and the worn flagstones, and left them duller, darker, sterner than before; there is no sort of doubt. The Temple fountain might have leaped up twenty feet to greet the spring of hopeful maidenhood, that in her person stole on, sparkling, through the dry and dusty channels of the Law; the chirping sparrows, bred in Temple chinks and crannies, might have held their peace to listen to imaginary skylarks, as so fresh a little creature passed; the dingy boughs, unused to droop, otherwise than in their puny growth might have bent down in a kindred gracefulness, to shed their benedictions on her graceful head; old love-letters, shut up in iron boxes in the neighbouring offices, and made of no account among the heaps of family papers into which they had strayed, and of which, in their degeneracy, they formed a part, might have stirred and fluttered with a moment's recollection of their ancient tenderness, as she went lightly by. Anything might have happened that did not happen, and never will, for the love of Ruth."[243]

This is far-fetched, without doubt. French taste, always measured, revolts against these affected strokes, these sickly prettinesses. And yet this affectation is natural; Dickens does not hunt after quaintnesses; they come to him. His excessive imagination is like a string too tightly stretched; it produces of itself, without any violent shock, sounds not heard elsewhere.

We shall see how it is excited. Imagine a shop, no matter what shop, the most repulsive; that of a mathematical-instrument maker. Dickens sees the barometers, chronometers, telescopes, compasses, charts, maps, sextants, speaking-trumpets, and so forth. He sees so many, sees them so clearly, they are crowded and crammed, they replace each other so forcibly in his brain, which they fill and obstruct; there are so many geographical and nautical ideas exposed under the glass cases hung from the ceiling, nailed to the wall, they swamp him from so many sides, and in such abundance, that he loses his judgment. "The shop itself, partaking of the general infection, seemed almost to become a snug, sea-going, ship-shape concern, wanting only good sea-room, in the event of an unexpected launch, to work its way securely to any desert island in the world."[244]

The difference between a madman and a man of genius is not very great. Napoleon, who knew men, said so to Esquirol.[245] The same faculty leads us to glory or throws us into a cell in a lunatic asylum. It is visionary imagination which forges the phantoms of the madman and creates the personages of an artist, and the classifications serving for the first may serve for the second. The imagination of Dickens is like that of monomaniacs. To plunge one's self into an idea, to be absorbed by it, to see nothing else, to repeat it under a hundred forms, to enlarge it, to carry it, thus enlarged, to the eye of the spectator, to dazzle and overwhelm him with it, to stamp it upon him so firmly and deeply that he can never again tear it from his memory— these are the great features of this imagination and style. In this, "David Copperfield" is a masterpiece. Never did objects remain more visible and présent to the memory of a reader than those which he describes. The old house, the parlor, the kitchen, Peggotty's boat, and above all the school play-ground, are interiors whose relief, energy, and precision are unequalled. Dickens has the passion and patience of the painters of his nation; he reckons his details one by one, notes the various hues of the old tree-trunks; sees the dilapidated cask, the greenish and broken flagstones, the chinks of the damp walls; he distinguishes the strange smells which rise from them; marks the size of the mildewed spots, reads the names of the scholars carved on the door, and dwells on the form of the letters. And this minute description has nothing cold about it; if it is thus detailed, it is because the contemplation was intense; it proves its passion by its exactness. We felt this passion without accounting for it; suddenly we find it at the end of a page; the boldness of the style renders it visible, and the violence of the phrase attests the violence of the impression. Excessive metaphors bring before the mind grotesque fancies. We feel ourselves beset by extravagant visions. Mr. Mell takes his flute, and blows on it, says Copperfield, "until I almost thought he would gradually blow his whole being into the large hole at the top, and ooze away at the keys."[246] Tom Pinch, disabused at last, discovers that his master Pecksniff is a hypocritical rogue. He "had so long been used to steep the Pecksniff of his fancy in his tea, and spread him out upon his toast, and take him as a relish with his beer, that he made but a poor breakfast on the first morning after his expulsion."[247] We think of Hoffman's fantastic tales; we are arrested by a fixed idea, and our head begins to ache. These eccentricities are in the style of sickness rather than of health.

Therefore Dickens is admirable in depicting hallucinations. We see that he feels himself those of his characters, that he is engrossed by their ideas, that he enters into their madness. As an Englishman and a moralist, he has described remorse frequently. Perhaps it may be said that he makes a scarecrow of it, and that an artist is wrong to transform himself into an assistant of the policeman and the preacher. What of that? The portrait of Jonas Chuzzlewit is so terrible that we may pardon it for being useful. Jonas, leaving his chamber secretly, has treacherously murdered his enemy, and thinks henceforth to breathe in peace; but the recollection of the murder gradually disorganizes his mind, like poison. He is no longer able to control his ideas; they bear him on with the fury of a terrified horse. He is forever thinking, and shuddering as he thinks, of the room where people believed he slept. He sees this room, counts the tiles of the floor, pictures the long folds of the dark curtains, the tumbled bed, the door at which some one might have knocked. The more he wants to escape from this vision, the more he is immersed in it; it is a burning abyss in which he rolls, struggling, with cries and sweats of agony. He fancies himself lying in his bed, as he ought to be, and an instant after he sees himself there. He fears this other self. The dream is so vivid that he is not sure that he is not in London. "He became, in a manner, his own ghost and phantom." And this imaginary being, like a mirror, only redoubles before his conscience the image of assassination and punishment. He returns, and shuffles, with pale face, to the door of his chamber. He, a man of business, a man of figures, a coarse machine of positive reasoning, has become as fanciful as a nervous woman. "He stole on, to the door, on tip-toe, as if he dreaded to disturb his own imaginary rest."

At the moment when he turns the key in the lock, "a monstrous fear beset his mind. What if the murdered man were there before him?" At last he enters, and tumbles into bed, burnt up with fever. "He buried himself beneath the blankets," so as to try not to see "that infernal room"; he sees it more clearly still. The rustling of the clothes, the buzz of an insect, the beatings of his heart, all cry to him Murderer! His mind fixed with "an agony of listening" on the door, he ends by thinking that people open it; he hears it creak. His senses are distorted; he dares not mistrust them, he dares no longer believe in them; and in this nightmare, in which drowned reason leaves nothing but a chaos of hideous forms, he finds no reality but the incessant burden of his convulsive despair. Thenceforth all his thoughts, dangers, the whole world disappears for him in "the one dread question only, When would they find the body in the wood?" He forces himself to distract his thoughts from this; they remain stamped and glued to it; they hold him to it as by a chain of iron. He continually figures himself going into the wood, "going softly about it and about it among the leaves, approaching it nearer and nearer through a gap in the boughs, and startling the very flies, that were thickly sprinkled all over it like heaps of dried currants." His mind was fixed and fastened on the discovery, for intelligence of which he listened intently to every cry and shout; listened when any one came in, or went out; watched from the window the people who passed up and down the street. At the same time, he has ever before his eyes that corpse "lying alone in the wood"; "he was forever showing and presenting it, as it were, to every creature whom he saw. 'Look here! do you know of this? Is it found? Do you suspect me?' If he had been condemned to bear the body in his arms, and lay it down for recognition at the feet of every one he met, it could not have been more constantly with him, or a cause of more monotonous and dismal occupation than it was in this state of his mind."[248]

Jonas is on the verge of madness. There are other characters quite mad. Dickens has drawn three or four portraits of madmen, very funny at first sight, but so true that they are in reality horrible. It needed an imagination like his, irregular, excessive, capable of fixed ideas, to exhibit the derangements of reason. Two especially there are, which make us laugh, and which make us shudder. Augustus, a gloomy maniac, who is on the point of marrying Miss Pecksniff; and poor Mr. Dick, partly an idiot, partly a monomaniac, who lives with Miss Trotwood. To understand these sudden exaltations, these unforeseen gloominesses, these incredible somersaults of perverted sensitiveness; to reproduce these hiatuses of thought, these interruptions of reasoning, this recurrence of a word, always the same, which breaks in upon a phrase attempted and overturns renascent reason; to see the stupid smile, the vacant look, the foolish and uneasy physiognomy of these haggard old children, who painfully grope about from one idea to another, and stumble at every step on the threshold of the truth which they cannot attain, is a faculty which Hoffman alone has possessed in an equal degree with Dickens. The play of these shattered reasons is like the creaking of a door on its rusty hinges; it makes one sick to hear it. We find in it, if we like, a discordant burst of laughter, but we discover still more easily a groan and a lamentation, and we are terrified to gauge the lucidity, strangeness, exaltation, violence of imagination which has produced such creations, which has carried them on and sustained them unbendingly to the end, and which found itself in its proper sphere in imitating and producing their irrationality.

Section III.—His Trivialities.—His Minuteness

To what can this force be applied? Imaginations differ not only in their nature, but also in their object; after having gauged their energy, we must define their domain; in the wide world the artist makes a world for himself; involuntarily he chooses a class of objects which he prefers; others do not warm his genius, and he does not perceive them. Dickens does not perceive great things; this is the second feature of his imagination. Enthusiasm seizes him in connection with everything, especially in connection with vulgar objects: a curiosity shop, a sign-post, a town-crier. He has vigor, he does not attain beauty. His instrument produces vibrating, but not harmonious sounds. If he is describing a house, he will draw it with geometrical clearness; he will put all its colors in relief, discover a face and thought in the shutters and the spouts; he will make a sort of human being out of the house, grimacing and forcible, which attracts our attention, and which we shall never forget; but he will not see the grandeur of the long monumental lines, the calm majesty of the broad shadows boldly divided by the white plaster; the cheerfulness of the light which covers them, and becomes palpable in the black niches in which it dives, as though to rest and to sleep. If he is painting a landscape, he will perceive the haws which dot with their red fruit the leafless hedges, the thin vapor steaming from a distant stream, the motion of an insect in the grass; but the deep poetry which the author of "Valentine" and "André"[249] would have felt, will escape him. He will be lost, like the painters of his country, in the minute and impassioned observation of small things; he will have no love of beautiful forms and fine colors. He will not perceive that the blue and the red, the straight line and the curve, are enough to compose vast concerts, which amidst so many various expressions maintain a grand serenity, and open up in the depths of the soul a spring of health and happiness. Happiness is lacking in him; his inspiration is a feverish rapture, which does not select its objects, which animates promiscuously the ugly, the vulgar, the ridiculous, and which communicating to his creations an indescribable jerkiness and violence, deprives them of the delight and harmony which in other hands they might have retained. Miss Ruth is a very pretty housekeeper; she puts on her apron; what a treasure this apron is! Dickens turns it over and over, like a milliner's shopman who wants to sell it.

She holds it in her hands, then she puts it round her waist, ties the strings, spreads it out, smoothes it that it may fall well. What does she not do with her apron? And how delighted is Dickens during these innocent occupations? He utters little exclamations of joyous fun. "Oh heaven, what a wicked little stomacher!" He apostrophizes a ring, he sports round Ruth, he is so delighted he claps his hands. It is much worse when she is making the pudding; there is a whole scene, dramatic and lyric, with exclamations, protasis, sudden inversions as complete as a Greek tragedy. These kitchen refinements and this waggery of imagination make us think, by way of contrast, of the household pictures of George Sand, of the room of Geneviève the flower-girl. She, like Ruth, is making a useful object, very useful, since she will sell it to-morrow for ten-pence; but this object is a full-blown rose, whose fragile petals are moulded by her fingers as by the fingers of a fairy, whose fresh corolla is purpled with a vermilion as tender as that of her cheeks; a fragile masterpiece which bloomed on an evening of poetic emotion, whilst from her window she beheld in the sky the piercing and divine eyes of the stars, and in the depths of her virgin heart murmured the first breath of love. Dickens does not need such a sight for his transports; a stagecoach throws him into dithyrambs; the wheels, the splashing, the cracking whip, the clatter of the horses, harness, the vehicle; here is enough to transport him. He feels sympathetically the motion of the coach; it bears him along with it; he hears the gallop of the horses in his brain, and goes off, uttering this ode, which seems to proceed from the guard's horn:

"Yoho, among the gathering shades; making of no account the deep reflections of the trees, but scampering on through light and darkness, all the same, as if the light of London, fifty miles away, were quite enough to travel by, and some to spare. Yoho, beside the village green, where cricket-players linger yet, and every little indentation made in the fresh grass by bat or wicket, ball or player's foot, sheds out its perfume on the night. Away with four fresh horses from the Baldfaced Stag, where topers congregate about the door admiring; and the last team, with traces hanging loose, go roaming off towards the pond, until observed and shouted after by a dozen throats, while volunteering boys pursue them. Now, with a clattering of hoofs and striking out of fiery sparks, across the old stone bridge, and down again into the shadowy road, and through the open gate, and far away, away into the wold. Yoho!

"Yoho, behind there, stop that bugle for a moment! Come creeping over to the front, along the coach-roof, guard, and make one at this basket! Not that we slacken in our pace the while, not we: we rather put the bits of blood upon their mettle, for the greater glory of the snack. Ah! It is long since this bottle of old wine was brought into contact with the mellow breath of night, you may depend, and rare good stuff it is to wet a bugler's whistle with. Only try it. Don't be afraid of turning up your finger, Bill, another pull! Now, take your breath, and try the bugle, Bill. There's music! There's a tone! 'Over the hills and far away,' indeed, Yoho! The skittish mare is all alive tonight. Yoho! Yoho!

"See the bright moon; high up before we know it; making the earth reflect the objects on its breast like water. Hedges, trees, low cottages, church steeples, blighted stumps and flourishing young slips, have all grown vain upon the sudden, and mean to contemplate their own fair images till morning. The poplars yonder rustle, that their quivering leaves may see themselves upon the ground. Not so the oak; trembling does not become him; and he watches himself in his stout old burly steadfastness, without the motion of a twig. The moss-grown gate, ill poised upon its creaking hinges, crippled and decayed, swings to and fro before its glass like some fantastic dowager; while our own ghostly likeness travels on, Yoho! Yoho! through ditch and brake, upon the ploughed land and the smooth, along the steep hill-side and steeper wall, as if it were a phantom-Hunter.

"Clouds too! And a mist upon the Hollow! Not a dull fog that hides it, but a light, airy, gauze-like mist, which in our eyes of modest admiration gives a now charm to the beauties it is spread before: as real gauze has done ere now, and would again, so please you, though we were the Pope. Yoho! Why, now we travel like the Moon herself. Hiding this minute in a grove of trees, next minute in a patch of vapour, emerging now upon our broad, clear course, withdrawing now, but always dashing on, our journey is a counterpart of hers. Yoho! A match against the Moon!

"The beauty of the night is hardly felt, when Day comes leaping up. Yoho! Two stages, and the country roads are almost changed to a continuous street. Yoho, past market gardens, rows of houses, villas, crescents, terraces, and squares; past wagons, coaches, carts; past early workmen, late stragglers, drunken men, and sober carriers of loads; past brick and mortar in its every shape; and in among the rattling pavements, where a jaunty-seat upon a coach is not so easy to preserve! Yoho down countless turnings, and through countless mazy ways, until an old Inn-yard is gained, and Tom Pinch, getting down, quite stunned and giddy, is in London!" [250]

All this to tell us that Tom Pinch is come to London! This fit of lyric poetry, in which the most poetic extravagances spring from the most vulgar commonplaces, like sickly flowers growing in a broken old flower-pot, displays in its natural and quaint contrasts all the sides of Dickens's imagination. We shall have his portrait if we picture to ourselves a man who, with a stew-pan in one hand and a postilion's whip in the other, took to making prophecies.

Section IV.—His Emotions.—His Pathos.—His Humor

The reader already foresees what vehement emotions this species of imagination will produce. The mode of conception in a man governs the mode of thought. When the mind, barely attentive, follows the indistinct outlines of a rough-sketched image, joy and grief glide past him with insensible touch. When the mind, with rapt attention, penetrates the minute details of a precise image, joy and grief shake the whole man.

Dickens has this attention, and sees these details: this is why he meets everywhere with objects of exaltation. He never abandons his impassioned tone; he never rests in a natural style and in simple narrative; he only rails or weeps; he writes but satires or elegies. He has the feverish sensibility of a woman who laughs loudly, or melts into tears at the sudden shock of the slightest occurrence. This impassioned style is extremely potent, and to it may be attributed half the glory of Dickens. The majority of men have only weak emotions. We labor mechanically, and yawn much; three-fourths of things leave us cold; we go to sleep by habit, and we no longer remark the household scenes, petty details, stale adventures, which are the basis of our existence. A man comes, who suddenly renders them interesting; nay, who makes them dramatic, changes them into objects of admiration, tenderness and dread. Without leaving the fireside or the omnibus, we are trembling, our eyes full of tears, or shaken by fits of inextinguishable laughter. We are transformed, our life is doubled; our soul has been vegetating; now it feels, suffers, loves. The contrast, the rapid succession, the number of the sentiments, add further to its trouble; we are immersed for two hundred pages in a torrent of new emotions, contrary and increasing, which communicates its violence to the mind, which carries it away in digressions and falls, and only casts it on the bank enchanted and exhausted. It is an intoxication, and on a delicate soul the effect would be too forcible; but it suits the English public, and that public has justified it.

This sensibility can hardly have more than two issues— laughter and tears. There are others, but they are only reached by lofty eloquence; they are the path to sublimity, and we have seen that for Dickens this path is cut off. Yet there is no writer who knows better how to touch and melt; he makes us weep, absolutely shed tears; before reading him we did not know there was so much pity in the heart. The grief of a child, who wishes to be loved by his father, and whom his father does not love; the despairing love and slow death of a poor half-imbecile young man; all these pictures of secret grief leave an ineffaceable impression. The tears which he sheds are genuine, and compassion is their only source. Balzac, George Sand, Stendhal have also recorded human miseries; is it possible to write without recording them? But they do not seek them out, they hit upon them; they do not dream of displaying them to us; they were going elsewhere, and met them on their way. They love art better than men. They delight only in setting in motion the springs of passions, in combining large systems of events, in constructing powerful characters: they do not write from sympathy with the wretched, but from love of beauty. When we have finished George Sand's "Mauprat," our emotion is not pure sympathy; we feel, in addition, a deep admiration for the greatness and the generosity of love. When we have come to the end of Balzac's "Le Père Goriot," our heart is pained by the tortures of that anguish; but the astonishing inventiveness, the accumulation of facts, the abundance of general ideas, the force of analysis, transport us into the world of science, and our painful sympathy is calmed by the spectacle of this physiology of the heart. Dickens never calms our sympathy; he selects subjects in which it alone, and more than elsewhere, is unfolded: the long oppression of children persecuted and starved by their schoolmaster; the life of a factory-hand Stephen, robbed and degraded by his wife, driven away by his fellow-workmen, accused of theft, lingering six days at the bottom of a pit into which he has fallen, maimed, consumed by fever, and dying when he is at length discovered. Rachael, his only friend, is there; and his delirium, his cries, the storm of despair in which Dickens envelops his characters, have prepared the way for the painful picture of this resigned death. The bucket brings up a poor, crushed human creature, and we see "the pale, worn, patient face looking up to the sky, whilst the right hand, shattered and hanging down, seems as if waiting to be taken by another hand." Yet he smiles, and feebly said "Rachael!" She stooped down, and bent over him until her eyes were between his and the sky, for he could not so much as turn them to look at her. Then in broken words he tells her of his long agony. Ever since he was born he has met with nothing but misery and injustice; it is the rule— the weak suffer, and are made to suffer. This pit into which he has fallen "has cost hundreds and hundreds o' men's lives— fathers, sons, brothers, dear to thousands an' thousands, an' keeping 'em fro' want and hunger.... The men that works in pits... ha' pray'n an' pray'n the lawmakers for Christ's sake not to let their work be murder to 'em, but to spare 'em for th' wives and children, that they loves as well as gentlefok loves theirs"; all in vain. "When the pit was in work, it killed wi'out need; when 't is let alone, it kills wi'out need."[251] Stephen says this without anger, quietly, merely as the truth. He has his calumniator before him; he does not get angry, accuses no one; he only charges old Gradgrind to clear him and make his name good with all men as soon as he shall be dead. His heart is up there in heaven, where he has seen a star shining. In his agony, on his bed of stones, he has gazed upon it, and the tender and touching glance of the divine star has calmed, by its mystical serenity, the anguish of mind and body.

"'It ha' shined in upon me,' he said reverently, 'in my pain and trouble down below. It ha' shined into my mind. I ha' lookn at't and thowt o' thee, Rachael, till the muddle in my mind have cleared awa, above a bit, I hope. If soom ha' been wantin' in unnerstan'in' me better, I, too, ha' been wantin' in unnerstan'in' them better.

"'In my pain an' trouble, lookin' up yonder— wi' it shinin' on me— I ha' seen more clear, and ha' made it my dyin' prayer that aw th' world may on'y coom toogether more, an' get a better unnerstan'in' o' one another, than when I were in't my own weak seln.

"'Often as I coom to myseln, and found it shinin' on me down there in my trouble, I thowt it were the star as guided to our Saviour's home. I awmust think it be the very star!'

"They carried him very gently along the fields, and down the lanes, and over the wide landscape; Rachael always holding the hand in hers. Very few whispers broke the mournful silence. It was soon a funeral procession. The star had shown him where to find the God of the poor; and through humility, and sorrow, and forgiveness, he had gone to his Redeemer's rest."[252]

This same writer is the most railing, the most comic, the most jocose of English authors. And it is moreover a singular gayety! It is the only kind which would harmonize with this impassioned sensibility. There is a laughter akin to tears. Satire is the sister of elegy: if the second pleads for the oppressed, the first combats the oppressors. Feeling painfully all the wrongs that are committed, and the vices that are practised, Dickens avenges himself by ridicule. He does not paint, he punishes. Nothing could be more damaging than those long chapters of sustained irony, in which the sarcasm is pressed, line after line, more sanguinary and piercing in the chosen adversary. There are five or six against the Americans— their venal newspapers, their drunken journalists, their cheating speculators, their women authors, their coarseness, their familiarity, their insolence, their brutality— enough to captivate an absolutist, and to justify the French Liberal who, returning from New York, embraced with tears in his eyes the first gendarme whom he saw on landing at Havre. Starting of commercial companies, interviews between a member of Parliament and his constituents, instructions of a member of the House of Commons to his secretary, the outward display of great banking-houses, the laying of the first stone of a public building, every kind of ceremony and lie of English society, are depicted with the fire and bitterness of Hogarth. There are parts where the comic element is so violent that it has the semblance of vengeance— as the story of Jonas Chuzzlewit. "The very first word which this excellent boy learnt to spell was gain, and the second (when he came into two syllables) was money." This fine education had unfortunately produced two results: first, that, "having been long taught by his father to overreach everybody, he had imperceptibly acquired a love of overreaching that venerable monitor himself"; secondly, that being taught to regard everything as a matter of property, "he had gradually come to look with impatience on his parent as a certain amount of personal estate," who would be very well "secured," in that particular description of strong-box which is commonly called a coffin, and banked in the grave.[253] "Is that my father snoring, Pecksniff?" asked Jonas; "tread upon his foot; will you be so good? The foot next you is the gouty one."[254] Young Chuzzlewit is introduced to us with this mark of attention; we may judge by this of his other feelings. In reality, Dickens is gloomy, like Hogarth; but, like Hogarth, he makes us burst with laughter by the buffoonery of his invention and the violence of his caricatures. He pushes his characters to absurdity with unwonted boldness. Pecksniff hits off moral phrases and sentimental actions in so grotesque a manner that they make him extravagant. Never were heard such monstrous oratorical displays. Sheridan had already painted an English hypocrite, Joseph Surface; but he differs from Pecksniff as much as a portrait of the eighteenth century differs from a cartoon of "Punch." Dickens makes hypocrisy so deformed and monstrous that his hypocrite ceases to resemble a man; we would call him one of those fantastic figures whose nose is greater than his body. This exaggerated comicality springs from excess of imagination. Dickens uses the same spring throughout. The better to make us see the object he shows us, he dazzles the reader's eyes with it; but the reader is amused by this irregular fancy; the fire of the execution makes him forget that the scene is improbable, and he laughs heartily as he listens to the undertaker, Mould, enumerating the consolations which filial piety, well backed by money, may find in his shop. What grief could not be softened by

"'Four horses to each vehicle... velvet trappings... drivers in cloth cloaks and top-boots... the plumage of the ostrich, dyed black... any number of walking attendants, dressed in the first style of funeral fashion, and carrying batons tipped with brass... a place in Westminster Abbey itself, if he choose to invest it in such a purchase. Oh! do not let us say that gold is dross, when it can buy such things as these. Ay, Mrs. Gamp, you are right,' rejoined the undertaker. 'We should be an honoured calling. We do good by stealth, and blush to have it mentioned in our little bills. How much consolation may I—even I,' cried Mr. Mould, 'have diffused among my fellow-creatures by means of my four long-tailed prancers, never harnessed under ten pund ten!'"[255]

Usually Dickens remains grave whilst drawing his caricatures. English wit consists in saying very jocular things in a solemn manner. Tone and ideas are then in contrast; every contrast makes a strong impression. Dickens loves to produce them, and his public to hear them.

If at times he forgets to castigate his neighbor, if he tries to sport, to amuse himself, he is not the more happy for all that. The chief element of the English character is its want of happiness. The ardent and tenacious imagination of Dickens is impressed with things too firmly to pass lightly and gayly over the surface. He leans too heavily on them, he penetrates, works into, hollows them out; all these violent actions are efforts, and all efforts are sufferings. To be happy, a man must be light-minded, as a Frenchman of the eighteenth century, or sensual, as an Italian of the sixteenth; a man must not get anxious about things, if he wishes to enjoy them. Dickens does get anxious and does not enjoy. Let us take a little comical accident, such as we meet with in the street— a gust of wind, which blows about the garments of a street-porter. Scaramouche will grin with good humor; Le Sage smile like a diverted man; both will pass by and think no more of it. Dickens muses over it for half a page. He sees so clearly all the effects of the wind, he puts himself so entirely in its place, he imagines for it a will so impassioned and precise, he shakes the clothes of the poor man hither and thither so violently and so long, he turns the gust into a tempest, into a persecution so great, that we are made giddy; and even whilst we laugh, we feel in ourselves too much emotion and compassion to laugh heartily:

"And a breezy, goose-skinned, blue-nosed, red-eyed, stony-toed, tooth-chattering place it was, to wait in, in the winter-time, as Toby Veck well knew. The wind came tearing round the corner— especially the east wind— as if it had sallied forth, express, from the confines of the earth, to have a blow at Toby. And often-times it seemed to come upon him sooner than it had expected; for, bouncing round the corner, and passing Toby, it would suddenly wheel round again, as if it cried":

"'Why, here he is!' Incontinently his little white apron would be caught up over his head like a naughty boy's garments, and his feeble little cane would be seen to wrestle and struggle unavailingly in his hand, and his legs would undergo tremendous agitation; and Toby himself, all aslant, and facing now in this direction, now in that, would be so banged and buffeted, and tousled, and worried, and hustled, and lifted off his feet, as to render it a state of things but one degree removed from a positive miracle that he wasn't carried up bodily into the air as a colony of frogs or snails or other portable creatures sometimes are, and rained down again, to the great astonishment of the natives, on some strange corner of the world where ticket-porters are unknown."[256]

If now we would picture in a glance this imagination— so lucid, so violent, so passionately fixed on the object selected, so deeply touched by little things, so wholly attached to the details and sentiments of vulgar life, so fertile in incessant emotions, so powerful in rousing painful pity, sarcastic raillery, nervous gayety— we must fancy a London street on a rainy winter's night. The flickering light of the gas dazzles our eyes, streams through the shop windows, floods over the passing forms; and its harsh light, settling upon their contracted features, brings out, with endless detail and damaging force, their wrinkles, deformities, troubled expression. If in this close and dirty crowd we discover the fresh face of a young girl, this artificial light covers it with false and excessive lights and shades; it makes it stand out against the rainy and cold blackness with a strange halo. The mind is struck with wonder; but we carry our hand to our eyes to cover them, and whilst we admire the force of this light, we involuntarily think of the real country sun and the tranquil beauty of day.

PART II.—THE PUBLIC

Section I.—The Morality of English Novels

Plant this talent on English soil; the literary opinion of the country will direct its growth and explain its fruits. For this public opinion is its private opinion; it does not submit to it as to an external constraint, but feels it inwardly as an inner persuasion; it does not hinder, but develops it, and only repeats aloud what it said to itself in a whisper.

The counsels of this public taste are somewhat like this; the more powerful because they agree with its natural inclination, and urge it upon its special course:

"Be moral. All your novels must be such as may be read by young girls. We are practical minds, and we would not have literature corrupt practical life. We believe in family life, and we would not have literature paint the passions which attack family life. We are Protestants, and we have preserved something of the severity of our fathers against enjoyment and passions. Amongst these, love is the worst. Beware of resembling in this respect the most illustrious of our neighbors. Love is the hero of all George Sand's novels. Married or not, she thinks it beautiful, holy, sublime in itself; and she says so. Don't believe this; and if you do believe it don't say it. It is a bad example. Love thus represented makes marriage a secondary matter. It ends in marriage, or destroys it, or does without it, according to circumstances; but whatever it does, it treats it as inferior; it does not recognize any holiness in it beyond that which love gives it, and holds it impious if it is excluded. A novel of this sort is a plea for the heart, the imagination, enthusiasm, nature; but it is also often a plea against society and law: we do not suffer society and law to be touched, directly or indirectly. To present a feeling as divine, to make all institutions bow before it, to carry it through a series of generous actions, to sing with a sort of heroic inspiration the combats which it wages and the attacks which it sustains, to enrich it with all the force of eloquence, to crown it with all the flowers of poetry, is to paint the life, which it results in, as more beautiful and loftier than others, to set it far above all passions and duties, in a sublime region, on a throne, whence it shines as a light, a consolation, a hope, and draws all hearts towards it. Perhaps this is the world of artists; it is not the world of ordinary men. Perhaps it is true to nature; we make nature give way before the interests of society. George Sand paints impassioned women; paint you for us good women. George Sand makes us desire to be in love; do you make us desire to be married.

"This has its disadvantages without doubt; art suffers by it, if the public gains. Though your characters give the best examples, your works will be of less value. No matter; you may console yourself with the thought that you are moral. Your lovers will be uninteresting; for the only interest natural to their age is the violence of passion, and you cannot paint passion. In 'Nicholas Nickleby' you will show two good young men, like all young men, marrying two good young women, like all young women; in 'Martin Chuzzlewit' you will show two more good young men, perfectly resembling the other two, marrying again two good young women, perfectly resembling the other two; in 'Dombey and Son' there will be only one good young man and one good young woman. Otherwise there is no difference. And so on. The number of your marriages is marvellous, and you marry enough couples to people England. What is more curious still, they are all disinterested, and the young man and young woman snap their fingers at money as sincerely as in the Opéra Comique. You will not cease to dwell on the pretty shynesses of the betrothed, the tears of the mothers, the tears of all the guests, the amusing and touching scenes of the dinner table; you will create a crowd of family pictures, all touching, and almost all as agreeable as screen-paintings. The reader is moved; he thinks he is beholding the innocent loves and virtuous attentions of a little boy and girl of ten. He should like to say to them: 'Good little people, continue to be very proper.' But the chief interest will be for young girls, who will learn in how devoted and yet suitable a manner a lover ought to court his intended. If you venture on a seduction, as in 'Copperfield,' you do not relate the progress, ardor, intoxication of love; you only depict its miseries, despair and remorse. If in 'Copperfield' and the 'Cricket on the Hearth' you present a troubled marriage and a suspected wife, you hasten to restore peace to the marriage and innocence to the wife; and you will deliver, by her mouth, so splendid a eulogy on marriage, that it might serve for a model to Émile Augier.[257] If in 'Hard Times' the wife treads on the border of crime, she shall check herself there. If in 'Dombey and Son' she flees from her husband's roof, she remains pure, only incurs the appearance of crime, and treats her lover in such a manner that the reader wishes to be the husband. If, lastly, in 'Copperfield' you relate the emotions and follies of love, you will rally this poor affection, depict its littlenesses, not venture to make us hear the ardent, generous, undisciplined blast of the all-powerful passion; you turn it into a toy for good children, or a pretty marriage-trinket. But marriage will compensate you. Your genius of observation and taste for details is exercised on the scenes of domestic life; you will excel in the picture of a fireside, family prattle, children on the knees of their mother, a husband watching by lamplight by the side of his sleeping wife, the heart full of joy and courage, because it feels that it is working for its own. You will describe charming or grave portraits of women; of Dora, who after marriage continues to be a little girl, whose pouting, prettinesses, childishnesses, laughter, make the house gay, like the chirping of a bird; Esther, whose perfect goodness and divine innocence cannot be affected by trials or years; Agnes, so calm, patient, sensible, pure, worthy of respect, a very model of a wife, sufficient in herself to claim for marriage the respect which we demand for it. And when it is necessary to show the beauty of these duties, the greatness of this conjugal love, the depth of the sentiment which ten years of confidence, cares, and reciprocal devotion have created, you will find in your sensibility, so long constrained, speeches as pathetic as the strongest words of love.[258]

"The worst novels are not those which glorify love. A man must live across the Channel to dare what the French have dared. In England, some admire Balzac; but no man would tolerate him. Some pretend that he is not immoral; but every one will recognize that he always and everywhere makes morality an abstraction. George Sand has only celebrated one passion; Balzac has celebrated them all. He has considered them as forces; and holding that force is beautiful, he has supported them by their causes, surrounded them by their circumstances, developed them in their effects, pushed them to an extreme, and magnified them so as to make them into sublime monsters, more systematic and more true than the truth. We do not admit that a man is only an artist, and nothing else. We would not have him separate himself from his conscience, and lose sight of the practical. We will never consent to see that such is the leading feature of our own Shakespeare; we will not recognize that he, like Balzac, brings his heroes to crime and monomania, and that, like him, he lives in a land of pure logic and imagination. We have changed much since the sixteenth century, and we condemn now what we approved formerly. We would not have the reader interested in a miser, an ambitious man, a rake. And he is interested in them when the writer, neither praising nor blaming, sets himself to unfold the mood, training, shape of the head, and habits of mind which have impressed in him this primitive inclination, to prove the necessity of its effects, to lead it through all its stages, to show the greater power which age and contentment give, to expose the irresistible fall which hurls man into madness or death. The reader, caught by this reasoning, admires the work which it has produced, and forgets to be indignant against the personage created. He says, What a splendid miser! and thinks not of the evils which avarice causes. He becomes a philosopher and an artist, and remembers not that he is an upright man. Always recollect that you are such, and renounce the beauties which may flourish on this evil soil.

"Amongst these, the first is greatness. A man must be interested in passions to comprehend their full effect, to count all their springs, to describe their whole course. They are diseases; if a man is content to blame them he will never know them; if you are not a physiologist, if you are not enamoured of them, if you do not make your heroes out of them, if you do not start with pleasure at the sight of a fine feature of avarice, as at the sight of a valuable symptom, you will not be able to unfold their vast system, and to display their fatal greatness. You will not have this immoral merit; and, moreover, it does not suit your species of mind. Your extreme sensibility, and ever-ready irony, must needs be exercised; you have not sufficient calmness to penetrate to the depths of a character, you prefer to weep over or to rail at it; you lay the blame on it, make it your friend or foe, render it touching or odious; you do not depict it; you are too impassioned, and not enough inquisitive. On the other hand, the tenacity of your imagination, the vehemence and fixity with which you impress your thought into the detail you wish to grasp, limit your knowledge, arrest you in a single feature, prevent you from reaching all the parts of a soul, and from sounding its depths. Your imagination is too lively, too meagre. These, then, are the characters you will outline. You will grasp a personage in a single attitude, you will see of him only that and you will impose it upon him from beginning to end. His face will always have the same expression, and this expression will be almost always a grimace. Your personages will have a sort of knack which will not quit them. Miss Mercy will laugh at every word; Mark Tapley will say 'jolly' in every scene; Mrs. Gamp will be ever talking of Mrs. Harris; Dr. Chillip will not venture a single action free from timidity; Mr. Micawber will speak through three volumes the same kind of emphatic phrases, and will pass five or six times, with comical suddenness, from joy to grief. Each of your characters will be a vice, a virtue, a ridicule personified; and the passion, with which you endow it, will be so frequent, so invariable, so absorbing, that it will no longer be like a living man, but an abstraction in man's clothes. The French have a Tartuffe like your Pecksniff, but the hypocrisy which he represents has not destroyed the other traits of his character; if he adds to the comedy by his vice, he belongs to humanity by his nature. He has, besides his ridiculous feature, a character and a mood; he is coarse, strong, red in the face, brutal, sensual; the vehemence of his blood makes him bold; his boldness makes him calm; his boldness, his calm, his quick decision, his scorn of men, make him a great politician. When he has entertained the public through five acts, he still offers to the psychologist and the physician more than one subject of study. Your Pecksniff will offer nothing to these. He will only serve to instruct and amuse the public. He will be a living satire of hypocrisy, and nothing more. If you give him a taste for brandy, it is gratuitously; in the mood which you assign to him, nothing requires it; he is so steeped in oily hypocrisy, in softness, in a flowing style, in literary phrases, in tender morality that the rest of his nature has disappeared; it is a mask, and not a man. But this mask is so grotesque and energetic that it will be useful to the public, and will diminish the number of hypocrites. It is our end and yours, and the list of your characters will have rather the effect of a book of satires than of a portrait gallery.

"For the same reason, these satires, though united, will continue effectually detached, and will not constitute a genuine collection. You began with essays, and your larger novels are only essays, tagged together. The only means of composing a natural and solid whole is to write the history of a passion or of a character, to take them up at their birth, to see them increase, alter, become destroyed, to understand the inner necessity for their development. You do not follow this development; you always keep your character in the same attitude; he is a miser, or a hypocrite, or a good man to the end, and always after the same fashion: thus he has no history. You can only change the circumstances in which he is met with, you do not change him; he remains motionless, and at every shock that touches him, emits the same sound. The variety of events which you contrive is, therefore, only an amusing phantasmagoria; they have no connection, they do not form a system, they are but a heap. You will only write lives, adventures, memoirs, sketches, collections of scenes, and you will not be able to compose an action. But if the literary taste of your nation, added to the natural direction of your genius, imposes upon you moral intentions, forbids you the lofty depicture of characters, vetoes the composition of united aggregates, it presents to your observation, sensibility and satire, a succession of original figures which belong only to England, which drawn by your hand, will form a unique gallery, and which, with the stamp of your genius, will offer that of your country and of your time."

Part III.—The Characters

Section I.—Dickens's Love for Natural Characters

Take away the grotesque characters, who are only introduced to fill up and to excite laughter, and you will find that all Dickens's characters, belong to two classes— people who have feelings and emotions, and people who have none. He contrasts the souls which nature creates with those which society deforms. One of his last novels, "Hard Times," is an abstract of all the rest. He there exalts instinct above reason, intuition of heart above positive knowledge; he attacks education built on statistics, figures, and facts; overwhelms the positive and mercantile spirit with misfortune and ridicule; combats the pride, harshness, selfishness of the merchant and the aristocrat; falls foul of manufacturing towns, towns of smoke and mud, which fetter the body in an artificial atmosphere, and the mind in a factitious existence. He seeks out poor artisans, mountebanks, a foundling, and crushes beneath their common-sense, generosity, delicacy, courage, and gentleness, the false science, false happiness, and false virtue of the rich and powerful who despise them. He satirizes oppressive society; mourns over oppressed nature; and his elegiac genius like his satirical genius, finds ready to his hand in the English world around him, the sphere which it needs for its development.

Section II.—The Hypocrite.—The Positive Man.—The Proud Man

The first fruits of English society is hypocrisy. It ripens here under the double breath of religion and morality; we know their popularity and sway across the Channel. In a country where it is shocking to laugh on Sunday, where the gloomy Puritan has preserved something of his old rancor against happiness, where the critics of ancient history insert dissertations on the relative virtue of Nebuchadnezzar, it is natural that the appearance of morality should be serviceable. It is a needful coin: those who lack good money coin bad; and the more public opinion declares it precious, the more it is counterfeited. This vice is therefore English. Mr. Pecksniff is not found in France. His speech would disgust Frenchmen. If they have an affectation, it is not of virtue, but of vice: if they wish to succeed, they would be wrong to speak of their principles: they prefer to confess their weaknesses; and if they have quacks, they are boasters of immorality. They had their hypocrites once, but it was when religion was popular. Since Voltaire, Tartuffe is impossible. Frenchmen no longer try to affect a piety which would deceive no one, and lead to nothing. Hypocrisy comes and goes, varying with the state of morals, religion, and mind; we can see, then, how Pecksniff's suits the dispositions of his country. English religion is not very dogmatical, but wholly moral. Therefore Pecksniff does not, like Tartuffe, utter theological phrases; he expands altogether in philanthropic tirades. He has progressed with the age; he has become a humanitarian philosopher. He calls his daughters Mercy and Charity. Fie is tender, he is kind, he gives vent to domestic effusions. He innocently exhibits, when visited, charming domestic scenes; he displays his paternal heart, marital sentiments, the kindly feeling of a good master. The family virtues are honored nowadays; he must muffle himself therewith. Orgon formerly said, as taught by Tartuffe:

> "My brother, children, mother, wife might die!
> You think I'll care; no surely, no! not I!"[259]

Modern virtue and English piety think otherwise; we must not despise this world in view of the next; we must improve it. Tartuffe speaks of his hair-shirt and his discipline; Pecksniff, of his comfortable little parlor, of the charm of friendship, the beauties of nature. He tries to make men "dwell in unity." He is like a member of the Peace Society. He develops the most touching considerations on the benefits and beauties of union among men. It will be impossible to hear him without being affected. Men are refined nowadays, they have read much elegiac poetry; their sensibility is more active; they can no longer be deceived by the coarse impudence of Tartuffe. This is why Mr. Pecksniff will use gestures of sublime long-suffering, smiles of ineffable compassion, starts, free and easy movements, graces, tendernesses which will seduce the most reserved and charm the most delicate. The English in their Parliament, meetings, associations, public ceremonies, have learned the oratorical phraseology, the abstract terms, the style of political economy, of the newspapers and the prospectus. Pecksniff talks like a prospectus. He possesses its obscurity, its wordiness, and its emphasis. He seems to soar above the earth, in the region of pure ideas, in the bosom of truth. He resembles an apostle, brought up in the "Times" office. He spouts general ideas on every occasion. He finds a moral lesson in the ham and eggs he has just eaten. As he folds his napkin, he rises to lofty contemplations:

"Even the worldly goods of which we have just disposed, even they have their moral. See how they come and go. Every pleasure is transitory."[260]

"'The process of digestion, as I have been informed by anatomical friends, is one of the most wonderful works of nature. I do not know how it may be with others, but it is a great satisfaction to me to know, when regaling on my humble fare, that I am putting in motion the most beautiful machinery with which we have any acquaintance. I really feel at such times as if I was doing a public service. When I have wound myself up, if I may employ such a term/ said Mr. Pecksniff with exquisite tenderness, 'and know that I am Going, I feel that in the lesson afforded by the works within me, I am a Benefactor to my Kind!'"[261]

We recognize a new species of hypocrisy. Vices, like virtues, change in every age.

The practical, as well as the moral spirit, is English; by commerce, labor, and government, this people has acquired the taste and talent for business; this is why they regard the French as children and madmen. The excess of this disposition is the destruction of imagination and sensibility. Man becomes a speculative machine, in which figures and facts are set in array; he denies the life of the mind and the joys of the heart; he sees in the world nothing but loss and gain; he becomes hard, harsh, greedy, and avaricious; he treats men as machinery; on a certain day he finds himself simply a merchant, banker, statistician; he has ceased to be a man. Dickens has multiplied portraits of the positive man— Ralph Nickleby, Scrooge, Anthony Chuzzlewit, Jonas Chuzzlewit, Alderman Cute, Mr. Murdstone and his sister, Bounderby, Gradgrind: we can find them in all his novels. Some are so by education, others by nature; but all are odious, for they all rail at and destroy kindness, sympathy, compassion, disinterested affections, religious emotions, a fanciful enthusiasm, all that is lovely in man. They oppress children, strike women, starve the poor, insult the wretched. The best are machines of polished steel, methodically performing their official duties, and not knowing that they make others suffer. These kinds of men are not found in France. Their rigidity is not in the French character. They are produced in England by a school which has its philosophy, its great men, its glory, and which has never been established amongst the French. More than once, it is true, French writers have depicted avaricious men, men of business, and shopkeepers: Balzac is full of them: but he explains them by their imbecility, or makes them monsters, like Grandet and Gobseck. Those of Dickens constitute a real class, and represent a national vice. Read this passage of "Hard Times," and see if, body and soul, Mr. Gradgrind is not wholly English:

"'Now, what I want is Facts. Teach these boys and girls nothing but Facts. Facts alone are wanted in life. Plant nothing else, and root out everything else. You can only form the minds of reasoning animals upon Facts: nothing else will ever be of any service to them. This is the principle on which I bring up my own children, and this is the principle on which I bring up these children. Stick to Facts, sir!'

"The scene was a plain, bare, monotonous vault of a school-room, and the speaker's square forefinger emphasized his observations by underscoring every sentence with a line on the schoolmaster's sleeve. The emphasis was helped by the speaker's square wall of a forehead, which had his eyebrows for its base, while his eyes found commodious cellarage in two dark caves, overshadowed by the wall. The emphasis was helped by the speaker's mouth, which was wide, thin, and hard set. The emphasis was helped by the speaker's voice, which was inflexible, dry, and dictatorial. The emphasis was helped by the speaker's hair, which bristled on the skirts of his bald head, a plantation of firs to keep the wind from its shining surface, all covered with knobs, like the crust of a plum-pie, as if the head had scarcely warehouse-room for the hard facts stored inside. The speaker's obstinate carriage, square coat, square legs, square shoulders— nay, his very neckcloth, trained to take him by the throat with an unaccommodating grasp, like a stubborn fact, as it was— all helped the emphasis.

"'In this life we want nothing but Facts, sir; nothing but Facts!'

"The speaker, and the schoolmaster, and the third grown person present, all backed a little, and swept with their eyes the inclined plane of little vessels then and there arranged in order, ready to have imperial gallons of facts poured into them until they were full to the brim.[262]

"'Thomas Gradgrind, sir! A man of realities. A man of facts and calculations. A man who proceeds upon the principle that two and two are four, and nothing over, and who is not to be talked into allowing for anything over. Thomas Gradgrind, sir— peremptorily Thomas— Thomas Gradgrind. With a rule and a pair of scales, and the multiplication table always in his pocket, sir, ready to weigh and measure any parcel of human nature, and tell you exactly what it comes to. It is a mere question of figures, a case of simple arithmetic. You might hope to get some other nonsensical belief into the head of George Gradgrind, or Augustus Gradgrind, or John Gradgind, or Joseph Gradgrind (all supposititious, non-existent persons), but into the head of Thomas Gradgrind— no, sir!'

"In such terms Mr. Gradgrind always mentally introduced himself, whether to his private circle of acquaintance, or to the public in general. In such terms, no doubt, substituting the words 'boys and girls' for 'sir,' Thomas Gradgrind now presented Thomas Gradgrind to the little pitchers before him, who were to be filled so full of facts."[263]

Another fault, arising from the habit of commanding and striving, is pride. It abounds in an aristocratic country, and no one has more soundly rated aristocracy than Dickens; all his portraits are sarcasms. James Harthouse, a dandy disgusted with everything, chiefly with himself, and rightly so; Lord Frederick Verisopht, a poor duped idiot, brutalized with drink, whose wit consists in staring at men and sucking his cane; Lord Feenix, a sort of mechanism of parliamentary phrases, out of order, and hardly able to finish the ridiculous periods into which he always takes care to lapse; Mrs. Skewton, a hideous old ruin, a coquette to the last, demanding rose-colored curtains for her death-bed, and parading her daughter through all the drawing-rooms of England, in order to sell her to some vain husband; Sir John Chester, a wretch of high society, who, for fear of compromising himself, refuses to save his natural son, and refuses it with all kinds of airs, as he finishes his chocolate. But the most complete and most English picture of the aristocratic spirit is the portrait of a London merchant, Mr. Dombey.

In France people do not look for types among the merchants, but they are found among that class in England, as forcible as in the proudest châteaux. Mr. Dombey loves his house as if he were a nobleman, as much as himself. If he neglects his daughter and longs for a son, it is to perpetuate the old name of his bank. He has his ancestors in commerce, and he likes to have his descendants in the same branch of business. He maintains traditions, and continues a power. At this height of opulence, and with this scope of action, he is a prince, and with a prince's position he has his feelings. We see there a character which could only be produced in a country whose commerce embraces the globe, where merchants are potentates, where a company of merchants has trafficked in continents, maintained wars, destroyed kingdoms, founded an empire of a hundred million men. The pride of such a man is not petty, but terrible; it is so calm and high that to find a parallel we must read again the memoirs of the Duke of Saint Simon. Mr. Dombey has always commanded, and it does not enter his mind that he could yield to anyone or anything. He receives flattery as a tribute to which he has a right, and sees men beneath him, at a vast distance, as beings made to beseech and obey him. His second wife, proud Edith Skewton, resists and scorns him; the pride of the merchant is pitted against the pride of the highborn woman, and the restrained outbursts of the growing opposition reveal an intensity of passion, which souls thus born and bred alone can feel. Edith, to avenge herself, flees on the anniversary of her marriage, and gives herself the appearance of being an adulteress. It is then that his inflexible pride asserts itself in all its rigidity. He has driven out of the house his daughter, whom he believes the accomplice of his wife; he forbids the one or the other to be recalled to his memory; he commands his sister and his friends to be silent; he receives guests with the same tone and the same coldness. With despair in his heart, and feeling bitterly the insult offered to him by his wife, the conscientiousness of his failure, and the idea of public ridicule, he remains as firm, as haughty, as calm as ever. He launches out more recklessly in speculations, and is ruined; he is on the point of suicide. Hitherto all was well: the bronze column continued whole and unbroken; but the exigencies of public morality mar the idea of the book. His daughter arrives in the nick of time. She entreats him; his feelings get the better of him, she carries him off; he becomes the best of fathers, and spoils a fine novel.

Section III.—Children

Let us look at some different personages. In contrast with these bad and factitious characters, produced by national institutions, we find good creatures such as nature made them; and first, children.

We have none in French literature. Racine's little Joas could only exist in a piece composed for the ladies' college of Saint Cyr; the little child speaks like a prince's son, with noble and acquired phrases, as if repeating his catechism.

Nowadays these portraits are only seen in France in New-Year's books, written as models for good children. Dickens painted his with special gratification; he did not think of edifying the public, and he has charmed it. All his children are of extreme sensibility; they love much, and they crave to be loved. To understand this gratification of the painter, and this choice of characters, we must think of their physical type. English children have a color so fresh, a complexion so delicate, a skin so transparent, eyes so blue and pure, that they are like beautiful flowers. No wonder if a novelist loves them, lends to their soul a sensibility and innocence which shine forth from their looks, if he thinks that these frail and charming roses are crushed by the coarse hands which try to bend them. We must also imagine to ourselves the households in which they grow up. When, at five o'clock, the merchant and the clerk leave their office and their business, they return as quickly as possible to the pretty cottage, where their children have played all day on the lawn. The fireside by which they will pass the evening is a sanctuary, and domestic tenderness is the only poetry they need. A child deprived of these affections and this happiness seems to be deprived of the air we breathe, and the novelist does not find a volume too much to explain its unhappiness. Dickens has recorded it in ten volumes, and at last he has written the history of "David Copperfield." David is loved by his mother, and by an honest servant girl, Peggotty; he plays with her in the garden; he watches her sew; he reads to her the natural history of crocodiles; he fears the hens and geese, which strut in a menacing and ferocious manner in the yard; he is perfectly happy. His mother marries again, and all changes. The father-in-law, Mr. Murdstone, and his sister Jane, are harsh, methodical, and cold beings. Poor little David is every moment wounded by harsh words. He dare not speak or move; he is afraid to kiss his mother; he feels himself weighed down, as by a leaden cloak, by the cold looks of the new master and mistress. He falls back on himself; mechanically studies the lessons assigned him; cannot learn them, so great is his dread of not knowing them. He is whipped, shut up with bread and water in a lonely room. He is terrified by night, and fears himself. He asks himself whether in fact he is not bad or wicked, and weeps. This incessant terror, hopeless and issueless, the spectacle of this wounded sensibility and stupefied intelligence, the long anxieties, the sleepless nights, the solitude of the poor, imprisoned child, his passionate desire to kiss his mother or to weep on the breast of his nurse— all this is sad to see. These children's griefs are as heartfelt as the sorrows of a man. It is the history of a frail plant, which was flourishing in a warm air, beneath a mild sun, and which, suddenly transplanted to the snow, sheds its leaves and withers.

The working-classes are like children, dependent, not very cultivated, akin to nature, and liable to oppression. And so Dickens extols them. That is not new in France; the novels of Eugène Sue have given us more than one example, and the theme is as old as Rousseau; but in the hands of the English writer it has acquired a singular force. His heroes possess feelings so delicate, and are so self-sacrificing, that we cannot admire them sufficiently. They have nothing vulgar but their pronunciation; the rest is but nobility and generosity. We see a mountebank abandon his daughter, his only joy, for fear of injuring her in any way. A young woman devotes herself to save the unworthy wife of a man who loves her, and whom she loves; the man dies; she continues, from pure self-sacrifice, to care for the degraded creature. A poor wagoner, who thinks his wife unfaithful, loudly pronounces her innocent, and all his vengeance is to think only of loading her with tenderness and kindness. None, according to Dickens, feel so strongly as they do the happiness of loving and being loved— the pure joys of domestic life. None have so much compassion for those poor, deformed and infirm creatures whom they so often bring into the world, and who seem only born to die. None have a juster and more inflexible moral sense. I confess that even Dickens's heroes unfortunately resemble the indignant fathers of French melodramas. When old Peggotty learns that his niece is seduced, he sets off, stick in hand, and walks over France, Germany, and Italy, to find her and bring her back to duty. But above all, they have an English sentiment, which fails in Frenchmen: they are Christians. It is not only women, as in France, who take refuge in the idea of another world; men turn also their thoughts towards it. In England, where there are so many sects, and everyone chooses his own, each one believes in the religion he has made for himself; and this noble sentiment raises still higher the throne upon which the uprightness of their resolution and the delicacy of their heart have placed them.

In reality, the novels of Dickens can all be reduced to one phrase, to-wit: Be good, and love; there is genuine joy only in the emotions of the heart; sensibility is the whole man. Leave science to the wise, pride to the nobles, luxury to the rich; have compassion on humble wretchedness; the smallest and most despised being may in himself be worth as much as thousands of the powerful and the proud. Take care not to bruise the delicate souls which flourish in all conditions, under all costumes, in all ages. Believe that humanity, pity, forgiveness, are the finest things in man; believe that intimacy, expansion, tenderness, tears, are the sweetest things in the world. To live is nothing; to be powerful, learned, illustrious, is little; to be useful is not enough. He alone has lived and is a man who has wept at the remembrance of a kind action which he himself has performed or received.

Section IV.—The Ideal Man

We do not believe that this contrast between the weak and the strong, or this outcry against society in favor of nature, are the caprice of an artist or the chance of the moment. When we penetrate deeply into the history of English genius, we find that its primitive foundation was impassioned sensibility, and that its natural expression was lyrical exaltation. Both were brought from

Germany, and make up the literature existing before the Conquest. After an interval you find them again in the sixteenth century, when the French literature, introduced from Normandy, had passed away: they are the very soul of the nation. But the education of this soul was opposite to its genius; its history contradicted its nature; and its primitive inclination has clashed with all the great events which it has created or suffered. The chance of a victorious invasion and an imposed aristocracy, whilst establishing the enjoyment of political liberty, has impressed on the character habits of strife and pride. The chance of an insular position, the necessity of commerce, the abundant possession of the first materials for industry, have developed the practical faculty and the positive mind. The acquisition of these habits, faculties, and mind, to which must be added former hostile feelings to Rome, and an inveterate hatred against an oppressive church, has given birth to a proud and reasoning religion, replacing submission by independence, poetic theology by practical morality, and faith by discussion. Politics, business, and religion, like three powerful machines, have created a new man above the old. Stern dignity, self-command, the need of authority, severity in its exercise, strict morality, without compromise or pity, a taste for figures and dry calculation, a dislike of facts not palpable and ideas not useful, ignorance of the invisible world, scorn of the weaknesses and tendernesses of the heart—such are the dispositions which the stream of facts and the ascendancy of institutions tend to confirm in their souls. But poetry and domestic life prove that they have only half succeeded. The old sensibility, oppressed and perverted, still lives and works. The poet subsists under the Puritan, the trader, the statesman. The social man has not destroyed the natural man. This frozen crust, this unsociable pride, this rigid attitude, often cover a good and tender nature. It is the English mask of a German head; and when a talented writer, often a writer of genius, reaches the sensibility which is bruised or buried by education and national institutions, he moves his reader in the most inner depths, and becomes the master of all hearts.

---

[238]Taine was not wrong in thinking so. In the "Life of Charles Dickens" by J. Forster we find (vol. I. p. 8) the following words: "And here I may at once expressly mention, what already has been hinted, that even as Fielding described himself and his belongings in Captain Booth and Amelia, and protested always that he had writ in his books nothing more than he had seen in life, so it may be said of Dickens, in more especial relation to David Copperfield. Many guesses have been made since his death, connecting David's autobiography with his own. ... There is not only truth in all this, but it will very shortly be seen that the identity went deeper than any had supposed, and covered experiences not less startling in the reality than they appear to be in the fiction."— Tr.

[239]"Martin Chuzzlewit," ch. XLII. The translator has used the "Charles Dickens" edition, 1868, 18 vols.

[240]"It was small tyranny for a respectable wind to go wreaking its vengeance on such poor creatures as the fallen leaves; but this wind happening to come up with a great heap of them just after venting its humour on the insulted Dragon, did so disperse and scatter them that they fled away, pell-mell, some here, some there, rolling over each other, whirling round and round upon their thin edges, taking frantic flights into the air, and playing all manner of extraordinary gambols in the extremity of their distress. Nor was this enough for its malicious fury: for, not content with driving them abroad, it charged small parties of them and hunted them into the wheel-wright's saw-pit, and below the planks and timbers in the yard, and, scattering the sawdust in the air, it looked for them underneath, and when it did meet with any, whew! how it drove them on and followed at their heels!

"The scared leaves only flew the faster for all this, and a giddy chase it was: for they got into unfrequented places, where there was no outlet, and where their pursuer kept them eddying round and round at his pleasure; and they crept under the eaves of houses, and clung tightly to the sides of hayricks, like bats; and tore in at open chamber windows, and cowered close to hedges; and, in short, went anywhere for safety."— "Martin Chuzzlewit," ch. II.

[241]"The Chimes," first quarter.
[242]"The Chimes," first quarter.
[243]"Martin Chuzzlewit." ch. XLV.
[244]"Dombey and Son," ch. IV.
[245]See ante, vol. I. note, page 393.
[246]"David Copperfield," ch. V.
[247]"Martin Chuzzlewit," ch. XXXVI.
[248]"Martin Chuzzlewit," ch. LI.
[249]Novels of George Sand.
[250]"Martin Chuzzlewit," ch. XXXVI.
[251]"Hard Times," bk. 3, ch. VI.
[252]Ibid.
[253]"Martin Chuzzlewit," ch. VIII.
[254]Ibid.
[255]"Martin Chuzzlewit," ch. XIX.
[256]"The Chimes," the first quarter.
[257]A living French author, whose dramas are all said to have a moral purpose.— Tr.
[258]"David Copperfield," ch. LXV; the scene between the doctor and his wife.
[259]"Et je verrais mourir frère, enfants, mère, et femme

Que je m'en soucierais autant que
de cela."

These lines, said by Orgon to his brother-in-law Cléante, are from Molière's "Tartuffe," I. 6.

[260]"Martin Chuzzlewit," ch. II.
[261]"Martin Chuzzlewit," ch. VIII.
[262]"Hard Times," book I. ch. I.
[263]Ibid, book I. ch. II.

PAGE FROM THE LETTERS OF ST. JEROME
Fac-simile example of Printing and Engraving in the Fifteenth Century.

Chapter Second. The Novel (Continued)—Thackeray

Comparison Between Dickens and Thackeray

The novel of manners in England multiplies, and for this there are several reasons: first, it is born there, and every plant thrives well in its own soil; secondly, it is a natural outlet: there is no music in England as in Germany, or conversation as in France; and men who must think and feel find in it a means of feeling and thinking. On the other hand, women take part in it with eagerness; amidst the stagnation of gallantry and the coldness of religion, it gives scope for imagination and dreams. Finally, by its minute details and practical counsels, it opens up a career to the precise and moral mind. The critic thus is, as it were, swamped in this copiousness; he must select in order to grasp the whole, and confine himself to a few in order to embrace all.

In this crowd two men have appeared of superior talent, original and contrasted, popular on the same grounds, ministers to the same cause, moralists in comedy and drama, defenders of natural sentiments against social institutions; who, by the precision of their pictures, the depth of their observations, the succession and bitterness of their attacks, have renewed, with other views and in another style, the old combative spirit of Swift and Fielding.

One, more ardent, more expansive, wholly given up to rapture, an impassioned painter of crude and dazzling pictures, a lyric prose-writer, omnipotent in laughter and tears, plunged into fantastic invention, painful sensibility, vehement buffoonery; and by the boldness of his style, the excess of his emotions, the grotesque familiarity of his caricatures, he has displayed all the forces and weaknesses of an artist, all the audacities, all the successes, and all the oddities of the imagination.

The other, more contained, better informed and stronger, a lover of moral dissertations, a counsellor of the public, a sort of lay preacher, less bent on defending the poor, more bent on censuring man, has brought to the aid of satire a sustained common-sense, a great knowledge of the heart, consummate cleverness, powerful reasoning, a treasure of meditated hatred, and has persecuted vice with all the weapons of reflection. By this contrast the one completes the other; and we may form an exact idea of English taste by placing the portrait of William Makepeace Thackeray by the side of that of Charles Dickens.

BOOK V — MODERN AUTHORS

PART I.—THE SATIRIST

Section I.—The English Satirist

No wonder if in England a novelist writes satires. A gloomy and reflective man is impelled to it by his character; he is still further impelled by the surrounding manners. He is not permitted to contemplate passions as poetic powers; he is bidden to appreciate them as moral qualities. His pictures become sentences; he is a counsellor rather than an observer, a judge rather than an artist. We see by what machinery Thackeray has changed novel into satire.

I open at random his three great works— "Pendennis, Vanity Fair, The Newcomes." Every scene sets in relief a moral truth: the author desires that at every page we should form a judgment on vice and virtue; he has blamed or approved beforehand, and the dialogues or portraits are to him only means by which he adds our approbation to his approbation, our blame to his blame. He is giving us lessons; and beneath the sentiments which he describes, as beneath the events which he relates, we continually discover rules for our conduct and the intentions of a reformer.

On the first page of "Pendennis" we see the portrait of an old major, a man of the world, selfish and vain, seated comfortably in his club, at the table by the fire, and near the window, envied by Surgeon Glowry, whom nobody ever invites, seeking in the records of aristocratic entertainments for his own name, gloriously placed amongst those of illustrious guests. A family letter arrives. Naturally he puts it aside and reads it, carelessly, last of all. He utters an exclamation of horror; his nephew wants to marry an actress. He has places booked in the coach (charging the sum which he disburses for the seats to the account of the widow and the young scape-grace of whom he is guardian), and hastens to save the young fool. If there were a low marriage, what would become of his invitations? The manifest conclusion is: Let us not be selfish, or vain, or fond of good living, like the major.

Chapter the second: Pendennis, the father of the young man in love, had "exercised the profession of apothecary and surgeon," but, being of good birth, his "secret ambition had always been to be a gentleman." He comes into money; is called Doctor, marries the very distant relative of a lord, tries to get acquainted with high families. He boasts to the last day of his life of having been invited by Sir Pepin Ribstone to an entertainment. He buys a small estate, tries to sink the apothecary, and shows off in the new glory of a landed proprietor. Each of these details is a concealed or evident sarcasm, which says to the reader: "My good friend, remain the honest John Tomkins that you are; and for the love of your son and yourself, avoid taking the airs of a great nobleman."

Old Pendennis dies. His son, the noble heir of the domain, "Prince of Pendennis and Grand Duke of Fairoaks," begins to reign over his mother, his cousin, and the servants. He sends wretched verses to the county papers, begins an epic poem, a tragedy in which sixteen persons die, a scathing history of the Jesuits, and defends church and king like a loyal Tory. He sighs after the ideal, wishes for an unknown maiden, and falls in love with an actress, a woman of thirty-two, who learns her parts mechanically, as ignorant and stupid as can be. Young folks, my dear friends, you are all affected, pretentious, dupes of yourselves and of others. Wait to judge the world until you have seen it, and do not think you are masters when you are scholars.

The lesson continues, and lasts as long as the life of Arthur. Like Le Sage in "Gil Blas," and Balzac in "Le Père Goriot," the author of "Pendennis" depicts a young man having some talent, endowed with good feelings, even generous, desiring to make a name, whilst, at the same time, he falls in with the maxims of the world; but Le Sage only wished to amuse us, and Balzac only wished to stir our passions: Thackeray, from beginning to end, labors to correct us.

This intention becomes still more evident if we examine in detail one of his dialogues and one of his pictures. We will not find there impartial energy, bent on copying nature, but attentive thoughtfulness, bent on transforming into satire objects, words, and events. All the words of the character are chosen and weighed so as to be odious or ridiculous. It accuses itself, is studious to display vice, and behind its voice we hear the voice of the writer who judges, unmasks, and punishes it. Miss Crawley, a rich old woman, falls ill.[264] Mrs. Bute Crawley, her relative, hastens to save her, and to save the inheritance. Her aim is to have excluded from the will a nephew, Captain Rawdon, an old favorite, presumptive heir of the old lady. This Rawdon is a stupid guardsman, a frequenter of taverns, a too clever gambler, a duellist, and a *roué*. Fancy the capital opportunity for Mrs. Bute, the respectable mother of a family, the worthy spouse of a clergyman, accustomed to write her husband's sermons! From sheer virtue she hates Captain Rawdon, and will not suffer that such a good sum of money should fall into such bad hands. Moreover, are we not responsible for our families? and is it not for us to publish the faults of our relatives? It is our strict duty, and Mrs. Bute acquits herself of hers conscientiously. She collects edifying stories of her nephew, and therewith she edifies the aunt. He has ruined so and so; he has wronged such a woman. He has duped this tradesman; he has killed this husband. And above all, unworthy man, he has mocked his aunt! Will that generous lady continue to cherish such a viper? Will she suffer her numberless sacrifices to be repaid by such ingratitude and such ridicule? We can imagine the ecclesiastical eloquence of Mrs. Bute. Seated at the foot of the bed, she keeps the patient in sight, plies her with draughts, enlivens her with terrible sermons, and mounts guard at the door against the probable invasion of the heir. The siege was well conducted, the legacy attacked so obstinately must be yielded up; the virtuous fingers of the matron grasped beforehand and by anticipation the substantial heap of shining sovereigns. And yet a carping spectator might have found some faults in her management. Mrs. Bute managed rather too well. She forgot that a woman persecuted with sermons, handled like a bale of goods, regulated like a clock, might take a dislike to so harassing an authority. What is worse, she forgot that a timid old woman, confined to the house, overwhelmed with preachings, poisoned with pills, might die before having changed her will, and leave all, alas, to her scoundrelly nephew. Instructive and formidable example! Mrs. Bute, the honor of her sex, the consoler of the sick, the counsellor of her family, having ruined her health to look after her beloved sister-in-law, and to preserve the inheritance, was just on the point, by her exemplary devotion, of putting the patient in her coffin, and the inheritance in the hands of her nephew.

Apothecary Clump arrives; he trembles for his dear client; she is worth to him two hundred a year; he is resolved to save this precious life, in spite of Mrs. Bute. Mrs. Bute interrupts him, and says: "I am sure, my dear Mr. Clump, no efforts of mine have been wanting to restore our dear invalid, whom the ingratitude of her nephew has laid on the bed of sickness. I never shrink from personal discomfort; I never refuse to sacrifice myself.... I would lay down my life for my duty, or for any member of my husband's family."[265] The disinterested apothecary returns to the charge heroically. Immediately she replies in the finest strain; her eloquence flows from her lips as from an over-full pitcher. She cries aloud: "Never, as long as nature supports me, will I desert the post of duty. As the mother of a family and the wife of an English clergyman, I humbly trust that my principles are good. When my poor James was in the small-pox, did I allow any hireling to nurse him? No!" The patient Clump scatters about sugared compliments, and pressing his point amidst interruptions, protestations, offers of sacrifice, railings against the nephew, at last hits the mark. He delicately insinuates that the patient "should have change, fresh air, gaiety. The sight of her horrible nephew casually in the Park, where I am told the wretch drives with the brazen partner of his crimes," Mrs. Bute said (letting the cat of selfishness out of the bag of secrecy), "would cause her such a shock that we should have to bring her back to bed again. She must not go out, Mr. Clump. She shall not go out as long as I remain to watch over her. And as for my health, what matters it? I give it cheerfully, sir. I sacrifice it at the altar of my duty." It is clear that the author attacks Mrs. Bute and all legacy-hunters. He gives her ridiculous airs, pompous phrases, a transparent, coarse, and blustering hypocrisy. The reader feels hatred and disgust for her the more she speaks. He would unmask her; he is pleased to see her assailed, driven into a corner, taken in by the polished manoeuvres of her adversary, and rejoices with the author, who tears from her and emphasizes the shameful confession of her tricks and her greed.

Having arrived so far, satirical reflection quits the literary form. In order the better to develop itself, it exhibits itself alone. Thackeray now attacks vice himself, and in his own name. No author is more fertile in dissertations; he constantly enters his story to reprimand or instruct us; he adds theoretical to active morality. We might glean from his novels one or two volumes of essays, in the manner of La Bruyère or of Addison. There are essays on love, on vanity, on hypocrisy, on meanness, on all the virtues, on all the vices; and turning over a few pages, we shall find one on the comedies of legacies, and on too attentive relatives:

"What a dignity it gives an old lady, that balance at the banker's! How tenderly we look at her faults, if she is a relative (and may every reader have a score of such), what a kind, good-natured old creature we find her! How the junior partner of Hobbs and Dobbs leads her smiling to the carriage, with the lozenge upon it, and the fat wheezy coachman! How, when she comes to pay us a visit, we generally find an opportunity to let our friends know her station in the world! We say (and with perfect truth) I wish I had Miss MacWhirter's signature to a cheque for five thousand pounds. She wouldn't miss it, says your wife. She is my aunt, say you, in an easy, careless way, when your friend asks if Miss MacWhirter is any relative? Your wife is perpetually sending her little testimonies of affection; your little girls work endless worsted baskets, cushions, and foot-stools for her. What a good fire there is in her room when she comes to pay you a visit, although your wife laces her stays without one! The house during her stay assumes a festive, neat, warm, jovial, snug appearance, not visible at other seasons. You yourself, dear sir, forget to go to sleep after dinner, and find yourself all of a sudden (though you invariably lose) very fond of rubber. What good dinners you have— game every day, Malmsey-Madeira, and no end of fish from London! Even the servants in the kitchen share in the general prosperity; and, somehow, during the stay of Miss MacWhirter's fat coachman, the beer is grown much stronger, and the consumption of tea and sugar in the nursery (where her maid takes her meals) is not regarded in the least. Is it so, or is it not so? I appeal to the middle classes. Ah, gracious powers! I wish you would send me an old aunt— a maiden aunt— an aunt with a lozenge on her carriage, and a front of light coffee-coloured hair— how my children should work workbags for her, and my Julia and I would make her comfortable! Sweet— sweet vision! Foolish— foolish dream!"[266]

There is no disguising it. The reader most resolved not to be warned, is warned. When we have an aunt with a good sum to leave, we shall value our attentions and our tenderness at their true worth. The author has taken the place of our conscience, and the novel, transformed by reflection, becomes a school of manners.

Section II.—The English Temperament

The lash is laid on very heavily in this school; it is the English taste. About tastes and whips there is no disputing; but without disputing we may understand, and the surest means of understanding the English taste is to compare it with the French taste.

I see in France, in a drawing-room of men of wit, or in an artist's studio, a score of lively people: they must be amused, that is their character. You may speak to them of human wickedness, but on condition of diverting them. If you get angry, they will be shocked; if you teach a lesson, they will yawn. Laugh, it is the rule here— not cruelly, or from manifest enmity, but in good humor and in lightness of spirit. This nimble wit must act; the discovery of a clean piece of folly is a fortunate hap for it. As a light flame, it glides and flickers in sudden outbreaks on the mere surface of things. Satisfy it by imitating it, and to please gay people be gay. Be polite, that is the second commandment, very like the other. You speak to sociable, delicate, vain men, whom you must take care not to offend, but whom you must flatter. You would wound them by trying to carry conviction by force, by dint of solid arguments, by a display of eloquence and indignation. Do them the honor of supposing that they understand you at the first word, that a hinted smile is to them as good as a sound syllogism, that a fine allusion caught on the wing reaches them better than the heavy onset of a dull geometrical satire. Think, lastly (between ourselves), that, in politics as in religion, they have been for a thousand years very well governed, over-governed; that when a man is bored he desires to be so no more; that a coat too tight splits at the elbows, and elsewhere. They are critics from choice; from choice they like to insinuate forbidden things; and often, by abuse of logic, by transport, by vivacity, from ill humor, they strike at society through government, at morality through religion. They are scholars who have been too long, under the rod; they break the windows in opening the doors. I dare not tell you to please them: I simply remark that, in order to please them, a grain of seditious humor will do no harm.

I cross seven leagues of sea, and here I am in a great unadorned hall, with a multitude of benches, with gas burners, swept, orderly, a debating club or a preaching-house. There are five hundred long faces, gloomy and subdued;[267] and at the first glance it is clear that they are not there to amuse themselves. In this land a grosser mood, overcharged with a heavier and stronger nourishment, has deprived impressions of their swift nobility, and thought, less facile and prompt, has lost its vivacity and its gayety. If we rail before them, we must think that we are speaking to attentive, concentrated men, capable of durable and profound sensations, incapable of changeable and sudden emotion. Those immobile and contracted faces will preserve the same attitude; they resist fleeting and half-formed smiles; they cannot unbend; and their laughter is a convulsion as stiff as their gravity. Let us not skim over our subject, but lay stress upon it; let us not pass over it lightly, but impress it; let us not dally, but strike; be assured that we must vehemently move vehement passions, and that shocks are needed to set these nerves in motion. Let us also not forget that our hearers are practical minds, lovers of the useful; that they come here to be taught; that we owe them solid truths; that their common-sense, somewhat contracted, does not fall in with hazardous extemporizations or doubtful hints; that they demand worked-out refutations and complete explanations; and that if they have paid to come in, it was to hear advice which they might apply, and satire founded on proof. Their mood requires strong emotions; their mind asks for precise demonstrations. To satisfy their mood, we must not merely scratch, but torture vice; to satisfy their mind, we must not rail in sallies, but by arguments. One word more: down there, in the midst of the assembly, behold that gilded, splendid book, resting royally on a velvet cushion. It is the Bible: around it there are fifty moralists, who awhile ago met at the theatre and pelted an actor off the stage, with apples, who was guilty of having the wife of a citizen for his mistress. If with our finger-tip, with all the compliments and disguises in the world, we touch a single sacred leaf, or the smallest moral conventionalism, immediately fifty hands will fasten themselves on our coat collar and put us out at the door. With Englishmen we must be English, with their passion and their common-sense adopt their leading-strings. Thus confined to recognize truths, satire will become more bitter, and will add the weight of public belief to the pressure of logic and the force of indignation.

Section III.—Superiority of Thackeray as a Satirist.—Literary Snobs

No writer was better gifted than Thackeray for this kind of satire, because no faculty is more proper to satire than reflection. Reflection is concentrated attention, and concentrated attention increases a hundredfold the force and duration of emotions. He who is immersed in the contemplation of a vice feels a hatred of vice, and the intensity of his hatred is measured by the intensity of his contemplation. At first, anger is a generous wine, which intoxicates and excites; when preserved and shut up, it becomes a liquor burning all that it touches, and corroding even the vessel which contains it. Of all satirists, Thackeray, after Swift, is the most gloomy. Even his countrymen have reproached him with depicting the world uglier than it is.[268] Indignation, grief, scorn, disgust, are his ordinary sentiments. When he digresses, and imagines tender souls, he exaggerates their sensibility, in order to render their oppression more odious. The selfishness which wounds them appears horrible, and their resigned sweetness is a mortal insult to their tyrants: it is the same hatred which has calculated the kindliness of the victims and the harshness of the persecutors.[269]

This anger, exasperated by reflection, is also armed by reflection. It is clear that the author is not carried away by passing indignation or pity. He has mastered himself before speaking. He has often weighed the rascality which he is about to describe. He is in possession of the motives, species, results, as a naturalist is of his classifications. He is sure of his judgment, and has matured it. He punishes like a man convinced, who has before him a heap of proofs, who advances nothing without a document or an argument, who has foreseen all objections and refuted all excuses, who will never pardon, who is right in being inflexible, who is conscious of his justice, and who rests his sentence and his vengeance on all the powers of meditation and equity. The effect of this justified and contained hatred is overwhelming. When we have read to the end of Balzac's novels, we feel the pleasure of a naturalist walking through a museum, past a fine collection of specimens and monstrosities. When we have read to the end of Thackeray, we feel the shudder of a stranger brought before a mattress in the operating-room of a hospital, on the day when cautery is applied or a limb is taken off.

In such a case the most natural weapon is serious irony, because it bears witness to concentrated hatred: he who employs it suppresses his first feeling; he feigns to be speaking against himself, and constrains himself to take the part of his adversary. On the other hand, this painful and voluntary attitude is the sign of excessive scorn; the protection which apparently is afforded to an enemy is the worst of insults. The author seems to say: "I am ashamed to attack you; you are so weak that, even supported, you must fall; your reasonings are your shame, and your excuses are your condemnation." Thus the more serious the irony, the stronger it is; the more you take care to defend your adversary, the more you degrade him; the more you seem to aid him the more you crush him. This is why Swift's grave sarcasm is so terrible; we think he is showing respect, and he slays; his approbation is a flagellation. Amongst Swift's pupils, Thackeray is the first. Several chapters in the "Book of Snobs"— that, for instance, on literary snobs— are worthy of Gulliver. The author has been passing in review all the snobs of England; what will he say of his colleagues, the literary snobs? Will he dare to speak of them? Certainly:

"My dear and excellent querist, whom does the Schoolmaster flog so resolutely as his own son? Didn't Brutus chop his offspring's head off? You have a very bad opinion indeed of the present state of Literature and of literary men, if you fancy that any one of us would hesitate to stick a knife into his neighbour penman, if the latter's death could do the State any service.

"But the fact is, that in the literary profession there are no Snobs. Look round at the whole body of British men of letters, and I defy you to point out among them a single instance of vulgarity, or envy, or assumption."

"Men and women, as far as I have known them, they are all modest in their demeanour, elegant in their manners, spotless in their lives, and honourable in their conduct to the world and to each other. You may occasionally, it is true, hear one literary man abusing his brother; but why? Not in the least out of malice; not at all from envy: merely from a sense of truth and public duty.

Suppose, for instance, I good-naturedly point out a blemish in my friend Mr. Punch's person, and say Mr. P. has a hump-back, and his nose and chin are more crooked than those features in the Apollo or Antinous, which we are accustomed to consider as our standards of beauty; does this argue malice on my part towards Mr. Punch? Not in the least. It is the critic's duty to point out defects as well as merits, and he invariably does his duty with the utmost gentleness and candour....

"That sense of equality and fraternity amongst Authors has always struck me as one of the most amiable characteristics of the class. It is because we know and respect each other, that the world respects us so much; that we hold such a good position in society, and demean ourselves so irreproachably when there.

"Literary persons are held in such esteem by the nation, that about two of them have been absolutely invited to Court during the present reign; and it is probable that towards the end of the season, one or two will be asked to dinner by Sir Robert Peel.

"They are such favourites with the public, that they are continually obliged to have their pictures taken and published; and one or two could be pointed out, of whom the nation insists upon having a fresh portrait every year. Nothing can be more gratifying than this proof of the affectionate regard which the people has for its instructors.

"Literature is held in such honour in England, that there is a sum of near twelve hundred pounds per annum set apart to pension deserving persons following that profession. And a great compliment this is, too, to the professors, and a proof of their generally prosperous and flourishing condition. They are generally so rich and thrifty, that scarcely any money is wanted to help them."[270]

We are tempted to make a mistake; and to comprehend this passage, we must remember that, in an aristocratical and monarchical society, amidst money-worship and adoration of rank, poor and low born talent is treated as its low birth and poverty deserve.[271] What makes these ironies yet stronger, is their length; some are prolonged during a whole tale, like the Fatal Boots. A Frenchman could not keep up a sarcasm so long. It would escape, right or left, through various emotions; it would change countenance, and not preserve so fixed an attitude— the mark of such a decided animosity, so calculated and bitter. There are characters which Thackeray develops through three volumes— Blanche Amory, Rebecca Sharp— and of whom he never speaks but with insult; both are base, and he never introduces them without plying them with tendernesses: dear Rebecca! tender Blanche! The tender Blanche is a sentimental and literary young creature, obliged to live with her parents, who do not understand her. She suffers so much that she ridicules them aloud before everybody; she is so oppressed by the folly of her mother and father-in-law that she never omits an opportunity of making them feel their folly. In good conscience, could she do otherwise? Would it not be on her part a lack of sincerity to affect a gayety which she has not, or a respect which she cannot feel? We understand that the poor child is in need of sympathy. When she gave up her dolls, this loving heart became first enamoured of Trenmor, a high-souled convict, the fiery Sténio, Prince Djalma, and other heroes of French novels. Alas! the imaginary world is not sufficient for wounded souls, and to satisfy the craving for the ideal, for satiety, the heart at last gives itself up to beings of this world. At eleven years of age Miss Blanche felt tender emotions towards a young Savoyard, an organ-grinder at Paris, whom she persisted in believing to be a prince carried off from his parents; at twelve, an old and hideous drawing-master had agitated her young heart; at Madame de Carmel's boarding-school a correspondence by letter took place with two young gentlemen at the College Charlemagne. Dear forlorn girl, her delicate feet are already wounded by the briers in her path of life; every day her illusions shed their leaves; in vain she puts them down in verse, in a little book bound in blue velvet, with a clasp of gold, entitled "Mes Larmes." In this isolation, what is she to do? She grows enthusiastic over the young ladies whom she meets, feels a magnetic attraction at sight of them, becomes their sister, except that she casts them aside to-morrow like an old dress: we cannot command our feelings, and nothing is more beautiful than the natural. Moreover, as the amiable child has much taste, a lively imagination, a poetic inclination for change, she keeps her maid Pincott at work day and night. Like a delicate person, a genuine dilettante and lover of the beautiful, she scolds her for her heavy eyes and her pale face:

"Our muse, with the candour which distinguished her, never failed to remind her attendant of the real state of matters. 'I should send you away, Pincott, for you are a great deal too weak, and your eyes are failing you, and you are always crying and snivelling, and wanting the doctor; but I wish that your parents at home should be supported, and I go on enduring, for their sake, mind,' the dear Blanche would say to her timid little attendant. Or, 'Pincott, your wretched appearance and slavish manner, and red eyes, positively give me the migraine; and I think I shall make you wear rouge, so that you may look a little cheerful'; or, 'Pincott, I can't bear, even for the sake of your starving parents, that you should tear my hair out of my head in that manner; and I will thank you to write them and say that I dispense with your services.'"[272]

This fool of a Pincott does not appreciate her good fortune. Can one be sad in serving such a superior being as Miss Blanche? How delightful to furnish her with subjects for her style! for, to confess the truth, Miss Blanche has not disdained to write "some very pretty verses about the lonely little tiring-maid, whose heart was far away, sad exile in a foreign land." Alas! the slightest event suffices to wound this too sensitive heart. At the least emotion her tears flow, her feelings are shaken, like a delicate butterfly, crushed as soon as touched. There she goes, aërial, her eyes fixed on heaven, a faint smile lingering round her rosy lips, a touching sylphide, so consoling to all who surround her that everyone wishes her at the bottom of a well.

One step added to serious irony leads us to serious caricature. Here, as before, the author pleads the rights of his neighbor; the only difference is, that he pleads them with too much warmth; it is insult upon insult. Under this head it abounds in Thackeray. Some of his grotesques are outrageous: for instance, M. Alcide de Mirobolant, a French cook, an artist in sauces, who declares his passion to Miss Blanche through the medium of symbolic dishes, and thinks himself a gentleman; Mrs. Major O'Dowd, a sort of female grenadier, the most pompous and talkative of Irishwomen, bent on ruling the regiment, and marrying the bachelors will they nill they; Miss Briggs, an old companion, born to receive insults, to make phrases and to shed tears; the Doctor, who proves to his scholars who write bad Greek, that habitual idleness and bad construing lead to the gallows. These calculated deformities only excite a sad smile. We always perceive behind the oddity of the character the sardonic air of the painter, and we conclude that the human race is base and stupid. Other figures, less exaggerated, are not more natural. We see that the author throws them expressly into palpable follies and marked contradictions. Such is Miss Crawley, an old maid, without any morals, and a free-thinker, who praises unequal marriages, and falls into a fit when on the next page her nephew makes one; who calls Rebecca Sharp her equal, and at the same time bids her "put some coals on the fire"; who, on learning the departure of her favorite, cries with despair: "Gracious goodness, and who's to make my chocolate"? These are comedy scenes, and not pictures of manners. There are twenty such. You see an excellent aunt, Mrs. Hoggarty, of Castle Hoggarty, settling down in the house of her nephew, Titmarsh, throw him into vast expenses, persecute his wife, drive away his friends, make his marriage unhappy. The poor ruined fellow is thrown into prison. She denounces him to the creditors with genuine indignation, and reproaches him with perfect sincerity. The wretch has been his aunt's executioner; she has been dragged by him from her home, tyrannized over by him, robbed by him, outraged by his wife. She writes:

"Such waist and extravygance never, never, never did I see. Butter waisted as if it had been dirt, coles flung away, candles burned at both ends;... and now you have the audassaty, being placed in prison justly for your crimes, for cheating me of £3000.... You come upon me to pay your detts! No, sir, it is quite enough that your mother should go on the parish, and that your wife should sweep the streets, to which you have indeed brought them; I at least... have some of the comforts to which my rank entitles me. The furniture in this house is mine; and as I presume you intend your lady to sleep in the streets, I give you warning that I shall remove it all to-morrow. Mr. Smithers will tell you that I had intended to leave you my intire fortune. I have this morning, in his presents, solamly toar up my will, and hereby renounce all connection with you and your beggarly family. P.S.— I took a viper into my bosom, and it stung me."[273]

This just and compassionate woman finds her match, a pious man, John Brough, Esquire, M.P., director of the Independent West Diddlesex Fire and Life Insurance Company. This virtuous Christian has sniffed from afar the cheering odor of her lands, houses, stocks, and other landed and personal property. He pounces upon the fine property of Mrs. Hoggarty, is sorry to see that it only brings that lady four per cent., and resolves to double her income. He calls upon her at her lodgings when her face was shockingly swelled and bitten by— never mind what:

"'Gracious heavens!' shouted John Brough, Esquire, 'a lady of your rank to suffer in this way!— the excellent relative of my dear boy, Titmarsh! Never, madam— never let it be said that Mrs. Hoggarty of Castle Hoggarty should be subject to such horrible humiliation, while John Brough has a home to offer her— a humble, happy Christian home, madam, though unlike, perhaps, the splendour to which you have been accustomed in the course of your distinguished career. Isabella, my love!— Belinda! speak to Mrs. Hoggarty. Tell her that John Brough's house is hers from garret to cellar. I repeat it, madam, from garret to cellar. I desire— I insist— I order, that Mrs. Hoggarty of Castle Hoggarty's trunks should be placed this instant in my carriage!'"[274]

This style raises a laugh, if you will, but a sad laugh. We have just learned that man is a hypocrite, unjust, tyrannical, blind. In our vexation we turn to the author, and we see on his lips only sarcasms, on his brow only chagrin.

Section IV.—Resemblance of Thackeray to Swift

Let us look carefully; perhaps in less grave matters we shall find subject of genuine laughter. Let us consider, not a rascality, but a misadventure; rascality revolts, a misadventure might amuse. But amusement alone is not here; even in a diversion the satire retains its force, because reflection retains its intensity. There is in English fun a seriousness, an effort, an application that is marvellous, and their comicalities are composed with as much knowledge as their sermons. The powerful attention decomposes its object in all its parts, and reproduces it with illusive detail and relief. Swift describes the land of speaking horses, the politics of Liliput, the inventors of the Flying Island, with details as precise and harmonious as an experienced traveller, an exact inquirer into manners and countries. Thus supported, the impossible monster and the literary grotesque enter upon actual existence, and the phantoms of imagination take the consistency of objects which we touch. Thackeray introduces this imperturbable gravity, this solid conception, this talent for illusion, into his farce. Let us study one of his moral essays; he wishes to prove that in the world we must conform to received customs, and he transforms this commonplace into an Oriental anecdote. Let us count up the details of manners, geography, chronology, cookery, the mathematical designation of every object, person, and gesture, the lucidity of imagination, the profusion of local truths; we will then understand why his raillery produces so original and biting an impression, and we will find here the same degree of study and the same attentive energy as in the foregoing ironies and exaggerations: his humor is as reflective as his hatred; he has changed his attitude, not his faculty:

"I am naturally averse to egotism, and hate self-laudation consumedly; but I can't help relating here a circumstance illustrative of the point in question, in which I must think I acted with considerable prudence.

"Being at Constantinople a few years since— (on a delicate mission)— the Russians were playing a double game, between ourselves, and it became necessary on our part to employ an extra negotiator— Leckerbiss Pasha of Roumelia, then Chief Galeongee of the Porte, gave a diplomatic banquet at his summer palace at Bujukdere. I was on the left of the Galeongee; and the Russian agent Count de Diddloff on his dexter side. Diddloff is a dandy who would die of a rose in aromatic pain: he had tried to have me assassinated three times in the course of the negotiation: but of course we were friends in public, and saluted each other in the most cordial and charming manner.

"The Galeongee is— or was, alas! for a bow-string has done for him— a staunch supporter of the old school of Turkish politics. We dined with our fingers, and had flaps of bread for plates; the only innovation he admitted was the use of European liquors, in which he indulged with great gusto. He was an enormous eater. Amongst the dishes a very large one was placed before him of a lamb dressed in its wool, stuffed with prunes, garlic, assafœtida, capsicums, and other condiments, the most abominable mixture that ever mortal smelt or tasted. The Galeongee ate of this hugely; and, pursuing the Eastern fashion, insisted on helping his friends right and left, and when he came to a particularly spicy morsel, would push it with his own hands into his guests' very mouths.

"I shall never forget the look of poor Diddloff, when his Excellency, rolling up a large quantity of this into a ball, and exclaiming, 'Buk Buk' (it is very good), administered the horrible bolus to Diddloff. The Russian's eyes rolled dreadfully as he received it: he swallowed it with a grimace that I thought must precede a convulsion, and seizing a bottle next him, which he thought was Sauterne, but which turned out to be French brandy, he drank off nearly a pint before he knew his error. It finished him; he was carried away from the dining-room almost dead, and laid out to cool in a summer-house on the Bosphorus.

"When it came to my turn, I took down the condiment with a smile, said 'Bismillah,' licked my lips with easy gratification, and when the next dish was served, made up a ball myself so dexterously, and popped it down the old Galeongee's mouth with so much grace, that his heart was won. Russia was put out of Court at once, and the treaty of Kabobanople was signed. As for Diddloff, all was over with him; he was recalled to St. Petersburg, and Sir Roderick Murchison saw him, under the No. 3,067, working in the Ural mines."[275]

The anecdote is evidently authentic; and when De Foe related the apparition of Mrs. Veal, he did not better imitate the style of an authenticated account.

Section V.—Thackeray's Misanthropy

Such attentive reflection is a source of sadness. To amuse ourselves with human passions, we must consider them as inquisitive men, like shifting puppets, or as learned men, like regulated wheels, or as artists, like powerful springs. If we only consider them as virtuous or vicious, our lost illusions will enchain us in gloomy thoughts, and we will find in man only weakness and ugliness. This is why Trackeray depreciates our whole nature. He does, as a novelist, what Hobbes does as a philosopher. Almost everywhere, when he describes fine sentiments, he derives them from an ugly source. Tenderness, kindness, love, are in his characters the effect of the nerves, of instinct, or of a moral disease. Amelia Sedley, his favorite, and one of his master-pieces, is a poor little woman, snivelling, incapable of reflection and decision, blind, a superstitious adorer of a coarse and selfish husband, always sacrificed by her own will and fault, whose love is made up of folly and weakness, often unjust, accustomed to see falsely, and more worthy of compassion than respect. Lady Castlewood, so good and tender, is enamoured, like Amelia, of a drunken and imbecile boor; and her wild jealousy, exasperated on the slightest suspicion, implacable against her husband, giving utterance violently to cruel words, shows that her love springs not from virtue but from mood. Helen Pendennis, a model mother, is a somewhat silly country prude, of narrow education, jealous also, and having in her jealousy all the harshness of Puritanism and passion. She faints on learning that her son has a mistress: it is "such a sin, such a dreadful sin. I can't bear to think that my boy should commit such a crime. I wish he had died, almost, before he had done it."[276] Whenever she is spoken to of little Fanny, "the widow's countenance, always soft and gentle, assumed a cruel and inexorable expression."[277]
Meeting Fanny at the bedside of the sick young man, she drives her away, as if she were a prostitute and a servant. Maternal love, in her as in the others, is an incurable blindness: her son is her idol; in her adoration she finds the means of making his lot unbearable, and himself unhappy. As to the love of the men for the women, if we judge from the pictures of the author, we can but feel pity for it, and look on it as ridiculous. At a certain age, according to Thackeray, nature speaks: we meet Somebody; a fool or not, good or bad, we adore her; it is a fever. At the age of six months dogs have their disease; man has his at twenty. If a man loves, it is not because the lady is lovable, but

because it is his nature so to do. "Do you suppose you would drink if you were not thirsty, or eat if you were not hungry?"[278]

He relates the history of this hunger and thirst with a bitter vigor. He seems like an intoxicated man grown sober, railing at drunkenness. He explains at length, in a half-sarcastic tone, the follies which Major Dobbin commits for the sake of Amelia; how the Major buys bad wines from her father; how he tells the postilions to make haste, how he rouses the servants, persecutes his friends, to see Amelia more quickly; how, after ten years of sacrifice, tenderness, and service, he sees that he is held second to an old portrait of a faithless, coarse, selfish, and dead husband. The saddest of these accounts is that of the first love of Pendennis— Miss Fotheringay, the actress, whom he loves, a matter-of-fact person, a good housekeeper, who has the mind and education of a kitchen-maid. She speaks to the young man of the fine weather, and the pie she has just been making: Pendennis discovers in these two phrases a wonderful depth of intellect and a superhuman majesty of devotion. He asks Miss Fotheringay, who has just been playing Ophelia, if the latter loved Hamlet. Miss Fotheringay answers:

"'In love with such a little ojous wretch as that stunted manager of a Bingley?' She bristled with indignation at the thought. Pen explained it was not of her he spoke, but of Ophelia of the play. 'Oh, indeed; if no offence was meant, none was taken: but as for Bingley, indeed, she did not value him— not that glass of punch.' Pen next tried her on Kotzebue. 'Kotzebue? who was he? The author of the play in which she had been performing so admirably. She did not know that— the man's name at the beginning of the book was Thompson,' she said. Pen laughed at her adorable simplicity."

"'How beautiful she is,' thought Pen, cantering homewards. 'Pendennis, Pendennis— how she spoke the word! Emily, Emily! how good, how noble, how beautiful, how perfect she is!'"[279]

The first volume runs wholly upon this contrast; it seems as though Thackeray says to his reader: "My dear brothers in humanity, we are rascals forty-nine days in fifty; in the fiftieth, if we escape pride, vanity, wickedness, selfishness, it is because we fall into a hot fever; our folly causes our devotion."

Section VI.—His Characters

Yet, short of being Swift, a man must love something; he cannot always be wounding and destroying; and the heart, wearied of scorn and hate, needs repose in praise and tenderness. Moreover, to blame a fault is to laud the contrary quality; and a man cannot sacrifice a victim without raising an altar: it is circumstance which fixes on the one, and which builds up the other; and the moralist who combats the dominant vice of his country and his age, preaches the virtue contrary to the vice of his age and his country. In an aristocratical and commercial society, this vice is selfishness and pride!

Thackeray therefore extols sweetness and tenderness. Let love and kindness be blind, instinctive, unreasoning, ridiculous, it matters little: such as they are, he adores them; and there is no more singular contrast than that of his heroes and of his admiration. He creates foolish women, and kneels before them; the artist within him contradicts the commentator: the first is ironical, the second laudatory; the first represents the pettiness of love, the second writes its panegyric; the top of a page is a satire in action, the bottom is a dithyramb in periods. The compliments which he lavishes on Amelia Sedley, Helen Pendennis, Laura, are infinite; no author ever more visibly and incessantly paid court to his female creations; he sacrifices his male creations to them, not once, but a hundred times:

"Very likely female pelicans like so to bleed under the selfish little beaks of their young ones: it is certain that women do. There must be some sort of pleasure which we men don't understand, which accompanies the pain of being sacrificed.[280]... Do not let us men despise these instincts because we cannot feel them. These women were made for our comfort and delectation, gentlemen— with all the rest of the minor animals.[281]... Be it for a reckless husband, a dissipated son, a darling scapegrace of a brother, how ready their hearts are to pour out their best treasures for the benefit of the cherished person; and what a deal of this sort of enjoyment are we on our side, ready to give the soft creatures! There is scarce a man that reads this, but has administered pleasure in that fashion to his womankind, and has treated them to the luxury of forgiving him."[282]

When he enters the room of a good mother, or of a young honest girl, he casts down his eyes as on the threshold of a sanctuary. In the presence of Laura resigned, pious, he checks himself:

"And as that duty was performed quite noiselessly— while the supplications which endowed her with the requisite strength for fulfilling it, also took place in her own chamber, away from all mortal sight— we, too, must be perforce silent about these virtues of hers, which no more bear public talking about than a flower will bear to bloom in a ballroom."[283]

Like Dickens, he has a reverence for the family, for tender and simple sentiments, calm and pure contentments, such as are relished by the fireside between a child and a wife. When this misanthrope, so reflective and harsh, lights upon a filial effusion or a maternal grief, he is wounded in a sensitive place, and, like Dickens, he makes us weep.[284]

We have enemies because we have friends, and aversions because we have preferences. If we prefer devoted kindliness and tender affections, we dislike arrogance and harshness; the cause of love is also the cause of hate; and sarcasm, like sympathy, is the criticism of a social form and a public vice. This is why Thackeray's novels are a war against aristocracy. Like Rousseau, he praised simple and affectionate manners; like Rousseau, he hated the distinction of ranks.

He wrote a whole book on this, a sort of moral and half political pamphlet, the "Book of Snobs." The word does not exist in France, because they have not the thing. The snob is a child of aristocratical societies; perched on his step of the long ladder, he respects the man on the step above him, and despises the man on the step below, without inquiring what they are worth, solely on account of their position; in his innermost heart he finds it natural to kiss the boots of the first, and to kick the second. Thackeray reckons up at length the degrees of this habit. Hear his conclusion:

"I can bear it no longer— this diabolical invention of gentility, which kills natural kindliness and honest friendship. Proper pride, indeed! Rank and precedence, forsooth! The table of ranks and degrees is a lie and should he flung into the fire. Organize rank and precedence! that was well for the masters of ceremonies of former ages. Come forward, some great marshal, and organize Equality in society."

Then he adds, with common-sense, altogether English bitterness and familiarity:

"If ever our cousins the Smigsmags asked me to meet Lord Longears, I would like to take an opportunity after dinner, and say, in the most good-natured way in the world:— Sir, Fortune makes you a present of a number of thousand pounds every year. The ineffable wisdom of our ancestors has placed you as a chief and hereditary legislator over me. Our admirable Constitution (the pride of Britons and envy of surrounding nations) obliges me to receive you as my senator, superior, and guardian. Your eldest son, Fitz-Heehaw, is sure of a place in Parliament; your younger sons, the De Brays, will kindly condescend to be post-captains and lieutenant-colonels, and to represent us in foreign courts, or to take a good living when it falls convenient. These prizes our admirable Constitution (the pride and envy of, etc.) pronounces to be your due; without count of your dulness, your vices, your selfishness; of your entire incapacity and folly. Dull as you may be (and we have as good a right to assume that my lord is an ass, as the other proposition, that he is an enlightened patriot);— dull, I say, as you may be, no one will accuse you of such monstrous folly, as to suppose that you are indifferent to the good luck which you possess, or have any inclination to part with it. No— and patriots as we are, under happier circumstances, Smith and I, I have no doubt, were we dukes ourselves, would stand by our order.

"We would submit good-naturedly to sit in a high place. We would acquiesce in that admirable Constitution (pride and envy of, etc.) which made us chiefs and the world our inferiors; we would not cavil particularly at that notion of hereditary superiority which brought so many simple people cringing to our knees. May be we would rally round the Corn-Laws; we would make a stand against the Reform Bill; we would die rather than repeal the acts against Catholics and Dissenters; we would, by our noble system of class-legislation, bring Ireland to its present admirable condition.

"But Smith and I are not Earls as yet. We don't believe that it is for the interest of Smith's army, that young De Bray should be a Colonel at five-and-twenty, of Smith's diplomatic relations, that Lord Longears should go ambassador to Constantinople— of our politics, that Longears should put his hereditary foot into them.

"This booing and cringing, Smith believes to be the act of Snobs; and he will do all in his might and main to be a Snob, and to submit to Snobs no longer. To Longears he says, 'We can't help seeing, Longears, that we are as good as you. We can spell even better; we can think quite as rightly; we will not have you for our master, or black your shoes any more.'"[285]

Thackeray's opinion on politics only continues his remarks as a moralist. If he hates aristocracy, it is less because it oppresses man than because it corrupts him; in deforming social life, it deforms private life; in establishing injustice, it establishes vice; after having made itself master of the government, it poisons the soul; and Thackeray finds its trace in the perversity and foolishness of all classes and all sentiments.

The king opens this list of vengeful portraits. It is George IV, "the first gentleman in Europe." This great monarch, so justly regretted, could cut out a coat, drive a four-in-hand nearly as well as the Brighton coachman, and play the fiddle well. "In the vigour of youth and the prime force of his invention, he invented Maraschino punch, a shoe-buckle, and a Chinese pavilion, the most hideous building in the world:"

"Two boys had leave from their loyal masters to go from Slaughter House School where they were educated, and to appear on Drury Lane stage, amongst a crowd which assembled there to greet the king. The king? There he was. Beef-eaters were before the august box: the Marquis of Steyne (Lord of the Powder Closet) and other great officers of state were behind the chair on which he sate, He sate— florid of face, portly of person, covered with orders, and in a rich curling head of hair— How we sang God save him! How the house rocked and shouted with that magnificent music. How they cheered, and cried, and waved handkerchiefs. Ladies wept: mothers clasped their children: some fainted with emotion.... Yes, we saw him. Fate cannot deprive us of that. Others have seen Napoleon. Some few still exist who have beheld Frederick the Great, Doctor Johnson, Marie Antoinette, etc.— be it our reasonable boast to our children, that we saw George the Good, the Magnificent, the Great."[286]

Dear prince! the virtues emanating from his heroic throne spread through the hearts of all his courtiers. Whoever presented a better example than the Marquis of Steyne? This lord, a king in his own house, tried to prove that he was so. He forces his wife to sit at table beside women without any character, his mistresses. Like a true prince, he had for his special enemy his eldest son, presumptive heir to the marquisate, whom he leaves to starve, and compels to run into debt. He is now making love to a charming person, Mrs. Rebecca

Crawley, whom he loves for her hypocrisy, coolness, and unequalled insensibility. The Marquis, by dint of debasing and oppressing all who surround him, ends by hating and despising men; he has no taste for anything but perfect rascalities. Rebecca rouses him; one day even she transports him with enthusiasm. She plays Clytemnestra in a charade, and her husband Agamemnon; she advances to the bed, a dagger in her hand; her eyes are lighted up with a smile so ghastly that people quake as they look at her; Brava! brava! old Steyne's strident voice was heard roaring over all the rest, "By— —, she'd do it too!" We can hear that he has the true conjugal feeling. His conversation is remarkably frank. "I can't send Briggs away," Becky said.— "You owe her her wages, I suppose," said the peer.— "Worse than that, I have ruined her."— "Ruined her? then why don't you turn her out?"

He is, moreover, an accomplished gentleman, of fascinating sweetness; he treats his women like a pacha, and his words are like blows. Let us read again the domestic scene in which he gives the order to invite Mrs. Crawley. Lady Gaunt, his daughter-in-law, says that she will not be present at dinner, and will go home. His lordship answered:

"I wish you would, and stay there. You will find the bailiffs at Bareacres very pleasant company, and I shall be freed from lending money to your relations, and from your own damned tragedy airs. Who are you to give orders here? You have no money. You've got no brains. You were here to have children, and you have not had any. Gaunt's tired of you; and George's wife is the only person in the family who doesn't wish you were dead. Gaunt would marry again if you were. ... You, forsooth, must give yourself airs of virtue.... Pray, madame, shall I tell you some little anecdotes about my Lady Bareacres, your mamma?"[287]

The rest is in the same style. His daughters-in-law, driven to despair, say they wish they were dead. This declaration rejoices him, and he concludes with these words; "This Temple of Virtue belongs to me. And if I invite all Newgate or all Bedlam here, by— —, they shall be welcome." The habit of despotism makes despots, and the best means of implanting despots in families is to preserve nobles in the State.

Let us take rest in the contemplation of the country gentleman. The innocence of the fields, hereditary respect, family traditions, the pursuit of agriculture, the exercise of local magistracy, must have produced these upright and sensible men, full of kindness and probity, protectors of their county, and servants of their country. Sir Pitt Crawley is a model; he has four thousand a year and two parliamentary boroughs. It is true that these are rotten boroughs, and that he sells the second for fifteen hundred a year. He is an excellent steward, and shears his farmers so close that he can only find bankrupt-tenants. A coach proprietor, a government contractor, a mine proprietor, he pays his subordinates so badly, and is so niggard in outlay, that his mines "are filled with water; and as for his coach-horses, every mail proprietor in the kingdom knew that he lost more horses than any man in the country"; the Government flung his contract of damaged beef upon his hands. A popular man, he always prefers the society of a horse-dealer to the company of a gentleman. "He was fond of drink, of swearing, of joking with the farmers' daughters;... would cut his joke and drink his glass with a tenant, and sell him up the next day; or have his laugh with the poacher he was transporting, with equal good humour." He speaks with a country accent, has the mind of a lackey, the habits of a boor. At table, waited on by three men and a butler, on massive silver, he inquires into the dishes, and the beasts which have furnished them. "What *ship* was it, Horrocks, and when did you kill? One of the black-faced Scotch, Sir Pitt: we killed on Thursday. Who took any? Steel of Mudbury took the saddle and two legs, Sir Pitt; but he says the last was too young and confounded woolly, Sir Pitt. What became of the shoulders?" The dialogue goes on in the same tone; after the Scotch mutton comes the Black Kentish pig: these animals might be Sir Pitt's family, so much is he interested in them. As for his daughters, he lets them stray to the gardener's cottage, where they pick up their education. As for his wife, he beats her from time to time. If he pays his people one farthing more than he owes them he asks it back. "A farthing a day is seven shillings a year; seven shillings a year is the interest of seven guineas. Take care of your farthings, old Tinker, and your guineas will come quite natural. He never gave away a farthing in his life," growled Tinker. "Never, and never will: it is against my principle." He is impudent, brutal, coarse, stingy, shrewd, extravagant; but is courted by ministers, is a high-sheriff, honored, powerful, he rolls in a gilded carriage, and is one of the pillars of the State.

These are the rich; probably money has corrupted them. Let us look for a poor aristocrat, free from temptations; his lofty mind, left to itself, will display all its native beauty. Sir Francis Clavering is in this case. He has played, drunk, and supped until he has nothing more left. Transactions at the gambling-table speedily effected his ruin; he had been forced to sell out of his regiment; had shown the white feather, and after frequenting all the billiard-rooms in Europe, been thrown into prison by his uncourteous creditors. To get out he married a good-natured Indian widow, who outrages spelling, and whose money was left her by her father, a disreputable old lawyer and indigo-smuggler. Clavering ruins her, goes on his knees to obtain gold and pardon, swears on the Bible to contract no more debts, and when he goes out runs straight to the money-lender. Of all the rascals that novelists have ever exhibited, he is the basest. He has neither resolution nor common-sense; he is simply a man in a state of dissolution. He swallows insults like water, weeps, begs pardon, and begins again. He debases himself, prostrates himself, and the next moment swears and storms, to fall back into the depths of the extremest cowardice. He implores, threatens, and in the same quarter of an hour accepts the threatened man as his intimate confidant and friend:

"Now, ain't it hard that she won't trust me with a single tea-spoon; ain't it ungentlemanlike, Altamont? You know my lady's of low birth— that is— I beg your pardon— hem— that is, it's most cruel of her not to show more confidence in me. And the very servants begin to laugh— the dam scoundrels!... They don't answer my bell; and— and my man was at Vauxhall last night with one of my dress shirts and my velvet waistcoat on, I know it was mine— the confounded impudent blackguard!— and he went on dancing before my eyes, confound him! I'm sure he'll live to be hanged— he deserves to be hanged— all those infernal rascals of valets!"[288]

His conversation is a compound of oaths, whines, and ravings; he is not a man, but the wreck of a man: there survive in him but the discordant remains of vile passions, like the fragments of a crushed snake, which, unable to bite, bruise themselves and wriggle about in their slaver and mud. The sight of a banknote makes him launch blindly into a mass of entreaties and lies. The future has disappeared for him, he sees but the present. He will sign a bill for twenty pounds at three months to get a sovereign. His degradation has become imbecility; his eyes are shut; he does not see that his protestations excite mistrust, that his lies excite disgust, that by his very baseness he loses the fruit of his baseness; so that when he comes in, a man feels a violent inclination to take the honorable baronet, the member of Parliament, the proud inhabitant of a historic house, by the neck, and pitch him, like a basket of rubbish, from the top of the stairs to the bottom.

We must stop. A volume would not exhaust the list of perfections which Thackeray discovers in the English aristocracy. The Marquis of Farintosh, twenty-fifth of his name, an illustrious fool, healthy and full of self-conceit, whom all the women ogle and all the men bow to; Lady Kew, an old woman of the world, tyrannical and corrupted, at enmity with her daughter, and a match-maker; Sir Barnes Newcome, one of the most cowardly of men, the wickedest, the falsest, the best-abused and beaten who has ever smiled in a drawing-room or spoken in Parliament. I see only one estimable character, and he is not in the front rank— Lord Kew, who, after many follies and excesses, is touched by his Puritan old mother, and repents. But these portraits are sweet, compared to the dissertations; the commentator is still more bitter than the artist; he wounds more in speaking than in making his personages speak. We must read his biting diatribes against marriages for the sake of money or rank, and against the sacrifice of girls; against the inequality of inheritance and the envy of younger sons; against the education of the nobles, and their traditional insolence; against the purchase of commissions in the army, the isolation of classes, the outrages on nature and family, invented by society and law. Behind this philosophy is shown a second gallery of portraits as insulting as the first: for inequality, having corrupted the great men whom it exalts, corrupts the small men whom it degrades; and the spectacle of envy or baseness in the small, is as ugly as that of insolence or despotism in the great. According to Thackeray, English society is a compound of flatteries and intrigues, each striving to hoist himself up a step higher on the social ladder and to push back those who are climbing. To be received at court, to see one's name in the papers amongst a list of illustrious guests, to give a cup of tea at home to some stupid and bloated peer; such is the supreme limit of human ambition and felicity. For one master there are always a hundred lackeys. Major Pendennis, a resolute man, cool and clever, has contracted this leprosy. His happiness to-day is to bow to a lord. He is only at peace in a drawing-room, or in a park of the aristocracy. He craves to be treated with that humiliating condescension wherewith the great overwhelm their inferiors. He pockets lack of attention with ease, and dines graciously at a noble board, where he is invited twice in three years, to stop a gap. He leaves a man of genius or a woman of wit to converse with a titled fool or a tipsy lord. He prefers being tolerated at a Marquis's to being respected at a commoner's. Having exalted these fine dispositions into principles, he inculcates them on his nephew, whom he loves, and to push him on in the world offers him in marriage a basely acquired fortune and the daughter of a convict. Others glide through the proud drawing-rooms, not with parasitic manners, but on account of their splendid balance at the banker's. Once upon a time in France the nobles manured their estates with the money of citizens; now, in England, the citizens ennoble their money by marrying a lady of noble birth. For a hundred thousand pounds to the father, Pump, the merchant, marries Lady Blanche Stiffneck, who, though married, remains my Lady. Naturally young Pump is scorned by her, as a tradesman, and moreover, hated for having made her half a woman of the people. He dare not see his own friends in his own house; they are too vulgar for his wife. He dare not visit the friends of his wife; they are too high for him. He is his wife's butler, the butt of his father-in-law, the servant of his son, and consoles himself by thinking that his grandsons, when they become Lord Pump, will blush for him and never mention his name.[289] A third means of entering the aristocracy is to ruin one's self, and never see anyone. This ingenious method is employed by Mrs. Major Ponto in the country. She has an incomparable governess for her daughters, who thinks that Dante is called Alighieri because he was born at Algiers, but who has educated two marchionesses and a countess.

"Some one wondered we were not enlivened by the appearance of some of the neighbours.— We can't in our position of life, we can't well associate with the attorney's family, as I leave you to suppose— and the Doctor— one may ask one's medical man to one's table, certainly: but his family.— The people in that large red house just outside of the town.— What! the *château-calicot*. That purse-proud ex-linendraper.— The parson— Oh! he used to preach in a surplice. He is a Puseyite!"

This sensible Ponto family yawns in solitude for six months, and the rest of the year enjoys the gluttony of the country squires whom they regale, and the rebuffs of the great lords whom they visit. The son, an officer of the hussars, requires to be kept in luxury so as to be on an equality with his noble comrades, and his tailor receives above three hundred a year out of the nine hundred which make up the whole family income.[290] I should never end, if I recounted all the villainies and miseries which Thackeray attributes to the aristocratic spirit, the division of families, the pride of the ennobled sister, the jealousy of the sister who has not been ennobled, the degradation of the characters trained up from school to reverence the little lords, the abasement of the daughters who strive to compass noble marriages, the rage of snubbed vanity, the meanness of the attentions offered, the triumph of folly, the scorn of talent, the consecrated injustice, the heart rendered unnatural, the morals perverted. Before this striking picture of truth and genius, we need remember that this injurious inequality is the cause of a wholesome liberty, that social injustice produces political welfare, that a class of hereditary nobles is a class of hereditary statesmen, that in a century and a half England has had a hundred and fifty years of good government, that in a century and a half France has had a hundred and fifty years of bad government, that all is compensated, and that it is possible to pay dearly for capable leaders, a consistent policy, free elections, and the control of the government by the nation. We must also remember that this talent, founded on intense reflection, concentrated in moral prejudices, could not but have transformed the picture of manners into a systematic and combative satire, exasperate satire into calculated and implacable animosity, blacken human nature, and attack again and again with studied, redoubled, and natural hatred, the chief vice of his country and of his time.

Part II.—The Artist

Section I—The Art of Thackeray

In literature as well as in politics, we cannot have everything. Talents, like happiness, do not always follow suit. Whatever constitution it selects, a people is always half unhappy; whatever genius he has, a writer is always half impotent. We cannot preserve at once more than a single attitude. To transform the novel is to deform it; he who, like Thackeray, gives to the novel satire for its object, ceases to give it art for its rule, and the complete strength of the satirist is the weakness of the novelist.

What is a novelist? In my opinion he is a psychologist, who naturally and involuntarily sets psychology at work; he is nothing else, nor more. He loves to picture feelings, to perceive their connections, their precedents, their consequences; and he indulges in this pleasure. In his eyes they are forces, having various directions and magnitudes. About their justice or injustice he troubles himself little. He introduces them in characters, conceives the dominant quality, perceives the traces which this leaves on the others, marks the discordant or harmonious influences of temperament, of education, of occupation, and labors to manifest the invisible world of inward inclinations and dispositions by the visible world of outward words and actions. To this is his labor reduced. Whatever these bents are, he cares little. A genuine painter sees with pleasure a well-shaped arm and vigorous muscles, even if they be employed in knocking down a man. A genuine novelist enjoys the contemplation of the greatness of a harmful sentiment, or the organized mechanism of a pernicious character. He has sympathy with talent, because it is the only faculty which exactly copies nature; occupied in experiencing the emotions of his personages, he only dreams of marking their vigor, kind, and mutual action. He represents them to us as they are, whole, not blaming, not punishing, not mutilating them; he transfers them to us intact and separate, and leaves to us the right of judging, if we desire it. His whole effort is to make them visible, to unravel the types darkened and altered by the accidents and imperfections of real life, to set in relief grand human passions, to be shaken by the greatness of the beings whom he animates, to raise us out of ourselves by the force of his creations. We recognize art in this creative power, impartial and universal as nature, freer and more potent than nature, taking up the rough-drawn or disfigured work of its rival in order to correct its faults and give effect to its conceptions.

All is changed by the intervention of satire; and more particularly, the part of the author. When, in an ordinary novel, he speaks in his own name, it is to explain a sentiment or mark the cause of a faculty; in a satirical novel it is to give us moral advice. It has been seen to how many lessons Thackeray subjects us. That they are good ones, no one disputes; but at least they take the place of useful explanations. A third of a volume, being occupied by warnings, is lost to art. Summoned to reflect on our faults, we know the character less. The author designedly neglects a hundred delicate shades which he might have discovered and shown to us. The character, less complete, is less lifelike; the interest, less concentrated, is less lively. Turned away from it, instead of brought back to it, our eyes wander and forget it; instead of being absorbed, we are absent in mind. And, what is worse, we end by experiencing some degree of weariness. We judge these sermons true, but repeated till we are sick of them, we fancy ourselves listening to college lectures, or handbooks for the use of young priests. We find similar things in books with gilt edges and pictured covers, given as Christmas presents to children. Are we much rejoiced to learn that marriages for the sake of money or rank have their inconvenience, that in the absence of a friend we readily speak evil of him, that a son often afflicts his mother by his irregularities, that selfishness is an ugly fault? All this is true; but it is too true. We listen in order to hear new things. These old moralities, though useful and well spoken, smack of the paid pedant, so common in England, the clergyman in white tie, standing bolt upright in his room, and droning, for three hundred a year, daily admonition to the young gentlemen whom parents have sent to his educational hot-house.

This regular presence of a moral intention spoils the novel as well as the novelist. It must be confessed, a volume of Thackeray has the cruel misfortune of recalling the novels of Miss Edgeworth or the stories of Canon Schmidt. Here is one which shows us Pendennis proud, extravagant, harebrained, lazy, shamefully plucked at his examination; whilst his companions, less intellectual but more studious, take high places in honors, or pass with decent credit. This edifying contrast does not warn us; we do not wish to go back to school; we shut the book, and recommend it, like medicine, to our little cousin. Other puerilities, less shocking, end in wearying us just as much. We do not like the prolonged contrast between good Colonel Newcome and his wicked relatives. The Colonel gives money and cakes to every child, money and shawls to all his cousins, money and kind words to all the servants; and these people only answer him with coldness and coarseness. It is clear, from the first page, that the author would persuade us to be affable, and we kick against the too matter-of-course invitation; we don't want to be scolded in a novel; we are in a bad humor with this invasion of pedagogy. We wanted to go to the theatre; we have been taken in by the outside bill, and we growl *sotto voce* to find ourselves at a sermon.

Let us console ourselves: the characters suffer as much as we; the author spoils them in preaching to us; they like us, are sacrificed to satire. He does not animate beings, he lets puppets act. He only combines their actions to make them ridiculous, odious, or disappointing. After a few scenes we recognize the spring, and thenceforth we are always foreseeing when it is going to act. This foresight deprives the character of half its truth, and the reader of half his illusion. Perfect fooleries, complete mischances, unmitigated wickednesses, are rare things. The events and feelings of real life are not so arranged as to make such calculated contrasts and such clever combinations. Nature does not invent these dramatic effects: we soon see that we are before the foot-lights, in front of bedizened actors, whose words are written for them, and their gestures arranged.

To bring before our mind exactly this alteration of truth and art, we must compare two characters step by step. There is a personage, unanimously recognized as Thackeray's masterpiece, Becky Sharp, an intriguante and a bad character, but a superior and well-mannered woman. Let us compare her to a similar personage of Balzac, in "Les Parents Pauvres," Valérie Marneffe. The difference of the two works will exhibit the difference of the two literatures. As the English excel as moralists and satirists, so the French excel as artists and novel-writers.

Balzac loves his Valérie; this is why he explains and magnifies her. He does not labor to make her odious, but intelligible. He gives her the education of a prostitute, a "husband as depraved as a prison full of galley-slaves," luxurious habits, recklessness, prodigality, womanly nerves, a pretty woman's dislikes, an artist's rapture. Thus born and bred, her corruption is natural. She needs elegance, as she needs air. She takes it, no matter whence, remorselessly, as we drink water from the first stream. She is not worse than her profession: she has all its innate and acquired excuses, of mood, tradition, circumstance, necessity; she has all its powers, abandon, charms, mad gayety, alternations of triviality and elegance, sudden audacity, comical devices, magnificence and success. She is perfect of her kind, like a proud and dangerous horse, which we admire while we fear it. Balzac delights to paint her only for the sake of his picture. He dresses her, lays on for her her patches, arranges her garments, trembles before her dancing-girl's motions. He details her gestures with as much pleasure and truth as if he were her waiting-woman. His artistic curiosity is fed on the least traits of character and manners. After a violent scene, he pauses at a spare moment, and shows her idle, stretched on her couch like a cat, yawning and basking in the sun. Like a physiologist, he knows that the nerves of the beast of prey are softened, and that it only ceases to bound in order to sleep. But what bounds! She dazzles, fascinates; she defends herself successively against three proved accusations, refutes evidence, alternately humiliates and glorifies herself, rails, adores, demonstrates, changing a score of times her voice, her ideas, tricks, and all this in one quarter of an hour. An old shopkeeper, protected against emotions by trade and avarice, trembles at her speech: "She sets her feet on my heart, crushes me, stuns me. Ah, what a woman! When she looks cold at me, it is worse than a stomach-ache.... How she tripped down the steps, making them bright with her looks!" Everywhere passion, force, atrocity, conceal the ugliness and corruption. Attacked in her fortune by a respectable woman, Mme. Marneffe gets up an incomparable comedy, played with a great poet's eloquence and exaltation, and broken suddenly by the burst of laughter and coarse triviality of a porter's daughter on the stage. Style and action are raised to the height of an epic. "When the words 'Hulot and two hundred thousand francs' were mentioned, Valérie gave a passing look from between her two long eyelids, like the glare of a cannon through its smoke." A little further, caught in the act by one of her lovers, a Brazilian, and quite capable of killing her, she blenched for an instant; but recovering the same moment, she checked her tears. "She came to him, and looked so fiercely that her eyes glittered like daggers." Danger roused and inspired her, and her excited nerves propel genius and courage to her brain. To complete the picture of this impetuous nature, superior and unstable, Balzac at the last moment makes her repent. To proportion her fortune to her vice, he leads her triumphantly through the ruin, death, or despair of twenty people, and shatters her in the supreme moment by a fall as terrible as her success.

Before such passion and logic, what is Becky Sharp? A calculating plotter, cool in temperament, full of common-sense, an ex-governess, having parsimonious habits, a genuine woman of business, always proper, always active, unsexed, void of the voluptuous softness and diabolical transport which can give brilliancy to her character and charm to her profession. She is not a prostitute, but a petticoated and heartless barrister. Nothing is more fit to inspire aversion. The author loses no opportunity of expressing his own; through two-thirds of the book he pursues her with sarcasms and misfortunes; he puts only false words, perfidious actions, revolting sentiments, in her mouth. From her coming on the stage, at the age of seventeen, treated with rare kindness by a simple-minded family, she lies from morning to night, and by coarse expedients tries to fish there for a husband. The better to crush her, Thackeray himself sets forth all this baseness, these lies, and indecencies. Rebecca ever so gently presses the hand of fat Joseph: "It was an advance, and as such, perhaps some ladies of indisputable correctness and gentility will condemn the action as immodest; but, you see, poor dear Rebecca had all this work to do for herself. If a person is too poor to keep a servant, though ever so elegant, he must sweep his own rooms: if a dear girl has no dear mamma to settle matters with the young man, she must do it for herself."[291] Whilst Becky was a governess at Sir Pitt Crawley's, she gains the friendship of her pupils, by reading to them the tales of Crébillon the younger, and of Voltaire. She writes to her friend Amelia: "The rector's wife paid me a score of compliments about the progress my pupils made, and thought, no doubt, to touch my heart— poor, simple, country soul! as if I cared a fig about my pupils."[292] This phrase is an imprudence hardly natural in so careful a person, and the author adds it gratuitously to her part, to make it odious. A little further Rebecca is grossly adulatory and mean to old Miss

Crawley; and her pompous periods, manifestly false, instead of exciting admiration, raise disgust. She is selfish and lying to her husband, and knowing that he is on the field of battle, busies herself only in getting together a little purse. Thackeray designedly dwells on the contrast: the heavy dragoon "went through the various items of his little catalogue of effects, striving to see how they might be turned into money for his wife's benefit, in case any accident should befall him. Faithful to his plan of economy, the captain dressed himself in his oldest and shabbiest uniform" to get killed in:

"And this famous dandy of Windsor and Hyde Park went off on his campaign... with something like a prayer on the lips for the woman he was leaving. He took her up from the ground, and held her in his arms for a minute, tight pressed against his strong beating heart.. His face was purple and his eyes dim, as he put her down and left her.... And Rebecca, as we have said, wisely determined not to give way to unavailing sentimentality on her husband's departure.... 'What a fright I seem,' she said, examining herself in the glass, 'and how pale this pink makes one look.' So she divested herself of this pink raiment;... then she put her bouquet of the ball into a glass of water, and went to bed, and slept very comfortably."[293]

From these examples, judge of the rest. Thackeray's whole business is to degrade Rebecca Sharp. He convicts her of being harsh to her son, robbing tradesmen, deceiving everybody. And after all, he makes her a dupe; whatever she does, comes to nothing. Compromised by the advances which she has lavished on foolish Joseph, she momentarily expects an offer of marriage. A letter comes, announcing that he has gone to Scotland, and presents his compliments to Miss Rebecca. Three months later she secretly marries Captain Rawdon, a poor dolt. Sir Pitt Crawley, Rawdon's father, throws himself at her feet, with four thousand a year, and offers her his hand. In her consternation she weeps despairingly. "Married, married, married already!" is her cry; and it is enough to pierce sensitive souls. Later, she tries to win her sister-in-law by passing for a good mother. "Why do you kiss me here?" asks her son; "you never kiss me at home." The consequence is, complete discredit; once more she is lost. The Marquis of Steyne, her lover, presents her to society, loads her with jewels, banknotes, and has her husband appointed to some island in the East. The husband enters at the wrong moment, knocks my lord down, restores the diamonds, and drives her away. Wandering on the Continent, she tries five or six times to grow rich and appear honest. Always, at the moment of success, accident brings her to the ground. Thackeray sports with her as a child with a cockchafer, letting her hoist herself painfully to the top of the ladder, in order to pluck her down by the foot and make her tumble disgracefully. He ends by dragging her through taverns and greenrooms, and pointing his finger at her from a distance, as a gamester, a drunkard: is unwilling to touch her further. On the last page he installs her vulgarly in a small fortune, plundered by doubtful devices, and leaves her in bad odor, uselessly hypocritical, abandoned to the shadiest society. Beneath this storm of irony and contempt, the heroine is dwarfed, illusion is weakened, interest diminished, art attenuated, poetry disappears, and the character, more useful, has become less true and beautiful.

Section II.—Portrait of Henry Esmond.—Historical Talent

Suppose that a happy chance lays aside these causes of weakness, and keeps open these sources of talent. Amongst all these transformed novels appears a single genuine one, elevated, touching, simple, original: the history of Henry Esmond. Thackeray has not written a less popular nor a more beautiful story.

This book comprises the fictitious memoirs of Colonel Esmond, a contemporary of Queen Anne, who, after a troubled life in Europe, retired with his wife to Virginia, and became a planter there. Esmond speaks; and the necessity of adapting the tone to the character suppresses the satirical style, the reiterated irony, the bitter sarcasm, the scenes contrived to ridicule folly, the events combined to crush vice. Thenceforth we enter the real world; we let illusion guide us, we rejoice in a varied spectacle, easily unfolded, without moral intention. We are no more harassed by personal advice; we remain in our place, calm, sure, no actor's finger pointed at us to warn us at an interesting moment that the piece is played on our account, and to do us good. At the same time, and unconsciously, we are at ease. Quitting bitter satire, pure narration charms us; we take rest from hating. We are like an army surgeon, who, after a day of fights and manœuvres, sits on a hillock and beholds the motion in the camp, the procession of carriages, and the distant horizon softened by the sombre tints of evening.

On the other hand, the long reflections, which seem vulgar and out of place under the pen of the writer, become natural and interesting in the mouth of the chief character in this novel. Esmond is an old man, writing for his children, and remarking upon his experience. He has a right to judge life; his maxims are suitable to his years: having passed into sketches of manners, they lose their pedantic air; we hear them complacently, and perceive, as we turn the page, the calm and sad smile which has dictated them.

With the reflections we endure the details. Elsewhere, the minute descriptions appear frequently puerile; we blamed the author for dwelling, with the preciseness of an English painter, on school adventures, coach scenes, inn episodes; we thought that this intense studiousness, unable, to grasp lofty themes of art, was compelled to stoop to microscopical observations and photographic details. Here, everything is changed. A writer of memoirs has a right to record his childish impressions. His distant recollections, mutilated remnants of a forgotten life, have a peculiar charm; we accompany him back to infancy. A Latin lesson, a soldier's march, a ride behind someone, become important events embellished by distance; we enjoy his peaceful and familiar pleasure, and feel with him a vast sweetness in seeing once more, with so much ease and in so clear a light, the well-known phantoms of the past. Minute detail adds to the interest in adding to the naturalness. Stories of campaign life, random opinions on the books and events of the time, a hundred petty scenes, a thousand petty facts, manifestly useless, are on that very account illusory. We forget the author, we listen to the old Colonel, we find ourselves carried back a hundred years, and we have the extreme pleasure, so uncommon, of believing in what we read.

Whilst the subject obviates the faults, or turns them into virtues, it offers for these virtues the very finest theme. A powerful reflection has decomposed and reproduced the manners of the time with a most astonishing fidelity. Thackeray knows Swift, Steele, Addison, St. John, Marlboro, as well as the most attentive and learned historian. He depicts their habits, household conversation, like Walter Scott himself; and, what Walter Scott could not do, he imitates their style so that we are deceived by it; and many of their authentic phrases, inwoven with the text, cannot be distinguished from it. This perfect imitation is not limited to a few select scenes, but pervades the whole volume. Colonel Esmond writes as people wrote in the year 1700. The feat, I was going to say the genius, is as great as the attempt of Paul Louis Courier, in imitating successfully the style of ancient Greece. The style of Esmond has the calmness, the exactness, the simplicity, the solidity of the classics. Our modern temerities, our prodigal imagery, our jostled figures, our habit of gesticulation, our striving for effect, all our bad literary customs have disappeared. Thackeray must have gone back to the primitive sense of words, discovered there forgotten shades of meaning, recomposed an obliterated state of intellect and a lost species of ideas, to make his copy approach so closely to the original. The imagination of Dickens himself would have failed in this. To attempt and accomplish this needed all the sagacity, calmness, and power of knowledge and meditation.

But the masterpiece of the work is the character of Esmond. Thackeray has endowed him with that tender kindliness, almost feminine, which he everywhere extols above all other human virtues, and that self-mastery which is the effect of habitual reflection. These are the finest qualities of his psychological armory; each by its contrast increases the value of the other. We see a hero, but original and new, English in his cool resolution, modern by the delicacy and sensibility of his heart.

Henry Esmond is a poor child, the supposed bastard of Lord Castlewood, brought up by his heirs. In the opening chapter we are touched by the modulated and noble emotion which we retain to the end of the work. Lady Castlewood, on her first visit to the castle, comes to him in the "book-room, or yellow gallery"; being informed by the house-keeper who the little boy is, she blushes and walks back; the next instant, touched by remorse, she returns:

"With a look of infinite pity and tenderness in her eyes, she took his hand again, placing her other fair hand on his head, and saying some words to him, which were so kind, and said in a voice so sweet, that the boy, who had never looked upon so much beauty before, felt as if the touch of a superior being or angel smote him down to the ground, and kissed the fair protecting hand as he knelt on one knee. To the very last hour of his life, Esmond remembered the lady as she then spoke and looked, the rings on her fair hands, the very scent of her robe, the beam of her eyes lighting up with surprise and kindness, her lips blooming in a smile, the sun making a golden halo round her hair.[294]... There seemed, as the boy thought, in every look or gesture of this fair creature, an angelical softness and bright pity— in motion or repose she seemed gracious alike; the tone of her voice, though she uttered words ever so trivial, gave him a pleasure that amounted almost to anguish. It cannot be called love, that a lad of twelve years of age, little more than a menial, felt for an exalted lady, his mistress; but it was worship."[295]

This noble and pure feeling is expanded by a series of devoted actions, related with extreme simplicity; in the least words, in the turn of a phrase, in a chance conversation, we perceive a great heart, passionately grateful, never tiring of doing a kindness, or a service, sympathizing, friendly, giving advice, defending the honor of the family and the fortune of the children. Twice Esmond interposed between Lord Castle wood and Mohun, the duellist; it was not his fault that the murderer's weapon did not reach his own breast. When Lord Castlewood on his death-bed revealed that Esmond was not a bastard, but that the title and fortune of Castlewood were lawfully his, the young man, without a word, burned the confession which would have rescued him from the poverty and humiliation in which he had so long pined. Insulted by the Lady Castlewood, sick of a wound received by his kinsman's side, accused of ingratitude and cowardice, he persisted in his silence with the justification in his hand: "And when the struggle was over in Harry's mind, a glow of righteous happiness filled it; and it was with grateful tears in his eyes that he returned thanks to God for that decision which he had been enabled to make."[296] Later, being in love, but sure not to marry if his birth remained under a cloud in the eyes of the world, having repaid his benefactress, whose son he had saved, entreated by her to resume the name which belonged to him, he smiled sweetly, and gravely replied:

"'It was settled twelve years since, by my dear lord's bedside,' says Colonel Esmond. 'The children must know nothing of this. Frank and his heirs after him must bear our name. 'Tis his rightfully; I have not even a proof of that marriage of my father and mother, though my poor lord, on His death-bed, told me that Father Holt had brought such a proof to Castlewood. I would not seek it when I was abroad. I went and looked at my poor mother's grave in her convent. What matter to her now? No court of law on earth, upon my mere word, would deprive my Lord Viscount and set me up. I am the head of the house, dear lady; but Frank is Viscount of Castlewood still. And rather than disturb him, I would turn monk, or disappear in America.'

"As he spoke so to his dearest mistress, for whom he would have been willing to give up his life, or to make any sacrifice any day, the fond creature flung herself down on her knees before him, and kissed both his hands in an outbreak of passionate love and gratitude, such as could not but melt his heart, and make him feel very proud and thankful that God had given him the power to show his love for her, and to prove it by some little sacrifice on his own part. To be able to bestow benefits or happiness on those one loves is sure the greatest blessing conferred upon a man— and what wealth or name, or gratification of ambition or vanity, could compare with the pleasure Esmond now had of being able to confer some kindness upon his best and dearest friends?

"'Dearest saint,' says he, 'purest soul, that has had so much to suffer, that has blest the poor lonely orphan with such a treasure of love. 'Tis for me to kneel, not for you: 'tis for me to be thankful that I can make you happy. Hath my life any other aim? Blessed be God that I can serve you!'" [297]

This noble tenderness seems still more touching when contrasted with the surrounding circumstances. Esmond goes to the wars, serves a political party, lives amidst dangers and bustle, judging revolutions and politics from a lofty point of view; he becomes a man of experience, well informed, learned, far-sighted, capable of great enterprises, possessing prudence and courage, harassed by his own thoughts and griefs, ever sad and ever strong. He ends by accompanying to England the Pretender, half-brother of Queen Anne, and keeps him, disguised, at Castlewood, awaiting the moment when the queen, dying and won over to the Tory cause, should declare him her heir. This young prince, a true Stuart, pays court to Lord Castlewood's daughter Beatrix, whom Esmond loves, and gets out at night to join her. Esmond, who waits for him, sees the crown lost and his house dishonored. His insulted honor and outraged love break forth in a proud and terrible rage. Pale, with set teeth, his brain on fire by four sleepless nights of anxiety, he keeps his mind clear, and his voice calm; he explains to the prince with perfect etiquette, and with the respectful coldness of an official messenger, the folly which the prince has committed, and the villainy which the prince contemplated. The scene must be read to show how much superiority and passion this calmness and bitterness imply:

"'What mean you, my lord?' says the Prince, and muttered something about a *guet-à-pens*, which Esmond caught up.

"'The snare, Sir,' said he, 'was not of our laying; it is not we that invited you. We came to avenge, and not to compass, the dishonor of our family.'

"'Dishonor! *Morbleu!* there has been no dishonor,' says the Prince, turning scarlet, 'only a little harmless playing.'

"'That was meant to end seriously.'

"'I swear,' the Prince broke out impetuously, 'upon the honor of a gentleman, my lords'—

"'That we arrived in time. No wrong hath been done, Frank,' says Colonel Esmond, turning round to young Castlewood, who stood at the door as the talk was going on. 'See! here is a paper whereon his Majesty hath deigned to commence some verses in honor, or dishonor, of Beatrix. Here is "Madame" and "Flamme, Cruelle" and "Rebelle," and "Amour" and "Jour," in the Royal writing and spelling. Had the Gracious lover been happy, he had not passed his time in sighing.' In fact, and actually as he was speaking, Esmond cast his eyes down towards the table, and saw a paper on which my young Prince had been scrawling a madrigal, that was to finish his charmer on the morrow.

"'Sir,' says the Prince, burning with rage (he had assumed his Royal coat unassisted by this time), 'did I come here to receive insults?'

"'To confer them, may it please your Majesty,' says the Colonel, with a very low bow, 'and the gentlemen of our family are come to thank you.'

"'*Malédiction!*' says the young man, tears starting into his eyes with helpless rage and mortification. 'What will you with me, gentlemen?'

"'If your Majesty will please to enter the next apartment,' says Esmond, preserving his grave tone, 'I have some papers there which I would gladly submit to you, and by your permission I will lead the way;' and taking the taper up, and backing before the Prince with very great ceremony, Mr. Esmond passed into the little Chaplain's room, through which we had just entered into the house:— 'Please to set a chair for his Majesty, Frank,' says the Colonel to his companion, who wondered almost as much at this scene, and was as much puzzled by it, as the other actor in it. Then going to the crypt over the mantelpiece, the Colonel opened it, and drew thence the papers which so long had lain there.

"'Here, may it please your Majesty,' says he, 'is the Patent of Marquis sent over by your Royal Father at St. Germain's to Viscount Castlewood, my father: here is the witnessed certificate of my father's marriage to my mother, and of my birth and christening; I was christened of that religion of which your sainted sire gave all through life so shining example. These are my titles, dear Frank, and this what I do with them: here go Baptism and Marriage, and here the Marquisate and the August Sign-Manual, with which your predecessor was pleased to honor our race.' And as Esmond spoke he set the papers burning in the brazier. 'You will please, sir, to remember,' he continued, 'that our family hath ruined itself by fidelity to yours; that my grandfather spent his estate, and gave his blood and his son to die for your service; that my dear lord's grandfather (for lord you are now, Frank, by right and title too) died for the same cause; that my poor kinswoman, my father's second wife, after giving away her honor to your wicked perjured race, sent all her wealth to the King, and got in return that precious title that lies in ashes, and this inestimable yard of blue riband. I lay this at your feet, and stamp upon it: I draw this sword, and break it and deny you; and had you completed the wrong you designed us, by Heaven I would have driven it through your heart, and no more pardoned you than your father pardoned Monmouth.'"[298]

Two pages later he speaks thus of his marriage to Lady Castlewood:

"That happiness which hath subsequently crowned it, cannot be written in words; 'tis of its nature sacred and secret, and not to be spoken of, though the heart be ever so full of thankfulness, save to Heaven and the One ear alone— to one fond being, the truest and tenderest and purest wife ever man was blessed with. As I think of the immense happiness which was in store for me, and of the depth and intensity of that love which, for so many years, hath blessed me, I own to a transport of wonder and gratitude for such a boon— nay, am thankful to have been endowed with a heart capable of feeling and knowing the immense beauty and value of the gift which God hath bestowed upon me. Sure, love, *vincit omnia*, is immeasurably above all ambition, more precious than wealth, more noble than name. He knows not life who knows not that: he hath not felt the highest faculty of the soul who hath not enjoyed it. In the name of my wife I write the completion of hope, and the summit of happiness. To have such a love is the one blessing, in comparison with which all earthly joy is of no value; and to think of her, is to praise God."

A character capable of such contrasts is a lofty work; it is to be remembered that Thackeray has produced no other; we regret that moral intentions have perverted these fine literary faculties; and we deplore that satire has robbed art of such talent.

Section III.—Literature the Definition of Man

Who is he; and what is the value of this literature of which he is one of the princes? At bottom, like every literature, it is a definition of man; and to judge it, we must compare it with man. We can do so now; we have just studied a mind, Thackeray himself; we have considered his faculties, their connections, results, their different degrees; we have before our eyes a model of human nature. We have a right to judge of the copy by the model, and to control the definition which his novels lay down by the definition which his character furnishes.

The two definitions are contrary, and his portrait is a criticism on his talent. We have seen that in him the same faculties produce the beautiful and the ugly, force and weakness, success and failure; that moral reflection, after having provided him with every satirical power, debases him in art; that, after having spread over his contemporary novels a tone of vulgarity and falseness, it raises his historical novel to the level of the finest productions; that the same constitution of mind teaches him the sarcastic and violent, as well as the modulated and simple style, the bitterness and harshness of hate with the effusion and delicacy of love. The evil and the good, the beautiful and the ugly, the repulsive and the agreeable, are in him then but remoter effects, of slight importance, born of changing circumstances, acquired and fortuitous qualities, not essential and primitive, different forms which different streams present in the same current. So it is with other men. Doubtless moral qualities are of the first rank; they are the motive power of civilization, and constitute the nobleness of the individual; society exists by them alone, and by them alone man is great. But if they are the finest fruit of the human plant, they are not its root; they give us our value, but do not constitute our elements. Neither the vices nor the virtues of man are his nature; to praise or to blame him is not to know him; approbation or disapprobation does not define him; the names of good or bad tell us nothing of what he is. Put the robber Cartouche in an Italian court of the fifteenth century: he would be a great statesman. Transport this nobleman, stingy and narrow-minded, into a shop; he will be an exemplary tradesman. This public man, of inflexible probity, is in his drawing-room an intolerable coxcomb. This father of a family, so humane, is an idiotic politician. Change a virtue in its circumstances, and it becomes a vice; change a vice in its circumstances, and it becomes a virtue. Regard the same quality from two sides: on one it is a fault, on the other a merit. The essential man is found concealed far below these moral badges; they only point out the useful or noxious effect of our inner constitution; they do not reveal our inner constitution. They are safety or advertising lights attached to our names, to warn the passer-by to avoid or approach us; they are not the explanatory chart of our being. Our true essence consists in the causes of our good or bad qualities, and these causes are discovered in the temperament, the species and degree of imagination, the amount and velocity of attention, the magnitude and direction of primitive passions. A character is a force, like gravity, or steam, capable, as it may happen, of pernicious or profitable effects, and which must be defined otherwise than by the amount of the weight it can lift or the havoc it can cause. It is therefore to ignore man, to reduce him, as Thackeray and English literature generally do, to an aggregate of virtues and vices; it is to lose sight in him of all but the exterior and social side; it is to neglect the inner and natural element. We will find the same fault in English criticism, always moral, never psychological, bent on exactly measuring the degree of human honesty, ignorant of the mechanism of our sentiments and faculties; we will find the same fault in English religion, which is but an emotion or a discipline; in their philosophy, destitute of metaphysics; and if we ascend to the source, according to the rule which derives vices from virtues, and virtues from vices, we will see all these weaknesses derived from their native energy, their practical education, and that kind of severe and religious poetic instinct which has in time past made them Protestant and Puritan.

[264]"Vanity Fair." Unless the original octavo edition is mentioned, the translator has always used the collected edition of Thackeray's works in small octavo, 1855-1868, 14 vols.

[265]"Vanity Fair," ch. XIX.

[266]"Vanity Fair," ch. IX.

[267]Thackeray, in his "Book of Snobs," says: "Their usual English expression of intense gloom and subdued agony."

[268]"The Edinburgh Review."

[269]See the character of Amelia in "Vanity Fair," and of Colonel Newcome in the "Newcomes."

[270]"The Book of Snobs," ch. XVI; On Literary Snobs.

[271]Stendhal says: "L'esprit et le génie perdent vingt-cinq pour cent de leur valeur en abordant en Angleterre."

[272]These remarks are only to be found in the octavo edition of "Pendennis."— Tr.

[273]"The History of Samuel Titmarsh and the Great Hoggarty Diamond," ch. XI.

[274]Ibid. ch. IX.

[275]"The Book of Snobs," ch. I., The Snob playfully dealt with.

[276]"Pendennis," ch. LIV.

[277]Ibid. ch. LII.

[278]Ibid. ch. LIII.

[279]Ibid. ch. V.

[280]"Pendennis," ch. XXI. This passage is only found in the octavo edition.— Tr.

[281]Ibid. ch. XXI.

[282]Ibid. ch. XXI. These words are only found in the octavo edition.— Tr.

[283]Ibid. ch. LI.

[284]See, for example, in the "Great Hoggarty Diamond," the death of the little child. The "Book of Snobs" ends thus: "Fun is good. Truth is still better, and Love best of all."

[285]"The Book of Snobs," last chapter.

[286]"Vanity Fair," ch. XLVIII. This passage is only found in the original octavo edition.— Tr.

[287]"Vanity Fair," ch. XLIX.

[288]"Pendennis," ch. LX.

[289]"The Book of Snobs," ch. VIII; Great City Snobs.

[290]"The Book of Snobs," ch. XXVI; On Some Country Snobs.

[291]"Vanity Fair," ch. IV.

[292]Ibid. ch. XI.

[293]"Vanity Fair," ch. XXX.

[294]"The History of Henry Esmond," bk. I. ch. I.

[295]Ibid. bk. I. ch. VII.
[296]Ibid. bk. II. ch. I.
[297]"The History of Henry Esmond," bk. III. ch. II.
[298]"The History of Henry Esmond," bk. III. ch. XIII.

BOOK V—MODERN AUTHORS

CHAPTER THIRD. CRITICISM AND HISTORY—MACAULAY

Section I.—His Position in England

I shall not here attempt to write the life of Lord Macaulay. It can only be related twenty years hence, when his friends shall have put together all their recollections of him. As to what is public now, it seems to me useless to recall it: everyone knows that his father was an abolitionist and a philanthropist; that Macaulay passed through a most brilliant and complete classical education; that at twenty-five his essay on Milton made him famous; that at thirty he entered Parliament, and took his standing there amongst the first orators; that he went to India to reform the law, and that on his return he was appointed to high offices; that on one occasion his liberal opinions in religious matters lost him his seat in Parliament; that he was re-elected amidst universal congratulations; that he continued to be the most celebrated publicist and the most accomplished writer of the Whig party; and that on this ground, towards the close of his life, the gratitude of his party and the public admiration made him a British peer. It will be a fine biography to write— a life of honor and happiness, devoted to noble ideas, and occupied by manly enterprises; literary in the first place, but sufficiently charged with action and immersed in business to furnish substance and solidity to his eloquence and style, to form the observer side by side with the artist, and the thinker side by side with the writer. On the present occasion I will only describe the thinker and writer: I leave the life, I take his works; and first his Essays.

Section II.—Essays

His Essays are a collection of articles from reviews: I confess to a fondness for books of this kind. In the first place we can throw down the volume after a score of pages, begin at the end, or in the middle; we are not its slave, but its master; we can treat it like a newspaper: in fact, it is the journal of a mind. In the second place, it is miscellaneous: in turning over a page, we pass from the Renaissance to the nineteenth century, from England to India: this diversity surprises and pleases. Lastly, involuntarily, the author is indiscreet; he displays himself to us, keeping back nothing; it is a familiar conversation, and no conversation is worth so much as that of England's greatest historian. We are pleased to mark the origin of this generous and powerful mind, to discover what faculties have nourished his talent, what researches have shaped his knowledge, what opinions he formed on philosophy, religion, the state, literature; what he was, and what he has become; what he wishes, and what he believes.

Seated in an arm-chair, with our feet on the fender, we see little by little, as we turn over the leaves of the book, an animated and thoughtful face arise before us; the countenance assumes expression and clearness; the different features are mutually explained and lightened up; presently the author lives again for us, and before us; we perceive the causes and birth of all his thoughts, we foresee what he is going to say; his bearing and mode of speech are as familiar to us as those of a man whom we see every day; his opinions correct and affect our own; he enters partly into our thoughts and our life; he is two hundred leagues away, and his book stamps his image on us, as the reflected light paints on the horizon the object from which it is emitted. Such is the charm of books which deal with all kinds of subjects, which give the author's opinions on all sorts of things, which lead us in all directions of his thoughts, and make us, so to speak, walk around his mind.

Macaulay treats philosophy in the English fashion, as a practical man. He is a disciple of Bacon, and sets him above all philosophers; he decides that genuine science dates from him; that the speculations of old thinkers are only witticisms; that for two thousand years the human mind was on a wrong tack; that only since Bacon it has discovered the goal to which it must turn, and the method by which it must arrive there. This goal is utility. The object of knowledge is not theory, but application. The object of mathematicians is not the satisfaction of an idle curiosity, but the invention of machines calculated to alleviate human labor, to increase the power of subduing nature, to render life more secure, commodious, and happy. The object of astronomy is not to furnish matter for vast calculations and poetical cosmogonies, but to subserve geography and to guide navigation. The object of anatomy and the zoological sciences is not to suggest eloquent systems on the nature of organization, or to set before the eyes the orders of the animal kingdom by an ingenious classification, but to conduct the surgeon's hand and the physician's prognosis. The object of every research and every study is to diminish pain, to augment comfort, to ameliorate the condition of man; theoretical laws are serviceable only in their practical use; the labors of the laboratory and the cabinet receive their sanction and value only through the use made of them by workshops and mills; the tree of knowledge must be estimated only by its fruits. If we wish to judge of a philosophy, we must observe its effects; its works are not its books, but its acts. The philosophy of the ancients produced fine writings, sublime phrases, infinite disputes, hollow dreams, systems displaced by systems, and left the world as ignorant, as unhappy, and as wicked as it found it. That of Bacon produced observations, experiments, discoveries, machines, entire arts and industries:

"It has lengthened life; it has mitigated pain; it has extinguished diseases; it has increased the fertility of the soil; it has given new securities to the mariner; it has furnished new arms to the warrior; it has spanned great rivers and estuaries with bridges of form unknown to our fathers; it has guided the thunderbolt innocuously from heaven to earth; it has lighted up the night with the splendor of the day; it has extended the range of the human vision; it has multiplied the power of the human muscles; it has accelerated motion; it has annihilated distance; it has facilitated intercourse, correspondence, all friendly offices, all despatch of business; it has enabled man to descend to the depths of the sea, to soar into the air, to penetrate securely into the noxious recesses of the earth, to traverse the land in cars which whirl along without horses, and the ocean in ships which run ten knots an hour against the wind."[299]

The first was consumed in solving unsolvable enigmas, fabricating portraits of an imaginary sage, mounting from hypothesis to hypothesis, tumbling from absurdity to absurdity; it despised what was practicable, promised what was impracticable; and because it disregarded the limits of the human mind, ignored its power. The other, measuring our force and weakness, diverted us from roads that were closed to us, to start us on roads that were open to us; it recognized facts and laws, because it resigned itself to remain ignorant of their essence and principles; it rendered man more happy because it has not pretended to render him perfect; it discovered great truths and produced great effects, because it had the courage and good sense to study small things, and to keep for a long time to petty vulgar experiments; it has become glorious and powerful, because it deigned to become humble and useful. Formerly, science furnished only vain pretensions and chimerical conceptions, whilst it held itself far aloof from practical existence, and styled itself the sovereign of man. Now, science possesses acquired truths, the hope of loftier discoveries, an ever-increasing authority, because it has entered upon active existence, and has declared itself the servant of man. Let it keep to its new functions; let it not try to penetrate the region of the invisible; let it renounce what must remain unknown; it does not contain its own issue, it is but a medium; man was not made for it, but science was made for man; it is like the thermometers and piles which it constructs for its own experiments; its whole glory, merit, and office, is to be an instrument:

"We have sometimes thought that an amusing fiction might be written, in which a disciple of Epictetus and a disciple of Bacon should be introduced as fellow-travellers. They come to a village where the small-pox has just begun to rage, and find houses shut up, intercourse suspended, the sick abandoned, mothers weeping in terror over their children. The Stoic assures the dismayed population that there is nothing bad in the small-pox, and that to a wise man disease, deformity, death, the loss of friends, are not evils. The Baconian takes out a lancet and begins to vaccinate. They find a body of miners in great dismay. An explosion of noisome vapours had just killed many of those who were at work; and the survivors are afraid to venture into the cavern. The Stoic assures them that such an accident is nothing but a mere ἀποπροηγμένον. The Baconian, who has no such fine word at his command, contents himself with devising a safety-lamp. They find a shipwrecked merchant wringing his hands on the shore. His vessel, with an inestimable cargo, had just gone down, and he is reduced in a moment from opulence to beggary. The Stoic exhorts him not to seek happiness in things which lie without himself, and repeats the whole chapter of Epictetus, πρὸς τοὺς τὴν απoριαν δεδοικότας. The Baconian constructs a diving-bell, goes down in it, and returns with the most precious effects from the wreck. It would be easy to multiply illustrations of the difference between the philosophy of thorns and the philosophy of fruit, the philosophy of words and the philosophy of works."[300]

It is not for me to discuss these opinions; it is for the reader to blame or praise them, if he sees fit: I do not wish to criticise doctrines, but to depict a man; and truly nothing could be more striking than this absolute scorn for speculation, and this absolute love for the practical. Such a mind is entirely suitable to the national genius: in England a barometer is still called a philosophical instrument; philosophy is there a thing unknown. The English have moralists, psychologists, but no metaphysicians: if there is one— Hamilton, for instance— he is a sceptic in metaphysics; he has only read the German philosophers to refute them; he regards speculative philosophy as an extravagance of visionaries, and is compelled to apologize to his readers for the strangeness of his subject, when he tries to make them understand somewhat of Hegel's conceptions. The positive and practical English, excellent politicians, administrators, fighters, and workers, are no more suited than the ancient Romans for the abstractions of subtle dialectics and grand systems; and Cicero, too, once excused himself when he tried to expound to his audience of senators and public men the deep and audacious deductions of the Stoics.

Section III.—His Critical Method

The only part of philosophy which pleases men of this kind is morality, because like them it is wholly practical, and only attends to actions. Nothing else was studied at Rome, and everyone knows what place it holds in English philosophy: Hutcheson, Price, Ferguson, Wollaston, Adam Smith, Bentham, Reid, and many others, have filled the last century with dissertations and discussions on the rule of duty and the faculty which discovers our duty; and Macaulay's Essays are a new example of this national and dominant inclination: his biographies are less portraits than judgments. What strictly is the degree of uprightness and dishonesty of the personage he describes, that is the important question for him; he makes all other questions refer to it; he applies himself throughout only to justify, excuse, accuse, or condemn. If he speaks of Lord Clive, Warren Hastings, Sir William Temple, Addison, Milton, or any other man, he devotes himself, first of all, to measure exactly the number and greatness of their faults and virtues; he interrupts himself, in the midst of a narration, to examine whether the action which he is relating is just or unjust; he considers it as a legist and a moralist, according to positive and natural law; he takes into account the state of public opinion, the examples which surrounded the accused, the principles he professed, the education he has received; he bases his opinion on analogies drawn from ordinary life, from the history of all peoples, the laws of all countries; he brings forward so many proofs, such certain facts, such conclusive reasonings, that the best advocate might find a model in him, and when at last he pronounces judgment, we think we are listening to the summing up of a judge. If he analyzes a literature— that of the Restoration, for instance— he impanels before the reader a sort of jury to judge it. He makes it appear at the bar, and reads the indictment; he then presents the plea of the defenders, who try to excuse its levities and indecencies: at last he begins to speak in his turn, and proves that the arguments set forth are not applicable to the case in question; that the accused writers have labored effectually and with premeditation to corrupt morals; that they not only employed unbecoming words, but that they designedly, and with deliberate intent, represented unbecoming things; that they always took care to conceal the hatefulness of vice, to render virtue ridiculous, to make adultery fashionable and a necessary exploit of a man of taste; that this intention was all the more manifest from its being in the spirit of the times, and that they were pandering to a crime of their age. If I dare employ, like Macaulay, religious comparisons, I should say that this criticism was like the Last Judgment, in which the diversity of talents, characters, ranks, employments, will disappear before the consideration of virtue and vice, and where there will be no more artists, but a judge of the righteous and the wicked.

In France, criticism has a freer gait; it is less subservient to morality, and more akin to art. When we try to relate a life, or paint the character of a man, we more readily consider him as a simple subject of painting or science: we only think of displaying the various feelings of his heart, the connection of his ideas and the necessity of his actions; we do not judge him, we only wish to represent him to the eyes, and make him intelligible to the reason. We are spectators, and nothing more. What matters it if Peter or Paul is a rascal? that is the business of his contemporaries: they suffered from his vices, and ought to think only of despising and condemning him. Now we are beyond his reach, and hatred has disappeared with danger. At this distance, and in the historic perspective, I see in him but a mental machine, provided with certain springs, animated by a primary impulse, affected by various circumstances. I calculate the play of his motives; I feel with him the impact of obstacles; I see beforehand the curve which his motion will trace out; I feel for him neither aversion nor disgust; I have left these feelings on the threshold of history, and I taste the very deep and pure pleasure of seeing a soul act after a definite law, in a fixed groove, with all the variety of human passions, with the succession and constraint, which the inner structure of man imposes on the external development of his passions.

In a country where men are so much occupied by morality, and so little by philosophy, there is much religion. For lack of natural theology they have a positive theology, and demand from the Bible the metaphysics not supplied by reason. Macaulay is a Protestant; and though a very candid and liberal man, he at times retains the English prejudices against the Roman-Catholic religion.[301] Popery in England always passes for an impious idolatry and for a degrading servitude. After two revolutions, Protestantism, allied to liberty, seemed to be the religion of liberty; and Roman-Catholicism, allied to despotism, seemed the religion of despotism: the two doctrines have both assumed the name of the cause which they supported. To the first has been transferred the love and veneration which were felt for the rights which it defended; on the second has been poured the scorn and hatred which were felt for the slavery which it would have introduced: political passions have inflamed religious beliefs; Protestantism has been confounded with the victorious fatherland, Roman-Catholicism, with the conquered enemy; prejudices survive when the strife is ended, and to this day English Protestants do not feel for the doctrines of Roman Catholics the same good-will or impartiality which French Roman Catholics feel for the doctrines of Protestants.

But these English opinions are moderated in Macaulay by an ardent love for justice. He is a liberal, in the largest and best sense of the word. He demands that all citizens should be equal before the law, that men of all sects should be declared capable to fill all public functions— that Roman Catholics and Jews may, as well as Lutherans, Anglicans, and Calvinists, sit in Parliament. He refutes Mr. Gladstone and the partisans of State religion with incomparable ardor and eloquence, abundance of proof, and force of argument; he clearly proves that the State is only a secular association, that its end is wholly temporal, that its single object is to protect the life, liberty, and property of the citizens; that in entrusting to it the defence of spiritual interests, we overturn the order of things; and that to attribute to it a religious belief, is as though a man, walking with his feet, should also confide to his feet the care of seeing and hearing. This question has often been discussed in France; it is so to this day; but no one has brought to it more common-sense, more practical reasoning, more palpable arguments. Macaulay withdraws the discussion from the region of metaphysics; he leads it back to the earth; he brings it home to all minds; he takes his proofs and examples from the best known facts of ordinary life; he addresses the shopkeeper, the citizen, the artist, the scholar, everyone; he connects the truth, which he asserts, with the familiar and intimate truths which no one can help admitting, and which are believed with all the force of experience and habit; he carries off and conquers our belief by such solid reasons that his adversaries will thank him for convincing them; and if by chance a few amongst us have need of a lesson on tolerance, they had better look for it in Macaulay's Essay on that subject.

Section IV—His Love of Political Liberty

This love of justice becomes a passion when political liberty is at stake; this is the sensitive point; and when we touch it, we touch the writer to the quick. Macaulay loves it interestedly, because it is the only guarantee of the properties, happiness, and life of individuals; he loves it from pride, because it is the honor of man: he loves it from patriotism, because it is a legacy left by preceding generations; because for two hundred years a succession of upright and great men have defended it against all attacks, and preserved it in all dangers; because it has made the power and glory of England; because in teaching the citizens to will and to decide for themselves, it adds to their dignity and intelligence; because in assuring internal peace and continuous progress, it guarantees the land against bloody revolutions and silent decay. All these advantages are perpetually present to his eyes; and whoever attacks the liberty, which forms their foundation, becomes at once his enemy. Macaulay cannot look calmly on the oppression of man; every outrage on human will hurts him like a personal outrage. At every step bitter words escape him, and the stale adulation of courtiers, which he meets with, brings to his lips a sarcasm the more violent from being the more deserved. Pitt, he says, at college wrote Latin verses on the death of George I. In this piece "the Muses are earnestly entreated to weep over the urn of Cæsar: for Cæsar, says the poet, loved the muses; Cæsar, who could not read a line of Pope, and who loved nothing but punch and fat women."[302] Elsewhere, in the biography of Miss Burney, he relates how the poor young lady, having become celebrated by her two first novels, received as a reward, and as a great favor, a place of keeper of the robes of Queen Charlotte; how, worn out with watching, sick, nearly dying, she asked as a favor the permission to depart; how "the sweet queen" was indignant at this impertinence, unable to understand that anyone could refuse to die in and for her service, or that a woman of letters should prefer health, life, and glory to the honor of folding her Majesty's dresses. But it is when Macaulay comes to the history of the Revolution that he hauls to justice and vengeance those men who violated the rights of the public, who hated and betrayed the national cause, who outraged liberty. He does not speak as a historian, but as a contemporary; it seems as though his life and his honor were at stake, that he pleaded for himself, that he was a member of the Long Parliament, that he heard at the door the muskets and swords of the guards sent to arrest Pym and Hampden. M. Guizot has related the same history; but we recognize in his book the calm judgment and impartial emotion of a philosopher. He does not condemn the actions of Strafford or Charles; he explains them; he shows in Strafford the imperious character, the domineering genius, which feels itself born to command and to crush opposition, whom an invincible bent rouses against the law or the right which restrains him, who oppresses from a sort of inner craving, and who is made to govern as a sword is to strike. He shows in Charles the innate respect for royalty, the belief in divine right, the rooted conviction that every remonstrance or demand is an insult to his crown, an outrage on his rights, an impious and criminal sedition. Thenceforth we see in the strife of king and parliament but the strife of two doctrines; we cease to take an interest in one or the other, to take an interest in both; we are spectators of a drama; we are no longer judges at a trial. But it is a trial which Macaulay conducts before us; he takes a side in it; his account is the address of a public prosecutor before the court, the most entrancing, the most acrimonious, the best reasoned, that was ever written. He approves of the condemnation of Strafford; he honors and admires Cromwell; he exalts the character of the Puritans; he praises Hampden to such a degree that he calls him the equal of Washington; he has no words scornful and insulting enough for Laud; and what is more terrible, each of his judgments is justified by as many quotations, authorities, historic precedents, arguments, conclusive proofs, as the vast erudition of Hallam, or the calm dialectics of Macintosh could have assembled. Judge of this transport of passion and this withering logic by a single passage:

"For more than ten years the people had seen the rights which were theirs by a double claim, by immemorial inheritance and by recent purchase, infringed by the perfidious King who had recognized them. At length circumstances compelled Charles to summon another parliament: another chance was given to our fathers: were they to throw it away as they had thrown away the former? Were they again to be cozened by *le Roi le veut?* Were they again to advance their money on pledges which had been forfeited over and over again? Were they to lay a second Petition of Right at the foot of the throne, to grant another lavish aid in exchange for another unmeaning ceremony, and then to take their departure, till, after ten years more of fraud and oppression, their prince should again require a supply and again repay it with a perjury? They were compelled to choose whether they would trust a tyrant, or conquer him. We think that they chose wisely and nobly.

"The advocates of Charles, like the advocates of other malefactors against whom overwhelming evidence is produced, generally decline all controversy about the facts, and content themselves with calling testimony to character. He had so many private virtues! And had James the Second no private virtues? Was Oliver Cromwell, his bitterest enemies themselves being judges, destitute of private virtues? And what, after all, are the virtues ascribed to Charles? A religious zeal, not more sincere than that of his son, and fully as weak and narrow-minded, and a few of the ordinary household decencies which half the tombstones in England claim for those who lie beneath them. A good father! A good husband! Ample apologies indeed for fifteen years of persecution, tyranny, and falsehood!

"We charge him with having broken his coronation oath; and we are told that he kept his marriage vow! We accuse him of having given up his people to the merciless inflictions of the most hot-headed and hard-hearted of prelates; and the defence is, that he took his little son on his knee and kissed him! We censure him for having violated the articles of the Petition of Right, after having, for good and valuable consideration, promised to observe them; and we are informed that he was accustomed to hear prayers at six o'clock in the morning! It is to such considerations as these, together with his Vandyke dress, his handsome face, and his peaked beard, that he owes, we verily believe, most of his popularity with the present generation.

"For ourselves, we own that we do not understand the common phrase, a good man, but a bad king. We can as easily conceive a good man and an unnatural father, or a good man and a treacherous friend. We cannot, in estimating the character of an individual, leave out of our consideration his conduct in the most important of all human relations; and if in that relation we find him to have been selfish, cruel, and deceitful, we shall take the liberty to call him a bad man, in spite of all his temperance at table, and all his regularity at chapel."[303]

This is for the father; now the son will receive something. The reader will perceive, by the furious invective, what excessive rancor the government of the Stuarts left in the heart of a patriot, a Whig, a Protestant, and an Englishman:

"Then came those days, never to be recalled without a blush, the days of servitude without loyalty and sensuality without love, of dwarfish talents and gigantic vices, the paradise of cold hearts and narrow minds, the golden age of the coward, the bigot, and the slave. The King cringed to his rival that he might trample on his people, sank into a viceroy of France, and pocketed, with complacent infamy, her degrading insults, and her more degrading gold. The caresses of harlots, and the jests of buffoons, regulated the policy of the state. The government had just ability enough to deceive, and just religion enough to persecute. The principles of liberty were the scoff of every grinning courtier, and the Anathema Maranatha of every fawning dean. In every high place, worship was paid to Charles and James, Belial and Moloch; and England propitiated those obscene and cruel idols with the blood of her best and bravest children. Crime succeeded to crime, and disgrace to disgrace, till the race accursed of God and man was a second time driven forth, to wander on the face of the earth, and to be a by-word and a shaking of the head to the nations."[304]

This piece, with all the biblical metaphors, which has preserved something of the tone of Milton and the Puritan prophets, shows to what an issue the various tendencies of this great mind were turning— what was its bent— how the practical spirit, science and historic talent, the unvaried presence of moral and religious ideas, love of country and justice, concurred to make of Macaulay the historian of liberty.

Section V.—Characteristics of Macaulay's Style

In this his talent assisted him: for his opinions are akin to his talent.

What first strikes us in him is the extreme solidity of his mind. He proves all that he says, with astonishing vigor and authority. We are almost certain never to go astray in following him. If he cites a witness, he begins by measuring the veracity and intelligence of the authors quoted, and by correcting the errors they may have committed, through negligence or partiality. If he pronounces a judgment, he relies on the most certain facts, the clearest principles, the simplest and most logical deductions. If he develops an argument, he never loses himself in a digression; he always has his goal before his eyes; he advances towards it by the surest and straightest road. If he rises to general considerations he mounts step by step through all the grades of generalization, without omitting one; he feels his way every instant; he neither adds nor subtracts from facts; he desires at the cost of every precaution and research to arrive at the precise truth. He knows an infinity of details of every kind; he owns a great number of philosophic ideas of every species; but his erudition is as well-tempered as his philosophy, and both constitute a coin worthy of circulation amongst all thinking minds. We feel that he believes nothing without reason; that if we doubted one of the facts which he advances, or one of the views which he propounds, we should at once encounter a multitude of authentic documents and a serried phalanx of convincing arguments. In France and Germany we are too much accustomed to receive hypotheses for historic laws, and doubtful anecdotes for attested events. We too often see whole systems established, from day to day, according to the caprice of a writer; a sort of castles in the air, whose regular arrangement stimulates the appearance of genuine edifices, and which vanish at a breath, when we come to touch them. We have all made theories, in a fireside discussion, in case of need, when for lack of argument we required some fictitious reasoning, like those Chinese generals who, to terrify their enemies, placed amongst their troops formidable monsters of painted card-board. We have judged men at random, under the impression of the moment, on a detached action, an isolated document; and we have dressed them up with vices or virtues, folly or genius, without controlling by logic or criticism the hazardous decisions to which our precipitation had carried us. Thus we feel a deep satisfaction and a sort of internal peace, on leaving so many doctrines of ephemeral bloom in our books or reviews, to follow the steady gait of a guide so clear-sighted, reflective, instructed, able to lead us aright. We understand why the English accuse the French of being frivolous, and the Germans of being chimerical. Macaulay brings to the moral sciences that spirit of circumspection, that desire for certainty, and that instinct of truth, which make up the practical mind, and which from the time of Bacon have constituted the scientific merit and power of his nation. If art and beauty lose by this, truth and certainty are gained; and no one, for instance, would blame our author for inserting the following demonstration in the life of Addison:

"He (Pope) asked Addison's advice. Addison said that the poem as it stood was a delicious little thing, and entreated Pope not to run the risk of marring what was so excellent in trying to mend it. Pope afterwards declared that this insidious counsel first opened his eyes to the baseness of him who gave it.

"Now there can be no doubt that Pope's plan was most ingenious, and that he afterwards executed it with great skill and success. But does it necessarily follow that Addison's advice was bad? And if Addison's advice was bad, does it necessarily follow that it was given from bad motives? If a friend were to ask us whether we would advise him to risk his all in a lottery, of which the chances were ten to one against him, we should do our best to dissuade him from running such a risk. Even if he were so lucky as to get the thirty thousand pound prize, we should not admit that we had counselled him ill; and we should certainly think it the height of injustice in him to accuse us of having been actuated by malice. We think Addison's advice good advice. It rested on a sound principle, the result of long and wide experience. The general rule undoubtedly is that when a successful work of the imagination has been produced, it should not be recast. We cannot, at this moment, call to mind a single instance in which this rule has been transgressed with happy effect, except the instance of the 'Rape of the Lock.' Tasso recast his 'Jerusalem,' Akenside recast his 'Pleasures of the Imagination' and his 'Epistle to Curio.' Pope himself, emboldened no doubt by the success with which he had expanded and remodelled the 'Rape of the Lock,' made the same experiment on the 'Dunciad.' All these attempts failed. Who was to foresee that Pope would, once in his life, be able to do what he could not himself do twice, and what nobody else has ever done?

"Addison's advice was good. But had it been bad, why should we pronounce it dishonest? Scott tells us that one of his best friends predicted the failure of Waverley. Herder adjured Goethe not to take so unpromising a subject as Faust. Hume tried to dissuade Robertson from writing the 'History of Charles the Fifth.' Nay, Pope himself was one of those who prophesied that Cato would never succeed on the stage, and advised Addison to print it without risking a representation. But Scott, Goethe, Robertson, Addison, had the good sense and generosity to give their advisers credit for the best intentions. Pope's heart was not of the same kind with theirs."[305]

What does the reader think of this dilemma, and this double series of inductions? The demonstrations would not be more studied or rigorous, if a physical law were in question.

This demonstrative talent was increased by his talent for development. Macaulay enlightens inattentive minds, as well as he convinces opposing minds; he manifests, as well as he persuades, and spreads as much evidence over obscure questions as certitude over doubtful points. It is impossible not to understand him; he approaches the subject under every aspect, he turns it over on every side; it seems as though he addressed himself to every spectator, and studied to make himself understood by every individual; he calculates the scope of every mind, and seeks for each a fit mode of exposition; he takes us all by the hand, and leads us alternately to the end which he has marked out beforehand. He sets out from the simplest facts, he descends to our level, he brings himself even with our mind; he spares us the pain of the slightest effort; then he leads us on, and smoothes the road throughout; we rise gradually, without perceiving the slope, and at the end we find ourselves at the top, after having walked as easily as on the plain. When a subject is obscure, he is not content with a first explanation; he gives a second, then a third: he sheds light in abundance from all sides, he searches for it in all regions of history; and the wonderful thing is, that he is never prolix. In reading him we find ourselves in our proper sphere; we feel as though we could understand; we are annoyed to have taken twilight so long for day; we rejoice to see this abounding light rising and leaping forth in torrents; the exact style, the antithesis of ideas, the harmonious construction, the artfully balanced paragraphs, the vigorous summaries, the regular sequence of thoughts, the frequent comparisons, the fine arrangement of the whole— not an idea or phrase of his writings in which the talent and the desire to explain, the characteristic of an orator, does not shine forth. Macaulay was a member of Parliament, and spoke so well, we are told, that he was listened to for the mere pleasure of listening. The habit of public speaking is, perhaps, the cause of this incomparable lucidity. To convince a great assembly, we must address all the members; to rivet the attention of absentminded and weary men, we must save them from all fatigue; they must take in too much in order to take in enough. Public speaking vulgarizes ideas; it drags truth from the height at which it dwells, with some thinkers, to bring it amongst the crowd: it reduces it to the level of ordinary minds, who, without this intervention, would only have seen it from afar, and high above them. Thus, when great orators consent to write, they are the most powerful of writers; they make philosophy popular; they lift all minds a stage higher, and seem to enlarge human intelligence. In the hands of Cicero, the dogmas of the Stoics and the dialectics of the Academicians lose their prickles. The subtle Greek arguments become united and easy; the hard problems of providence, immortality, highest good, become public property. Senators, men of business, lawyers, lovers of formulas and procedure, the massive and narrow intelligence of publicists, comprehend the deductions of Chrysippus; and the book "De Officiis" has made the morality of Panætius popular. In our days, M. Thiers, in his two great histories, has placed within reach of everybody the most involved questions of strategy and finance; if he would write a course of political economy for street-porters, I am sure he would be understood; and pupils of the lower classes at school have been able to read M. Guizot's "History of Civilization."

When, with the faculty for proof and explanation, a man feels the desire of proving, he arrives at vehemence. These serried and multiplied arguments which all tend to a single aim, these reiterated logical points, returning every instant, one upon the other, to shake the opponent, give heat and passion to the style. Rarely was eloquence more captivating than Macaulay's. He has the oratorical afflatus; all his phrases have a tone; we feel that he would govern minds, that he is irritated by resistance, that he fights as he discusses. In his books the discussion always seizes and carries away the reader; it advances evenly, with accumulating force, straightforward, like those great American rivers, impetuous as a torrent and wide as a sea. This abundance of thought and style, this multitude of explanations, ideas, and facts, this vast aggregate of historical knowledge goes rolling on, urged forward by internal passion, sweeping away objections in its course, and adding to the dash of eloquence the irresistible force of its mass and weight. We might say that the history of James II. is a discourse in two volumes, spoken without stopping, and with never-failing voice. We see the oppression and discontent begin, increase, widen, the partisans of James abandoning him one by one, the idea of revolution arise in all hearts, confirmed, fixed, the preparations made, the event approaching, growing imminent, then suddenly falling on the blind and unjust monarch, and sweeping away his throne and dynasty, with the violence of a foreseen and fatal tempest. True eloquence is that which thus perfects argument by emotion, which reproduces the unity of events by the unity of passion, which repeats the motion and the chain of facts by the motion and the chain of ideas. It is a genuine imitation of nature; more complete than pure analysis; it reanimates beings; its dash and vehemence form part of science and of truth. Of whatever subject Macaulay treats, political economy, morality, philosophy, literature, history, he is impassioned for his subject. The current which bears away events, excites in him, as soon as he sees it, a current which bears forward his thought. He does not set forth his opinion; he pleads it. He has that energetic, sustained, and vibrating tone which bows down opposition and conquers belief. His thought is an active force; it is imposed on the hearer; it attacks him with such superiority, falls upon him with such a train of proofs, such a manifest and legitimate authority, such a powerful impulse, that we never think of resisting it; and it masters the heart by its vehemence, whilst at the same time it masters the reason by its evidence.

All these gifts are common to orators; they are found in different proportions and degrees, in men like Cicero and Livy, Bourdaloue and Bossuet, Fox and Burke. These fine and solid minds form a natural family, and all have for their chief feature the habit and talent of passing from particular to general ideas, orderly and successively, as we climb a ladder by setting our feet one after the other on every round. The inconvenience of this art is the use of commonplace. They who practise it do not depict objects with precision; they fall easily into vague rhetoric. They hold in their hands ready-made developments, a sort of portable scales, equally applicable on both sides of the same and every question. They continue willingly in a middle region, amongst the tirades and arguments of the special pleader, with an indifferent knowledge of the human heart, and a fair number of amplifications on that which is useful and just. In France and at Rome, amongst the Latin races, especially in the seventeenth century, these men love to hover above the earth, amidst grand words or general considerations, in the style of the drawing-room and the academy. They do not descend to minor facts, convincing details, circumstantial examples of every-day life. They are more inclined to plead than to prove. In this Macaulay is distinguished from them. His principle is, that a special fact has more hold on the mind than a general reflection. He knows that, to give men a clear and vivid idea, they must be brought back to their personal experience. He remarks[306] that, in order to make them realize a storm, the only method is to recall to them some storm which they have themselves seen and heard, with which their memory is still charged, and which still re-echoes through all their senses. He practises, in his style, the philosophy of Bacon and Locke. With him, as well as with them, the origin of every idea is a sensation. Every complicated argument, every entire conception, has certain particular facts for its only support. It is so for every structure of ideas, as well as for a scientific theory. Beneath long calculations, algebraical formulas, subtle deductions, written volumes which contain the combinations and elaborations of learned minds, there are two or three sensible experiences, two or three little facts on which we may lay our finger, a turn of the wheel in a machine, a scalpel-cut in a living body, an unlooked-for color in a liquid. These are decisive specimens. The whole substance of theory, the whole force of proof, is contained in this. Truth is here, as a nut in its shell: painful and ingenious discussion adds nothing thereto; it only extracts the nut. Thus, if we would rightly prove, we must before everything present these specimens, insist upon them, make them visible and tangible to the reader, as far as may be done in words. This is difficult, for words are not things. The only resource of the writer is to employ words which bring things before the eyes. For this he must appeal to the reader's personal observation, set out from his experience, compare the unknown objects presented to him with the known objects which he sees every day: place past events beside contemporary events. Macaulay always has before his mind English imaginations, full of English images: I mean full of the detailed and present recollections of a London street, a dram-shop, a wretched alley, an afternoon in Hyde Park, a moist green landscape, a white ivy-covered country-house, a clergyman in a white tie, a sailor in a sou'-wester. He has recourse to such recollections; he makes them still more precise by descriptions and statistics; he notes colors and qualities; he has a passion for exactness; his descriptions are worthy both of a painter and a topographer; he writes like a man who sees a physical and sensible object, and who at the same time classifies and weighs it. We will see him carry his figures even to moral or literary worth, assign to an action, a virtue, a book, a talent, its compartment and its step in the scale, with such clearness and relief, that we could easily imagine ourselves in a classified museum, not of stuffed skins, but of feeling, suffering, living animals.

Consider, for instance, these phrases, by which he tries to render visible to an English public, events in India:

"During that interval the business of a servant of the Company was simply to wring out of the natives a hundred or two hundred thousand pounds as speedily as possible, that he might return home before his constitution had suffered from the heat, to marry a peer's daughter, to buy rotten boroughs in Cornwall, and to give balls in St. James's Square.[307]... There was still a nabob of Bengal, who stood to the English rulers of his country in the same relation in which Augustulus stood to Odoacer, or the last Merovingians to Charles Martel and Pepin. He lived at Moorshedabad, surrounded by princely magnificence. He was approached with outward marks of reverence, and his name was used in public instruments. But in the government of the country he had less real share than the youngest writer or cadet in the Company's service."[308]

Of Nuncomar, the native servant of the Company, he writes:

"Of his moral character it is difficult to give a notion to those who are acquainted with human nature only as it appears in our island. What the Italian is to the Englishman, what the Hindoo is to the Italian, what the Bengalee is to other Hindoos, that was Nuncomar to other Bengalees. The physical organization of the Bengalee is feeble, even to effeminacy. He lives in a constant vapour bath. His pursuits are sedentary, his limbs delicate, his movements languid. During many ages he has been trampled upon by men of bolder and more hardy breeds. Courage, independence, veracity, are qualities to which his constitution and his situation are equally unfavorable. His mind bears a singular analogy to his body. It is weak even to helplessness, for purposes of manly resistance; but its suppleness and its tact move the children of sterner climates to admiration not unmingled with contempt. All those arts which are the natural defence of the weak are more familiar to this subtle race than to the Ionian of the time of Juvenal, or to the Jew of the dark ages. What the horns are to the buffalo, what the paw is to the tiger, what the sting is to the bee, what beauty, according to the old Greek song, is to woman, deceit is to the Bengalee. Large promises, smooth excuses, elaborate tissues of circumstantial falsehood, chicanery, perjury, forgery, are the weapons, offensive and defensive, of the people of the Lower Ganges. All those millions do not furnish one sepoy to the armies of the Company. But as usurers, as money-changers, as sharp legal practitioners, no class of human beings can bear a comparison with them."[309]

It was such men and such affairs, which were to provide Burke with the amplest and most brilliant subject-matter for his eloquence; and when Macaulay described the distinctive talent of the great orator, he described his own:

"He (Burke) had, in the highest degree, that noble faculty whereby man is able to live in the past and in the future, in the distant and in the unreal. India and its inhabitants were not to him, as to most Englishmen, mere names and abstractions, but a real country and a real people. The burning sun, the strange vegetation of the palm and the cocoa-tree, the rice-field, the tank, the huge trees, older than the Mogul empire, under which the village crowds assemble; the thatched roof of the peasant's hut; the rich tracery of the mosque where the imaum prays with his face to Mecca, the drums, and banners, and gaudy idols, the devotee swinging in the air, the graceful maiden, with the pitcher on her head, descending the steps to the river-side, the black faces, the long beards, the yellow streaks of sect, the turbans and the flowing robes, the spears and the silver maces, the elephants with their canopies of state, the gorgeous palanquin of the prince, and the close litter of the noble lady, all those things were to him as the objects amidst which his own life had been passed, as the objects which lay on the road between Beaconsfield and St. James's Street. All India was present to the eye of his mind, from the halls where suitors laid gold and perfumes at the feet of sovereigns, to the wild moor where the gipsy camp was pitched, from the bazaar, humming like a bee-hive with the crowd of buyers and sellers, to the jungle where the lonely courier shakes his bunch of iron rings to scare away the hyenas. He had just as lively an idea of the insurrection at Benares as of Lord George Gordon's riots, and of the execution of Nuncomar as of the execution of Dr. Dodd. Oppression in Bengal was to him the same thing as oppression in the streets of London."[310]

Section VI.—His Rudeness and Humor

Other forms of his talent are more peculiarly English. Macaulay has a rough touch; when he strikes, he knocks down. Béranger sings:

> "*Chez nous, point.*
> *Point de ces coups de poing*
> *Qui font tant d'honneur à l'Angleterre.*"[311]

And a French reader would be astonished if he heard a great historian treat an illustrious poet in this style:

"But in all those works in which Mr. Southey has completely abandoned narration, and has undertaken to argue moral and political questions, his failure has been complete and ignominious. On such occasions his writings are rescued from utter contempt and derision solely by the beauty and purity of the English. We find, we confess, so great a charm in Mr. Southey's style that, even when he writes nonsense, we generally read it with pleasure, except indeed when he tries to be droll. A more insufferable jester never existed. He very often attempts to be humorous, and yet we do not remember a single occasion on which he has succeeded, further than to be quaintly and flippantly dull. In one of his works he tells us that Bishop Spratt was very properly so-called, inasmuch as he was a very small poet. And in the book now before us he cannot quote Francis Bugg, the renegade Quaker, without a remark on his unsavoury name. A wise man might talk folly like this by his own fireside; but that any human being, after having made such a joke should write it down, and copy it out, and transmit it to the printer, and correct the proof-sheets, and send it forth into the world, is enough to make us ashamed of our species."[312]

We may imagine that Macaulay does not treat the dead better than the living. Thus he speaks of Archbishop Laud:

"The severest punishment which the two Houses could have inflicted on him would have been to set him at liberty and send him to Oxford. There he might have staid, tortured by his own diabolical temper, hungering for Puritans to pillory and mangle, plaguing the Cavaliers, for want of somebody else to plague, with his peevishness and absurdity, performing grimaces and antics in the cathedral, continuing that incomparable diary, which we never see without forgetting the vices of his heart in the imbecility of his intellect, minuting down his dreams, counting the drops of blood which fell from his nose, watching the direction of the salt, and listening for the note of the screech-owls. Contemptuous mercy was the only vengeance which it became the Parliament to take on such a ridiculous old bigot."[313]

While he jests he remains grave, as do almost all the writers of his country. Humor consists in saying extremely comical things in a solemn tone, and in preserving a lofty style and ample phraseology, at the very moment when the author is making all his hearers laugh. Such is the beginning of an article on a new historian of Burleigh:

"The work of Dr. Nares has filled us with astonishment similar to that which Captain Lemuel Gulliver felt when first he landed in Brobdingnag, and saw corn as high as the oaks in the New Forest, thimbles as large as buckets, and wrens of the bulk of turkeys. The whole book, and every component part of it, is on a gigantic scale. The title is as long as an ordinary preface; the prefatory matter would furnish out an ordinary book: and the book contains as much reading as an ordinary library. We cannot sum up the merits of the stupendous mass of paper which lies before us better than by saying that it consists of about two thousand closely printed quarto pages, that it occupies fifteen hundred inches cubic measure, and that it weighs sixty pounds avoir-du-pois. Such a book might, before the deluge, have been considered as light reading by Hilpah and Shalum. But unhappily the life of man is now threescore years and ten; and we cannot but think it somewhat unfair in Dr. Nares to demand from us so large a portion of so short an existence."[314]

This comparison, borrowed from Swift, is a mockery in Swift's taste. Mathematics become in English hands an excellent means of raillery; and we remember how the Dean, comparing Roman and English generosity by numbers, overwhelmed Marlborough by a sum in addition. Humor employs against the people it attacks, positive facts, commercial arguments, odd contrasts drawn from ordinary life. This surprises and perplexes the reader, without warning; he falls abruptly into some familiar and grotesque detail; the shock is violent; he bursts out laughing without being much amused; the trigger is pulled so suddenly and so roughly that it is like a knockdown blow. For instance, Macaulay is refuting those who would not print the indecent classical authors:

"We find it difficult to believe that, in a world so full of temptations as this, any gentleman whose life would have been virtuous if he had not read Aristophanes and Juvenal will be made vicious by reading them. A man who, exposed to all the influences of such a state of society as that in which we live, is yet afraid of exposing himself to the influence of a few Greek or Latin verses, acts, we think, much like the felon who begged the sheriffs to let him have an umbrella held over his head from the door of Newgate to the gallows, because it was a drizzling morning, and he was apt to take cold."[315]

Irony, sarcasm, the bitterest kinds of pleasantry, are the rule with Englishmen. They tear when they scratch. To be convinced of this, we should compare French scandal, as Molière represents it in the "Misanthrope," with English scandal as Sheridan represents it, imitating Molière and the "Misanthrope." Célimène pricks, but does not wound; Lady Sneerwell's friends wound, and leave bloody marks on all the reputations which they handle. The raillery, which I am about to give, is one of Macaulay's tenderest:

"They (the ministers) therefore gave the command to Lord Galway, an experienced veteran, a man who was in war what Molière's doctors were in medicine, who thought it much more honorable to fail according to rule, than to succeed by innovation, and who would have been very much ashamed of himself if he had taken Monjuich by means so strange as those which Peterborough employed. This great commander conducted the campaign of 1707 in the most scientific manner. On the plain of Almanza he encountered the army of the Bourbons. He drew up his troops according to the methods prescribed by the best writers, and in a few hours lost eighteen thousand men, a hundred and twenty standards, all his baggage and all his artillery."[316]

These incivilities are all the stronger, because the ordinary tone is noble and serious.

Hitherto we have seen only the reasoner, the scholar, the orator, and the wit: there is still in Macaulay a poet; and if we had not read his "Lays of Ancient Rome," it would suffice to read a few of his periods, in which the imagination, long held in check by the severity of the proof, breaks out suddenly in splendid metaphors, and expands into magnificent comparisons, worthy by their amplitude of being introduced into an epic:

"Ariosto tells a pretty story of a fairy, who, by some mysterious law of her nature, was condemned to appear at certain seasons in the form of a foul and poisonous snake. Those who injured her during the period of her disguise were forever excluded from participation in the blessings which she bestowed. But to those who, in spite of her loathsome aspect, pitied and protected her, she afterwards revealed herself in the beautiful and celestial form which was natural to her, accompanied their steps, granted all their wishes, filled their houses with wealth, made them happy in love and victorious in war. Such a spirit is Liberty. At times she takes the form of a hateful reptile. She grovels, she hisses, she stings. But woe to those who in disgust shall venture to crush her! And happy are those who, having dared to receive her in her degraded and frightful shape, shall at length be rewarded by her in the time of her beauty and her glory!"[317]

These noble words come from the heart; the fount is full, and though it flows, it never becomes dry. As soon as the writer speaks of a cause which he loves, as soon as he sees Liberty rise before him, with Humanity and Justice, Poetry bursts forth spontaneously from his soul and sets her crown on the brows of her noble sisters:

"The Reformation is an event long past. That volcano has spent its rage. The wide waste produced by its outbreak is forgotten. The landmarks which were swept away have been replaced. The ruined edifices have been repaired. The lava has covered with a rich incrustation the fields which it once devastated, and, after having turned a beautiful and fruitful garden into a desert, has again turned the desert into a still more beautiful and fruitful garden. The second great eruption is not yet over. The marks of its ravages are still all around us. The ashes are still hot beneath our feet. In some directions, the deluge of fire still continues to spread. Yet experience surely entitles us to believe that this explosion, like that which preceded it, will fertilize the soil which it has devastated. Already, in those parts which have suffered most severely, rich cultivation and secure dwellings have begun to appear amidst the waste. The more we read of the history of past ages, the more we observe the signs of our own times, the more do we feel our hearts filled and swelled up by a good hope for the future destinies of the human race."[318]

I ought, perhaps, in concluding this analysis, to point out the imperfections caused by these high qualities; how ease, charm, a vein of amiability, variety, simplicity, playfulness, are wanting in this manly eloquence, this solid reasoning, and this glowing dialectic; why the art of writing and classical purity are not always found in this partisan, fighting from his platform; in short, why an Englishman is not a Frenchman or an Athenian. I prefer to transcribe another passage, the solemnity and magnificence of which will give some idea of the grave and rich ornament, which Macaulay throws over his narrative, a sort of potent vegetation, flowers of brilliant purple, like those which are spread over every page of "Paradise Lost" and "Childe Harold." Warren Hastings had returned from India, and had just been placed on his trial:

PAGE FROM THE PRAYER-BOOK OF JUANA OF CASTILE
Fac-simile example of Book Illumination in the Sixteenth Century.

"On the thirteenth of February, 1788, the sittings of the Court commenced. There have been spectacles more dazzling to the eye, more gorgeous with jewellery and cloth of gold, more attractive to grown-up children, than that which was then exhibited at Westminster; but, perhaps, there never was a spectacle so well calculated to strike a highly cultivated, a reflecting, an imaginative mind. All the various kinds of interests which belong to the near and to the distant, to the present and to the past, were collected on one spot, and in one hour. All the talents and all the accomplishments which are developed by liberty and civilization were now displayed, with every advantage that could be derived both from co-operation and from contrast. Every step in the proceedings carried the mind either backward, through many troubled centuries, to the days when the foundations of our constitution were laid; or far away, over boundless seas and deserts, to dusky nations living under strange stars, worshipping strange gods, and writing strange characters from right to left. The High Court of Parliament was to sit, according to forms handed down from the days of the Plantagenets, on an Englishman accused of exercising tyranny over the lord of the holy city of Benares, and over the ladies of the princely house of Oude.

"The place was worthy of such a trial. It was the great Hall of William Rufus, the hall which had resounded with acclamations at the inauguration of thirty kings, the hall which had witnessed the just sentence of Bacon and the just absolution of Somers, the hall where the eloquence of Strafford had for a moment awed and melted a victorious party inflamed with just resentment, the hall where Charles had confronted the High Court of Justice with the placid courage which has half redeemed his fame. Neither military nor civil pomp was wanting. The avenues were lined with grenadiers. The streets were kept clear by cavalry. The peers, robed in gold and ermine, were marshalled by the heralds under Garter King at-arms. The judges in their vestments of state attended to give advice on points of law. Near a hundred and seventy lords, three-fourths of the Upper House as the Upper House then was, walked in solemn order from their usual place of assembling to the tribunal. The junior baron present led the way, George Eliot Lord Heathfield, recently ennobled for his memorable defence of Gibraltar against the fleets and armies of France and Spain. The long procession was closed by the Duke of Norfolk, Earl Marshal of the realm, by the great dignitaries, and by the brothers and sons of the King. Last of all came the Prince of Wales, conspicuous by his fine person and noble bearing. The gray old walls were hung with scarlet. The long galleries were crowded by an audience such as has rarely excited the fears or the emulation of an orator. There were gathered together, from all parts of a great, free, enlightened, and prosperous empire, grace and female loveliness, wit and learning, the representatives of every science and of every art. There were seated round the Queen the fair-haired young daughters of the house of Brunswick. There the Ambassadors of great Kings and Commonwealths gazed with admiration on a spectacle which no other country in the world could present. There Siddons, in the prime of her majestic beauty, looked with emotion on a scene surpassing all the imitations of the stage. There the historian of the Roman Empire thought of the days when Cicero pleaded the cause of Sicily against Verres, and when, before a senate which still retained some show of freedom, Tacitus thundered against the oppressor of Africa. There were seen, side by side, the greatest painter and the greatest scholar of the age. The spectacle had allured Reynolds from that easel which has preserved to us the thoughtful foreheads of so many writers and statesmen, and the sweet smiles of so many noble matrons. It had induced Parr to suspend his labors in that dark and profound mine from which he had extracted a vast treasure of erudition, a treasure too often buried in the earth, too often paraded with injudicious and inelegant ostentation, but still precious, massive, and splendid. There appeared the voluptuous charms of her to whom the heir of the throne had in secret plighted his faith. There too was she, the beautiful mother of a beautiful race, the Saint Cecilia whose delicate features, lighted up by love and music, art has rescued from the common decay. There were the members of that brilliant society which quoted, criticised, and exchanged repartees, under the rich peacock-hangings of Mrs. Montague. And there the ladies whose lips, more persuasive than those of Fox himself, had carried the Westminster election against palace and treasury, shone round Georgiana, Duchess of Devonshire."[319]

This evocation of the national history, glory, and constitution forms a picture of a unique kind. The species of patriotism and poetry which it reveals is an abstract of Macaulay's talent; and the talent, like the picture, is thoroughly English.

Section VII.—Estimate of Macaulay's Work

Thus prepared, he entered upon the history of England; and he chose therefrom the period best suited to his political opinions, his style, his passion, his knowledge, the national taste, the sympathy of Europe. He related the establishment of the English constitution, and concentrated all the rest of history about this unique event, "the finest in the world," to the mind of an Englishman and a politician. He brought to this work a new method of great beauty, extreme power; its success has been extraordinary. When the second volume appeared, 30,000 copies were ordered beforehand. Let us try to describe this history, to connect it with that method, and that method to that order of mind.

The history is universal and not broken. It comprehends events of every kind, and treats of them simultaneously. Some have related the history of races, others of classes, others of governments, others of sentiments, ideas, and manner; Macaulay has related all.

"I should very imperfectly execute the task which I have undertaken if I were merely to treat of battles and sieges, of the rise and fall of administrations, of intrigues in the palace, and of debates in the parliament. It will be my endeavor to relate the history of the people as well as the history of the government, to trace the progress of useful and ornamental arts, to describe the rise of religious sects and the changes of literary taste, to portray the manners of successive generations, and not to pass by with neglect even the revolutions which have taken place in dress, furniture, repasts, and public amusements. I shall cheerfully bear the reproach of having descended below the dignity of history, if I can succeed in placing before the English of the nineteenth century a true picture of the life of their ancestors."[320]

He kept his word. He has omitted nothing, and passed nothing by. His portraits are mingled with his narrative. We find those of Danby, Nottingham, Shrewsbury, Howe, during the account of a session, between two parliamentary divisions. Short, curious anecdotes, domestic details, the description of furniture, intersect without disjointing, the record of a war. Quitting the narrative of important business, we gladly look upon the Dutch tastes of William, the Chinese museum, the grottoes, the mazes, aviaries, ponds, geometrical garden-beds, with which he defaced Hampton Court. A political dissertation precedes or follows the relation of a battle; at other times the author is a tourist or a psychologist before becoming a politician or a tactician. He describes the Highlands of Scotland, semi-papistical and semi-pagan, the seers wrapped in bulls' hides to await the moment of inspiration, Christians making libations of milk or beer to the demons of the place; pregnant women, girls of eighteen, working a wretched patch of oats, whilst their husbands or fathers, athletic men, basked in the sun; robbery and barbarities looked upon as honorable deeds; men stabbed from behind or burnt alive; repulsive food, coarse oats, and cakes made of the blood of a live cow, offered to guests as a mark of favor and politeness; infected hovels where men lay on the bare ground, and where they woke up half smothered, half blinded by the smoke, and half mad with the itch. The next instant he stops to mark a change in the public taste, the horror then experienced on account of these brigands' retreats, this country of wild rocks and barren moors; the admiration now felt for this land of heroic warriors, this country of grand mountains, seething waterfalls, picturesque defiles. He finds in the progress of physical welfare the causes of this moral revolution, and concludes that, if we praise mountains and an uncivilized life, it is because we are satiated with security. He is successively an economist, a literary man, a publicist, an artist, a historian, a biographer, a story-teller, even a philosopher; by this diversity of parts he imitates the diversity of human life, and presents to the eyes, heart, mind, all the faculties of man, the complete history of the civilization of his country.

Others, like Hume, have tried, or are trying to do it. They set forth now religious matters, a little further political events, then literary details, finally general considerations on the change of society and government, believing that a collection of histories is history, and that parts joined endwise are a body. Macaulay did not believe it and he did well. Though English, he had the spirit of harmony. So many accumulated events form with him not a total, but a whole. Explanations, accounts, dissertations, anecdotes, illustrations, comparisons, allusions to modern events, everything is connected in his book. It is because everything is connected in his mind. He had a most lively consciousness of causes; and causes unite facts. By them scattered events are assembled into a single event; they unite them because they produce them, and the historian, who seeks them all out, cannot fail to perceive or to feel the unity which is their effect. Read, for instance, the voyage of James II to Ireland: no picture is more curious. Is it, however, nothing more than a curious picture? When the king arrived at Cork there were no horses to be found. The country is a desert. No more industry, cultivation, civilization, since the English and Protestant colonists were driven out, robbed and slain. James was received between two hedges of half-naked Rapparees, armed with skeans, stakes, and half-pikes; under his horse's feet they spread by way of carpet the rough frieze mantles, such as the brigands and shepherds wore. He was offered garlands of cabbage stalks for crowns of laurel. In a large district he only found two carts. The palace of the lord-lieutenant in Dublin was so ill-built that the rain drenched the rooms. The king left for Ulster; the French officers thought they were travelling "through the deserts of Arabia." The Count d'Avaux wrote to the French court that to get one truss of hay they had to send five or six miles. At Charlemont, with great difficulty, as a matter of favor, they obtained a bag of oatmeal for the French legation. The superior officers lay in dens which they would have thought too foul for their dogs. The Irish soldiers were half-savage marauders, who could only shout, cut throats, and disband. Ill fed on potatoes and sour milk, they cast themselves like starved men on the great flocks belonging to the Protestants. They greedily tore the flesh of oxen and sheep, and swallowed it half raw and half rotten. For lack of kettles, they cooked it in the skin. When Lent began, the plunderers generally ceased to devour, but continued to destroy. A peasant would kill a cow merely in order to get a pair of brogues. At times a band slaughtered fifty or sixty beasts, took the skins, and left the bodies to poison the air. The French ambassador reckoned that in six weeks there had been slain 50,000 horned cattle, which were rotting on the ground. They counted the number of the sheep and lambs slain at 400,000. Cannot the result of the rebellion be seen before-hand? What could be expected of these gluttonous serfs, so stupid and savage? What could be drawn from a devastated land, peopled with robbers? To what kind of discipline could these marauders and butchers be subjected? What resistance will they make on the Boyne, when they see William's old regiments, the furious squadrons of French refugees, the enraged and insulted Protestants of Londonderry and Enniskillen, leap into the river and run with uplifted swords against their muskets? They will flee, the king at their head; and the minute anecdotes scattered amidst the account of receptions, voyages, and ceremonies, will have announced the victory of the Protestants. The history of manners is thus seen to be involved in the history of events; the one is the cause of the other, and the description explains the narrative.

It is not enough to see some causes; we must see a great many of them. Every event has a multitude. Is it enough for me, if I wish to understand the action of Marlborough or of James, to be reminded of a disposition or a quality which explains it? No; for, since it has for a cause a whole situation and a whole character, I must see at one glance and in abstract the whole character and situation which produced it. Genius concentrates. It is measured by the number of recollections and ideas which it assembles in one point. That which Macaulay has assembled is enormous. I know no historian who has a surer, better furnished, better regulated memory. When he is relating the actions of a man or a party, he sees in an instant all the events of his history, and all the*maxims of his conduct; he has all the details present; he remembers them every moment, and a great many of them. He has forgotten nothing; he runs through them as easily, as completely, as surely, as on the day when he enumerated or wrote them. No one has so well taught or known history. He is as much steeped in it as his personages. The ardent Whig or Tory, experienced, trained to business, who rose and shook the House, had not more numerous, better arranged, more precise arguments. He did not better know the strength and weakness of his cause; he was not more familiar with the intrigues, rancors, variation of parties, the chances of the strife, individual and public interests. The great novelists penetrate the soul of their characters, assume their feelings, ideas, language; it seems as if Balzac had been a commercial traveller, a female doorkeeper, a courtesan, an old maid, a poet, and that he had spent his life in being each of these personages: his existence is multiplied, and his name is legion. With a different talent, Macaulay has the same power: an incomparable advocate, he pleads an infinite number of causes; and he is master of each cause, as fully as his client. He has answers for all objections, explanations for all obscurities, reasons for all tribunals. He is ready at every moment, and on all parts of his case. It seems as if he had been Whig, Tory, Puritan, Member of the Privy Council, Ambassador. He is not a poet like Michelet; he is not a philosopher like Guizot; but he possesses so well all the oratorical powers, he accumulates and arranges so many facts, he holds them so closely in his hand, he manages them with so much ease and vigor, that he succeeds in recomposing the whole and harmonious woof of history, not losing or separating one thread. The poet reanimates the dead; the philosopher formulates creative laws; the orator knows, expounds, and pleads causes. The poet resuscitates souls, the philosopher composes a system, the orator redisposes chains of arguments; but all three march towards the same end by different routes, and the orator, as well as his rivals, and by other means than his rivals, reproduces in his work the unity and complexity of life.

A second feature of this history is clearness. It is popular; no one explains better, or so much, as Macaulay. It seems as if he were making a wager with his reader, and said to him: Be as absent in mind, as stupid, as ignorant as you please; in vain you will be absent in mind, you shall listen to me; in vain you will be stupid, you shall understand; in vain you will be ignorant, you shall learn. I will repeat the same idea in so many different forms, I will make it sensible by such familiar and precise examples, I will announce it so clearly at the beginning, I will resumé it so carefully at the end, I will mark the divisions so well, follow the order of ideas so exactly, I will display so great a desire to enlighten and convince you, that you cannot help being enlightened and convinced. He certainly thought thus when he was preparing the following passage on the law which, for the first time, granted to Dissenters the liberty of exercising their worship:

"Of all the Acts that have ever been passed by Parliament, the Toleration Act is perhaps that which most strikingly illustrates the peculiar vices and the peculiar excellences of English legislation. The science of Politics bears in one respect a close analogy to the science of Mechanics. The mathematician can easily demonstrate that a certain power, applied by means of a certain lever or of a certain system of pulleys, will suffice to raise a certain weight. But his demonstration proceeds on the supposition that the machinery is such as no load will bend or break. If the engineer, who has to lift a great mass of real granite by the instrumentality of real timber and real hemp, should absolutely rely on the propositions which he finds in treatises on Dynamics, and should make no allowance for the imperfection of his materials, his whole apparatus of beams, wheels, and ropes would soon come down in ruin, and, with all his geometrical skill, he would be found a far inferior builder to those painted barbarians who, though they never heard of the parallelogram of forces, managed to pile up Stonehenge. What the engineer is to the mathematician, the active statesman is to the contemplative statesman. It is indeed most important that legislators and administrators should be versed in the philosophy of government, as it is most important that the architect who has to fix an obelisk on its pedestal, or to hang a tubular bridge over an estuary, should be versed in the philosophy of equilibrium and motion. But, as he who has actually to build must bear in mind many things never noticed by D'Alembert and Euler, so must he who has actually to govern be perpetually guided by considerations to which no allusion can be found in the writings of Adam Smith or Jeremy Bentham. The perfect law-giver is a just temper between the mere man of theory, who can see nothing but general principles, and the mere man of business, who can see nothing but particular circumstances. Of law-givers, in whom the speculative element has prevailed to the exclusion of the practical, the world has during the last eighty years been singularly fruitful. To their wisdom Europe and America have owed scores of abortive constitutions, scores of constitutions which have lived just long enough to make a miserable noise, and have then gone off in convulsions. But in English legislation the practical element has always predominated, and not seldom unduly predominated, over the speculative. To think nothing of symmetry and much of convenience; never to remove an anomaly merely because it is an anomaly; never to innovate except when some grievance is felt; never to innovate except so far as to get rid of the grievance; never to lay down any proposition of wider extent than the particular case for which it is necessary to provide; these are the rules which have, from the age of John to the age of Victoria, generally guided the deliberations of our two hundred and fifty Parliaments."[321]

Is the idea still obscure or doubtful? Does it still need proofs, illustrations? Do we wish for anything more? You answer, No; Macaulay answers, Yes. After the general explanation comes the particular; after the theory, the application; after the theoretical demonstration, the practical. We would fain stop; but he proceeds:

"The Toleration Act approaches very near to the idea of a great English law. To a jurist, versed in the theory of legislation, but not intimately acquainted with the temper of the sects and parties into which the nation was divided at the time of the Revolution, that Act would seem to be a mere chaos of absurdities and contradictions. It will not bear to be tried by sound general principles. Nay, it will not bear to be tried by any principle, sound or unsound. The sound principle undoubtedly is, that mere theological error ought not to be punished by the civil magistrate. This principle the Toleration Act not only does not recognize, but positively disclaims. Not a single one of the cruel laws enacted against non-conformists by the Tudors or the Stuarts is repealed. Persecution continues to be the general rule. Toleration is the exception. Nor is this all. The freedom which is given to conscience is given in the most capricious manner. A Quaker, by making a declaration of faith in general terms, obtains the full benefit of the Act without signing one of the thirty-nine Articles. An Independent minister, who is perfectly willing to make the declaration required from the Quaker, but who has doubts about six or seven of the Articles, remains still subject to the penal laws. Howe is liable to punishment if he preaches before he has solemnly declared his assent to the Anglican doctrine touching the Eucharist. Penn, who altogether rejects the Eucharist, is at perfect liberty to preach without making any declaration whatever on the subject.

"These are some of the obvious faults which must strike every person who examines the Toleration Act by that standard of just reason which is the same in all countries and in all ages. But these very faults may perhaps appear to be merits, when we take into consideration the passions and prejudices of those for whom the Toleration Act was framed. This law, abounding with contradictions which every smatterer in political philosophy can detect, did what a law framed by the utmost skill of the greatest masters of political philosophy might have failed to do. That the provisions which have been recapitulated are cumbrous, puerile, inconsistent with each other, inconsistent with the true theory of religious liberty, must be acknowledged. All that can be said in their defence is this: that they removed a vast mass of evil, without shocking a vast mass of prejudice; that they put an end, at once and forever, without one division in either House of Parliament, without one riot in the streets, with scarcely one audible murmur even from the classes most deeply tainted with bigotry, to a persecution which had raged during four generations, which had broken innumerable hearts, which had made innumerable firesides desolate, which had filled the prisons with men of whom the world was not worthy, which had driven thousands of those honest, diligent and god-fearing yeomen and artisans, who are the true strength of a nation, to seek a refuge beyond the ocean among the wigwams of red Indians and the lairs of panthers. Such a defence, however weak it may appear to some shallow speculators, will probably be thought complete by statesmen."[322]

What I find complete in this, is the art of developing. This antithesis of ideas, sustained by the antithesis of words, the symmetrical periods, the expressions designedly repeated to attract attention, the exhaustion of proof, set before our eyes the special-pleader's and oratorical talent, which we just before encountered in the art of pleading all causes, of employing an infinite number of methods, of mastering them all and always, during every incident of the lawsuit. The final manifestation of a mind of this sort is the faults into which its talent draws it. By dint of development, he protracts. More than once his explications are commonplace. He proves what all allow. He makes clear what is already clear. In one of his works there is a passage on the necessity of reactions which reads like the verbosity of a clever schoolboy. Other passages, excellent and novel, can only be read with pleasure once. On the second reading they appear too true; we have seen it all at a glance, and are wearied. I have omitted one-third of the passage on the Act of Toleration, and acute minds will think that I ought to have omitted another third.

The last feature, the most singular, the least English of this history, is, that it is interesting. Macaulay wrote, in the "Edinburgh Review," several volumes of essays; and everyone knows that the first merit of a reviewer or a journalist is to make himself readable. A thick volume naturally bores us; it is not thick for nothing; its bulk demands at the outset the attention of him who opens it. The solid binding, the table of contents, the preface, the substantial chapters, drawn up like soldiers in battle-array, all bid us take an arm-chair, put on a dressing-gown, place our feet on the fender, and study; we owe no less to the grave man who presents himself to us, armed with 600 pages of text and three years of reflection. But a newspaper which we glance at in a club, a review which we finger in a drawing-room in the evening, before sitting down to dinner, must needs attract the eyes, overcome absence of mind, conquer readers. Macaulay attained, through practice, this gift of readableness, and he retains in his history the habits which he acquired in periodicals. He employs every means of keeping up attention, good or indifferent, worthy or unworthy of his great talent; amongst others, allusion to actual circumstances. You may have heard the saying of an editor, to whom Pierre Leroux offered an article on God, "God! there is no actuality about it!" Macaulay profits by this remark. He never forgets the actual. If he mentions a regiment, he points out in a few lines the splendid deeds which it has done since its formation up to our own day; thus the officers of this regiment, encamped in the Crimea, stationed at Malta, or at Calcutta, are obliged to read his history. He relates the reception of Schomberg in the House: who is interested in Schomberg? Forthwith he adds that Wellington, a hundred years later, was received, under like circumstances, with a ceremony copied from the first: what Englishman is not interested in Wellington? He relates the siege of Londonderry, he points out the spot which the ancient bastions occupy in the present town, the field which was covered by the Irish camp, the well at which the besiegers drank: what citizen of Londonderry can help buying his book? Whatever town he comes upon, he notes the changes which it has undergone, the new streets added, the buildings repaired or constructed, the increase of commerce, the introduction of new industries: hence all the aldermen and merchants are constrained to subscribe to his work. Elsewhere we find an anecdote of an actor and actress: as the superlative degree is interesting, he begins by saying that William Mountford was the most agreeable comedian, that Anne Bracegirdle was the most popular actress of the time. If he introduces a statesman, he always announces him by some great word: he was the most insinuating, or the most equitable, or the best informed, or the most inveterately debauched, of all the politicians of the day. But Macaulay's great qualities serve him as well in this matter as his literary machinery: a little too manifest, a little too copious, a little too coarse. The astonishing number of details, the medley of psychological and moral dissertations, descriptions, relations, opinions, pleadings, portraits, beyond all, good composition and the continuous stream of eloquence, seize and retain the attention to the end. We have hard work to finish a volume of Lingard or Robertson; we should have hard work not to finish a volume of Macaulay.

Here is a detached narrative which shows very well, and in the abstract, the means of interesting which he employs, and the great interest which he excites. The subject is the Massacre of Glencoe. Macaulay begins by describing the spot like a traveller who has seen it, and points it out to the bands of tourists and dilettanti, historians and antiquarians, who every year start from London:

"Mac Ian dwelt in the mouth of a ravine situated not far from the southern shore of Loch Leven, an arm of the sea which deeply indents the western coast of Scotland, and separates Argyleshire from Inverness-shire. Near his house were two or three small hamlets inhabited by his tribe. The whole population which he governed was not supposed to exceed two hundred souls. In the neighbourhood of the little cluster of villages was some copsewood and some pasture land: but a little further up the defile no sign of population or of fruitfulness was to be seen. In the Gaelic tongue, Glencoe signifies the Glen of Weeping: and, in truth, that pass is the most dreary and melancholy of all the Scottish passes, the very Valley of the Shadow of Death. Mists and storms brood over it through the greater part of the finest summer; and even on those rare days when the sun is bright, and when there is no cloud in the sky, the impression made by the landscape is sad and awful. The path lies along a stream which issues from the most sullen and gloomy of mountain pools. Huge precipices of naked stone frown on both sides. Even in July the streaks of snow may often be discerned in the rifts near the summits. All down the sides of the crags heaps of ruin mark the headlong paths of the torrents. Mile after mile the traveller looks in vain for the smoke of one hut, or for one human form wrapped in a plaid, and listens in vain for the bark of a shepherd's dog, or the bleat of a lamb. Mile after mile the only sound that indicates life is the faint cry of a bird of prey from some stormbeaten pinnacle of rock. The progress of civilization, which has turned so many wastes into fields yellow with harvests or gay with apple blossoms, has only made Glencoe more desolate. All the science and industry of a peaceful age can extract nothing valuable from that wilderness: but, in an age of violence and rapine, the wilderness itself was valued on account of the shelter which it afforded to the plunderer and his plunder."[323]

The description, though very beautiful, is written for effect. The final antithesis explains it; the author has made it in order to show that the Macdonalds were the greatest brigands of the country.

The Master of Stair, who represented William III in Scotland, relying on the fact that Mac Ian had not taken the oath of allegiance on the appointed day, determined to destroy the chief and his clan. He was not urged by hereditary hate nor by private interest; he was a man of taste, polished and amiable. He did this crime out of humanity, persuaded that there was no other way of pacifying the Highlands. Thereupon Macaulay inserts a dissertation of four pages, very well written, full of interest and knowledge, whose diversity affords us rest, which leads us over all kinds of historical examples, and moral lessons:

"We daily see men do for their party, for their sect, for their country, for their favorite schemes of political and social reform, what they would not do to enrich or to avenge themselves. At a temptation directly addressed to our private cupidity or to our private animosity, whatever virtue we have takes the alarm. But virtue itself may contribute to the fall of him who imagines that it is in his power, by violating some general rule of morality, to confer an important benefit on a church, on a commonwealth, on mankind. He silences the remonstrances of conscience, and hardens his heart against the most touching spectacles of misery, by repeating to himself that his intentions are pure, that his objects are noble, that he is doing a little evil for the sake of a great good. By degrees he comes altogether to forget the turpitude of the means in the excellence of the end, and at length perpetrates without one internal twinge acts which would shock a buccaneer. There is no reason to believe that Dominic would, for the best archbishopric in Christendom, have incited ferocious marauders to plunder and slaughter a peaceful and industrious population, that Edward Digby would, for a dukedom, have blown a large assembly of people into the air, or that Robespierre would have murdered for hire one of the thousands whom he murdered from philanthropy."[324]

Do we not recognize here the Englishman brought up on psychological and moral essays and sermons, who involuntarily and every instant spreads one over the paper? This species of literature is unknown in French lecture-rooms and reviews; this is why it is unknown in French histories. When we wish to enter English history, we have only to step down from the pulpit and the newspaper.

I do not transcribe the sequel of the explanation, the examples of James V, Sixtus V, and so many others, whom Macaulay cites to find precedents for the Master of Stair. Then follows a very circumstantial and very solid discussion, to prove that William III was not responsible for the massacre. It is clear that Macaulay's object, here as elsewhere, is less to draw a picture than to suggest a judgment. He desires that we should have an opinion on the morality of the act, that we should attribute it to its real authors, that each should bear exactly his own share, and no more. A little further, when the question of the punishment of the crime arises, and William, having severely chastised the executioners, contents himself with recalling the Master of Stair, Macaulay writes a dissertation of several pages to consider this injustice and to blame the king. Here, as elsewhere, he is still an orator and a moralist; nothing has more power to interest an English reader. Happily for us, he at length becomes once more a narrator; the petty details which he then selects fix the attention, and place the scene before our eyes:

"The sight of the red coats approaching caused some anxiety among the population of the valley. John, the eldest son of the Chief, came, accompanied by twenty clansmen, to meet the strangers, and asked what this visit meant. Lieutenant Lindsay answered that the soldiers came as friends, and wanted nothing but quarters. They were kindly received, and were lodged under the thatched roofs of the little community. Glenlyon and several of his men were taken into the house of a tacksman who was named from the cluster of cabins over which he exercised authority, Inverriggen. Lindsay was accommodated nearer to the abode of the old chief. Auchintriater, one of the principal men of the clan, who governed the small hamlet of Auchnaion, found room there for a party commanded by a sergeant named Barbour. Provisions were liberally supplied. There was no want of beef, which had probably fattened in distant pastures: nor was any payment demanded: for in hospitality, as in thievery, the Gaelic marauders rivalled the Bedouins. During twelve days the soldiers lived familiarly with the people of the glen. Old Mac Ian, who had before felt many misgivings as to the relation in which he stood to the government, seems to have been pleased with the visit. The officers passed much of their time with him and his family. The long evenings were cheerfully spent by the peat fire, with the help of some packs of cards which had found their way to that remote corner of the world, and of some French brandy which was probably part of James's farewell gift to his Highland supporters. Glenlyon appeared to be warmly attached to his niece and her husband Alexander. Every day he came to their house to take his morning draught. Meanwhile he observed with minute attention all the avenues by which, when the signal for the slaughter should be given, the Macdonalds might attempt to escape to the hills; and he reported the result of his observations to Hamilton....

"The night was rough. Hamilton and his troops made slow progress, and were long after their time. While they were contending with the wind and snow, Glenlyon was supping and playing at cards with those whom he meant to butcher before daybreak. He and Lieutenant Lindsay had engaged themselves to dine with the old Chief on the morrow.

"Late in the evening a vague suspicion that some evil was intended crossed the mind of the Chief's eldest son. The soldiers were evidently in a restless state; and some of them uttered strange exclamations. Two men, it is said, were overheard whispering: 'I do not like this job,' one of them muttered; 'I should be glad to fight the Macdonalds. But to kill men in their beds— We must do as we are bid,' answered another voice. 'If there is anything wrong, our officers must answer for it.' John Macdonald was so uneasy, that, soon after midnight, he went to Glenlyon's quarters. Glenlyon and his men were all up, and seemed to be getting their arms ready for action. John, much alarmed, asked what these preparations meant. Glenlyon was profuse of friendly assurances. 'Some of Glengarry's people have been harrying the country. We are getting ready to march against them. You are quite safe. Do you think that, if you were in any danger, I should not have given a hint to your brother Sandy and his wife?' John's suspicions were quieted. He returned to his house, and lay down to rest."[325]

On the next day, at five in the morning, the old chieftain was assassinated: his men shot in their beds or by the fireside. Women were butchered; a boy twelve years old, who begged his life on his knees, was slain; they who fled half-naked, women and children, died of cold and hunger in the snow.

These precise details, these soldiers' conversations, this picture of evenings by the fireside, give to history the animation and life of a novel. And still the historian remains an orator: for he has chosen all these facts to exhibit the perfidy of the assassins and the horrible nature of the massacre; and he will make use of them later on, to demand, with all the power and passion of logic, the punishment of the criminals.

Section VIII.—Comparison of Macaulay with French Historians

Thus this History, whose qualities seem so little English, bears throughout the mark of genuine English talent. Universal, connected, it embraces all the facts in its vast, undivided, and unbroken woof. Developed, abundant, it enlightens obscure facts, and opens up to the most ignorant the most complicated questions. Interesting, varied, it attracts and preserves the attention. It has life, clearness, unity, qualities which appear to be wholly French. It seems as if the author were a popularizer like Thiers, a philosopher like Guizot, an artist like Thierry. The truth is, that he is an orator, and that after the fashion of his country; but, as he possesses in the highest degree the oratorical faculties, and possesses them with a national tendency and instincts, he seems to supplement through them the faculties which he has not. He is not genuinely philosophical; the mediocrity of his earlier chapters on the ancient history of England proves this sufficiently; but his force of reasoning, his habits of classification and order, bestow unity upon his History. He is not a genuine artist; when he draws a picture, he is always thinking of proving something; he inserts dissertations in the most interesting and affecting places; he has neither charm, lightness, vivacity, nor *finesse*, but a marvellous memory, vast knowledge, an ardent, political passion, a great legal talent for expounding and pleading every cause, a precise knowledge of precise and petty facts which rivet the attention, charm, diversify, animate, and warm a narrative. He is not simply a popularizer; he is too ardent, too eager to prove, to conquer belief, to beat down his foes, to have only the limpid talent of a man who explains and expounds, with no other end than to explain and expound, which spreads light throughout, and never spreads heat; but he is so well provided with details and reasons, so anxious to convince, so rich in his expositions, that he cannot fail to be popular. By this breadth of knowledge, this power of reasoning and passion, he has produced one of the finest books of the age, whilst manifesting the genius of his nation. This solidity, this energy, this deep political passion, these moral prepossessions, these oratorical habits, this limited philosophical power, this somewhat uniform style, without flexibility or sweetness, this eternal gravity, this geometrical progress to a settled end, announce in him the English mind. But if he is English to the French, he is not so to his nation. The animation, interest, clearness, unity of his narrative, astonish them. They think him brilliant, rapid, bold; it is, they say, a French mind. Doubtless he is so, in many respects: if he understands Racine badly, he admires Pascal and Bossuet; his friends say that he used daily to read Mme de Sévigné. Nay more, by the structure of his mind, by his eloquence and rhetoric, he is Latin; so that the inner structure of his talent places him amongst the classics; it is only by his lively appreciation, of special, complex, and sensible facts, by his energy and fierceness, by the rather heavy richness of his imagination, by the depth of his coloring, that he belongs to his race. Like Addison and Burke, he resembles a strange graft, fed and transformed by the sap of the national stock. At all events, this judgment is the strongest mark of the difference between the two nations. To reach the English intellect, a Frenchman must make two voyages. When he has crossed the first interval, which is wide, he comes upon Macaulay. Let him re-embark; he must accomplish a second passage, just as long, to arrive at Carlyle for instance— a mind fundamentally Germanic, on the genuine English soil.

---

[299]Macaulay's Works, ed. Lady Trevelyan, 8 vols. 1866; "Essay on Bacon," VI. 222.

[300]Macaulay's Works; "Essay on Bacon," VI. 223.

[301]"Charles himself, and his creature Laud, while they abjured the innocent badges of Popery, retained all its worst vices— a complete subjection of reason to authority, a weak preference of form to substance, a childish passion for mummeries, an idolatrous veneration for the priestly character, and, above all, a merciless intolerance."— Macaulay, V. 24; Milton.

"It is difficult to relate without a pitying smile, that in the sacrifice of the mass, Loyola saw transubstantiation take place, and that, as he stood praying on the steps of the Church of St. Dominic, he saw the Trinity in Unity, and wept aloud with joy and wonder."— Macaulay, VI. 468; Ranke, "History of the Popes."

[302]Macaulay, VI. 39; An Essay on William Pitt, Earl of Chatham.

[303]Macaulay, V. 27; Milton.

[304]Macaulay, V. 35; Milton.

[305]Macaulay, VII. 109; "Life and Writings of Addison."

[306]See in his "Essay on the Life and Writings of Addison" (VII. 78) Macaulay's observations on the "Campaign."

[307]Macaulay, VI. 549; "Warren Hastings."

[308]Ibid. 553.

[309]Macaulay, VI. 555; "Warren Hastings."

[310]Ibid. VI. 619; "Warren Hastings."

[311]Béranger, "Chansons," 2 vols. 1853; Les Boxeurs, ou L'Anglomane.

[312]Macaulay, V. 333; "Southey's Colloquies on Society."

[313]Macaulay, V. 204; "Hallam's Constitutional History."

[314]Ibid. 587; "Burleigh and his Times."

[315]Macaulay, VI. 491; "Comic Dramatists of the Restoration."

[316]Ibid. V. 672; "Lord Mahon's War of the Succession in Spain."
[317]Macaulay, V. 31; "Milton."
[318]Ibid. 595; "Burleigh and his Times."
[319]Macaulay, VI. 628; "Warren Hastings."
[320]Macaulay, I. 2; "History of England before the Restoration," ch. I.
[321]Macaulay, II. 463, "History of England," ch. XI.
[322]Macaulay, II. 465, "History of England," ch. XI.
[323]Macaulay, III. 513, "History of England," ch. XVIII.
[324]Macaulay, III. 519, "History of England," ch. XVIII.
[325]Macaulay, III. 526, "History of England," ch. XVIII.

Chapter Fourth. Philosophy and History—Carlyle

When we ask Englishmen, especially those under forty, who amongst them are the great thinkers, they first mention Carlyle; but at the same time they advise us not to read him, warning us that we will not understand him at all. Then, of course, we hasten to get the twenty volumes of Carlyle— criticism, history, pamphlets, fantasies, philosophy; we read them with very strange emotions, contradicting every morning our opinion of the night before. We discover at last that we are in presence of a strange animal, a relic of a lost family, a sort of mastodon, who has strayed in a world not made for him. We rejoice in this zoological good luck, and dissect him with minute curiosity, telling ourselves that we shall probably never find another like him.

Part I.—Style and Mind

Section I.—Carlyle's Obscurity and Crudeness

We are at first put out. All is new here— ideas, style, tone, the shape of the phrases, and the very vocabulary. He takes everything in a contrary meaning, does violence to everything, to expressions as well as to things. With him paradoxes are set down for principles; common-sense takes the form of absurdity. We are, as it were, carried into an unknown world, whose inhabitants walk head downwards, feet in the air, dressed in motley, as great lords and maniacs, with contortions, jerks, and cries; we are grievously stunned by these extravagant and discordant sounds; we want to stop our ears, we have a headache, we are obliged to decipher a new language. We see upon the table volumes which ought to be as clear as possible— "The History of the French Revolution," for instance; and there we read these headings to the chapters: "Realized Ideals— Viaticum— Astræa Redux— Petition in Hieroglyphs— Windbags— Mercury de Brézé— Broglie the War-God." We ask ourselves what connection there can be between these riddles and such simple events as we all know. We then perceive that Carlyle always speaks in riddles. "Logic-choppers" is the name he gives to the analysts of the eighteenth century; "Beaver science" is his word for the catalogues and classifications of our modern men of science; "Transcendental moonshine" signifies the philosophical and sentimental dreams imported from Germany. The religion of the "rotary calabash" means external and mechanical religion.[326] He cannot be contented with a simple expression; he employs figures at every step; he embodies all his ideas; he must touch forms. We see that he is besieged and haunted by brilliant or gloomy visions; every thought with him is a shock; a stream of misty passion comes bubbling into his overflowing brain, and the torrent of images breaks forth and rolls on amidst every kind of mud and magnificence. He cannot reason, he must paint. If he wants to explain the embarrassment of a young man obliged to choose a career amongst the lusts and doubts of the age, in which we live, he tells you of

"A world all rocking and plunging, like that old Roman one when the measure of its iniquities was full; the abysses, and subterranean and supernal deluges, plainly broken loose; in the wild dim-lighted chaos all stars of Heaven gone out. No star of Heaven visible, hardly now to any man; the pestiferous fogs and foul exhalations grown continual, have, except on the highest mountain-tops, blotted out all stars: will-o'-wisps, of various course and colour, take the place of stars. Over the wild surging chaos, in the leaden air, are only sudden glares of revolutionary lightning; then mere darkness, with philanthropistic phosphorescences, empty meteoric lights; here and there an ecclesiastical luminary still hovering, hanging on to its old quaking fixtures, pretending still to be a Moon or Sun— though visibly it is but a Chinese Lantern made of paper mainly, with candle-end foully dying in the heart of it."[327]

Imagine a volume, twenty volumes, made up of such pictures, united by exclamations and apostrophes; even history— that of the French Revolution— is like a delirium. Carlyle is a Puritan seer, before whose eyes pass scaffolds, orgies, massacres, battles, and who, beset by furious or bloody phantoms, prophesies, encourages, or curses. If we do not throw down the book from anger or weariness, we will become dazed; our ideas leave us, nightmare seizes us, a medley of grinning and ferocious figures whirl about in our head; we hear the howls of insurrection, cries of war; we are sick; we are like those hearers of the Covenanters whom the preaching filled with disgust or enthusiasm, and who broke the head of their prophet, if they did not take him for their leader.

These violent outbursts will seem to us still more violent if we mark the breadth of the field which they traverse. From the sublime to the ignoble, from the pathetic to the grotesque, is but a step with Carlyle. At one and the same time he touches the two extremes. His adorations end in sarcasms. The Universe is for him an oracle and a temple, as well as a kitchen and a stable. He moves freely about, and is at his ease in mysticism, as well as in brutality. Speaking of the setting sun at the North Cape, he writes:

"Silence as of death; for Midnight, even in the Arctic latitudes, has its character: nothing but the granite cliffs ruddy-tinged, the peaceable gurgle of that slow-heaving Polar Ocean, over which in the utmost North the great Sun hangs low and lazy, as if he too were slumbering. Yet is his cloud-couch wrought of crimson and cloth-of-gold; yet does his light stream over the mirror of waters, like a tremulous fire-pillar, shooting downwards to the abyss, and hide itself under my feet. In such moments, Solitude also is invaluable; for who would speak, or be looked on, when behind him lies all

Europe and Africa, fast asleep, except the watchmen; and before him the silent Immensity, and Palace of the Eternal, whereof our Sun is but a porch-lamp?"[328]

Such splendors he sees whenever he is face to face with nature. No one has contemplated with a more powerful emotion the silent stars which roll eternally in the pale firmament and envelop our little world. No one has contemplated with more of religious awe the infinite obscurity in which our slender thought appears for an instant like a gleam, and by our side the gloomy abyss in which the hot frenzy of life is to be extinguished. His eyes are habitually fixed on this vast Darkness, and he paints with a shudder of veneration and hope the effort which religions have made to pierce it:

"In the heart of the remotest mountains rises the little Kirk; the Dead all slumbering round it, under their white memorial stones, 'in hope of a happy resurrection';— dull wert thou, O Reader, if never in any hour (say of moaning midnight, when such Kirk hung spectral in the sky, and Being was as if swallowed up of Darkness) it spoke to thee— things unspeakable, that went to thy soul's soul. Strong was he that had a Church, what we can call a Church: he stood thereby, though 'in the centre of Immensities, in the conflux of Eternities,' yet manlike towards God and man: the vague shoreless Universe had become for him a firm city, and dwelling which he knew."[329]

Rembrandt alone has beheld these sombre visions drowned in shade, traversed by mystic rays: look, for example, at the church which he has painted; glance at the mysterious floating apparition, full of radiant forms, which he has set in the summit of the heavens, above the stormy night and the terror which shakes mortality.[330] The two imaginations have the same painful grandeur, the same scintillations, the same agony, and both sink with like facility into triviality and crudeness. No ulcer, no filth, is repulsive enough to disgust Carlyle. On occasion he will compare the politician who seeks popularity to "the dog that was drowned last summer, and that floats up and down the Thames with ebb and flood.... You get to know him by sight... with a painful oppression of nose.... Daily you may see him,... and daily the odour of him is getting more intolerable."[331] Absurdities, incongruities, abound in his style. When the frivolous Cardinal de Loménie proposed to convoke a Plenary Court, he compares him to "trained canary birds, that would fly cheerfully with lighted matches and fire cannon; fire whole powder magazines."[332] At need, he turns to funny images. He ends a dithyramb with a caricature: he bespatters magnificence with eccentric and coarse language: he couples poetry with puns:

"The Genius of England no longer soars Sunward, world defiant, like an Eagle through the storms, 'mewing her mighty youth,' as John Milton saw her do: the Genius of England, much liker a greedy Ostrich intent on provender and a whole skin mainly, stands with its other extremity Sunward; with its Ostrich-head stuck into the readiest bush, of old Church-tippets, King-cloaks, or what other 'sheltering Fallacy' there may be, and so awaits the issue. The issue has been slow; but it is now seen to have been inevitable. No Ostrich, intent on gross terrene provender, and sticking its head into Fallacies, but will be awakened one day— in a terrible *à-posteriori* manner, if not otherwise?"[333]

With such buffoonery he concludes his best book, never quitting his tone of gravity and gloom, in the midst of anathemas and prophecies. He needs these great shocks. He cannot remain quiet, or stick to one literary province at a time. He leaps in unimpeded jerks from one end of the field of ideas to the other; he confounds all styles, jumbles all forms, heaps together pagan allusions, Bible reminiscences, German abstractions, technical terms, poetry, slang, mathematics, physiology, archaic words, neologies. There is nothing he does not tread down and ravage. The symmetrical constructions of human art and thought, dispersed and upset, are piled under his hands into a vast mass of shapeless ruins, from the top of which he gesticulates and fights, like a conquering savage.

Section II.—The Humor of Carlyle

This kind of mind produces humor, a word untranslatable in French, because in France they have not the idea. Humor is a species of talent which amuses Germans, Northmen; it suits their mind, as beer and brandy suit their palate. For men of another race it is disagreeable; they often find it too harsh and bitter. Amongst other things, this talent embraces a taste for contrasts. Swift jokes with the serious mien of an ecclesiastic, performing religious rites, and develops the most grotesque absurdities, like a convinced man. Hamlet, shaken with terror and despair, bristles with buffooneries. Heine mocks his own emotions, even whilst he displays them. These men love travesties, put a solemn garb over comic ideas, a clown's jacket over grave ones. Another feature of humor is that the author forgets the public for whom he writes. He tells us that he does not care for us, that he needs neither to be understood nor approved, that he thinks and amuses himself by himself, and that if his taste and ideas displease us we have only to take ourselves off. He wishes to be refined and original at his ease; he is at home in his book, and with closed doors, he gets into his slippers, dressing-gown, often with his feet in the air, sometimes without a shirt. Carlyle has a style of his own, and marks his idea in his own fashion; it is our business to understand it. He alludes to a saying of Goethe, or Shakespeare, or to an anecdote which strikes him at the moment; so much the worse for us if we do not know it. He shouts when the fancy takes him; the worse for us if our ears do not like it. He writes on the caprice of his imagination, with all the starts of invention; the worse for us if our mind goes at a different pace. He catches on the wing all the shades, all the oddities of his conception; the worse for us if ours cannot reach them. A last feature of humor is the irruption of violent joviality, buried under a heap of sadness. Absurd incongruity appears unexpected. Physical nature, hidden and oppressed under habits of melancholic reflection, is laid bare for an instant. We see a grimace, a clown's gesture, then everything resumes its wonted gravity. Add lastly the unforeseen flashes of imagination. The humorist covers a poet; suddenly, in the monotonous mist of prose, at the end of an argument, a vista opens up; beautiful or ugly, it matters not; it is enough that it strikes our eyes. These inequalities fairly paint the solitary, energetic, imaginative German, a lover of violent contrasts, based on personal and gloomy reflection, with sudden up-wellings of physical instinct, so different from the Latin and classical races, races of orators or artists, where they never write but with an eye to the public, where they relish only consequent ideas, are only happy in the spectacle of harmonious forms, where the fancy is regulated, and voluptuousness appears natural. Carlyle is profoundly German, nearer to the primitive stock than any of his contemporaries, strange and unexampled in his fancies and his pleasantries; he calls himself "a bemired aurochs or urus of the German woods,... the poor wood-ox so bemired in the forests."[334] For instance, his first book, "Sartor Resartus," which is a clothes-philosophy, contains, *à propos* of aprons and breeches, metaphysics, politics, psychology. Man, according to him, is a dressed animal. Society has clothes for its foundation. "How, without Clothes, could we possess the master-organ, soul's seat, and true pineal gland of the Body social: I mean a PURSE:"[335]

"To the eye of vulgar Logic," says he, "what is man? An omnivorous Biped that wears Breeches. To the eye of Pure Reason what is he? A Soul, a Spirit, and divine Apparition. Round his mysterious Me, there lies, under all those wool-rags, a Garment of Flesh (or of Senses) contextured in the Loom of Heaven; whereby he is revealed to his like, and dwells with them in UNION and DIVISION; and sees and fashions for himself a Universe, with azure Starry Spaces, and long Thousands of Years. Deep-hidden is he under that strange Garment; amid Sounds and Colours and Forms, as it were, swathed-in, and inextricably over-shrouded: yet it is skywoven, and worthy of a God."[336]

The paradox continues, at once eccentric and mystical, hiding theories under follies, mixing together fierce ironies, tender pastorals, love-stories, explosions of rage, and carnival pictures. He says well:

"Perhaps the most remarkable incident in Modern History is not the Diet of Worms, still less the battle of Austerlitz, Wagram, Waterloo, Peterloo, or any other Battle; but an incident passed carelessly over by most Historians, and treated with some degree of ridicule by others: namely, George Fox's making to himself a suit of Leather."[337]

For, thus clothed for the rest of his life, lodging in a tree and eating wild berries, man could remain idle and invent Puritanism, that is, conscience-worship, at his leisure. This is how Carlyle treats the ideas which are dearest to him. He jests in connection with the doctrine, which was to employ his life and occupy his whole soul.

Should we like an abstract of his politics, and his opinion about his country? He proves that in the modern transformation of religions two principal sects have risen, especially in England; the one of "Poor Slaves" the other of Dandies. Of the first he says:

"Something Monastic there appears to be in their Constitution: we find them bound by the two Monastic Vows, of Poverty and Obedience; which Vows, especially the former, it is said, they observe with great strictness; nay, as I have understood it, they are pledged, and be it by any solemn Nazarene ordination or not, irrevocably consecrated thereto, even *before* birth. That the third Monastic Vow, of Chastity, is rigidly enforced among them, I find no ground to conjecture.

"Furthermore, they appear to imitate the Dandiacal Sect in their grand principle of wearing a peculiar Costume.... Their raiment consists of innumerable skirts, lappets, and irregular wings, of all cloths and of all colours; through the labyrinthic intricacies of which their bodies are introduced by some unknown process. It is fastened together by a multiplex combination of buttons, thrums, and skewers; to which frequently is added a girdle of leather, of hempen or even of straw rope, round the loins. To straw rope, indeed, they seem partial, and often wear it by way of sandals....

"One might fancy them worshippers of Hertha, or the Earth: for they dig and affectionately work continually in her bosom; or else, shut up in private Oratories, meditate and manipulate the substances derived from her; seldom looking-up towards the Heavenly Luminaries, and then with comparative indifference. Like the Druids, on the other hand, they live in dark dwellings; often even breaking their glass-windows, where they find such, and stuffing them up with pieces of raiment, or other opaque substances, till the fit obscurity is restored....

"In respect of diet they have also their observances. All Poor Slaves are Rhizophagous (or Root-eaters); a few are Ichthyophagous, and use Salted Herrings; other animal food they abstain from; except indeed, with perhaps some strange inverted fragment of a Brahminical feeling, such animals as die a natural death. Their universal sustenance is the root named Potato, cooked by fire alone.... In all their Religious Solemnities, Potheen is said to be an indispensable requisite, and largely consumed."[338]

Of the other sect he says:

"A certain touch of Manicheism, not indeed in the Gnostic shape, is discernible enough: also (for human error walks in a cycle, and reappears at intervals) a not-inconsiderable resemblance to that Superstition of the Athos Monks, who by fasting from all nourishment, and looking intensely for a length of time into their own navels, came to discern therein the true Apocalypse of Nature, and Heaven Unveiled. To my own surmise, it appears as if this Dandiacal Sect were but a new modification, adapted to the new time, of that primeval Superstition, *Self-worship*....

"They affect great purity and separatism; distinguish themselves by a particular costume (whereof some notices were given in the earlier part of this Volume); likewise, so far as possible, by a particular speech (apparently some broken *Lingua-franca*, or English-French); and, on the whole, strive to maintain a true Nazarene deportment, and keep themselves unspotted from the world."

"They have their Temples, whereof the chief, as the Jewish Temple did, stands in their metropolis; and is named *Almack's*, a word of uncertain etymology. They worship principally by night; and have their Highpriests and Highpriestesses, who, however, do not continue for life. The rites, by some supposed to be of the Menadic sort, or perhaps with an Elusinian or Cabiric character, are held strictly secret. Nor are Sacred Books wanting to the Sect; these they call *Fashionable Novels*: however, the Canon is not completed, and some are canonical, and others not...."[339]

Their chief articles of faith are:

"1. Coats should have nothing of the triangle about them; at the same time, wrinkles behind should be carefully avoided.

"2. The collar is a very important point: it should be low behind, and slightly rolled.

"3. No licence of fashion can allow a man of delicate taste to adopt the posterial luxuriance of a Hottentot.

"4. There is safety in a swallow-tail.

"5. The good sense of a gentleman is nowhere more finely developed than in his rings.

"6. It is permitted to mankind, under certain restrictions, to wear white waistcoats.

"7. The trousers must be exceedingly tight across the hips.

"All which Propositions I, for the present, content myself with modestly but peremptorily and irrevocably denying."[340]

This premised, he draws conclusions:

"I might call them two boundless and indeed unexampled Electric Machines (turned by the 'Machinery of Society'), with batteries of opposite quality; Drudgism the Negative, Dandyism the Positive: one attracts hourly towards it and appropriates all the Positive Electricity of the nation (namely, the Money thereof); the other is equally busy with the Negative (that is to say the Hunger), which is equally potent. Hitherto you see only partial, transient sparkles and sputters: but wait a little, till the entire nation is in an electric state; till your whole vital Electricity, no longer healthfully Neutral, is cut into two isolated portions of Positive and Negative (of Money and of Hunger); and stands there bottled-up in two World-Batteries! The stirring of a child's finger brings the two together; and then— What then? The Earth is but shivered into impalpable smoke by that Doom's thunder-peal: the Sun misses one of his Planets in Space, and thenceforth there are no eclipses of the Moon. Or better still, I might liken— — "[341]

He stops suddenly, and leaves you to your conjectures. This bitter pleasantry is that of an enraged or despairing man, who designedly, and simply by reason of the violence of his passion, would restrain it and force himself to laugh; but whom a sudden shudder at the end reveals just as he is. In one place Carlyle says that there is, at the bottom of the English character, underneath all its habits of calculation and coolness, an inextinguishable furnace:

"Deep hidden it lies, far down in the centre, like genial central fire, with stratum after stratum of arrangement, traditionary method, composed productiveness, all built above it, vivified and rendered fertile by it: justice, clearness, silence, perseverance unhasting, unresting diligence, hatred of disorder, hatred of injustice, which is the worst disorder, characterise this people: the inward fire we say, as all such fires would be, is hidden in the centre. Deep hidden, but awakenable, but immeasurable; let no man awaken it."

It is a fire of extraordinary fierceness, as the rage of devoted Berserkirs, who, once rushing to the heat of the battle, felt no more their wounds, and lived, fought, and killed, pierced with strokes, the least of which would have been mortal to an ordinary man. It is this destructive frenzy, this rousing of inward unknown powers, this loosening of a ferocity, enthusiasm, and imagination disordered and not to be bridled, which appeared in these men at the Renaissance and the Reformation, and a remnant of which still endures in Carlyle. Here is a vestige of it, in a passage almost worthy of Swift, which is the abstract of his customary emotions, and at the same time his conclusion on the age in which we live:

"Supposing swine (I mean four-footed swine), of sensibility and superior logical parts, had attained such culture; and could, after survey and reflection, jot down for us their notion of the Universe, and of their interests and duties there— might it not well interest a discerning public, perhaps in unexpected ways, and give a stimulus to the languishing book-trade? The votes of all creatures, it is understood at present, ought to be had; that you may 'legislate' for them with better insight. 'How can you govern a thing,' say many, 'without first asking its vote?' Unless, indeed, you already chance to know its vote— and even something more, namely, what you are to think of its vote; what *it* wants by its vote; and, still more important, what Nature wants— which latter, at the end of the account— the only thing that will be got!— — Pig Propositions, in a rough form, are somewhat as follows:

"1. The Universe, so far as sane conjecture can go, is an immeasurable Swine's-trough, consisting of solid and liquid, and of other contrasts and kinds;— especially consisting of attainable and unattainable, the latter in immensely greater quantities for most pigs.

"2. Moral evil is unattainability of Pig's-wash; moral good, attainability of ditto.

"3. 'What is Paradise, or the State of Innocence?' Paradise, called also State of Innocence, Age of Gold, and other names, *was* (according to Pigs of weak judgment) unlimited attainability of Pig's-wash; perfect fulfilment of one's wishes, so that the Pig's imagination could not outrun reality; a fable and an impossibility, as Pigs of sense now see.

"4. 'Define the Whole Duty of Pigs.' It is the mission of universal Pighood, and the duty of all Pigs, at all times, to diminish the quantity of unattainable and increase that of attainable. All knowledge and device and effort ought to be directed thither and thither only: Pig science, Pig enthusiasm and Devotion have this one aim. It is the Whole Duty of Pigs.

"5. Pig Poetry ought to consist of universal recognition of the excellence of Pig's-wash and ground barley, and the felicity of Pigs whose trough is in order, and who have had enough: Hrumph!

"6. The Pig knows the weather; he ought to look out what kind of weather it will be.

"7. 'Who made the Pig?' Unknown;— perhaps the Pork-butcher.

"8. 'Have you Law and Justice in Pigdom?' Pigs of observation have discerned that there is, or was once supposed to be, a thing called Justice. Undeniably at least there is a sentiment in Pig-nature called indignation, revenge, etc., which, if one Pig provoke another, comes out in a more or less destructive manner: hence laws are necessary, amazing quantities of laws. For quarrelling is attended with loss of blood, of life, at any rate with frightful effusion of the general stock of Hog's-wash, and ruin (temporary ruin) to large sections of the universal Swine's trough: wherefore let justice be observed, that so quarrelling be avoided.

"9. 'What is justice?' Your own share of the general Swine's-trough; not any portion of my share.

"10. 'But what is "my" share?' Ah! there, in fact, lies the grand difficulty; upon which Pig science, meditating this long while, can settle absolutely nothing. My share— hrumph!— my share is, on the whole, whatever I can contrive to get without being hanged or sent to the hulks."[342]

Such is the mire in which he plunges modern life, and, beyond all others, English life; drowning at the same time, and in the same filth, the positive mind, the love of comfort, industrial science, Church, State, philosophy, and law. This cynical catechism thrown in amidst furious declamations, gives, I think, the dominant note of this strange mind: it is this mad tension which constitutes his talent; which produces and explains his images and incongruities, his laughter and his rages. There is an English expression which cannot be translated into French, but which depicts this condition, and illustrates the whole physical constitution of the race: His blood is up. In fact, the cold and phlegmatic temperature covers the surface; but when the roused blood has swept through the veins, the fevered animal can only be glutted by devastation, and be satiated by excess.

Section III.—Perception of the Real and the Sublime

It seems as though a soul so violent, so enthusiastic, so savage, so abandoned to imaginative follies, so entirely without taste, order, and measure, would be capable only of rambling, and expending itself in hallucinations, full of sorrow and danger. In fact, many of those who had this temperament, and who were his genuine forefathers— the Norse pirates, the poets of the sixteenth century, the Puritans of the seventeenth— were madmen, hurting others and themselves, bent on devastating things and ideas, destroying the public security and their own heart. Two entirely English barriers have restrained and directed Carlyle: the sentiment of actuality, which is the positive spirit, and of the sublime, which makes the religious spirit; the first turned him to real things, the other furnished him with the interpretation of real things: instead of being sickly and visionary, he became a philosopher and a historian.

Section IV.—His Passion for Actuality

We must read his history of Cromwell to understand how far this sentiment of actuality penetrates him; with what knowledge it endows him; how he rectifies dates and texts; how he verifies traditions and genealogies; how he visits places, examines the trees, looks at the brooks, knows the agriculture, prices, the whole domestic and rural economy, all the political and literary circumstances; with what minuteness, precision, and vehemence he reconstructs before his eyes and before ours the external picture of objects and affairs, the internal picture of ideas and emotions. And it is not simply on his part conscience, habit, or prudence, but need and passion. In this great obscure void of the past, his eyes fix upon the rare luminous points as on a treasure. The black sea of oblivion has swallowed up the rest: the million thoughts and actions of so many million beings have disappeared, and no power will make them rise again to the light. These few points subsist alone, like the summits of the highest rocks of a submerged continent. With what ardor, what deep feeling for the destroyed worlds, of which these rocks are the remains, does the historian lay upon them his eager hands, to discover from their nature and structure some revelation of the great drowned regions, which no eye shall ever see again! A number, a trifling detail about expense, a petty phrase of barbarous Latin, is priceless in the sight of Carlyle. I should like you to read the commentary with which he surrounds the chronicle of the monk Jocelin of Brakelond,[343] to show you the impression which a proved fact produces on such a soul; all the attention and emotion that an old barbarous word, a bill from the kitchen summons up:

"Behold, therefore, this England of the year 1200 was no chimerical vacuity or dreamland, peopled with mere vaporous Fantasms, Rymer's Fœdera, and Doctrines of the Constitution; but a green solid place, that grew corn and several other things. The sun shone on it; the vicissitude of seasons and human fortunes. Cloth was woven and worn; ditches were dug, furrow-fields ploughed, and houses built. Day by day all men and cattle rose to labour, and night by night returned home weary, to their several lairs.... The *Dominus Rex*, at departing, gave us 'thirteen *sterlingii*,' one shilling and one penny, to say a mass for him.... For king Lackland *was* there, verily he.... There, we say, is the grand peculiarity; the immeasurable one; distinguishing to a really infinite degree, the poorest historical Fact from all Fiction whatsoever. 'Fiction,' 'Imagination, Imaginative poetry,' etc., etc., except as the vehicle for truth, or is fact of some sort... what is it?[344]... And yet these grim old walls are not a dilettantism and dubiety; they are an earnest fact. It was a most real and serious purpose they were built for! Yes, another world it was, when these black ruins, white in their new mortar and fresh chiselling, first saw the sun as walls, long ago.... Their architecture, belfries, land-carucates? Yes— and that is but a small item of the matter. Does it never give thee pause, this other strange item of it, that men then had a *soul*— not by hearsay alone, and as a figure of speech; but as a truth that they *knew* and practically went upon!"[345]

And then he tries to resuscitate this soul before our eyes; for this is his special feature, the special feature of every historian who has the sentiment of actuality, to understand that parchments, walls, dress, bodies themselves, are only cloaks and documents; that the true fact is the inner feeling of men who have lived, that the only important fact is the state and structure of their soul, that the first and sole business is to reach that inner feeling, for that all else diverges from it. We must tell ourselves this fact over and over again; history is but the history of the heart; we have to search out the feelings of past generations, and nothing else. This is what Carlyle perceives; man is before him, risen from the dead; he penetrates within him, sees that he feels, suffers, and wills, in that special and individual manner, now absolutely lost and extinguished, in which he did feel, suffer, and will. And he looks upon this sight, not coldly, like a man who only half sees things in a gray mist, indistinctly and uncertain, but with all the force of his heart and sympathy, like a convinced spectator, for whom past things, once proved, are as present and visible as the corporeal objects which his hand handles and touches, at the very moment. He feels this fact so clearly that he bases upon it all his philosophy of history. In his opinion, great men, kings, writers, prophets, and poets, are only great in this sense: "It is the property of the hero, in every time, in every place, in every situation, that he comes back to reality; that he stands upon things and not shows of things."[346] The great man discovers some unknown or neglected fact, proclaims it; men hear him, follow him; and this is the whole of history. And not only does he discover and proclaim it, but he believes and sees it. He believes it, not as hearsay or conjecture, like a truth simply probable and handed down; he sees it personally, face to face with absolute and indomitable faith; he deserts opinion for conviction, tradition for intuition. Carlyle is so steeped in his process, that he imputes it to all great men. And he is not wrong, for there is none more potent. Wherever he penetrates with this lamp, he carries a light not known before. He pierces mountains of paper erudition, and enters into the hearts of men. Everywhere he goes beyond political and conventional history. He divines characters, comprehends the spirit of extinguished ages, feels, better than any Englishman, better than Macaulay himself, the great revolutions of the soul. He is almost German in his power of imagination, his antiquarian perspicacity, his broad general views, and yet he is no dealer in guesses. The national common-sense and the energetic craving for profound belief retain him on the limits of supposition; when he does guess, he gives it for what it is worth. He has no taste for hazardous history. He rejects hearsay and legends; he accepts only partially, and under reserve, the Germanic etymologies and hypotheses. He wishes to draw from history a positive and active law for himself and us. He expels and tears away from it all the doubtful and agreeable additions which scientific curiosity and romantic imagination accumulate. He puts aside this parasitic growth to seize the useful and solid wood. And when he has seized it, he drags it so energetically before us, in order to make us touch it, he handles it in so violent a manner, he places it under such a glaring light, he illuminates it by such coarse contrasts of extraordinary images, that we are infected, and in spite of ourselves reach the intensity of his belief and vision.

He goes beyond, or rather is carried beyond this. The facts seized upon by this vehement imagination are melted in it as in a fire. Beneath this fury of conception, everything wavers. Ideas, changed into hallucinations, lose their solidity, realities are like dreams; the world, appearing in a nightmare, seems no more than a nightmare; the attestation of the bodily senses loses its weight before inner visions as lucid as itself. Man finds no longer a difference between his dreams and his perceptions. Mysticism enters like smoke within the over-heated walls of a collapsing imagination. It was thus that it once penetrated into the ecstasies of ascetic Hindoos, and into the philosophy of our first two centuries. Throughout, the same state of the imagination has produced the same teaching. The Puritans, Carlyle's true ancestors, were inclined to it. Shakespeare reached it by the prodigious tension of his poetic dreams, and Carlyle ceaselessly repeats after him that "we are such stuff as dreams are made of." This real world, these events so harshly followed up, circumscribed, and handled, are to him only apparitions; the universe is divine. "Thy daily life is girt with wonder, and based on wonder; thy very blankets and breeches are miracles.... The unspeakable divine significance, full of splendour, and wonder, and terror, lies in the being of every man and of everything; the presence of God who made every man and thing."

"Atheistic science babbles poorly of it, with scientific nomenclatures, experiments, and what-not, as if it were a poor dead thing, to be bottled up in Leyden jars, and sold over counters: but the natural sense of man, in all times, if he will honestly apply his sense, proclaims it to be a living thing—ah, an unspeakable, godlike thing; towards which the best attitude for us, after never so much science, is awe, devout prostration and humility of soul: worship, if not in words, then in silence."[347]

In fact, this is the ordinary position of Carlyle. It ends in wonder. Beyond and beneath objects, he perceives as it were an abyss, and is interrupted by shudderings. A score of times, a hundred times in the "History of the French Revolution," we have him suspending his narrative, and falling into a reverie. The immensity of the black night in which the human apparitions rise for an instant, the fatality of the crime which, once committed, remains attached to the chain of events as by a link of iron, the mysterious conduct which impels these floating masses to an unknown but inevitable end, are the great and sinister images which haunt him. He dreams anxiously of this focus of existence, of which we are only the reflection. He walks fearfully amongst this people of shadows, and tells himself that he too is a shadow. He is troubled by the thought that these human phantoms have their substance elsewhere, and will answer to eternity for their short passage. He exclaims and trembles at the idea of this motionless world, of which ours is but the mutable figure. He divines in it something august and terrible. For he shapes it, and he shapes our world according to his own mind; he defines it by the emotions which he draws from it, and figures it by the impressions which he receives from it. A moving chaos of splendid visions, of infinite perspectives, stirs and boils within him at the least event which he touches; ideas abound, violent, mutually jostling, driven from all sides of the horizon amidst darkness and flashes of lightning; his thought is a tempest, and he attributes to the universe the magnificence, the obscurities, and the terrors of a tempest. Such a conception is the true source of religious and moral sentiment. The man who is penetrated by them passes his life, like a Puritan, in veneration and fear. Carlyle passes his in expressing and impressing veneration and fear, and all his books are preachings.

Section V.—His Mode of Thought

Here truly is a strange mind, and one which makes us reflect. Nothing is more calculated to manifest truths than these eccentric beings. It will not be time misspent to discover the true position of this mind, and to explain for what reasons, and in what measure, he must fail to possess, or must attain to, beauty and truth.

As soon as we wish to begin to think, we have before us a whole and distinct object— that is, an aggregate of details connected amongst themselves, and separated from their surroundings. Whatever the object, tree, animal, sentiment, event, it is always the same; it always has parts, and these parts always form a whole: this group, more or less vast, comprises others, and is comprised in others, so that the smallest portion of the universe is, like the entire universe, a group. Thus the whole employment of human thought is to reproduce groups. According as a mind is fit for this or not, it is capable or incapable. According as it can reproduce great or small groups, it is great or small. According as it can produce complete groups, or only some of their parts, it is complete or partial.

What is it, then, to reproduce a group? It is first to separate therefrom all the parts, then to arrange them in ranks according to their resemblances, then to form these ranks into families, lastly to combine the whole under some general and dominant mark; in short, to imitate the hierarchical classifications of science. But the task is not ended there: this hierarchy is not an artificial and external arrangement, but a natural and internal necessity. Things are not dead, but living; there is in them a force which produces and organizes this group, which binds together the details and the whole, which repeats the type in all its parts. It is this force which the mind must reproduce in itself, with all its effects; it must perceive it by rebound and sympathy: this force must engender in the mind the entire group, and must be developed within it as without it: the series of internal ideas must imitate the series of external; the emotion must follow the conception, vision must complete analysis; the mind must become, like nature, creative. Then only can we say: We know.

All minds take one or other of these routes, and are divided by them into two great classes, corresponding to opposite temperaments. In the first are the plain men of science, the popularizes, orators, writers— in general, the classical ages and the Latin races; in the second are the poets, prophets, commonly the inventors— in general, the romantic ages and the Germanic races. The first proceed gradually from one idea to the next: they are methodical and cautious; they speak for the world at large, and prove what they say; they divide the field which they would traverse into preliminary sections, in order to exhaust their subject; they march on straight and level roads, so as to be sure never to fall; they proceed by transitions, enumerations, summaries; they advance from general to still more general conclusions; they form the exact and complete classification of a group. When they go beyond simple analysis, their whole talent consists in eloquently pleading a thesis. Amongst the contemporaries of Carlyle, Macaulay is the most complete model of this species of mind. The others, after having violently and confusedly rummaged amongst the details of a group, rush with a sudden spring into the mother-notion. They see it then in its entirety; they perceive the powers which organize it; they reproduce it by divination; they depict it, abridged by the most expressive and strangest words; they are not capable of decomposing it into regular series, they always perceive in a lump. They think only sudden concentrations of vehement ideas. They have a vision of distant effects or living actions; they are revealers or poets. Michelet, amongst the French, is the best example of this form of intellect, and Carlyle is an English Michelet.

He knows it, and argues plausibly that genius is an intuition, an insight: "Our Professor's method is not, in any case, that of common school Logic, where the truths all stand in a row, each holding by the skirts of the other; but at best that of practical Reason, proceeding by large Intuition over whole systematic groups and kingdoms; whereby we might say, a noble complexity, almost like that of Nature, reigns in his Philosophy, or spiritual Picture of Nature: a mighty maze, yet, as faith whispers, not without a plan."[348] Doubtless, but disadvantages, nevertheless, are not wanting; and, in the first place, obscurity and barbarism. In order to understand him, we must study laboriously, or else have precisely the same kind of mind as he. But few men are critics by profession, or natural seers; in general, an author writes to be understood, and it is annoying to end in enigmas. On the other hand, this visionary process is hazardous: when we wish to leap immediately into the inner and generative idea, we run the risk of falling short; the gradual progress is slower, but more sure. The methodical people, so much ridiculed by Carlyle, have at least the advantage over him in being able to verify all their steps. Moreover, these vehement divinations and assertions are very often void of proof. Carlyle leaves the reader to search for them: the reader at times does not search for them, and refuses to believe the soothsayer on his word. Consider, again, that affectation infallibly enters into this style. It must assuredly be inevitable, since Shakespeare is full of it. The simple writer, prosaic and rational, can always reason and stick to his prose; his inspiration has no gaps, and demands no efforts. On the contrary, prophecy is a violent condition which does not sustain itself. When it fails, it is replaced by grand gesticulation. Carlyle gets up the steam in order to continue glowing. He struggles hard; and this forced, perpetual epilepsy is a most shocking spectacle. We cannot endure a man who wanders, repeats himself, returns to oddities and exaggerations which he had already employed; makes a jargon of them, declaims, exclaims, and makes it a point, like a wretched bombastic comedian, to upset our nerves. Finally, when this species of mind coincides in a lofty mind with the habits of a gloomy preacher, it results in objectionable manners. Many will find Carlyle presumptuous, coarse; they will suspect from his theories, and also from his way of speaking, that he looks upon himself as a great man, neglected, of the race of heroes; that, in his opinion, the human race ought to put themselves in his hands, and trust him with their business. Certainly he lectures us, and with contempt. He despises his epoch; he has a sulky, sour tone; he keeps purposely on stilts. He disdains objections. In his eyes, opponents are not up to his form. He abuses his predecessors: when he speaks of Cromwell's biographers, he takes the tone of a man of genius astray amongst pedants. He has the superior smile, the resigned condescension of a hero who feels himself a martyr, and he only quits it, to shout at the top of his voice, like an ill-bred plebeian.

All this is redeemed, and more, by rare merits. He speaks truly: minds like his are the most fertile. They are almost the only ones which make discoveries. Pure classifiers do not invent: they are too dry. "To know a thing, what we can call knowing, a man must first *love* the thing, sympathize with it. Fantasy is the organ of the Godlike, the understanding is indeed thy window; too clear thou canst not make it; but fantasy is thy eye, with its color-giving retina, healthy or diseased." In more simple language, this means that every object, animate or inanimate, is gifted with powers which constitute its nature and produce its development; that, in order to know it, we must recreate it in ourselves, with the train of its potentialities, and that we only know it entirely by inwardly perceiving all its tendencies, and inwardly seeing all its effects. And verily this process, which is the imitation of nature, is the only one by which we can penetrate nature; Shakespeare had it as an instinct, and Goethe as a method. There is none so powerful or delicate, so fitted to the complexity of things and to the structure of our mind. There is none more proper to renew our ideas, to withdraw us from formulas, to deliver us from the prejudices with which education involves us, to overthrow the barriers in which our surroundings enclose us. It is by this that Carlyle escaped from conventional English ideas, penetrated into the philosophy and science of Germany, to think out again, in his own manner, the Germanic discoveries, and to give an original theory of man and of the universe.

PART II—VOCATION

It is from Germany that Carlyle has drawn his greatest ideas. He studied there, he knows perfectly its literature and language, he sets this literature in the highest rank: he translated "Wilhelm Meister," he wrote upon the German writers a long series of critical articles, he has just written a life of Frederick the Great. He is the best accredited and most original of the interpreters who have introduced the German mind into England. This is no small thing to do, for it is in such a work that every thinking person is now laboring.

Section I.—The Appearance and Development of Original Minds

From 1780-1830 Germany has produced all the ideas of our historic age; and for half a century still, perhaps for a whole century, our great work will be to think them out again. The thoughts which have been born and have blossomed in a country, never fail to propagate themselves in neighboring countries, and to be engrafted there for a season. That which is happening to us has happened twenty times already in the world; the growth of the mind has always been the same, and we may, with some assurance, foresee for the future what we observe in the past. At certain times appears an original form of mind, which produces a philosophy, a literature, an art, a science, and which, having renewed the form of man's thought, slowly and infallibly renews all his thoughts. All minds, which seek and find, are in the current; they only advance through it: if they oppose it, they are checked; if they deviate, they are slackened; if they assist it, they are carried beyond the rest. And the movement goes on so long as there remains anything to be discovered. When art has given all its works, philosophy all its theories, science all its discoveries, it stops; another form of mind takes the sway, or man ceases to think. Thus at the Renaissance appeared the artistic and poetic genius, which, born in Italy and carried into Spain, was there extinguished, after a century and a half, in the universal extinction, and which, with other characteristics, transplanted into France and England, ended after a hundred years in the refinements of mannerists and the follies of sectarians, having produced the Reformation, confirmed free thought, and founded science. Thus with Dryden in England, and with Malherbe in France, was born the oratorical and classical spirit, which, having produced the literature of the seventeenth century and the philosophy of the eighteenth, dried up under the successors of Voltaire and Pope, and died after two hundred years, having polished Europe and raised the French Revolution. Thus at the end of the last century arose the philosophic German genus, which, having engendered a new metaphysics, theology, poetry, literature, linguistic science, an exegesis, erudition, descends now into the sciences and continues its evolution. No more original spirit, more universal, more fertile in consequences of every scope and species, more capable of transforming and reforming everything, has appeared for three hundred years. It is of the same order as that of the Renaissance and of the Classical Age. It, like them, connects itself with the great works of contemporary intelligence, appears in all civilized lands, is propagated with the same inward qualities, but under different forms. It, like them, is one of the epochs of the world's history. It is encountered in the same civilization and in the same races. We may then conjecture, without too much rashness, that it will have a like duration and destiny. We thus succeed in fixing, with some precision, our place in the endless stream of events and things. We know that we are almost in the midst of one of the partial currents which compose it. We can perceive the form of mind which directs it, and seek beforehand the ideas to which it conducts us.

Section II.—Characteristics of the German Form of Mind

Wherein consists this form? In the power of discovering general ideas. No nation and no age has possessed it in so high a degree as the Germans. This is their governing faculty; it is by this power that they have produced all that they have done. This gift is properly that of comprehension (*Begreifen*). By it we find the aggregate conceptions (*Begriffe*); we reduce under one ruling idea all the scattered parts of a subject; we perceive, under the divisions of a group, the common bond which unites them; we conciliate objections; we bring down apparent contrasts to a profound unity. It is the pre-eminent philosophical faculty; and, in fact, it is the philosophical faculty which has impressed its seal on all their works. By it, they vivified dry studies, which seemed only fit to occupy pedants of the academy or seminary. By it, they divined the involuntary and primitive logic which created and organized languages, the great ideas which are hidden at the bottom of every work of art, the secret poetic emotions and vague metaphysical intuitions which engendered religions and myths. By it, they perceived the spirit of ages, civilizations, and races, and transformed into a system of laws the history which was but a heap of facts. By it, they rediscovered or renewed the sense of dogmas, connected God with the world, man with nature, spirit with matter, perceived the successive chain and the original necessity of the forms, whereof the aggregate is the universe. By it, they created a science of linguistics, a mythology, a criticism, an aesthetics, an exegesis, a history, a theology and metaphysics, so new that they continued long
incomprehensible, and could only be expressed by a special language. And this bent was so dominant that it subjected to its empire even art and poetry. The poets by it have become erudite, philosophical; they constructed their dramas, epics, and odes, after prearranged theories, and in order to manifest general ideas. They rendered moral theses, historical periods, sensible; they created and applied aesthetics; they had no artlessness, or made their artlessness an instrument of reflection; they loved not their characters for themselves, they ended by transforming them into symbols; their

philosophical ideas broke, every instant, out of the poetic shape in which they tried to enclose them; they have been all critics,[349] bent on constructing or reconstructing, possessing erudition and method, attracted to imagination by art and study, incapable of producing living beings unless by science and artifice, really systematical men, who, to express their abstract conceptions, employed, in place of formulas, the actions of personages and the music of verse.

Section III.—German Aptitude for General Ideas

From this aptitude to conceive the aggregate, one sole idea could be produced— the idea of aggregates. In fact, all the ideas worked out for fifty years in Germany are reduced to one only, that of development (*Entwickelung*), which consists in representing all the parts of a group as jointly responsible and complemental, so that each necessitates the rest, and that, all combined, they manifest, by their succession and their contrasts, the inner quality which assembles and produces them. A score of systems, a hundred dreams, a hundred thousand metaphors, have variously figured or disfigured this fundamental idea. Despoiled of its trappings, it merely affirms the mutual dependence which unites the term, of a series, and attaches them all to some abstract property within them. If we apply it to Nature, we come to consider the world as a scale of forms, and, as it were, a succession of conditions, having in themselves the reason for their succession and for their existence, containing in their nature the necessity for their decay and their limitation, composing by their union an invisible whole, which, sufficing for itself, exhausting all possibilities, and connecting all things, from time and space to existence and thought, resembles by its harmony and its magnificence some omnipotent and immortal god. If we apply it to man, we come to consider sentiments and thoughts as natural and necessary products, linked amongst themselves like the transformations of an animal or plant; which leads us to conceive religions, philosophies, literatures, all human conceptions and emotions, as necessary series of a state of mind which carries them away on its passage, which, if it returns, brings them back, and which, if we can reproduce it, gives us in consequence the means of reproducing them at will. These are the two doctrines which run through the writings of the two chief thinkers of the century, Hegel and Goethe. They have used them throughout as a method: Hegel to grasp the formula of everything, Goethe to obtain the vision of everything; they steeped themselves therein so thoroughly that they have drawn thence their inner and habitual sentiments, their morality and their conduct. We may consider them to be the two philosophical legacies which modern Germany has left to the human race.

Section IV.—Faults of the German Form of Thought

But these legacies have not been unmixed, and this passion for aggregate views has marred its proper work by its excess. It is rarely that the mind can grasp aggregates: we are imprisoned in too narrow a corner of time and space: our senses perceive only the surface of things; our instruments have but a small scope; we have only been experimentalizing for three centuries; our memory is short, and the documents by which we dive into the past are only doubtful lights, scattered over an immense region, which they show by glimpses without illuminating them. To bind together the small fragments which we are able to attain, we have generally to guess the causes, or to employ general ideas so vast that they might suit all facts; we must have recourse either to hypothesis or abstraction, invent arbitrary explanations, or be lost in vague ones. These, in fact, are the two vices which have corrupted German thought. Conjecture and formula have abounded. Systems have multiplied, some above the others, and broken out into an inextricable growth, into which no stranger dare enter, having found that every morning brought a new budding, and that the definitive discovery proclaimed overnight was about to be choked by another infallible discovery, capable at most of lasting till the morning after. The public of Europe was astonished to see so much imagination and so little common-sense, pretensions so ambitious and theories so hollow, such an invasion of chimerical existences and such an overflow of useless abstractions, so strange a lack of discernment and so great a luxuriance of irrationality. The fact was, that folly and genius flowed from the same source; a like faculty, excessive and all-powerful, produced discoveries and errors. If to-day we behold the workshop of human ideas, overcharged as it is and encumbered by its works, we may compare it to some blast-furnace, a monstrous machine which day and night has flamed unwearyingly, half darkened by choking vapors, and in which the raw ore, piled heaps on heaps, has descended, bubbling in glowing streams, into the channels in which it has become hard. No other furnace could have melted the shapeless mass, crusted over with the primitive scoriæ; this obstinate elaboration and this intense heat were necessary to overcome it. Now the heavy castings burden the earth; their weight discourages the hands which touch them; if we would turn them to some use, they defy us or break: as they are, they are of no use; and yet as they are, they are the material for every tool, and the instrument of every work; it is our business to cast them over again. Every mind must carry them back to the forge, purify them, temper them, recast them, and extract the pure metal from the rough mass.

Section V.—How Ideas are Reshaped

But every mind will re-forge them according to its own inner warmth; for every nation has its original genius, in which it moulds the ideas elsewhere derived. Thus Spain, in the sixteenth and seventeenth centuries, renewed in a different spirit Italian painting and poetry. Thus the Puritans and Jansenists thought out in new shapes primitive Protestantism; thus the French of the eighteenth century widened and put forth the liberal ideas which the English had applied or proposed in religion and politics. It is so in the present day. The French cannot at once reach, like the Germans, lofty aggregate conceptions. They can only march step by step, starting from concrete ideas, rising gradually to abstract ideas, after the progressive methods and gradual analysis of Condillac and Descartes. But this slower route leads almost as far as the other; and, in addition, it avoids many wrong steps. It is by this route that we succeed in correcting and comprehending the views of Hegel and Goethe; and if we look around us, at the ideas which are gaining ground, we find that we are already arriving thither. Positivism, based on all modern experience, and freed since the death of its founder from his social and religious fancies, has assumed a new life, by reducing itself to noting the connection of natural groups and the chain of established sciences. On the other hand, history, novels, and criticism, sharpened by the refinements of Parisian culture, have made us acquainted with the laws of human events; nature has been shown to be an order of facts, man a continuation of nature; and we have seen a superior mind, the most delicate, the most lofty of our own time, resuming and modifying the German divinations, expounding in the French manner everything which the science of myth, religion, and language had stored up, beyond the Rhine, during the last sixty years.[350]

Section VI.—Growth of German Ideas in England

The growth in England is more difficult; for the aptitude for general ideas is less, and the mistrust of general ideas is greater: they reject at once all that remotely or nearly seems capable of injuring practical morality or established dogma. The positive spirit seems as if it must exclude all German ideas; and yet it is the positive spirit which introduces them. Thus theologians,[351] having desired to represent to themselves with entire clearness and certitude the characters of the New Testament, have suppressed the halo and mist in which distance enveloped them; they have figured them with their garments, gestures, accent, all the shades of emotion of their style, with the species of imagination which their age has imposed, amidst the scenery which they have looked upon, amongst the mains of former ages before which they have spoken, with all the circumstances, physical or moral, which learning and travel can render sensible, with all the comparisons which modern physiology and psychology could suggest; they have given us their precise and demonstrated, colored and graphic, idea; they have seen these personages, not through ideas and as myths, but face to face, and as men. They have applied Macaulay's art to exegesis; and if the entire German erudition could pass unmutilated through this crucible, its solidity, as well as its value, would be doubled.

But there is another wholly Germanic route by which German ideas may become English. This is the road which Carlyle has taken; by this, religion and poetry in the two countries are alike; by it, the two nations are sisters. The sentiment of internal things (insight) is in the race, and this sentiment is a sort of philosophical divination. At need, the heart takes the place of the brain. The inspired, impassioned man penetrates into things; perceives the cause by the shock which he feels from it; he embraces aggregates by the lucidity and velocity of his creative imagination; he discovers the unity of a group by the unity of the emotion which he receives from it. For as soon as we create, we feel within ourselves the force which acts in the objects of our thought; our sympathy reveals to us their sense and connection; intuition is a finished and living analysis; poets and prophets, Shakespeare and Dante, St. Paul and Luther, have been systematic theorists, without wishing it, and their visions comprise general conceptions of man and the universe. Carlyle's mysticism is a power of the same kind. He translates, into a poetic and religious style, German philosophy. He speaks, like Fichte, of the divine idea of the world, the reality which lies at the bottom of every apparition. He speaks, like Goethe, of the spirit which eternally weaves the living robe of Divinity. He borrows their metaphors, only he takes them literally. He considers the god, which they consider as a form or a law, as a mysterious and' sublime being. He conceives by exaltation, by painful reverie, by a confused sentiment of the interweaving of existences, that unity of nature which they arrive at by dint of reasonings and abstractions. Here is a last route, steep doubtless, and little frequented, for reaching the summits from which German thought at first issued forth. Methodical analysis added to the co-ordination of the positive sciences; French criticism, refined by literary taste and worldly observation; English criticism, supported by practical common-sense and positive intuition; lastly, in a niche apart, sympathetic and poetic imagination; these are the four routes by which the human mind is now proceeding to reconquer the sublime heights to which it believed itself carried, and which it has lost. These routes all conduct to the same summit, but with different prospects. That by which Carlyle has advanced, being the lengthiest, has led him to the strangest perspective. I will let him speak for himself; he will tell the reader what he has seen.

Part III.—Philosophy, Morality, and Criticism

"However it may be with Metaphysics, and other abstract Science originating in the Head (*Verstand*) alone, no Life-Philosophy (*Lebensphilosophie*), such as this of Clothes pretends to be, which originates equally in the Character (*Gemüth*), and equally speaks thereto, can attain its significance till the Character itself is known and seen."[352]

Carlyle has related, under the name of Teufelsdroeckh, all the succession of emotions which lead to this Life-Philosophy. They are those of a modern Puritan; the same doubts, despairs, inner conflicts, exaltations, and pangs, by which the old Puritans arrived at faith: it is their faith under other forms. With him, as with them, the spiritual and inner man frees himself from the exterior and carnal; perceives duty amidst the solicitations of pleasure; discovers God through the appearances of nature; and, beyond the world and the instincts of sense, sees a supernatural world and instinct.

Section I.—Carlyle's Metaphysics

The specialty of Carlyle, as of every mystic, is to see a double meaning in everything. For him texts and objects are capable of two interpretations: the one gross, open to all, serviceable for ordinary life; the other sublime, open to a few, serviceable to a higher life. Carlyle says:

"To the eye of vulgar Logic, what is man? An omnivorous Biped that wears Breeches. To the eye of Pure Reason what is he? A Soul, a Spirit, and divine Apparition. Round his mysterious Me, there lies, under all those wool-rags, a Garment of Flesh (or of Senses), contextured in the Loom of Heaven.... Deep-hidden is he under that strange Garment; amid Sounds and Colours and Forms, as it were, swathed-in, and inextricably over-shrouded: yet it is skywoven, and worthy of a God."[353]

"For Matter, were it never so despicable, is Spirit, the manifestation of Spirit: were it never so honourable, can it be more? The thing Visible, nay, the thing Imagined, the thing in any way conceived as Visible, what is it but a Garment, a Clothing of the higher, celestial, Invisible, 'unimaginable, formless, dark with excess of bright?'"[354]

"All visible things are emblems; what thou seest is not there on its own account; strictly taken, is not there at all: Matter exists only spiritually, and to represent some Idea, and *body* it forth."[355]

Language, poetry, arts, church, state, are only symbols:

"In the Symbol proper, what we can call a Symbol, there is ever, more or less distinctly and directly, some embodiment and revelation of the Infinite; the Infinite is made to blend itself with the Finite, to stand visible, and as it were, attainable there. By Symbols, accordingly, is man guided and commanded, made happy, made wretched. He everywhere finds himself encompassed with Symbols, recognised as such or not recognised: the

Universe is but one vast Symbol of God; nay, if thou wilt have it, what is man himself but a Symbol of God; is not all that he does symbolical; a revelation to Sense of the mystic god-given force that is in him?"[356]

Let us rise higher still and regard Time and Space, those two abysses which it seems nothing could fill up or destroy, and over which hover our life and our universe. "They are but forms of our thought.... There is neither Time nor Space; they are but two grand fundamental, world-enveloping appearances, SPACE and TIME. These as spun and woven for us from before Birth itself, to clothe our celestial Me for dwelling here, and yet to blind it— lie all-embracing, as the universal canvas, or warp and woof, whereby all minor illusions, in this Phantasm and Existence, weave and paint themselves."[357] Our root is in eternity; we seem to be born to die, but actually, *we are.*

"Know of a truth that only the Time-shadows have perished, or are perishable; that the real Being of whatever was, and whatever is, and whatever will be, is even now and for ever.... Are we not Spirits, that are shaped into a body, into an appearance; and that fade away again into air and Invisibility?"[358] "O Heaven, it is mysterious, it is awful, to consider that we not only carry each a future Ghost within him; but are, in very deed, Ghosts! These Limbs, whence had we them; this stormy Force; this life-blood with its burning Passion? They are dust and shadow; a Shadow-system gathered round our Me; wherein, through some moments or years, the Divine Essence is to be revealed in the Flesh.

"And again, do we not squeak and gibber (in our discordant, screech-owlish debatings and recriminatings); and glide bodeful, and feeble, and fearful; or uproar (*poltern*), and revel in our mad Dance of the Dead— till the scent of the morning air summons us to our still Home; and dreamy Night becomes awake and Day?"[359]

What is there, then, beneath all these empty appearances? What is this motionless existence, whereof nature is but the "changing and living robe"? None knows; if the heart divines it, the mind perceives it not. "Creation, says one, lies before us like a glorious rainbow; but the sun that made it lies behind us, hidden from us." We have only the sentiment thereof, not the idea. We feel that this universe is beautiful and terrible, but its essence will remain ever unnamed. We have only to fall on our knees before this veiled face; wonder and adoration are our true attitude:

"The man who cannot wonder, who does not habitually wonder (and worship), were he President of innumerable Royal Societies, and carried the whole *Mécanique Céleste* and *Hegel's Philosophy*, and the epitome of all Laboratories and Observatories, with their results, in his single head— is but a Pair of Spectacles behind which there is no Eye. Let those who have Eyes look through him, then he may be useful.

"Thou wilt have no Mystery and Mysticism; wilt walk through thy world by the sunshine of what thou callest Truth, or even by the handlamp of what I call Attorney-Logic: and 'explain' all, 'account' for all, or believe nothing of it. Nay, thou wilt attempt laughter; who so recognises the unfathomable, all-pervading domain of Mystery, which is everywhere under our feet and among our hands; to whom the Universe is an oracle and Temple, as well as a Kitchen and Cattle-stall— he shall be a delirious Mystic; to him thou, with sniffing charity, wilt protrusively proffer thy Hand-lamp, and shriek, as one injured, when he kicks his foot through it."[360]

"We speak of the Volume of Nature; and truly a Volume it is— whose Author and Writer is God. To read it! Dost thou, does man, so much as well know the Alphabet thereof? With its Words, Sentences, and grand descriptive Pages, poetical and philosophical, spread out through Solar Systems, and Thousands of Years, we shall not try thee. It is a Volume written in celestial hieroglyphs, in the true Sacred-writing; of which even Prophets are happy that they can read here a line and there a line. As for your Institutes, and Academies of Science, they strive bravely, and from amid the thick-crowded, inextricably intertwisted hieroglyphic writing, pick out, by dexterous combination, some Letters in the vulgar Character and therefrom put together this and the other economic Recipe, of high avail in Practice."[361]

Do we believe, perhaps,

"That Nature is more than some boundless Volume of such Recipes, or huge, well-nigh inexhaustible Domestic-Cookery Book, of which the whole secret will in this manner one day evolve itself?..."[362]

"And what is that Science, which the scientific head alone, were it screwed off, and (like the Doctor's in the Arabian tale) set in a basin, to keep it alive, could prosecute without shadow of a heart, but one other of the mechanical and menial handicrafts, for which the Scientific Head (having a soul in it) is too noble an organ? I mean that Thought, without Reverence, is barren, perhaps poisonous."[363]

Let the scales drop from our eyes, and let us look:

"Then sawest thou that this fair-Universe, were it in the meanest province thereof, is in very deed the star-domed City of God; that through every star, through every grass-blade, and most through every Living Soul, the glory of a present God still beams."[364]

"Generation after generation takes to itself the form of a Body; and forth-issuing from Cimmerian Night, on Heaven's mission appears. What Force and Fire is in each he expends: one grinding in the mill of Industry; one, hunter-like, climbing the giddy Alpine heights of Science; one, madly dashed in pieces on the rocks of Strife, in war with his fellow:— and then the Heaven-sent is recalled; his earthly Vesture falls away, and soon even to Sense becomes a vanished Shadow. Thus, like some wild-flaming, wild-thundering train of Heaven's Artillery, does this mysterious MANKIND thunder and flame, in long-drawn, quick-succeeding grandeur, through the unknown Deep. Thus, like a God-created, fire-breathing Spirit-ho§t, we emerge from the Inane; haste stormfully across the astonished Earth, then plunge again into the Inane.... But whence?— O Heaven, whither? Sense knows not; Faith knows not; only that it is through Mystery to Mystery, from God and to God."[365]

Section II.—His Transposition of German Metaphysics into English Puritanism

This vehement religious poetry, charged as it is with memories of Milton and Shakespeare, is but an English transcription of German ideas. There is a fixed rule for transposing— that is, for converting into one another the ideas of a positivist, a pantheist, a spiritualist, a mystic, a poet, a head given to images, and a head given to formulas. We may mark all the steps which lead simple philosophical conception to its extreme and violent state. Take the world as science shows it; it is a regular group or series, which has a law; according to science, it is nothing more. As from the law we deduce the series, we may say that the law engenders it, and consider this law as a force. If we are an artist, we will seize in the aggregate the force, the series of effects, and the fine regular manner in which force produces the series. To my mind, this sympathetic representation is of all the most exact and complete: knowledge is limited, as long as it does not arrive at this, and it is complete when it has arrived there. But beyond, there commence the phantoms which the mind creates, and by which it dupes itself. If we have a little imagination, we will make of this force a distinct existence, situated beyond the reach of experience, spiritual, the principle and the substance of concrete things. That is a metaphysical existence. Let us add one degree to our imagination and enthusiasm, and we will say that this spirit, situated beyond time and space, is manifested through these: that it subsists and animates everything, that we have in it motion, existence, and life. When carried to the limits of vision and ecstasy, we will declare that this principle is the only reality, that the rest is but appearance: thenceforth we are deprived of all the means of defining it; we can affirm nothing of it, but that it is the source of things, and that nothing can be affirmed of it; we consider it as a grand unfathomable abyss; we seek, in order to come at it, a path other than that of clear ideas; we extol sentiment, exaltation. If we have a gloomy temperament, we seek it, like the sectarians, painfully, amongst prostrations and agonies. By this scale of transformations, the general idea becomes a poetical, then a philosophical, then a mystical existence; and German metaphysics, concentrated and heated, is changed into English Puritanism.

Section III.—Conception of God and Duty

What distinguishes this mysticism from others, is its practicality. The Puritan is troubled not only about what he ought to believe, but about what he ought to do; he craves an answer to his doubts, but especially a rule for his conduct; he is tormented by the notion of his ignorance, as well as by the horror of his vices; he seeks God, but duty also. In his eyes the two are but one; moral sense is the promoter and guide of philosophy:

"Is there no God, then: but at best an absentee God, sitting idle, ever since the first Sabbath, at the outside of his Universe, and *seeing* it go? Has the word Duty no meaning; is what we call Duty no divine Messenger and Guide, but a false earthly Fantasm, made-up of Desire and Fear, of emanations from the gallows and from Dr. Graham's Celestial-Bed? Happiness of an approving Conscience! Did not Paul of Tarsus, whom admiring men have since named Saint, feel that *he* was the 'chief of sinners;' and Nero of Rome, jocund in spirit (*wohlgemuth*), spend much of his time in fiddling? Foolish Word-monger and Motive-grinder, who in thy Logic-mill hast an earthly mechanism for the Godlike itself, and wouldst fain grind me out Virtue from the husks of pleasure— I tell thee, Nay!"[366]

There is an instinct within us which says Nay. We discover within us something higher than love of happiness— the love of sacrifice. That is the divine part of our soul. We perceive in it and by it the God, who otherwise would continue ever unknown. By it we penetrate an unknown and sublime world. There is an extraordinary state of the soul, by which it leaves selfishness, renounces pleasure, cares no more for itself, adores pain, comprehends holiness.[367]

This obscure beyond, which the senses cannot reach, the reason cannot define, which the imagination figures as a king and a person; this is holiness, this is the sublime. "The hero is he who lives in the inward sphere of things, in the True, Divine, Eternal, which exists always, unseen to most under the Temporary, Trivial; his being is in that.... His life is a piece of the everlasting heart of nature itself."[368] Virtue is a revelation, heroism is a light, conscience a philosophy; and we shall express in the abstract this moral mysticism, by saying that God, for Carlyle, is a mystery whose only name is the Ideal.

Section IV.—Conception of Christianity

This faculty for perceiving the inner sense of things and this disposition to search out the moral sense of things, have produced in him all his doctrines, and first his Christianity. This Christianity is very broad: Carlyle takes religion in the German manner: after a symbolical fashion. This is why he is called a Pantheist, which in plain language means a madman, or a rogue. In England, too, he is exorcised. His friend Sterling sent him long dissertations, to bring him back to a personal God. Every moment he wounds to the quick the theologians, who make of the prime cause an architect or an administrator. He shocks them still more when he touches upon dogma; he considers Christianity as a myth, of which the essence is the Worship of Sorrow:

"Knowest thou that '*Worship of sorrow*'? The Temple thereof founded some eighteen centuries ago, now lies in ruins, overgrown with jungle, the habitation of doleful creatures: nevertheless, venture forward; in a low crypt, arched out of falling fragments, thou findest the Altar still there, and its sacred Lamp perennially burning."[369]

But its guardians know it no more. A frippery of conventional adornments hides it from the eyes of men. The Protestant Church in the nineteenth century, like the Catholic Church in the sixteenth, needs a reformation. We want a new Luther:

"For if Government is, so to speak, the outward SKIN of the Body Politic, holding the whole together and protecting it; and if all your Craft-Guilds and Associations for Industry, of hand or of head, are the Fleshly Clothes, the muscular and osseous Tissues (lying *under* such SKIN), whereby Society stands and works;— then is Religion the inmost Pericardial and Nervous Tissue which ministers Life and warm Circulation to the whole...

"Meanwhile, in our era of the World, those same Church Clothes have gone sorrowfully out-at-elbows: nay, far worse, many of them have become mere hollow Shapes, or Masks, under which no living Figure or Spirit any longer dwells; but only spiders and unclean beetles, in horrid accumulation, drive their trade; and the mask still glares on you with its glass-eyes, in ghastly affectation of Life— some generation and half after Religion has quite withdrawn from it, and in unnoticed nooks is weaving for herself new Vestures, wherewith to reappear and bless us, or our sons or grandsons."[370]

Christianity, once reduced to the sentiment of abnegation, other religions resume, in consequence, dignity and importance. They are, like Christianity, forms of universal religion. "They have all had a truth in them, or men would not have taken them up."[371] They are no quack's imposture or poet's dream. They are an existence, more or less troubled by the mystery august and infinite, which is at the bottom of the universe:

"Canopus shining down over the desert, with its blue diamond brightness (that wild blue spirit-like brightness, far brighter than we ever witness here), would pierce into the heart of the wild Ishmaelitish man, whom it was guiding through the solitary waste there. To his wild heart, with all feelings in it, with no *speech* for any feeling, it might seem a little eye, that Canopus, glancing-out on him from the great deep Eternity; revealing the inner Splendour to him."[372]

"Grand Lamaism," Popery itself, interpret after their fashion the sentiment of the divine; therefore Popery itself is to be respected. "While a pious life remains capable of being led by it,... let it last as long as it can."[373] What matters if people call it idolatry?

"Idol is *Eidolon*, a thing seen, a symbol. It is not God, but a symbol of God.... Is not all worship whatsoever a worship by Symbols, by *eidola*, or things seen?... The most rigorous Puritan has his Confession of Faith, and intellectual Representation of Divine things, and worships thereby.... All creeds, liturgies, religious forms, conceptions that fitly invest religious feelings, are in this sense *eidola*, things seen. All worship whatsoever must proceed by Symbols, by Idols:— we may say, all Idolatry is comparative, and the worst Idolatry is only more idolatrous."[374]

The only detestable idolatry is that from which the sentiment has departed, which consists only in ceremonies learned by rote, in mechanical repetition of prayers, in decent profession of formulas not understood. The deep veneration of a monk of the twelfth century, prostrated before the relics of St. Edmund, was worth more than the conventional piety and cold philosophical religion of a Protestant of to-day. Whatever the worship, it is the sentiment which gives it its whole value. And this sentiment is that of morality:

"The one end, essence, and use of all religion, past, present, and to come, was this only: To keep that same Moral Conscience, or Inner Light of ours, alive and shining.... All religion was here to remind us, better or worse, of what we already know better or worse, of the quite *infinite* difference there is between a Good man and a Bad; to bid us love infinitely the one, abhor and avoid infinitely the other— strive infinitely to *be* the one, and not to be the other. 'All religion issues in due Practical Hero-worship.'"[375]

"All true Work is religion; and whatsoever religion is not Work may go and dwell among the Brahmins, Antinomians, Spinning Dervishes, or where it will; with me it shall have no harbour."[376]

Though it has "no harbour" with Carlyle, it has elsewhere. We touch here the English and narrow feature of this German and broad conception. There are many religions which are not moral; there are more still which are not practical. Carlyle would reduce the heart of man to the English sentiment of duty, and his imagination to the English sentiment of respect. The half of human poetry escapes his grasp. For if a part of ourselves raises us to abnegation and virtue, another part leads us to enjoyment and pleasure. Man is pagan as well as Christian; nature has two faces: several races, India, Greece, Italy, have only comprehended the second, and have had for religions merely the adoration of overflowing force and the ecstasy of grand imagination; or otherwise the admiration of harmonious form, with the culture of pleasure, beauty, and happiness.

Section V.—Carlyle's Criticism

His criticism of literary works is of the same character and violence, and has the same scope and the same limits, the same principle and the same conclusions, as his criticism of religious works. Carlyle has introduced the great ideas of Hegel and Goethe, and has confined them under the narrow discipline of Puritan sentiment.[377] He considers the poet, the writer, the artist, as an interpreter of "The Divine Idea of the World, that which lies at the bottom of Appearance;" as a revealer of the infinite, as representing his century, his nation, his age: we recognize here all the German formulas. They signify that the artist detects and expresses better than anyone, the salient and durable features of the world which surrounds him, so that we might draw from his work a theory of man and of nature, together with a picture of his race and of his time. This discovery has renewed criticism. Carlyle owes to it his finest views, his lessons on Shakespeare and Dante, his studies on Goethe, Dr. Johnson, Burns, and Rousseau. Thus, by a natural enthusiasm, he becomes the herald of German literature; he makes himself the apostle of Goethe; he has praised him with a neophyte's fervor, to the extent of lacking on this subject skill and perspicacity; he calls him a Hero, presents his life as an example to all the men of our century; he will not see his paganism, manifest as it is, and so repellent to a Puritan. Through the same causes, he has made of Jean-Paul Richter, an affected clown, and an extravagant humorist: "a giant," a sort of prophet; he has heaped eulogy on Novalis and the mystic dreamers; he has set the democrat Burns above Byron; he has exalted Dr. Johnson, that honest pedant, the most grotesque of literary behemoths. His principle is, that in a work of the mind, form is little: the basis alone is important. As soon as a man has a profound sentiment, a strong conviction, his book is beautiful. A writing, be it what it will, only manifests the soul: if the soul is serious, if it is intimately and habitually shaken by the grave thoughts which ought to preoccupy a soul; if it loves what is good, is devoted, endeavors with its whole effort, without any mental reservation of interest or self-love, to publish the truth which strikes it, it has reached its goal. We have nothing to do with the talent; we need not to be pleased by beautiful forms; our sole object is to find ourselves face to face with the sublime; the whole destiny of man is to perceive heroism; poetry and art have no other employment or merit. We see how far and with what excess Carlyle possesses the Germanic sentiment, why he loves the mystics, humorists, prophets, illiterate writers, and men of action, spontaneous poets, all who violate regular beauty through ignorance, brutality, folly, or deliberately. He goes so far as to excuse the rhetoric of Dr. Johnson because Johnson was loyal and sincere; he does not distinguish in him the literary man from the practical; he avoids seeing the classic declaimer, a strange compound of Scaliger, Boileau, and La Harpe, majestically decked out in the Ciceronian gown, in order to see only a man of faith and conviction. Such a habit prevents a man seeing one-half of things. Carlyle speaks with scornful indifference[378] of modern dilettanteism, seems to despise painters, admits no sensible beauty. Wholly on the side of the authors, he neglects the artists; for the source of art is the sentiment of form; and the greatest artists, the Italians, the Greeks, did not know, like their priests and poets, any beauty beyond that of voluptuousness and force. Thence also it comes that he has no taste for French literature. The exact order, the fine proportions, the perpetual regard for the agreeable and proper, the harmonious structure of clear and consecutive ideas, the delicate picture of society, the perfection of style— nothing which moves us has attraction for him. His mode of comprehending life is too far removed from ours. In vain he tries to understand Voltaire, all he can do is to slander him:

"We find no heroism of character in him, from first to last; nay, there is not, that we know of, one great thought in all his six-and-thirty quartos.... He sees but a little way into Nature; the mighty All, in its beauty and infinite mysterious grandeur, humbling the small *me* into nothingness, has never even for moments been revealed to him; only this and that other atom of it, and the differences and discrepancies of these two, has he looked into and noted down. His theory of the world, his picture of man and man's life is little; for a poet and philosopher, even pitiful. 'The Divine idea, that which lies at the bottom of appearances,' was never more invisible to any man. He reads history, not with the eyes of a devout seer, or even of a critic, but through a pair of mere anticatholic spectacles. It is not a mighty drama enacted on the theatre of Infinitude, with suns for lamps and Eternity as a background,... but a poor wearisome debating-club dispute, spun through ten centuries, between the *Encyclopédie* and the *Sorbonne*.... God's Universe is a larger patrimony of St. Peter, from which it were well and pleasant to hunt out the Pope.... The still higher praise of having had a right or noble aim cannot be conceded him without many limitations, and may, plausibly enough, be altogether denied.... The force necessary for him was nowise a great and noble one; but small, in some respects a mean one, to be nimbly and seasonably put into use. The Ephesian temple, which it had employed many wise heads and strong arms for a lifetime to build, could be *un*built by one madman, in a single hour."[379]

These are big words; we will not employ the like. I will simply say, that if a man were to judge Carlyle, as a Frenchman, as he judges Voltaire as an Englishman, he would draw a different picture of Carlyle from that which I am trying here to draw.

Section VI.—The Future of Criticism

This trade of calumny was in vogue fifty years ago: in fifty more it will probably have altogether ceased. The French are beginning to comprehend the gravity of the Puritans; perhaps the English will end by comprehending the gayety of Voltaire: the first are laboring to appreciate Shakespeare; the second will doubtless attempt to appreciate Racine. Goethe, the master of all modern minds, knew well how to appreciate both.[380] The critic must add to his natural and national soul five or six artificial and acquired souls, and his flexible sympathy must introduce him to extinct or foreign sentiments. The best fruit of criticism is to detach ourselves from ourselves, to constrain us to make allowance for the surroundings in which we live, to teach us to distinguish objects themselves through the transient appearances, with which our character and our age never fail to clothe them. Each person regards them through glasses of diverse focus and hue, and no one can reach the truth save by taking into account the form and tint which his glasses give to the objects which he sees. Hitherto we have been wrangling and pommelling one another— this man declaring that things are green, another that they are yellow; others, again, that they are red; each accusing his neighbor of seeing wrong, and being disingenuous. Now, at last, we are learning moral optics; we are finding that the color is not in the objects, but in ourselves; we pardon our neighbors for seeing differently from us; we recognize that they may see red what to us appears blue, green what to us appears yellow; we can even define the kind of glasses which produces yellow; and the kind which produces green, divine their effects from their nature, predict to people the tint under which the object we are about to present to them will appear, construct beforehand the system of every mind, and perhaps one day free ourselves from every system. "As a poet," said Goethe, "I am a polytheist; as a naturalist, a pantheist; as a moral man, a deist; and in order to express my mind, I need all these forms." In fact, all these glasses are serviceable, for they all show us some new aspect of things. The important point is to have not one, but several, to employ each at the suitable moment: not to mind the particular color of these glasses, but to know that behind these million moving poetical tints, optics only prove transformations, governed by a law.

Part IV.—Conception of History

Section I.—Great Men

"Universal History, the history of what man has accomplished in this world, is at bottom the History of the Great Men who have worked here. They were the leaders of men, these great ones; the modellers, patterns, and in a wide sense creators, of whatsoever the general mass of men contrived to do, or to attain; all things that we see standing accomplished in the world are properly the outer material result, the practical realisation and embodiment of Thoughts that dwelt in the Great Men sent into the world; the soul of the whole world's history, it may justly be considered, were the history of these."[381]

Whatever they be, poets, reformers, writers, men of action, revealers, he gives them all a mystical character;

"Such a man is what we call an original man; he comes to us at first-hand. A messenger he, sent from the Infinite Unknown with tidings to us.... Direct from the Inner Fact of things;— he lives, and has to live, in daily communion with that. Hearsays cannot hide it from him; he is blind, homeless, miserable, following hearsays; it glares in upon him.... It is from the heart of the world that he comes; he is portion of the primal reality of things."[382]

In vain the ignorance of his age and his own imperfections mar the purity of his original vision; he ever attains some immutable and life-giving truth; for this truth he is listened to, and by this truth he is powerful. That which he has discovered is immortal and efficacious:

"The works of a man, bury them under what guano-mountains and obscene owl-droppings you will, do not perish, cannot perish. What of Heroism, what of Eternal Light was in a Man and his Life, is with very great exactness added to the Eternities; remains forever a new divine portion of the Sum of things."[383]

"No nobler feeling than this, of admiration for one higher than himself, dwells in the breast of man. It is to this hour, and at all hours, the vivifying influence in man's life. Religion, I find, stands upon it ... What, therefore, is loyalty proper, the life-breath of all society, but an effluence of Hero-worship, submissive admiration for the truly great? Society is founded on Hero-worship."[384]

This feeling is the deepest part of man. It exists even in this levelling and destructive age: "I seem to see in this indestructibility of Hero-worship the everlasting adamant, lower than which the confused wreck of revolutionary things cannot fall."[381]

Section II.—Wherein Carlyle is Original

We have here a German theory, but transformed, made precise, thickened after the English manner. The Germans said that every nation, period, civilization, has its idea; that is, its chief feature, from which the rest were derived; so that philosophy, religion, arts, and morals, all the elements of thought and action, could be deduced from some original and fundamental quality, from which all proceeded and in which all ended. Where Hegel proposed an idea, Carlyle proposes a heroic sentiment. It is more palpable and moral. To complete his escape from the vague, he considers this sentiment in a hero. He must give to abstractions a body and soul; he is not at ease in pure conceptions, and wishes to touch a real being.

But this being, as he conceives it, is an abstract of the rest. For according to him, the hero contains and represents the civilization in which he is comprised; he has discovered, proclaimed or practised an original conception, and in this his age has followed him. The knowledge of a heroic sentiment, thus gives us a knowledge of a whole age. By this method Carlyle has emerged beyond biography. He has rediscovered the grand views of his masters. He has felt, like them, that a civilization, vast and dispersed as it is over time and space, forms an indivisible whole. He has combined, in a system of hero-worship, the scattered fragments which Hegel united by a law. He has derived from a common sentiment the events which the Germans derived from a common definition. He has comprehended the deep and distant connection of things, such as bind a great man to his time, such as connect the works of accomplished thought with the stutterings of infant thought, such as link the wise inventions of modern constitutions to the disorderly furies of primitive barbarism:

"Silent, with closed lips, as I fancy them, unconscious that they were specially brave; defying the wild ocean with its monsters, and all men and things;— progenitors of our own Blakes and Nelsons. ... Hrolf or Rollo, Duke of Normandy, the wild Sea-king, has a share in governing England at this hour."[386]

"No wild Saint Dominies and Thebaïd Eremites, there had been no melodious Dante; rough Practical Endeavour, Scandinavian and other, from Odin to Walter Raleigh, from Ulfila to Cranmer, enabled Shakespeare to speak. Nay, the finished Poet, I remark sometimes, is a symptom that his epoch itself has reached perfection and is finished; that before long there will be a new epoch, new Reformers needed."[387]

His great poetical or practical works only publish or apply this dominant idea; the historian makes use of it to rediscover the primitive sentiment which engenders them, and to form the segregate conception which unites them.

CHRIST CROWNED WITH THORNS
Fac-simile example of Printing and Engraving in the Sixteenth Century.

Section III.—In What Genuine History Consists

Hence, a new fashion of writing history. Since the heroic sentiment is the cause of the other sentiments, it is to this the historian must devote himself. Since it is the source of civilization, the mover of revolutions, the master and regenerator of human life, it is in this that he must observe civilization, revolutions and human life. Since it is the spring of every movement, it is by this that we shall understand every movement. Let the metaphysicians draw up deductions and formulas, or the politicians expound situations and constitutions. Man is not an inert being, moulded by a constitution, nor a lifeless being expressed by formula; he is an active and living soul, capable of acting, discovering, creating, devoting himself, and before all, of daring; genuine history is an epic of heroism. This idea is, in my opinion, brilliant and luminous. For men have not done great things without great emotions. The first and sovereign motive of an extraordinary revolution is an extraordinary sentiment. Then we see appear and swell a lofty and all-powerful passion, which has burst the old dykes, and hurled the current of things into a new bed. All starts from this, and it is this which we must observe. Let us leave metaphysical formulas and political considerations, and regard the inner state of every mind. Let us quit bare narrative, forget abstract explanations, and study impassioned souls. A revolution is only the birth of a great sentiment. What is this sentiment, how is it bound to others, what is its degree, source, effect, how does it transform the imagination, understanding, common inclinations; what passions feed it, what proportion of folly and reason does it embrace— these are the main questions. If anyone wishes to represent to me the history of Buddhism, he must show me the calm despair of the ascetics who, deadened by the contemplation of the infinite void, and by the expectation of final annihilation, attain in their monotonous quietude the sentiment of universal fraternity. If anyone wishes to represent to me the history of Christianity, he must show me the soul of a Saint John or Saint Paul, the sudden renewal of the conscience, the faith in visible things, the transformation of a soul penetrated by the presence of a paternal God, the irruption of tenderness, generosity, abnegation, trust, and hope, which rescued the wretches oppressed under the Roman tyranny and decline. To explain a revolution is to write a partial psychology; the analysis of critics and the divination of artists are the only instruments which can attain to it: if we would have it precise and profound we must ask it of those who, through their profession or their genius, possess a knowledge of the soul— Shakespeare, Saint-Simon, Balzac, Stendhal. This is why we may occasionally ask it of Carlyle. And there is a history which we may ask of him in preference to all others, that of the Revolution which had conscience for its source, which set God in the councils of the state, which imposed strict duty, which provoked severe heroism. The best historian of Puritanism is a Puritan.

Section IV.—Carlyle's History of Cromwell

The history of Cromwell, Carlyle's masterpiece, is but a collection of letters and speeches, commented on and united by a continuous narrative. The impression which they leave is extraordinary. Grave constitutional histories hang heavy after this compilation. The author wished to make us comprehend a soul: the soul of Cromwell, the greatest of the Puritans, their chief, their abstract, their hero, and their model. His narrative resembles that of an eye-witness. A covenanter who should have collected letters, scraps of newspapers, and daily added reflections, interpretations, notes, and anecdotes, might have written just such a book. At last we are face to face with Cromwell. We have his words, we can hear his tone of voice; we seize, around each action, the circumstances which produced it: we see him in his tent, in council, with the proper background, with his face and costume: every detail, the most minute, is here. And the sincerity is as great as the sympathy; the biographer confesses his ignorance, the lack of documents, the uncertainty; he is perfectly loyal, though a poet and a sectarian. With him we simultaneously restrain and give free play to our conjectures; and we feel at every step, amidst our affirmations and our reservations, that we are firmly planting our feet upon the truth. Would that all history were like this, a selection of texts provided with a commentary! I would exchange, for such a history, all the regular arguments, all the beautiful, colorless narrations of Robertson and Hume. I can verify the judgment of the author whilst reading this; I no more think after him, but for myself; the historian does not obtrude himself between me and his subject. I see a fact, and not an account of a'fact; the oratorical and personal envelope, with which a narrative covers the truth, disappears; I can touch the truth itself. And this Cromwell, with his Puritans, comes forth from the test, recreated and renewed. We divined pretty well already that he was not a mere man of ambition, a hypocrite, but we took him for a fanatic and hateful disputant. We consider these Puritans as gloomy madmen, shallow brains, and full of scruples. Let us quit our French and modern ideas, and enter into these souls: we shall find there something else than hypochondria, namely, a grand sentiment— am I a just man? And if God, who is perfect justice, were to judge me at this moment, what sentence would he pass upon me?— Such is the original idea of the Puritans, and through them came the Revolution into England. The feeling of the difference there is between good and evil, filled for them all time and space, and became incarnate, and expressed for them, by such words as Heaven and Hell. They were struck by the idea of duty. They examined themselves by this light, severely and without intermission; they conceived the sublime model of infallible and complete virtue; they were imbued therewith; they drowned in this absorbing thought all worldly prejudices and all inclinations of the senses; they conceived a horror even of imperceptible faults, which an honest mind will excuse in itself; they exacted from themselves absolute and continuous perfection, and they entered into life with a fixed resolve to suffer and do all, rather than deviate one step. We laugh at a revolution about surplices and chasubles; there was a sentiment of the divine, underneath all these disputes about vestments. These poor folk, shopkeepers and farmers, believed, with all their heart, in a sublime and terrible God, and the manner how to worship Him was not a trifling thing for them:

"Suppose now it were some matter of vital concernment, some transcendent matter (as Divine worship is), about which your whole soul, struck dumb with its excess of feeling, knew not how to *form* itself into utterance at all, and preferred formless silence to any utterance there possible— what should we say of a man coming forward to represent or utter it for you in the way of upholsterer-mummery? Such a man— let him depart swiftly, if he love himself! You have lost your only son; are mute, struck down, without even tears: an importunate man importunately offers to celebrate Funeral Games for him in the manner of the Greeks."[388]

This has caused the Revolution, and not the Writ of Ship-money, or any other political vexation. "You may take my purse,... but the Self is mine and God my Maker's."[389] And the same sentiment which made them rebels, made them conquerors. Men could not understand how discipline could exist in an army in which an inspired corporal would reproach a lukewarm general. They thought it strange that generals, who sought the Lord with tears, had learned administration and strategy in the Bible. They wondered that madmen could be men of business. The truth is, that they were not madmen, but men of business. The whole difference between them and practical men whom we know, is that they had a conscience; this conscience was their flame; mysticism and dreams were but the smoke. They sought the true, the just; and their long prayers, their nasal preaching, their quotations from the Bible, their tears, their anguish, only mark the sincerity and ardor with which they applied themselves to the search. They read their duty in themselves; the Bible only aided them. At need they did violence to it, when they wished to verify by texts the suggestions of their own hearts. It was this sentiment of duty which united, inspired, and sustained them, which made their discipline, courage, and boldness; which raised to ancient heroism Hutchinson, Milton, and Cromwell; which instigated all decisive deeds, grand resolves, marvellous successes, the declaration of war, the trial of the king, the purge of Parliament, the humiliation of Europe, the protection of Protestantism, the sway of the seas. These men are the true heroes of England; they display, in high relief, the original characteristics and noblest features of England— practical piety, the rule of conscience, manly resolution, indomitable energy. They founded England, in spite of the corruption of the Stuarts and the relaxation of modern manners, by the exercise of duty, by the practice of justice, by obstinate toil, by vindication of right, by resistance to oppression, by the conquest of liberty, by the repression of vice. They founded Scotland, they founded the United States; at this day they are, by their descendants, founding Australia and colonizing the world. Carlyle is so much their brother that he excuses or admires their excesses— the execution of the king, the mutilation of Parliament, their intolerance, inquisition, the despotism of Cromwell, the theocracy of Knox. He sets them before us as models, and judges both past and present by them alone.

Section V.—His History of the French Revolution

Hence, he saw nothing but evil in the French Revolution. He judges it as unjustly as he judges Voltaire, and for the same reasons. He understands our manner of acting no better than our manner of thinking. He looks for Puritan sentiment; and, as he does not find it, he condemns us. The idea of duty, the religious spirit, self-government, the authority of an austere conscience, can alone, in his opinion, reform a corrupt society; and none of all these are to be met with in French society. The philosophy which has produced and guided the Revolution was simply destructive, proclaiming no other gospel but "that a lie cannot be believed! Philosophy knows only this: Her other relief is mainly that in spiritual, supra-sensual matters, no belief is possible." The theory of the Rights of Man, borrowed from Rousseau, is only a logical game, a pedantry almost as opportune as a "Theory of Irregular Verbs." The manners in vogue were the epicurism of Faublas. The morality in vogue was the promise of universal happiness. Incredulity, hollow rant, sensuality, were the mainsprings of this reformation. Men let loose their instincts and overturned the barriers. They replaced corrupt authority by unchecked anarchy. In what could a jacquerie of brutalized peasants, impelled by ecclesiastical arguments, end?

"For ourselves, we answer that French Revolution means here the open violent Rebellion, and Victory, of disimprisoned Anarchy against corrupt, worn-out Authority...."[390]

"So thousandfold complex a Society, ready to burst up from its infinite depths; and these men its rulers and healers, without life-rule for themselves— other life-rule than a Gospel according to Jean Jacques! To the wisest of them, what we must call the wisest, man is properly an accident under the sky. Man is without duty round him, except it be to make the Constitution. He is without Heaven above him, or Hell beneath him; he has no God in the world.

"While hollow languor and vacuity is the lot of the upper, and want and stagnation of the lower, and universal misery is very certain, what other thing is certain?... What will remain? The five unsatiated senses will remain, the sixth insatiable sense (of vanity); the whole *dæmoniac* nature of man will remain.

"Man is not what we call a happy animal; his appetite for sweet victual is too enormous.... (He cannot subsist) except by girding himself together for continual endeavour and endurance."[391]

But set the good beside the evil; put down virtues beside vices. These sceptics believed in demonstrated truth, and would have her alone for mistress. These logicians founded society only on justice, and risked their lives rather than renounce an established theorem. These epicureans embraced in their sympathies entire humanity. These furious men, these workmen, these hungry, threadbare peasants, fought on the frontiers for humanitarian interests and abstract principles. Generosity and enthusiasm abounded in

France, as well as in England; acknowledge them under a form which is not English. These men were devoted to abstract truth, as the Puritan to divine truth; they followed philosophy, as the Puritans followed religion; they had for their aim universal salvation, as the Puritans had individual salvation. They fought against evil in society, as the Puritans fought it in the soul. They were generous, as the Puritans were virtuous. They had, like them, a heroism, but sympathetic, sociable, ready to proselytize, which reformed Europe, whilst the English one only served England.

Section VI.—His Opinion of Modern England

This exaggerated Puritanism, which revolted Carlyle against the French Revolution, revolts him against modern England:

"We have forgotten God;— in the most modern dialect and very truth of the matter, we have taken up the Fact of this Universe as it is *not*. We have quietly closed our eyes to the eternal Substance of things, and opened them only to the Shows and Shams of things. We quietly believe this Universe to be intrinsically a great unintelligible PERHAPS; extrinsically, clear enough, it is a great, most extensive Cattlefold and Workhouse, with most extensive Kitchen-ranges, Dining-tables— whereat he is wise who can find a place! All the Truth of this Universe is uncertain; only the profit and loss of it, the pudding and praise of it, are and remain very visible to the practical man.

"There is no longer any God for us! God's Laws are become a Greatest-Happiness Principle, a Parliamentary Expediency; the Heavens overarch, us only as an Astronomical Timekeeper; a butt for Herschel-telescopes to shoot science at, to shoot sentimentalities at: in our and old Jonson's dialect, man has lost the *soul* out of him; and now, after the due period— begins to find the want of it! This is verily the plague-spot; centre of the universal Social Gangrene, threatening all modern things with frightful death. To him that will consider it, here is the stem, with its roots and taproot, with its worldwide upas-boughs and accursed poison-exudations, under which the world lies writhing in atrophy and agony. You touch the focal-centre of all our disease, of our frightful nosology of diseases, when you lay your hand on this. There is no religion: there is no God; man has lost his soul, and vainly seeks antiseptic salt. Vainly: in killing Kings, in passing Reform bills, in French Revolutions, Manchester Insurrections, is found no remedy. The foul elephantine leprosy, alleviated for an hour, reappears in new force and desperateness next hour."[392]

Since the return of the Stuarts, we are utilitarians or sceptics. We believe only in observation, statistics, gross and concrete truth; or else we doubt, half believe, on hearsay, with reserve. We have no moral convictions, and we have only floating convictions. We have lost the mainspring of action; we no longer set duty in the midst of our resolve, as the sole and undisturbed foundation of life; we are caught by all kinds of little experimental and positive receipts, and we amuse ourselves with all kinds of pretty pleasures, well chosen and arranged. We are egotists or dilettanti. We no longer look on life as an august temple, but as a machine for solid profits, or as a hall for refined amusements. We have our rich men, our manufacturers, our bankers, who preach the gospel of gold; we have gentlemen, dandies, lords, who preach the gospel of manners. We overwork ourselves to heap up guineas, or else we make ourselves insipid to attain an elegant dignity. Our hell is no longer, as under Cromwell, the dread of being found guilty before the just Judge, but the dread of making a bad speculation, or of transgressing etiquette. We have for our aristocracy greedy shopkeepers, who reduce life to a calculation of cost and sale-prices; and idle amateurs, whose great business in life is to preserve the game on their estates. We are no longer governed. Our government has no other ambition than to preserve the public peace, and to get in the taxes. Our constitution lays it down as a principle that, in order to discover the true and the good, we have only to make two million imbeciles vote. Our Parliament is a great word-mill, where plotters out-bawl each other for the sake of making a noise.[393]

Under this thin cloak of conventionalities and phrases, ominously growls the irresistible democracy. England perishes if she ever ceases to be able to sell a yard of cotton at a farthing less than others. At the least check in the manufactures, 1,500,000 workmen,[394] without work, live upon public charity. The formidable masses, given up to the hazards of industry, urged by lust, impelled by hunger, oscillate between the fragile cracking barriers; we are nearing the final breaking-up, which will be open anarchy, and the democracy will heave amidst the ruins, until the sentiment of the divine and of duty has rallied them around the worship of heroism; until it has discovered the means of calling to power the most virtuous and the most capable;[395] until it has given its guidance into their hands, instead of making them subject to its caprices; until it has recognized and reverenced its Luther and its Cromwell, its priest and its king.

Section VII.—The Dangers of Enthusiasm.—Comparison of Carlyle and Macaulay

Nowadays, doubtless, in the whole civilized world, democracy is swelling or overflowing, and all the channels in which it flows are fragile or temporary. But it is a strange offer to present for its issue the fanaticism and tyranny of the Puritans. The society and spirit which Carlyle proposes, as models for human nature, lasted but an hour, and could not last longer. The asceticism of the Republic produced the debauchery of the Restoration; Harrison preceded Rochester, men like Bunyan raised up men like Hobbes; and the sectaries, in instituting the despotism of enthusiasm, established by reaction the authority of the positive mind, and the worship of gross pleasure. Exaltation is not stable, and it cannot be exacted from man without injustice and danger. The sympathetic generosity of the French Revolution ended in the cynicism of the Directory and the slaughters of the empire. The chivalric and poetic piety of the great Spanish monarchy emptied Spain of men and of thought. The primacy of genius, taste, and intellect in Italy, reduced her at the end of a century to voluptuous sloth and political slavery. "What makes the angel makes the beast;" and perfect heroism, like all excesses, ends in stupor. Human nature has its explosions, but with intervals: mysticism is serviceable but when it is short. Violent circumstances produce extreme conditions; great evils are necessary in order to raise great men, and you are obliged to look for shipwrecks when you wish to behold rescuers. If enthusiasm is beautiful, its results and its originating circumstances are sad; it is but a crisis, and a healthy state is better. In this respect, Carlyle himself may serve for a proof. There is, perhaps, less genius in Macaulay than in Carlyle; but when we have fed for some time on this exaggerated and demoniacal style, this marvellous and sickly philosophy, this contorted and prophetic history, these sinister and furious politics, we gladly return to the continuous eloquence, to the vigorous reasoning, to the moderate prognostications, to the demonstrated theories, of the generous and solid mind which Europe has just lost, who brought honor to England, and whose place none can fill.

———

[326]Because the Kalmucks put written prayers into a calabash turned by the wind, which in their opinion produces a perpetual adoration. In the same way are the prayer-mills of Thibet used.

[327]The "Life of John Sterling," ch. V; "A Profession."
[328]"Sartor Resartus," 1868, bk. II. ch. VIII; Centre of Indifference.
[329]"History of the French Révolution," bk. I. ch. II; Realised Ideals.
[330]In the "Adoration of the Magi."
[331]"Latter-Day Pamphlets," 1850; Stump Orator, 35.
[332]"The French Revolution," I. bk. III. ch. VII; Internecine.
[333]"Cromwell's Letters and Speeches," III. X; the end.
[334]"Life of Sterling."
[335]"Sartor Resartus," bk. I. ch. X; Pure Reason.
[336]Ibid.
[337]Ibid. bk. III. ch. I; Incident in Modern History.
[338]"Sailor Resartus," bk. III. ch. X; The Dandiacal Body.
[339]"Sailor Resartus," bk. III. ch. X; The Dandiacal Body.
[340]Ibid.
[341]Ibid.
[342]"Latter-Day Pamphlets," 1850; Jesuitism, 28.
[343]In "Past and Present," bk. II.
[344]Ibid. ch. I; Jocelin of Brakelond.
[345]Ibid. ch. II; St. Edmondsbury.
[346]"Lectures on Heroes," 1868.

[347]"Lectures on Heroes," I: The Hero as Divinity.
[348]"Sartor Resartus," bk. I, ch, VIII; The World out of Clothes.
[349]Goethe, the greatest of them all.
[350]M. Renan.
[351]In particular, Stanley and Jowett.
[352]"Sartor Resartus," bk. I. ch. XI; Prospective.
[353]Ibid. bk. I. ch. X; Pure Reason.
[354]Ibid.
[355]Ibid. bk. I. ch. XI; Prospective.
[356]"Sartor Resartus," bk. III. ch. III; Symbols.
[357]Ibid. bk. III. ch. VIII; Natural Supernaturalism.
[358]Ibid.
[359]Ibid.
[360]"Sartor Resartus," bk. I. ch. X; Pure Reason.
[361]Ibid. bk. III. ch. VIII; Natural Supernaturalism.
[362]Ibid.
[363]"Sartor Resartus," bk. I. ch. X; Pre Reason.
[364]Ibid. bk. III. ch. VIII; Natural Supernaturalism.
[365]Ibid.
[366]"Sartor Resartus," bk. II. ch. VII; The Everlasting No.
[367]"Only this I know: If what thou namest Happiness be our true aim, then are we all astray. With Stupidity and sound Digestion man may front much. But what, in these dull, unimaginative days, are the terrors of Conscience to the diseases of the Liver! Not on Morality, but on Cookery, let us build our stronghold: there brandishing our frying-pan, as censer, let us offer sweet incense to the Devil, and live at ease on the fat things he has provided for his Elect!"— "Sartor Resartus," bk. II. ch. VII.
[368]"Lectures on Heroes."
[369]"Sartor Resartus," bk. II. ch. IX; The Everlasting Yea.
[370]Ibid. bk. III. ch. II; Church Clothes.
[371]"Lectures on Heroes," I; The Hero as Divinity.
[372]"Lectures on Heroes," I; The Hero as Divinity.
[373]Ibid, IV; The Hero as Priest.
[374]Ibid.
[375]"Past and Present," bk. III. ch. XV; Morrison Again.
[376]Ibid. bk. III. ch. XII; Reward.
[377]"Lectures on Heroes;" Miscellanies, passim.
[378]"Life of Sterling."
[379]"Critical and Miscellaneous Essays," 4 vols.; II. Voltaire.
[380]See this double praise in "Wilhelm Meister."
[381]"Lectures on Heroes," I; The Hero as Divinity.
[382]Ibid. II; The Hero as Prophet.

[383]"Cromwell's Letters and Speeches," III. part X; Death of the Protector.
[384]"Lectures on Heroes," I; The Hero as Divinity.
[385]Ibid.
[386]"Lectures on Heroes," I; The Hero as Divinity.
[387]Ibid. IV; The Hero as Priest.
[388]"Lectures on Heroes," VI; The Hero as King.
[389]Ibid.
[390]"The French Revolution," I. bk. VI. ch. I; Make the Constitution.
[391]Ibid.
[392]"Past and Present," bk. III. ch. I; Phenomena.
[393]"It is his effort and desire to teach this and the other thinking British man that said finale, the advent namely of actual open Anarchy, cannot be distant, now when virtual disguised Anarchy, long-continued, and waxing daily, has got to such a height; and that the one method of staving off the fatal consummation, and steering towards the Continents of the Future, lies not in the direction of reforming Parliament, but of what he calls reforming Downing Street; a thing infinitely urgent to be begun, and to be strenuously carried on. To find a Parliament more and more the express image of the People, could, unless the people chanced to be wise as well as miserable, give him no satisfaction. Not this at all; but to find some sort of King, made in the image of God, who could a little achieve for the People, if not their spoken wishes, yet their dumb wants, and what they would at last find to have been their instinctive will— which is a far different matter usually, in this babbling world of ours."— Parliaments, in "Latter-Day Pamphlets."

"A king or leader, then, in all bodies of men, there must be; be their work what it may, there is one man here who by character, faculty, position, is fittest of all to do it.

"He who is to be my ruler, whose will is to be higher than my will, was chosen for me in Heaven. Neither, except in such obedience to the Heaven-chosen, is freedom so much as conceivable."

[394]Official Report, 1842.
[395]"Latter-Day Pamphlets;" Parliaments.

Chapter Fifth. Philosophy—Stuart Mill

Section I.—Lack of General Ideas

When at Oxford, some years ago, during the meeting of the British Association, I met, amongst the few students still in residence, a young Englishman, a man of intelligence, with whom I became intimate.[396] He took me in the evening to the New Museum, well filled with specimens. Here short lectures were delivered, new models of machinery were set to work; ladies were present and took an interest in the experiments; on the last day, full of enthusiasm, "God Save the Queen" was sung. I admired this zeal, this solidity of mind, this organization of science, these voluntary subscriptions, this aptitude for association and for labor, this great machine pushed on by so many arms, and so well fitted to accumulate, criticise, and classify facts. But yet in this abundance, there was a void; when I read the Transactions, I thought I was present at a congress of heads of manufactories. All these learned men verified details and exchanged recipes. It was as though I listened to foremen, busy in communicating their processes for tanning leather, or dyeing cotton: general ideas were wanting. I used to regret this to my friend; and in the evening, by his lamp, amidst that great silence in which the university town lay wrapped, we both tried to discover its reasons.

Section II.—Why Metaphysics are Lacking

One day I said to him: You lack philosophy— I mean, what the Germans call metaphysics. You have learned men, but you have no thinkers. Your God impedes you. He is the Supreme Cause, and you dare not reason on causes, out of respect for him. He is the most important personage in England, and I see clearly that he merits his position; for he forms part of your constitution, he is the guardian of your morality, he judges in final appeal on all questions whatsoever, he replaces with advantage the prefects and gendarmes with whom the nations on the Continent are still encumbered. Yet, this high rank has the inconvenience of all official positions; it produces a cant, prejudices, intolerance, and courtiers. Here, close by us, is poor Mr. Max Müller, who, in order to acclimatize the study of Sanscrit, was compelled to discover in the Vedas the worship of a moral God, that is to say, the religion of Paley and Addison. Some time ago, in London, I read a proclamation of the Queen, forbidding people to play cards, even in their own houses, on Sundays.[397] It seems that, if I were robbed, I could not bring my thief to justice without taking a preliminary religious oath; for the judge has been known to send a complainant away who refused to take the oath, deny him justice, and insult him into the bargain. Every year, when we read the Queen's speech in your papers, we find there the compulsory mention of Divine Providence, which comes in mechanically, like the invocation to the immortal gods on the fourth page of a rhetorical declamation; and you remember that once, the pious phrase having been omitted, a second communication was made to Parliament for the express purpose of supplying it. All these cavillings and pedantries indicate to my mind a celestial monarchy; naturally it resembles all others; I mean that it relies more willingly on tradition and custom than on examination and reason. A monarchy never invited men to verify its credentials. As yours is, however, useful, well adapted to you, and moral, you are not revolted by it; you submit to it without difficulty, you are, at heart, attached to it; you would fear, in touching it, to disturb the constitution and morality. You leave it in the clouds, amidst public homage. You fall back upon yourselves, confine yourselves to matters of fact, to minute dissections, to experiments in the laboratory. You go culling plants and collecting shells. Science is deprived of its head; but all is for the best, for practical life is improved, and dogma remains intact.

Section III.—Mill's Philosophical Method

You are truly French, he answered; you ignore facts, and all at once find yourself settled in a theory. I assure you that there are thinkers amongst us, and not far from hence, at Christ Church, for instance. One of them, the professor of Greek, has spoken so deeply on inspiration, the creation and final causes, that he is out of favor. Look at this little collection which has recently appeared, "Essays and Reviews;" your philosophic freedom of the last century, the latest conclusions of geology and cosmogony, the boldness of German exegesis, are here in abstract. Some things are wanting, amongst others the waggeries of Voltaire, the misty jargon of Germany, and the prosaic coarseness of Comte; to my mind, the loss is small. Wait twenty years, and you will find in London the ideas of Paris and Berlin.— But they will still be the ideas of Paris and Berlin. Whom have you that is original?— Stuart Mill.— Who is he?— A political writer. His little book "On Liberty" is as admirable as Rousseau's "Contrat Social" is bad.— That is a bold assertion.— No, for Mill decides as strongly for the independence of the individual as Rousseau for the despotism of the State.— Very well, but that is not enough to make a philosopher. What besides is he?— An economist who goes beyond his science, and subordinates production to man, instead of man to production.— Well, but this is not enough to make a philosopher. Is he anything else?— A logician.— Very good; but of what school?— Of his own. I told you he was original.— Is he Hegelian?— By no means; he is too fond of facts and proofs.— Does he follow Port-Royal?— Still less; he is too well acquainted with modern sciences.— Does he imitate Condillac?— Certainly not; Condillac has only taught him to write well.— Who, then, are his friends?— Locke and Comte in the first rank; then Hume and Newton.— Is he a system-monger, a speculative reformer?— He has too much sense for that; he only arranges the best theories, and explains the best methods. He does not attitudinize majestically in the character of a restorer of science; he does not declare, like your Germans, that his book will open up a new era for humanity. He proceeds gradually, somewhat slowly, often creepingly, through a multitude of particular facts. He excels in giving precision to an idea, in disentangling a principle, in discovering it amongst a number of different facts; in refuting, distinguishing, arguing. He has the astuteness, patience, method, and sagacity of a lawyer.— Very well, you admit that I was right. A lawyer, an ally of Locke, Newton, Comte, and Hume; we have here only English philosophy; but no matter. Has he reached a grand conception of the universe?— Yes.— Has he an individual and complete idea of nature and the mind?— Yes.— Has he combined the operations and discoveries of the intellect under a single principle which puts them all in a new light?— Yes; but we have to discover this principle.— That is your business, and I hope you will undertake it.— But I shall fall into abstract generalities.— There is no harm in that?— But this close reasoning will be like a quick-set hedge. We will prick our fingers with it.— But three men out of four would cast aside such speculations as idle.— So much the worse for them. For in what does the life of a nation or a century consist, except in the formation of such theories? We are not thoroughly men unless so engaged. If some dweller in another planet were to come down here to ask us the nature of our race, we should have to show him the five or six great ideas which we have formed of the mind and the world. That alone would give him the measure of our intelligence. Expound to me your theory, and I shall go away better instructed than after having seen the masses of brick, which you call London and Manchester.

PART I.—EXPERIENCE

Section I.—The Object of Logic

Let us begin, then, at the beginning, like logicians. Mill has written on logic. What is logic? It is a science. What is its object? The sciences; for, suppose that you have traversed the universe, and that you know it thoroughly: stars, earth, sun, heat, gravity, chemical affinities, the species of minerals, geological revolutions, plants, animals, human events, all that classifications and theories explain and embrace, there still remain these classifications and theories to be learnt. Not only is there an order of beings, but also an order of the thoughts which represent them; not only plants and animals, but also botany and zoology; not only lines, surfaces, volumes, and numbers, but also geometry and arithmetic. Sciences, then, are as real things as facts themselves, and therefore, as well as facts, become the subject of study. We can analyze them as we analyze facts, investigate their elements, composition, order, relations, and object. There is, therefore, a science of sciences; this science is called logic, and is the subject of Mill's work. It is no part of logic to analyze the operations of the mind, memory, the association of ideas, external perception, etc.; that is the business of psychology. We do not discuss the value of such operations, the veracity of our consciousness, the absolute certainty of our elementary knowledge; this belongs to metaphysics. We suppose our faculties to be at work, and we admit their primary discoveries. We take the instrument as nature has provided it, and we trust to its accuracy. We leave to others the task of taking its mechanism to pieces, and the curiosity which criticises its results. Setting out from its primitive operations, we inquire how they are added to each other; how they are combined; how one is convertible into another; how, by dint of additions, combinations, and transformations, they finally compose a system of connected and developed truths. We construct a theory of science, as others construct theories of vegetation, of the mind, or of numbers. Such is the idea of logic; and it is plain that it has, as other sciences, a real subject-matter, its distinct province, its manifest importance, its special method, and a certain future

Section II.—Discussion of Ideas

Having premised so much, we observe that all these sciences which form the subject of logic are but collections of propositions, and that each proposition merely connects or separates a subject and an attribute, that is, two names, a quality and a substance; that is to say, a thing and another thing. We must then ask what we understand by a thing, what we indicate by a name; in other words, what it is we recognize in objects, what we connect or separate, what is the subject-matter of all our propositions and all our science.

There is a point in which all our several items of knowledge resemble one another. There is a common element which, continually repeated, constitutes all our ideas. There is, as it were, a minute primitive crystal which, indefinitely and variously repeating itself, forms the whole mass, and which, once known, teaches us beforehand the laws and composition of the complex bodies which it has formed.

Now, when we attentively consider the idea which we form of anything, what do we find in it? Take first, substances: that is to say, Bodies and Minds.[398] This table is brown, long, wide, three feet high, judging by the eye: that is, it forms a little spot in the field of vision; in other words, it produces a certain sensation on the optic nerve. It weighs ten pounds: that is, it would require to lift it an effort less than for a weight of eleven pounds, and greater than for a weight of nine pounds; in other words, it produces a certain muscular sensation. It is hard and square, which means that, if first pushed, and then run over by the hand, it will excite two distinct kinds of muscular sensations. And so on. When I examine closely what I know of it, I find that I know nothing else except the impressions it makes upon me. Our idea of a body comprises nothing else than this: we know nothing of it but the sensations it excites in us; we determine it by the nature, number, and order of these sensations; we know nothing of its inner nature, nor whether it has one; we simply affirm that it is the unknown cause of these sensations. When we say that a body has existed in the absence of our sensations we mean simply that if, during that time, we had been within reach of it, we should have had sensations which we have not had. We never define it save by our present or past, future or possible, complex or simple impressions. This is so true, that philosophers like Berkeley have maintained, with some show of truth, that matter is a creature of the imagination, and that the whole universe of sense is reducible to an order of sensations. It is at least so, as far as our knowledge is concerned; and the judgments which compose our sciences have reference only to the impressions by which things are manifested to us.

So, again, with the mind. We may well admit that there is in us a soul, an "ego," a subject or recipient of our sensations, and of our other modes of being, distinct from those sensations and modes of existence; but we know nothing of it. Mr. Mill says:

"For, as our conception of a body is that of an unknown exciting cause of sensations, so our conception of a mind is that of an unknown recipient, or percipient, of them; and not of them alone, but of all our other feelings. As body is the mysterious something which excites the mind to feel, so mind is the mysterious something which feels, and thinks. It is unnecessary to give in the case of mind, as we gave in the case of matter, a particular statement of the sceptical system by which its existence as a Thing in itself, distinct from the series of what are denominated its states, is called in question. But it is necessary to remark, that on the inmost nature of the thinking principle, as well as on the inmost nature of matter, we are, and with our faculties must always remain, entirely in the dark. All which we are aware of, even in our own minds, is a certain 'thread of consciousness'; a series of feelings, that is, of sensations, thoughts, emotions, and volitions, more or less numerous and complicated."[399]

We have no clearer idea of mind than of matter; we can say nothing more about it than about matter. So that substances, of whatever kind, bodies or minds, within or without us, are never for us more than tissues, more or less complex, more or less regular, of which our impressions and modes of being form all the threads.

This is still more evident in the case of attributes than of substances. When I say that snow is white, I mean that, when snow is presented to my sight, I have the sensation of whiteness. When I say that fire is hot, I mean that, when near the fire, I have the sensation of heat. We call a mind devout, superstitious, meditative, or gay, simply meaning that the ideas, the emotions, the volitions, designated by these words, recur frequently in the series of its modes of being.[400] When we say that bodies are heavy, divisible, movable, we mean simply that, left to themselves, they will fall; when cut, they will separate; or, when pushed, they will move: that is, under such and such circumstances they will produce such and such a sensation in our muscles, or our sight. An attribute always designates a mode of our being, or a series of our modes of being. In vain we disguise these modes by grouping, concealing them under abstract words, dividing and transforming them, so that we are frequently puzzled to recognize them: whenever we pierce to the basis of our words and ideas, we find them and nothing but them. Mill says:

"Take the following example: A generous person is worthy of honour. Who would expect to recognize here a case of coexistence between phenomena? But so it is. The attribute which causes a person to be termed generous is ascribed to him on the ground of states of his mind, and particulars of his conduct; both are phenomena; the former are facts of internal consciousness, the latter, so far as distinct from the former, are physical facts, or perceptions of the senses. Worthy of honour, admits of a similar analysis. Honour, as here used, means a state of approving and admiring emotion, followed on occasion by corresponding outward acts. 'Worthy of honour' connotes all this, together with an approval of the act of showing honour. All these are phenomena; states of internal consciousness, accompanied or followed by physical facts. When we say, A generous person is worthy of honour, we affirm coexistence between the two complicated phenomena connoted by the two terms respectively. We affirm, that wherever and whenever the inward feelings and outward facts implied in the word generosity have place, then and there the existence and manifestation of an inward feeling, honour, would be followed in our minds by another inward feeling, approval."[401]

In vain we turn about as we please, we remain still in the same circle. Whether the object be an attribute or a substance, complex or abstract, compound or simple, its material is to us always the same; it is made up only of our modes of being. Our mind is to nature what a thermometer is to a boiler: we define the properties of nature by the impressions of our mind, as we indicate the conditions of the boiling water by the changes of the thermometer. Of both we know but condition and changes; both are made up of isolated and transient facts; a thing is for us but an aggregate of phenomena. These are the sole elements of our knowledge: consequently the whole effort of science will be to link facts to facts.

Section III.—The Two Corner-Stones of Logic

This brief phrase is the abstract of the whole system. Let us master it, for it explains all Mill's theories. He has defined and restated everything, from this starting-point. In all forms and all degrees of knowledge, he has recognized only the knowledge of facts, and of their relations.

Now we know that logic has two corner-stones: the Theories of Definition and of Proof. From the days of Aristotle logicians have spent their time in polishing them. They have only dared to touch them respectfully, as if they were sacred. At most, from time to time, some innovator ventured to turn them over cautiously, to put them in a better light. Mill shapes, cuts, turns them over, and replaces them both in a similar manner and by the same means.

Section IV.—Theory of Definitions

I am quite aware that nowadays men laugh at those who reason on definitions; the laughers deserve to be laughed at. There is no theory more fertile in universal and important results; it is the root by which the whole tree of human science grows and lives. For to define things is to mark out their nature. To introduce a new idea of definition is to introduce a new idea of the nature of things; it is to tell us what beings are, of what they are composed, into what elements they are capable of being resolved. In this lies the merit of these dry speculations; the philosopher seems occupied with arranging mere formulas; the fact is, that in them he encloses the universe.

Take, say logicians, an animal, a plant, a feeling, a geometrical figure, an object or group of objects of any kind. Doubtless the object has its properties, but it has also its essence. It is manifested to the outer world by an indefinite number of effects and qualities; but all these modes of being are the results or products of its inner nature. There is within it a certain hidden substratum which alone is primitive and important, without which it can neither exist nor be conceived, and which constitutes its being and our notion of it.[402] They call the propositions which denote this essence definitions, and assert that the best part of our knowledge consists of such propositions.

On the other hand, Mill says that these kinds of propositions teach us nothing; they show the mere sense of a word, and are purely verbal.[403] What do I learn by being told that man is a rational animal, or that a triangle is a space contained by three lines? The first part of such a phrase expresses, by an abbreviative word, what the second part expresses in a developed phrase. You tell me the same thing twice over; you put the same fact into two different expressions; you do not add one fact to another, but you go from one fact to its equivalent. Your proposition is not instructive. You might collect a million such, my mind would remain entirely void; I should have read a dictionary, but not have acquired a single piece of knowledge. Instead of saying that essential propositions are important, and those relating to qualities merely accessory, you ought to say that the first are accessory, and the second important. I learn nothing by being told that a circle is a figure formed by the revolution of a straight line about one of its points as centre; I do learn something when told that the chords which subtend equal arcs in the circle are themselves equal, or that three given points determine the circumference. What we call the nature of a being is the connected system of facts which constitutes that being. The nature of a carnivorous mammal consists in the fact that the property of giving milk, and all its implied peculiarities of structure, are combined with the possession of sharp teeth, instincts of prey, and the corresponding faculties. Such are the elements which compose its nature. They are facts linked together as mesh to mesh in a net. We perceive a few of them; and we know that beyond our present knowledge and our future experience, the network extends to infinity its interwoven and manifold threads. The essence or nature of a being is the indefinite sum of its properties. Mill says:

"The definition, they say, unfolds the nature of the thing: but no definition can unfold its whole nature; and every proposition in which any quality whatever is predicated of the thing, unfolds some part of its nature. The true state of the case we take to be this: All definitions are of names, and of names only; but in some definitions it is clearly apparent, that nothing is intended except to explain the meaning of the word; while in others, besides explaining the meaning of the word, it is intended to be implied that there exists a thing, corresponding to the word."[404]

Abandon, then, the vain hope of eliminating from properties some primitive and mysterious being, the source and abstract of the whole; leave entities to Duns Scotus; do not fancy that, by probing your ideas in the German fashion, by classifying objects according to genera and species like the schoolmen, by reviving the nominalism of the Middle Ages or the riddles of Hegelian metaphysics, you will ever supply the want of experience. There are no definitions of things; if there are definitions, they only define names.

No phrase can tell me what a horse is; but there are phrases which will inform me what is meant by these five letters. No phrase can exhaust the inexhaustible sum of qualities which make up a being; but several phrases may point out the facts corresponding to a word. In this case definition is possible, because we can always make an analysis, which will enable us to pass from the abstract and summary term to the attributes which it represents, and from these attributes to the inner or concrete feelings which constitute their foundation. From the term "dog" it enables us to rise to the attributes "mammiferous, carnivorous," and others which it represents; and from these attributes to the sensations of sight, of touch, of the dissecting knife, on which they are founded. It reduces the compound to the simple, the derived to the primitive. It brings back our knowledge to its origin. It transforms words into facts. If some definitions, such as those of geometry, seem capable of giving rise to long sequences of new truths,[405] it is because, in addition to the explanation of a word, they contain the affirmation of a thing. In the definition of a triangle there are two distinct propositions— the one stating that "there may exist a figure bounded by three straight lines"; the other, that "such a figure may be termed a triangle." The first is a postulate, the second a definition. The first is hidden, the second evident; the first may be true or false, the second can be neither. The first is the source of all possible theorems as to triangles, the second only resumes in a word the facts contained in the other. The first is a truth, the second is a convention; the first is a part of science, the second an expedient of language. The first expresses a possible relation between three straight lines, the second gives a name to this relation. The first alone is fruitful, because it alone conforms to the nature of every fruitful proposition, and connects two facts. Let us, then, understand exactly the nature of our knowledge: it relates either to words or to things, or to both at once. If it is a matter of words, as in the definition of names, it attempts to refer words to our primitive feelings: that is to say, to the facts which form their elements. If it relates to beings, as in propositions about things, its whole effort is to link fact to fact, in order to connect the finite number of known properties with the infinite number to be known. If both are involved, as in the definitions of names which conceal a proposition relating to things, it attempts to do both. Everywhere its operation is the same. The whole matter, in any case, is to understand each other— that is, to revert to facts, or to learn— that is, to add facts to facts.

Section V.—Theory of Proof

The first rampart is destroyed; our adversaries take refuge behind the second— the Theory of Proof. This theory has passed for two thousand years for a substantiated, definite, unassailable truth. Many have deemed it useless, but no one has dared to call it false. On all sides it has been considered as an established theorem. Let us examine it closely and attentively. What is a proof? According to logicians, it is a syllogism. And what is a syllogism? A group of three propositions of this kind: "All men are mortal; Prince Albert is a man; therefore Prince Albert is mortal." Here we have the type of a proof, and every complete proof is conformable to this type. Now what is there, according to logicians, in this proof? A general proposition concerning all men, which gives rise to a particular proposition concerning a certain man. From the first we pass to the second, because the second is contained in the first; from the general to the particular, because the particular is comprised in the general. The second is but an instance of the first; its truth is contained beforehand in that of the first, and this is why it is a truth. In fact, as soon as the conclusion is no longer contained in the premises, the reasoning is false, and all the complicated rules of the Middle Ages have been reduced by the Port-Royalists to this single rule, "The conclusion must be contained in the premises." Thus the entire process of the human mind in its reasonings, consists in recognizing in individuals what is known of a whole class; in affirming in detail what has been established for the aggregate; in laying down a second time, and piecemeal, what has been laid down once for all at first.

By no means, replies Mill; for if it were so, our reasoning would be good for nothing. It would not be a progress, but a repetition. When I have affirmed that all men are mortal, I have affirmed implicitly that Prince Albert is mortal. In speaking of the whole class, that is to say, of all the individuals of the class, I have spoken of each individual, and therefore of Prince Albert, who is one of them. I say nothing new, then, when I now mention him expressly. My conclusion teaches me nothing; it adds nothing to my positive knowledge; it only puts in another shape a knowledge which I already possessed. It is not fruitful, but purely verbal. If, then, reasoning be what logicians represent it, it is not instructive. I know as much of the subject at the beginning of my reasoning as at the end. I have transformed words into other words; I have been moving, without gaining ground. Now this cannot be the case; for, in fact, reasoning does teach us new truths. I learn a new truth when I discover that Prince Albert is mortal, and I discover it by dint of reasoning; for, since he is still alive, I cannot have learnt it by direct observation. Thus logicians are mistaken; and beyond the scholastic theory of syllogism, which reduces reasoning to substitutions of words, we must look for a positive theory of proof, which shall explain how it is that, by the process of reasoning, we discover facts.

For this purpose, it is sufficient to observe that general propositions are not the true proof of particular propositions. They seem so, but are not. It is not from the mortality of all men that I conclude Prince Albert to be mortal; the premises are elsewhere, and in the background. The general proposition is but a memento^ a sort of abbreviative register, to which I have consigned the fruit of my experience. This memento may be regarded as a notebook, to which we refer to refresh our memory; but it is not from the book that we draw our knowledge, but from the objects which we have seen. My memento is valuable, only for the facts which it recalls. My general proposition has no value, except for the particular facts which it sums up.

"The mortality of John, Thomas, and company, is, after all, the whole evidence we have for the mortality of the Duke of Wellington. Not one iota is added to the proof by interpolating a general proposition. Since the individual cases are all the evidence we can possess, evidence which no logical form into which we choose to throw it can make greater than it is; and since that evidence is either sufficient in itself, or, if insufficient for the one purpose, cannot be sufficient for the other; I am unable to see why we should be forbidden to take the shortest cut from these sufficient premisses to the conclusion, and constrained to travel the 'high priori road' by the arbitrary fiat of logicians."[406]

"The true reason which makes us believe that Prince Albert will die is, that his ancestors, and our ancestors, and all the other persons who were their contemporaries, are dead. These facts are the true premises of our reasoning." It is from them that we have drawn the general proposition; they have taught us its scope and truth; it confines itself to mentioning them in a shorter form; it receives its whole substance from them; they act by it and through it, to lead us to the conclusion to which it seems to give rise. It is only their representative, and on occasion they do without it. Children, ignorant people, animals, know that the sun will rise, that water will drown them, that fire will burn them, without employing this general proposition. They reason, and we reason, too, not from the general to the particular, but from particular to particular:

"All inference is from particulars to particulars; general propositions are merely registers of such inferences already made, and short formulæ for making more: The major premiss of a syllogism, consequently, is a formula of this description: and the conclusion is not an inference drawn from the formula, but an inference drawn according to the formula: the real logical antecedent, or premisses, being the particular facts from which the general proposition was collected by induction. Those facts, and the individual instances which supplied them, may have been forgotten; but a record remains, not indeed descriptive of the facts themselves, but showing how those cases may be distinguished respecting which the facts, when known, were considered to warrant a given inference. According to the indications of this record we draw our conclusion; which is to all intents and purposes, a conclusion from the forgotten facts. For this it is essential that we should read the record correctly: and the rules of the syllogism are a set of precautions to ensure our doing so."[407]

"If we had sufficiently capacious memories, and a sufficient power of maintaining order among a huge mass of details, the reasoning could go on without any general propositions; they are mere formulae for inferring particulars from particulars."[408]

Here, as before, logicians are mistaken: they gave the highest place to verbal operations, and left the really fruitful operations in the background. They gave the preference to words over facts. They perpetuated the nominalism of the Middle Ages. They mistook the explanation of names for the nature of things, and the transformation of ideas for the progress of the mind. It is for us to overturn this order in logic, as we have overturned it in science, to exalt particular and instructive facts, and to give them in our theories that superiority and importance which our practice has conferred upon them for three centuries past.

Section VI.—Theory of Axioms

There remains a kind of philosophical fortress in which the Idealists have taken refuge. At the origin of all proof are Axioms, from which all proofs are derived. Two straight lines cannot enclose a space; two things, equal to a third, are equal to one another; if equals be added to equals, the wholes are equal. These are instructive propositions, for they express, not the meanings of words, but the relations of things. And, moreover, they are fertile propositions; for arithmetic, algebra, and geometry are all the result of their truth. On the other hand, they are not the work of experience, for we need not actually see with our eyes two straight lines in order to know that they cannot enclose a space; it is enough for us to refer to the inner mental conception which we have of them: the evidence of our senses is not needed for this purpose; our belief arises wholly, with its full force, from the simple comparison of our ideas. Moreover, experience follows these two lines only to a limited distance, ten, a hundred, a thousand feet; and the axiom is true for a thousand, a hundred thousand, a million miles, and for an unlimited distance. Thus, beyond the point at which experience ceases, it is no longer experience which establishes the axiom. Finally, the axiom is a necessary truth; that is to say, the contrary is inconceivable. We cannot imagine a space enclosed by two straight lines: as soon as we imagine the space enclosed, the two lines cease to be straight; and as soon as we imagine the two lines to be straight, the space ceases to be enclosed. In the assertion of axioms, the constituent ideas are irresistibly drawn together. In the negation of axioms, the constituent ideas inevitably repel each other. Now this does not happen with truths of experience: they state an accidental relation, not a necessary connection; they lay down that two facts are connected, and not that they must be connected; they show us that bodies are heavy, not that they must be heavy. Thus, axioms are not, and cannot be the results of experience. They are not so, because we can form them mentally without the aid of experience; they cannot be so, because the nature and scope of their truths lie beyond the limits of experience. They have another and a deeper source. They have a wider scope, and they come from elsewhere.

Not so, answers Mill. Here again you reason like a schoolman; you forget the facts concealed behind your conceptions; for examine your first argument. Doubtless you can discover, without making use of your eyes, and by purely mental contemplation, that two straight lines cannot enclose a space; but this contemplation is but a displaced experiment. Imaginary lines here replace real lines: you construct the figure in your mind instead of on paper: your imagination fulfils the office of a diagram on paper: you trust to it as you trust to the diagram, and it is as good as the other; for in regard to figures and lines the imagination exactly reproduces the sensation. What you have seen with your eyes open, you will see again exactly the same a minute afterwards with your eyes closed; and you can study geometrical properties, transferred to the field of mental vision, as accurately as if they existed in the field of actual sight. There are, therefore, experiments of the brain as there are ocular ones; and it is after just such an experiment that you deny to two straight lines, indefinitely prolonged, the property of enclosing a space. You need not, for this purpose, pursue them to infinity: you need only transfer yourself in imagination to the point where they converge, and there you have the impression of a bent line, that is of one which ceases to be straight.[409] Your presence there, in imagination, takes the place of an actual presence; you can affirm by it what you affirmed by your actual presence, and as positively. The first is only the second in a more commodious form, with greater flexibility and scope. It is like using a telescope instead of the naked eye; the revelations of the telescope are propositions of experience; so are those of the imagination. As to the argument which distinguishes axioms from propositions of experience under the pretext that the contraries of the latter are conceivable, while the contraries of axioms are inconceivable, it is nugatory, for this distinction does not exist. Nothing prevents the contraries of certain propositions of experience from being conceivable, and the contraries of others inconceivable. That depends on the constitution of our minds. It may be that in some cases the mind may contradict its experience, and in others not. It is possible that in certain cases our conceptions may differ from our perceptions, and sometimes not. It may be that, in certain cases, external sight is opposed to internal, and in certain others not. Now, we have already seen that in the case of figures, the internal sight exactly reproduces the external. Therefore, in axioms of figures, the mental sight cannot be opposed to the actual; imagination cannot contradict sensation. In other words, the contraries of such axioms will be inconceivable. Thus axioms, although their contraries are inconceivable, are experiments of a certain class, and it is because they are so that their contraries are inconceivable. At every point there results this conclusion, which is the abstract of the system: every instructive or fruitful proposition is derived from experience, and is simply a connecting together of facts.

Section VII.—Theory of Induction

Hence it follows that Induction is the only key to nature. This theory is Mill's masterpiece. Only so thorough-going a partisan of experience could have constructed the theory of Induction.

What, then, is Induction?

"Induction is that operation of the mind by which we infer that what we know to be true in a particular case or cases, will be true in all cases which resemble the former in certain assignable respects. In other words, Induction is the process by which we conclude that what is true of certain individuals of a class is true of the whole class, or that what is true at certain times will be true in similar circumstances at all times."[410]

This is the reasoning by which, having observed that Peter, John, and a greater or less number of men have died, we conclude that all men will die. In short, induction connects "mortality" with the quality of "man"; that is to say, connects two general facts ordinarily successive, and asserts that the first is the Cause of the second.

This amounts to saying that the course of nature is uniform. But induction does not set out from this axiom, it leads up to it; we do not find it at the beginning, but at the end of our researches.[411] Fundamentally, experience presupposes nothing beyond itself. No *à priori* principle comes to authorize or guide her. We observe that this stone has fallen, that this hot coal has burnt us, that this man has died, and we have no other means of induction except the addition and comparison of these little isolated and transient facts. We learn by simple practical experience that the sun gives light, that bodies fall, that water quenches thirst, and we have no other means of extending or criticising these inductions than by other like inductions. Every observation and every induction draws its value from itself, and from similar ones. It is always experience which judges of experience, and induction of induction. The body of our truths has not, then, a soul distinct from it, and vivifying it; it subsists by the harmony of all its parts taken as a whole, and by the vitality of each part taken separately.

"Why is it that, with exactly the same amount of evidence, both negative and positive, we did not reject the assertion that there are black swans, while we should refuse credence to any testimony which asserted that there were men wearing their heads underneath their shoulders? The first assertion was more credible than the latter. But why more credible? So long as neither phenomenon had been actually witnessed, what reason was there for finding the one harder to be believed than the other? Apparently because there is less constancy in the colours of animals than in the general structure of their internal anatomy. But how do we know this? Doubtless from experience. It appears, then, that we need experience to inform us in what degree, and in what cases, or sorts of cases, experience is to be relied on. Experience must be consulted in order to learn from it under what circumstances arguments from it will be valid. We have no ulterior test to which we subject experience in general; but we make experience its own test. Experience testifies, that among the uniformities which it exhibits, or seems to exhibit, some are more to be relied on than others; and uniformity, therefore, may be presumed, from any given number of instances, with a greater degree of assurance, in proportion as the case belongs to a class in which the uniformities have hitherto been found more uniform."[412]

Experience is the only test, and it is to be found everywhere.

Let us then consider how, without any help but that of experience, we can form general propositions, especially the most numerous and important of all, those which connect two successive events, by saying that the first is the cause of the second.

Cause is a great word; let us examine it. It carries in itself a whole philosophy. From the idea we have of Cause depend all our notions of nature. To give a new idea of Causation is to transform human thought; and we shall see how Mill, like Hume and Comte, but better than they, has put this idea into a new shape.

What is a cause? When Mill says that the contact of iron with moist air produces rust, or that heat dilates bodies, he does not speak of the mysterious bond by which metaphysicians connect cause and effect. He does not busy himself with the intimate force and generative virtue which certain philosophers insert between the thing producing and the product. Mill says:

"The only notion of a cause, which the theory of induction requires, is such a notion as can be gained from experience. The Law of Causation, the recognition of which is the main pillar of inductive science, is but the familiar truth, that invariability of succession is found by observation to obtain between every fact in nature and some other fact which has preceded it; independently of all consideration respecting the ulterior mode of production of phenomena, and of every other question regarding the nature of 'Things in themselves.'"[413]

No other foundation underlies these two expressions. We mean simply, that everywhere, always, the contact of iron with the moist air will be followed by the appearance of rust; the application of heat by the dilatation of bodies: "The real cause is the whole of these antecedents."[414] "There is no scientific foundation for distinguishing between the cause of a phenomenon and the conditions of its happening.... The distinction drawn between the patient and the agent is purely verbal. The cause, then, philosophically speaking, is the sum total of the conditions, positive and negative, taken together; the whole of the contingencies of every description, which being realized, the consequent invariably follows."[415] Much argument has been expended on the word necessary: "If there be any meaning which confessedly belongs to the term necessity, it is *unconditionalness.* That which is necessary, that which must be, means that which will be, whatever supposition we may make in regard to all other things."[416] This is all we mean, when we assert that the notion of cause includes the notion of necessity. We mean that the antecedent is sufficient and complete, that there is no need to suppose any additional antecedent, that it contains all requisite conditions, and that no other condition need exist. To follow unconditionally, then, is the whole notion of cause and effect. We have none else. Philosophers are mistaken when they discover in our will a different type of causation, and declare it an example of efficient cause in act and in exercise. We sec nothing of the kind, but there, as elsewhere, we find only continuous successions. We do not see a fact engendering another fact, but a fact accompanying another. "Our will," says Mill, "produces our bodily actions as cold produces ice, or as a spark produces an explosion of gunpowder." There is here, as elsewhere, an antecedent, the resolution or state of mind, and a consequent, the effort or physical sensation. Experience connects them, and enables us to foresee that the effort will follow the resolution, as it enables us to foresee that the explosion of gunpowder will follow the contact of the spark. Let us then have done with all these psychological illusions, and seek only, under the names of cause and effect, for phenomena which form pairs without exception or condition.

Now, to establish these connections of phenomena, Mill discovers four methods, and only four— namely, the Methods of Agreement,[417] of Difference,[418] of Residues,[419] and of Concomitant Variations.[420] These are the only ways by which we can penetrate into nature. There are no other, and these are everywhere. And they all employ the same artifice, that is to say, elimination; for, in fact, induction is nothing else. You have two groups, one of antecedents, the other of consequents, each of them containing more or fewer elements, ten, for example. To what antecedent is each consequent joined? Is the first consequent joined to the first antecedent, or to the third, or sixth? The whole difficulty and the only possible solution lie there. To resolve the difficulty, and to effect the solution, we must eliminate, that is, exclude those antecedents which are not connected with the consequent we are considering.[421] But as we cannot exclude them effectually, and as in nature the pair of phenomena we are seeking is always surrounded with circumstances, we collect collect various cases, which by their diversity enable the mind to lop off these circumstances, and to discover the pair of phenomena distinctly. In short, we can only perform induction by discovering pairs of phenomena; we form these only by isolation; we isolate only by means of comparisons.

Section VIII.—Applications of the Theory of Induction

These are the rules; an example will make them clearer. We will show you the methods in exercise; here is an example which combines nearly the whole of them, namely, Dr. Well's theory of dew. I will give it to you in Mill's own words, which are so clear that you must have the pleasure of pondering over them: "We must separate dew from rain and the moisture of fogs, and limit the application of the term to what is really meant, which is, the spontaneous appearance of moisture on substances exposed in the open air when no rain or visible wet is falling."[422] What is the cause of the phenomena we have thus defined, and how was that cause discovered?

"'Now, here we have analogous phenomena, in the moisture which bedews a cold metal or stone when we breathe upon it; that which appears on a glass of water fresh from the well in hot weather; that which appears on the inside of windows when sudden rain or hail chills the external air; that which runs down our walls when, after a long frost, a warm moist thaw comes on.' Comparing these cases, we find that they all contain the phenomenon which was proposed as the subject of investigation. Now 'all these instances agree in one point: the coldness of the object dewed, in comparison with the air in contact with it.' But there still remains the most important case of all, that of nocturnal dew: does the same circumstance exist in this case? 'Is it a fact that the object dewed is colder than the air? Certainly not, one would at first be inclined to say; for what is to make it so? But ... the experiment is easy; we have only to lay a thermometer in contact with the dewed substance, and hang one at a little distance above it, out of reach of its influence. The experiment has been therefore made; the question has been asked, and the answer has been invariably in the affirmative. Whenever an object contracts dew, it is colder than the air.'

"Here then is a complete application of the Method of Agreement, establishing the fact of an invariable connection between the deposition of dew on a surface, and the coldness of that surface, compared with the external air. But which of these is cause, and which effect? or are they both effects of something else? On this subject the Method of Agreement can afford us no light: we must call in a more potent method. 'We must collect more facts, or, which comes to the same thing, vary the circumstances; since every instance in which the circumstances differ is a fresh fact: and especially, we must note the contrary or negative cases, i.e., where no dew is produced': for a comparison between instances of dew and instances of no dew, is the condition necessary to bring the Method of Difference into play.

"'Now, first, no dew is produced on the surface of polished metals, but it is very copiously on glass, both exposed with their faces upwards, and in some cases the under side of a horizontal plate of glass is also dewed.' Here is an instance in which the effect is produced, and another instance in which it is not produced; but we cannot yet pronounce, as the canon of the Method of

Difference requires, that the latter instance agrees with the former in all its circumstances except one: for the differences between glass and polished metals are manifold, and the only thing we can as yet be sure of is, that the cause of dew will be found among the circumstances by which the former substance is distinguished from the latter."

To detect this particular circumstance of difference, we have but one practicable method, that of Concomitant Variations:

"'In the cases of polished metal and polished glass, the contrast shows evidently that the substance has much to do with the phenomenon; therefore let the substance alone be diversified as much as possible, by exposing polished surfaces of various kinds. This done, a scale of intensity becomes obvious. Those polished substances are found to be most strongly dewed which conduct heat worst, while those which conduct well resist dew most effectually....'

"The conclusion obtained is, that *cæteris paribus* the deposition of dew is in some proportion to the power which the body possesses of resisting the passage of heat; and that this, therefore (or something connected with this), must be at least one of the causes which assist in producing the deposition of dew on the surface.

"'But if we expose rough surfaces instead of polished, we sometimes find this law interfered with. Thus, roughened iron, especially if painted over or blackened, becomes dewed sooner than varnished paper: the kind of surface, therefore, has a great influence. Expose, then, the same material in very diversified states as to surface' (that is, employ the Method of Difference to ascertain concomitance of variations),' and another scale of intensity becomes at once apparent; those surfaces which part with their heat most readily by radiation, are found to contract dew most copiously....'

"The conclusion obtained by this new application of the method is, that *cæteris paribus* the deposition of dew is also in some proportion to the power of radiating heat; and that the quality of doing this abundantly (or some cause on which that quality depends) is another of the causes which promote the deposition of dew on the substance.

"'Again, the influence ascertained to exist of substance and surface, leads us to consider that of texture; and here, again, we are presented on trial with remarkable differences, and with a third scale of intensity, pointing out substances of a close firm texture, such as stones, metals, etc., as unfavourable, but those of a loose one, as cloth, velvet, wool, eiderdown, cotton, etc., as eminently favourable to the contraction of dew.' The Method of Concomitant Variations is here, for the third time, had recourse to; and, as before, from necessity, since the texture of no substance is absolutely firm or absolutely loose. Looseness of texture, therefore, or something which is the cause of that quality, is another circumstance which promotes the deposition of dew; but this third cause resolves itself into the first, viz., the quality of resisting the passage of heat: for substances of loose texture 'are precisely those which are best adapted for clothing, or for impeding the free passage of heat from the skin into the air, so as to allow their outer surfaces to be very cold, while they remain warm within....'

"It thus appears that the instances in which much dew is deposited, which are very various, agree in this, and, so far as we are able to observe, in this only, that they either radiate heat rapidly or conduct it slowly: qualities between which there is no other circumstance of agreement than that by virtue of either, the body tends to lose heat from the surface more rapidly than it can be restored from within. The instances, on the contrary, in which no dew, or but a small quantity of it, is formed, and which are also extremely various, agree (so far as we can observe) in nothing except in not having this same property....

"This doubt we are now able to resolve. We have found that in every such instance, the substance must be one which, by its own properties or laws, would, if exposed in the night, become colder than the surrounding air. The coldness, therefore, being accounted for independently of the dew, while it is proved that there is a connection between the two, it must be the dew which depends on the coldness; or, in other words, the coldness is the cause of the dew.

"This law of causation, already so amply established, admits, however, of efficient additional corroboration in no less than three ways. First, by deduction from the known laws of aqueous vapour when diffused through air or any other gas, and though we have not yet come to the Deductive Method, we will not omit what is necessary to render this speculation complete. It is known, by direct experiment, that only a limited quantity of water can remain suspended in the state of vapour at each degree of temperature, and that this maximum grows less and less, as the temperature diminishes. From this it follows deductively, that if there is already as much vapour suspended as the air will contain at its existing temperature, any lowering of that temperature will cause a portion of the vapour to be condensed, and become water. But, again, we know deductively, from the laws of heat, that the contact of the air with a body colder than itself, will necessarily lower the temperature of the stratum of air immediately applied to its surface; and will therefore cause it to part with a portion of its water, which accordingly will, by the ordinary laws of gravitation or cohesion, attach itself to the surface of the body, thereby constituting dew. This deductive proof, it will have been seen, has the advantage of proving at once causation as well as coexistence; and it has the additional advantage that it also accounts for the exceptions to the occurrence of the phenomenon, the cases in which, although the body is colder than the air, yet no dew is deposited, by showing that this will necessarily be the case when the air is so under-supplied with aqueous vapour, comparatively to its temperature, that even when somewhat cooled by the contact of the colder body, it can still continue to hold in suspension all the vapour which was previously suspended in it: thus, in a very dry summer there are no dews, in a very dry winter no hoar frost....

"The second corroboration of the theory is by direct experiment, according to the canon of the Method of Difference. We can, by cooling the surface of any body, find in all cases some temperature (more or less inferior to that of the surrounding air, according to its hygrometric condition) at which dew will begin to be deposited. Here, too, therefore, the causation is directly proved. We can, it is true, accomplish this only on a small scale; but we have ample reason to conclude that the same operation, if conducted in Nature's great laboratory, would equally produce the effect.

"And, finally, even on that great scale we are able to verify the result. The case is one of those rare cases, as we have shown them to be, in which nature works the experiment for us in the same manner in which we ourselves perform it; introducing into the previous state of things a single and perfectly definite new circumstance, and manifesting the effect so rapidly that there is not time for any other material change in the pre-existing circumstances. 'It is observed that dew is never copiously deposited in situations much screened from the open sky, and not at all in a cloudy night; but if the clouds withdraw even for a few minutes, and leave a clear opening, a deposition of dew presently begins, and goes on increasing.... Dew formed in clear intervals will often even evaporate again when the sky becomes thickly overcast.' The proof, therefore, is complete, that the presence or absence of an uninterrupted communication with the sky causes the deposition or non-deposition of dew. Now, since a clear sky is nothing but the absence of clouds, and it is a known property of clouds, as of all other bodies between which and any given object nothing intervenes but an elastic fluid, that they tend to raise or keep up the superficial temperature of the object by radiating heat to it, we see at once that the disappearance of clouds will cause the surface to cool; so that Nature, in this case, produces a change in the antecedent by definite and known means, and the consequent follows accordingly: a natural experiment which satisfies the requisitions of the Method of Difference."

Section IX.—The Province and Method of Deduction

These four are not all the scientific methods, but they lead up to the rest. They are all linked together, and no one has shown their connection better than Mill. In many cases these processes of isolation are powerless; namely, in those in which the effect, being produced by a concourse of causes, cannot be reduced into its elements. Methods of isolation are then impracticable. We cannot eliminate, and consequently we cannot perform induction. This serious difficulty presents itself in almost all cases of motion, for almost every movement is the effect of a concurrence of forces; and the respective effects of the various forces are found so mixed up in it that we cannot separate them without destroying it, so that it seems impossible to tell what part each force has in the production of the movement. Take a body acted upon by two forces whose directions form an angle: it moves along the diagonal; each part, each moment, each position, each element of its movement, is the combined effect of the two impelling forces. The two effects are so commingled that we cannot isolate either of them, and refer it to its source. In order to perceive each effect separately, we should have to consider the movements apart, that is, to suppress the actual movement, and to replace it by others. Neither the Method of Agreement, nor of Difference, nor of Residues, nor of Concomitant Variations, which are all decomposing and eliminative, can avail against a phenomenon which by its nature excludes all elimination and decomposition. We must, therefore, evade the obstacle; and it is here that the last key of nature appears, the Method of Deduction. We quit the study of the actual phenomenon to observe other and simpler cases; we establish their laws, and we connect each with its cause by the ordinary methods of induction. Then, assuming the concurrence of two or of several of these causes, we conclude from their known laws what will be their total effect. We next satisfy ourselves as to whether the actual movement exactly coincides with the movement foretold; and if this is so, we attribute it to the causes from which we have deduced it. Thus, in order to discover the causes of the planetary motions, we seek by simple induction the laws of two causes: first, the force of primitive impulsion in the direction of the tangent; next, an accelerative attracting force. From these inductive laws we deduce by calculation the motion of a body submitted to their combined influence; and satisfying ourselves that the planetary motions observed coincide exactly with the predicted movements, we conclude that the two forces in question are actually the causes of the planetary motions. "To the Deductive Method," says Mill, "the human mind is indebted for its most conspicuous triumphs in the investigation of nature. To it we owe all the theories by which vast and complicated phenomena are embraced under a few simple laws." Our deviations have led us further than the direct path; we have derived efficiency from imperfection.

Section X.—Comparison of the Methods of Induction and Deduction

If we now compare the two methods, their aptness, function, and provinces, we shall find, as in an abstract, the history, divisions, hopes, and limits of human science. The first appears at the beginning, the second at the end. The first, necessarily, gained ascendancy in Bacon's time,[423] and now begins to lose it; the second, necessarily, lost ascendancy in Bacon's time, and now begins to regain it. So that science, after having passed from the deductive to the experimental state, is now passing from the experimental to the deductive. Induction has for its province phenomena which are capable of being decomposed', and on which we can experiment. Deduction has for its province indecomposable phenomena, or those on which we cannot experiment. The first is efficacious in physics, chemistry, zoology, and botany, in the earlier stages of every science, and also whenever phenomena are but slightly complicated, within our reach, capable of being modified by means at our disposal. The second is efficacious in astronomy, in the higher branches of physics, in physiology, history, in the higher grades of every science, whenever phenomena are very complicated, as in animal and social life, or lie beyond our reach, as the motions of the heavenly bodies and the changes of the atmosphere. When the proper method is not employed, science is at a stand-still: when it is employed, science progresses. Here lies the whole secret of its past and its present. If the physical sciences remained stationary till the time of Bacon, it is because men used deduction when they should have used induction. If physiology and the moral sciences are now making slow progress, it is because we employ induction when deduction should be used. It is by deduction, and according to physical and chemical laws, that we shall be enabled to explain physiological phenomena. It is by deduction, and according to mental laws, that we shall be enabled to explain historical phenomena.[424] And that which has become the instrument of these two sciences, it is the object of all the others to employ. All tend to become deductive, and aim at being summed up in certain general propositions, from which the rest may be deduced. The less numerous these propositions are, the more science advances. The fewer suppositions and postulates a science requires, the more perfect it is become. Such a reduction is its final condition. Astronomy, acoustics, optics, present its models; we shall know nature when we shall have deduced her millions of facts from two or three laws.

I venture to say that the theory which you have just heard is perfect. I have omitted several of its characteristics, but you have seen enough to recognize that induction has nowhere been explained in so complete and precise a manner, with such an abundance of fine and just distinctions, with such extensive and exact applications, with such a knowledge of the practical methods and ascertained results of science, with so complete an exclusion of metaphysical principles and arbitrary suppositions, and in a spirit more in conformity with the rigorous procedure of modern experimental science. You asked me just now, what Englishmen have effected in philosophy; I answer, the theory of Induction. Mill is the last of that great line of philosophers, which begins at Bacon, and which, through Hobbes, Newton, Locke, Hume, Herschel, is continued down to our own times. They have carried our national spirit into philosophy; they have been positive and practical; they have not soared above facts; they have not attempted out-of-the-way paths; they have cleared the human mind of its illusions, presumptions, and fancies. They have employed it in the only direction in which it can act; they only wished to mark out and light up the already well-trodden ways of the progressive sciences.

They have not been willing to spend their labor vainly in other than explored and verified paths; they have aided in the great modern work, the discovery of applicable laws; they have contributed, as men of special attainments do, to the increase of man's power. Can you find many philosophers who have done as much?

Section XI.—Limits of Our Knowledge

You will tell me that our philosopher has clipped his wings, in order to strengthen his legs. Certainly; and he has acted wisely. Experience limits the career which it opens to us; it has given us our goal, but also our boundaries. We have only to observe the elements of which our experience is composed, and the facts from which it sets out, to understand that its range is limited. Its nature and its method confine its progress to a few steps. And, in the first place,[425] the ultimate laws of nature cannot be less numerous than the several distinct species of our sensations. We can easily reduce a movement to another movement, but not the sensation of heat to that of smell, or of color, or of sound, nor either of these to a movement. We can easily connect together phenomena of different degrees, but not phenomena differing in species. We find distinct sensations at the bottom of all our knowledge, as simple indecomposable elements, separated absolutely one from another, absolutely incapable of being reduced one to another. Let experience do what she will, she cannot suppress these diversities which constitute her foundation. On the other hand, experience, do what she will, cannot escape from the conditions under which she acts. Whatever be her province, it is bounded by time and space; the fact which she observes is limited and influenced by an infinite number of other facts to which she cannot attain. She is obliged to suppose or recognize some primordial condition from whence she starts, and which she does not explain.[426] Every problem has its accidental or arbitrary data: we deduce the rest from these, but there is nothing from which these can be deduced. The sun, the earth, the planets, the initial impulse of the heavenly bodies, the primitive chemical properties of substances, are such data.[427] If we possessed them all we could explain everything by them, but we could not explain these themselves. Mill says:

"Why these particular natural agents existed originally and no others, or why they are commingled in such and such proportions, and distributed in such and such a manner throughout space, is a question we cannot answer. More than this: we can discover nothing regular in the distribution itself; we can reduce it to no uniformity, to no law. There are no means by which, from the distribution of these causes, or agents, in one part of space, we could conjecture whether a similar distribution prevails in another."[428]

And astronomy, which just now afforded us the model of a perfect science, now affords us an example of a limited science. We can predict the numberless positions of all the planetary bodies; but we are obliged to assume, beside the primitive impulse and its amount, not only the force of attraction and its law, but also the masses and distances of all the bodies in question. We understand millions of facts, but it is by means of a hundred facts which we do not comprehend; we arrive at necessary results, but it is only by means of accidental antecedents; so that if the theory of our universe were completed there would still remain two great voids: one at the commencement of the physical world, the other at the beginning of the moral world; the one comprising the elements of being, the other embracing the elements of experience; one containing primary sensations, the other primitive agents. "Our knowledge," says Royer-Collard, "consists in tracing ignorance as far back as possible."

Can we at least affirm that these irreducible data are so only in appearance, and in relation to our mind? Can we say that they have causes, like the derived facts of which they are the causes? Can we conclude that every event, always and everywhere, happens according to laws, and that this little world of ours, so well-regulated, is a sort of epitome of the universe? Can we by aid of the axioms, quit our narrow confines, and affirm anything of the universe? In no wise; and it is here that Mill pushes his principles to their furthest consequences: for the law which attributes a cause to every event, has to him no other foundation, worth, or scope, than what it derives from experience. It has no inherent necessity; it draws its whole authority from the great number of cases in which we have recognized it to be true; it only sums up a mass of observations; it unites two data, which, considered in themselves, have no intimate connection; it joins antecedents generally to consequents generally, just as the law of gravitation joins a particular antecedent to a particular consequent; it determines a couple, as do all experimental laws, and shares in their uncertainty and in their restrictions. Listen to this bold assertion:

"I am convinced that anyone accustomed to abstraction and analysis, who will fairly exert his faculties for the purpose, will, when his imagination has once learnt to entertain the notion, find no difficulty in conceiving that in some one, for instance, of the many firmaments into which sidereal astronomy now divides the universe, events may succeed one another at random, without any fixed law; nor can anything in our experience, or in our mental nature, constitute a sufficient, or indeed any, reason for believing that this is nowhere the case. The grounds, therefore, which warrant us in rejecting such a supposition with respect to any of the phenomena of which we have experience, must be sought elsewhere than in any supposed necessity of our intellectual faculties."[429]

Practically, we may trust in so well-established a law; but

"In distant parts of the stellar regions, where the phenomena may be entirely unlike those with which we are acquainted, it would be folly to affirm confidently that this general law prevails, any more than those special ones which we have found to hold universally on our own planet. The uniformity in the succession of events, otherwise called the law of causation, must be received not as a law of the universe, but of that portion of it only which is within the range of our means of sure observation, with a reasonable degree of extension to adjacent cases. To extend it further is to make a supposition without evidence, and to which, in the absence of any ground from experience for estimating its degree of probability, it would be idle to attempt to assign any."[430]

We are, then, irrevocably driven back from the infinite: our faculties and our assertions cannot attain to it; we remain confined in a small circle; our mind reaches not beyond its experience; we can establish no universal and necessary connection between facts; such a connection probably does not even exist. Mill stops here; but certainly, by carrying out his idea to its full extent, we should arrive at the conception of the world as a mere collection of facts; no internal necessity would induce their connection or their existence; they would be simple, arbitrary, accidentally-existing facts. Sometimes, as in our system, they would be found assembled in such a manner as to give rise to regular recurrences; sometimes they would be so assembled that nothing of the sort would occur. Chance, as Democritus taught, would be at the foundation of all things. Laws would be the result of chance, and sometimes we should find them, sometimes not. It would be with existences as with numbers— decimal fractions, for instance, which, according to the chance of their two primitive factors, sometimes recur regularly, and sometimes not. This is certainly an original and lofty conception. It is the final consequence of the primitive and dominant idea, which we have discovered at the beginning of the system, which has transformed the theories of Definition, of Propositions, and of the Syllogism; which has reduced axioms to experimental truths; which has developed and perfected the theory of induction; which has established the goal, the limits, the province, and the methods of science; which everywhere, in nature and in science, has suppressed interior connections; which has replaced the necessary by the accidental; cause by antecedent; and which consists in affirming that every assertion which is not merely verbal forms in effect a couple, that is to say, joins together two facts which were separate by their nature.

PART II.—ABSTRACTION

Section I.—Agreement of this Philosophy with the English Mind

An abyss of chance and an abyss of ignorance. The prospect is gloomy: no matter, if it be true. At all events, this theory of science is a theory of English science. Rarely, I grant you, has a thinker better summed up in his teaching the practice of his country; seldom has a man better represented, by his negations and his discoveries, the limits and scope of his race. The operations, of which he constructs science, are those in which the English excel all others, and those which he excludes from science are precisely those in which the English are deficient, more than any other nation. He has described the English mind, whilst he thought to describe the human mind. That is his glory, but it is also his weakness. There is in your idea of knowledge a flaw, of which the incessant repetition ends by creating the gulf of chance, from which, according to him, all things arise, and the gulf of ignorance, at whose brink, according to him, our knowledge ends. And see what comes of it. By cutting away from science the knowledge of first causes, that is, of divine things, you reduce men to become sceptical, positive, utilitarian, if they are cool-headed; or mystical, enthusiastic, methodistical, if they have lively imaginations. In this huge unknown void, which you place beyond our little world, passionate men and uneasy consciences find room for all their dreams; and men of cold judgment, despairing of arriving at any certain knowledge, have nothing left but to sink down to the search for practical means which may serve for the amelioration of our condition. It seems to me that these two dispositions are most frequently met with in an English mind. The religious and the positive spirit dwell there side by side, but separate. This produces an odd medley, and I confess that I prefer the way in which the Germans have reconciled science with faith.— But their philosophy is but badly written poetry.— Perhaps so.— But what they call reason, or intuition of principles, is only the faculty of building up hypotheses.— Perhaps so.— But the systems which they have constructed have not held their ground before experience.— I do not defend what they have done.— But their absolute, their subject, their object, and the rest, are but big words.— I do not defend their style.— What, then, do you defend?— Their idea of Causation.— You believe with them that causes are discovered by a revelation of the reason?— By no means.— You believe with us that our knowledge of causes is based on simple experience?— Still less.— You think, then, that there is a faculty, other than experience and reason, capable of discovering causes?— Yes.— You think there is an intermediate course between intuition and observation, capable of arriving at principles, as it is affirmed that the first is, capable of arriving at truths, as we find that the second is?— Yes.— What is it? Abstraction. Let us return to your original idea; I will endeavor to show in what I think it incomplete, and how you seem to me to mutilate the human mind. But my argument will be the formal one of an advocate, and requires to be stated at length.

Section II.—The Nature of Abstraction

Your starting-point is good: man, in fact, does not know anything of substances; he knows neither minds nor bodies; he perceives only transient, isolated, internal conditions; he makes use of these to affirm and name exterior states, positions, movements, changes, and avails himself of them for nothing else. He can only attain to facts, whether within or without, sometimes transient, when his impression is not repeated; sometimes permanent, when his impression, many times repeated, makes him suppose that it will be repeated as often as he wishes to experience it. He only grasps colors, sounds, resistances, movements: sometimes momentary and variable, sometimes like one another, and renewed. To group these facts more advantageously, he supposes, by an artifice of language, qualities and properties. We go even further than you: we think that there are neither minds nor bodies, but simply groups of present or possible movements or thoughts. We believe that there are no substances, but only systems of facts. We regard the idea of substance as a psychological illusion. We consider substance, force, and all the modern metaphysical existences, as the remains of scholastic entities. We think that there exists nothing but facts and laws, that is, events and the relations between them; and we recognize, with you, that all knowledge consists, first of all, in connecting or adding fact to fact. But when this is done, a new operation begins, the most fertile of all, which consists in reducing these complex into simple facts. A splendid faculty appears, the source of language, the interpreter of nature, the parent of religions and philosophies, the only genuine distinction, which according to its degree, separates man from the brute, and great from little men. I mean Abstraction, which is the power of isolating the elements of facts, and of considering them one by one. My eyes follow the outline of a square, and abstraction isolates its two constituent properties, the equality of its sides and angles. My fingers touch the surface of a cylinder, and abstraction isolates its two generative elements, the idea of a rectangle, and of the revolution of this rectangle about one of its sides as an axis. A hundred thousand experiments develop for me, by an infinite number of details, the series of physiological operations which constitute life; and abstraction isolates the law of this series, which is a round of constant loss and continual reparation. Twelve hundred pages teach me Mill's opinion on the various facts of science, and abstraction isolates his fundamental idea, namely, that the only fertile propositions are those which connect a fact with another not contained in the first. Everywhere the case is the same. A fact, or a series of facts, can always be resolved into its components. It is this resolution which forms our problem, when we ask what is the nature of an object. It is these components we look for when we wish to penetrate into the inner nature of a being. These we designate under the names of forces, causes, laws, essences, primitive properties. They are not new facts added to the first, but an essence or extract from them; they are contained in the first, they have no existence apart from the facts themselves. When we discover them, we do not pass from one fact to another, but from one to another aspect of the same fact; from the whole to a part, from the compound to the components. We only see the same thing under two forms; first, as a whole, then as divided: we only translate the same idea from one language into another, from the language of the senses into abstract language, just as we express a curve by an equation, or a cube as a function of its side. It signifies little whether this translation be difficult or not; or that we generally need the accumulation or comparison of a vast number of facts to arrive at it, and whether our mind may not often succumb before accomplishing it. However this may be, in this operation, which is evidently fertile, instead of proceeding from one fact to another, we go from the same to the same; instead of adding experiment to experiment, we set aside some portion of the first; instead of advancing, we pause to examine the ground we stand on. There are, thus, fruitful judgments, which, however, are not the results of experience: there are essential propositions, which, however, are not merely verbal: there is, thus, an operation, differing from experience, which acts by cutting down, instead of by addition; which, instead of acquiring, devotes itself to acquired data; and which, going further than observation, opening a new field to the sciences, defines their nature, determines their progress, completes their resources, and marks out their end.

This is the great omission of your system. Abstraction is left in the background, barely mentioned, concealed by the other operations of the mind, treated as an appendage of Experience; we have but to re-establish it in the general theory, in order to reform the particular theories in which it is absent.

Section III.—Definitions Explain the Abstract Generating Elements of Things

To begin with Definitions. Mill teaches that there is no definition of things, and that when you define a sphere as the solid generated by the revolution of a semicircle about its diameter, you only define a name. Doubtless you tell me by this the meaning of a name, but you also teach me a good deal more. You state that all the properties of every sphere are derived from this generating formula; you reduce an infinitely complex system of facts to two elements; you transform sensible into abstract data; you express the essence of the sphere, that is to say, the inner and primordial cause of all its properties. Such is the nature of every true definition; it is not content with explaining a name, it is not a mere description; it does not simply indicate a distinctive property;

it does not limit itself to that ticketing of an object which will cause it to be distinguished from all others. There are, besides its definition, several other ways of causing the object to be recognized; there are other properties belonging to it exclusively: we might describe a sphere by saying that, of all bodies having an equal surface, it occupies the most space; or in many other ways. But such descriptions are not definitions; they lay down a characteristic and derived property, not a generating and primitive one; they do not reduce the thing to its factors, and reconstruct it before our eyes; they do not show its inner nature and its irreducible elements. A definition is a proposition which marks in an object that quality from which its others are derived, but which is not derived from others. Such a proposition is not verbal, for it teaches the quality of a thing. It is not the affirmation of an ordinary quality, for it reveals to us the quality which is the source of the rest. It is an assertion of an extraordinary kind, the most fertile and valuable of all, which sums up a whole science, and in which it is the aim of every science to be summed up. There is a definition in every science, and one for each object. We do not, in every case, possess it, but we search for it everywhere. We have arrived at defining the planetary motion by the tangential force and attraction which compose it; we can already partially define a chemical body by the notion of equivalent, and a living body by the notion of type. We are striving to transform every group of phenomena into certain laws, forces, or abstract notions. We endeavor to attain in every object the generating elements, as we do attain them in the sphere, the cylinder, the circle, the cone, and in all mathematical loci. We reduce natural bodies to two or three kinds of movement— attraction, vibration, polarization— as we reduce geometrical bodies to two or three kinds of elements— the point, the movement, the line; and we consider our science partial or complete, provisional or definite, according as this reduction is approximate or absolute, imperfect or complete.

Section IV.—The Basis of Proof in Syllogism is an Abstract Law

The same alteration is required in the Theory of Proof. According to Mill, we do not prove that Prince Albert will die by premising that all men are mortal, for that would be asserting the same thing twice over; but from the facts that John, Peter, and others, in short, all men of whom we have ever heard, have died.— I reply that the real source of our inference lies neither in the mortality of John, Peter, and company, nor in the mortality of all men, but elsewhere. We prove a fact, says Aristotle,[431] by showing its cause. We shall therefore prove the mortality of Prince Albert, by showing the cause which produces his death. And why will he die? Because the human body, being an unstable chemical compound, must in time be resolved; in other words, because mortality is added to the quality of man. Here is the cause and the proof. It is this abstract law which, present in nature, will cause the death of the prince, and which, being present to my mind, shows me that he will die. It is this abstract proposition which is demonstrative; it is neither the particular nor the general propositions. In fact the abstract proposition proves the others. If John, Peter, and others, are dead, it is because mortality is added to the quality of man. If all men are dead, or will die, it is still because mortality is added to the quality, of man. Here, again, the part played by Abstraction has been overlooked. Mill has confounded it with Experience: he has not distinguished the proof from the materials of the proof, the abstract law from the finite or indefinite number of its applications. The applications contain the law and the proof, but are themselves neither law nor proof. The examples of Peter, John, and others, contain the cause, but they are not the cause. It is not sufficient to add up the cases, we must extract from them the law. It is not enough to experimentalize, we must abstract. This is the great scientific operation. Syllogism does not proceed from the particular to the particular, as Mill says, nor from the general to the particular, as the ordinary logicians teach, but from the abstract to the concrete; that is to say, from cause to effect. It is on this ground that it forms part of science, the links of which it makes and marks out; it connects principles with effects; it brings together definitions and phenomena. It diffuses through the whole range of science that Abstraction which definition has carried to its summit.

Section V.—Axioms are Relations between Abstract Truths

Abstraction explains also axioms. According to Mill, if we know that when equal magnitudes are added to equal magnitudes the wholes are equal, or that two straight lines cannot enclose a space, it is by external ocular experiment, or by an internal experiment, by the aid of imagination. Doubtless we may thus arrive at the conclusion that two straight lines cannot enclose a space, but we might recognize it also in another manner. We might represent a straight line in imagination, and we may also form a conception of it by reason. We may either study its form or its definition. We can observe it in itself, or in its generating elements. I can represent to myself a line ready drawn, but I can also resolve it into its elements. I can go back to its formation, and discover the abstract elements which produce it, as I have watched the formation of the cylinder and discover the revolution of the rectangle which generated it. It will not do to say that a straight line is the shortest from one point to another, for that is a derived property; but I may say that it is the line described by a point, tending to approach towards another point, and towards that point only: which amounts to saying that two points suffice to determine a straight line; in other words, that two straight lines, having two points in common, coincide in their entire length; from which we see that if two straight lines approach to enclose a space, they would form but one straight line, and enclose nothing at all. Here is a second method of arriving at a knowledge of the axiom, and it is clear that it differs much from the first. In the first we verify; in the second we deduce it. In the first we find by experience that it is true; in the second we prove it to be true. In the first we admit the truth; in the second we explain it. In the first we merely remark that the contrary of the axiom is inconceivable; in the second we discover, in addition, that the contrary of the axiom is contradictory. Having given the definition of the straight line, we find that the axiom that two straight lines cannot enclose a space is comprised in it, and may be derived from it, as a consequent from a principle. In fact, it is nothing more than an identical proposition, which means that the subject contains its attribute; it does not connect two separate terms, irreducible one to the other; it unites two terms, of which the second is a part of the first. It is a simple analysis, and so are all axioms. We have only to decompose them, in order to see that they do not proceed from one object to a different one, but are concerned with one object only. We have but to resolve the notions of equality, cause, substance, time, and space into their abstracts, in order to demonstrate the axioms of equality, substance, cause, time, and space. There is but one axiom, that of identity. The others are only its applications or its consequences. When this is admitted, we at once see that the range of our mind is altered. We are no longer merely capable of relative and limited knowledge, but also of absolute and infinite knowledge; we possess in axioms facts which not only accompany one another, but one of which includes the other. If, as Mill says, they merely accompanied one another, we should be obliged to conclude with him, that perhaps this might not always be the case. We should not see the inner necessity for their connection, and should only admit it as far as our experience went; we should say that, the two facts being isolated in their nature, circumstances might arise in which they would be separate; we should affirm the truth of axioms only in reference to our world and mind. If, on the contrary, the two facts are such that the first contains the second, we should establish on this very ground the necessity of their connection; wheresoever the first may be found, it will carry the second with it, since the second is a part of it, and cannot be separated from it. Nothing can exist between them and divide them, for they are but one thing under different aspects. Their connection is therefore absolute and universal; and we possess truths which admit neither doubt nor limitation, nor condition, nor restriction. Abstraction restores to axioms their value, whilst it shows their origin; and we restore to science her dispossessed dominion, by restoring to the mind the faculty of which it had been deprived.

Section VI.—The Methods of Induction

Induction remains to be considered: which seems to be the triumph of pure experience, while it is in reality, the triumph of abstraction. When I discover, by induction, that cold produces dew, or that the passage from the liquid to the solid state produces crystallization, I establish a connection between two abstract facts. Neither cold, nor dew, nor the passage from the liquid to the solid state, nor crystallization, exist in themselves. They are parts of phenomena, extracts from complex cases, simple elements included in compound aggregates. I withdraw and isolate them; I isolate dew in general from all local, temporary, special dews which I observe; I isolate cold in general from all special, various distinct colds, which may be produced by all varieties of texture, all diversities of substance, all inequalities of temperature, all complications of circumstances. I join an abstract antecedent to an abstract consequent, and I connect them, as Mill himself shows, by subtractions, suppressions, eliminations; I expel from the two groups, containing them, all the proximate circumstances; I discover the couple under the surroundings which obscure it; I detach, by a series of comparisons and experiments, all the subsidiary accidental circumstances which have clung to it, and thus I end by laying it bare. I seem to be considering twenty different cases, and in reality I only consider one; I appear to proceed by addition, and in fact I am performing subtraction. All the methods of Induction, therefore, are methods of Abstraction, and all the work of Induction is the connection of abstract facts.

Section VII.—Experience and Abstraction

We see now the two great moving powers of science, and the two great manifestations of nature. There are two operations, experience and abstraction; there are two kingdoms, that of complex facts, and that of simple elements. The first is the effect, the second the cause. The first is contained in the second, and is deduced from it, as a consequent from its principle. The two are equivalent: they are one and the same thing considered under two aspects. This magnificent moving universe, this tumultuous chaos of mutually dependent events, this incessant life, infinitely varied and multiplied, may be all reduced to a few elements and their relations. Our whole efforts result in passing from one to the other, from the complex to the simple, from facts to laws, from experiences to formulas. And the reason of this is evident; for this fact, which I perceive by the senses or the consciousness, is but a fragment, arbitrarily severed by my senses or my consciousness, from the infinite and continuous woof of existence. If they were differently constituted, they would intercept other fragments; it is the chance of their structure which determines what is actually perceived. They are like open compasses, which might be more or less extended; and the area of the circle which they describe is not natural, but artificial. It is so in two ways, both externally and internally. For, when I consider an event, I isolate it artificially from its natural surroundings, and I compose it artificially of elements which do not form a natural group. When I see a falling stone, I separate the fall from the anterior circumstances which are really connected with it; and I put together the fall, the form, the structure, the color, the sound, and twenty other circumstances which are really not connected with it. A fact, then, is an arbitrary aggregate, and at the same time an arbitrary severing;[432] that is to say, a factitious group, which separates things connected, and connects things that are separate. Thus, so long as we only regard nature by observation, we do not see it as it is: we have only a provisional and illusory idea of it. Nature is, in reality, a tapestry, of which we only see the reverse; this is why we try to turn it. We strive to discover laws; that is, the natural groups which are really distinct from their surroundings, and composed of elements really connected. We discover couples; that is to say, real compounds and real connections. We pass from the accidental to the necessary, from the relative to the absolute, from the appearance to the reality; and having found these first couples, we practice upon them the same operation as we did upon facts, for, though in a less degree, they are of the same nature. Though more abstract, they are still complex. They may be decomposed and explained. There is some ulterior reason for their existence. There is some cause or other which constructs and unites them. In their case, as well as for facts, we can search for generating elements into which they may be resolved, and from which they may be deduced. And this operation may be continued until we have arrived at elements wholly simple; that is to say, such that their decomposition would involve a contradiction. Whether we can find them or not, they exist; the axiom of causation would be falsified if they were absent. There are, then, indecomposable elements, from which are derived more general laws; and from these, again, more special laws; and from these the facts which we observe; just as in geometry there are two or three primitive notions, from which are deduced the properties of lines, and from these the properties of surfaces, solids, and the numberless forms which nature can produce, or the mind imagine. We can now comprehend the value and meaning of that axiom of causation which governs all things, and which Mill has mutilated. There is an inner constraining force which gives rise to every event, which unites every compound, which engenders every actual fact. This signifies, on the one hand, that there is a reason for everything; that every fact has its law; that every compound can be reduced to simple elements; that every product implies factors; that every quality and every being must be reducible from some superior and anterior term. And it signifies, on the other hand, that the product is equivalent to the factors, that both are but the same thing under different aspects; that the cause does not differ in nature from the effect; that the generating powers are but elementary properties; that the active force, by which we represent Nature to our minds, is but the logical necessity which mutually transforms the compound and the simple, the fact and the law. Thus we determine beforehand the limits of every science; and we possess the potent formula, which, establishing the invincible connection and the spontaneous production of existences, places in Nature the moving spring of Nature, whilst it drives home and fixes in the heart of every living thing the iron fangs of necessity.

Section VIII.—Idea and Limits of Metaphysics

Can we arrive at a knowledge of these primary elements? For my part, I think we can; and the reason is, that, being abstractions, they are not beyond the region of facts, but are comprised in them, so that we have only to extract them from the facts. Besides, being the most abstract, that is, the most general of all things, there are no facts which do not comprise them, and from which we cannot extract them. However limited our experience may be, we can arrive at these primary notions; and it is from this observation that the modern German metaphysicians have started, in attempting their vast constructions. They understood that there are simple notions, that is to say, indecomposable abstract facts, that the combinations of these engender all others, and that the laws for their mutual union or contrarieties, are the primary laws of the universe. They tried to attain to these ideas, and to evolve, by pure reason, the world as observation shows it to us. They have partly failed; and their gigantic edifice, factitious and fragile, hangs in ruins, reminding one of those temporary scaffoldings which only serve to mark out the plan of a future building. The reason is, that with a high notion of our powers, they had no exact view of their limits. For we are outflanked on all sides by the infinity of time and space; we find ourselves thrown in the midst of this monstrous universe like a shell on the beach, or an ant at the foot of a steep slope. Here Mill is right. Chance is at the end of all our knowledge, as on the threshold of all our postulates: we vainly try to rise, and that by conjecture, to an initial state; but this state depends on the preceding one, which depends on another, and so on; and thus we are forced to accept it as a pure postulate, and to give up the hope of deducing it, though we know that it ought to be deduced. It is so in all sciences, in geology, natural history, physics, chemistry, psychology, history, and the primitive accidental fact extends its effects into all parts of the sphere in which it is comprised. If it had been otherwise, we should have neither the same planets, nor the same chemical compounds, nor the same vegetables, nor the same animals, nor the same races of men, nor, perhaps, any of these kinds of beings. If an ant were taken into another country, it would see neither the same trees, nor insects, nor dispositions of the soil, nor changes of the atmosphere, nor, perhaps, any of these forms of existence. There is, then, in every fact and in every object, an accidental and local part, a vast portion, which, like the rest, depends on primitive laws, but not directly, only through an infinite circuit of consequences in such a way that between it and the primitive laws there is an infinite hiatus, which can only be bridged over by an infinite series of deductions.

Such is the inexplicable part of phenomena, and this is what the German metaphysicians tried to explain. They wished to deduce from their elementary theorems the form of the planetary system, the various laws of physics and chemistry, the main types of life, the progress of human civilizations and thought. They contorted their universal formulae with the view of deriving from them particular cases; they took indirect and remote consequences as direct and proximate ones; they omitted or suppressed the great work which is interposed between the first laws and the final consequences; they discarded Chance from their construction, as a basis unworthy of science; and the void so left, badly filled up by deceptive materials, caused the whole edifice to fall to ruins.

Does this amount to saying, that in the facts with which this little corner of the universe furnishes us, everything is local? By no means. If an ant were capable of making experiments, it might attain to the idea of a physical law, a living form, a representative sensation, an abstract thought; for a foot of ground, on which there is a thinking brain, includes all these. Therefore, however limited be the field of the mind, it contains general facts; that is, facts spread over very vast external territories, into which its limitation prevents it from penetrating. If the ant were capable of reasoning, it might construct arithmetic, algebra, geometry, mechanics; for a movement of half an inch contains in the abstract, time, space, number, and force: all the materials of mathematics: therefore, however limited the field of a mind's researches be, it includes universal data; that is, facts spread over the whole region of time and space. Again, if the ant were a philosopher, it might evolve the ideas of existence, of nothingness, and all the materials of metaphysics; for any phenomenon, interior or exterior, suffices to present these materials: therefore, however limited the field of a mind be, it contains absolute truths; that is, such that there is no object from which they could be absent. And this must necessarily be so; for the more general a fact is, the fewer objects need we examine to meet with it. If it is universal, we meet with it everywhere; if it is absolute, we cannot escape meeting it. This is why, in spite of the narrowness of our experience, metaphysics, I mean the search for first causes, is possible, but on condition that we remain at a great height, that we do not descend into details, that we consider only the most simple elements of existence, and the most general tendencies of nature. If anyone were to collect the three or four great ideas in which our sciences result, and the three or four kinds of existence which make up our universe; if he were to compare those two strange quantities which we call duration and extension, those principal forms or determinations of quantity which we call physical laws, chemical types, and living species, and that marvellous representative power, the Mind, which, without falling into quantity, reproduces the other two and itself; if he discovered among these three terms— the pure quantity, the determined quantity, and the suppressed quantity[433]— such an order that the first must require the second, and the second the third; if he thus established that the pure quantity is the necessary commencement of Nature, and that Thought is the extreme term at which Nature is wholly suspended; if, again, isolating the elements of these data, he showed that they must be combined just as they are combined, and not otherwise: if he proved, moreover, that there are no other elements, and that there can be no other, he would have sketched out a system of metaphysics without encroaching on the positive sciences, and have attained the source, without being obliged to descend to trace the various streams.

In my opinion, these two great operations, Experience as you have described it, and Abstraction, as I have tried to define it, comprise in themselves all the resources of the human mind, the one in its practical, the other in its speculative direction. The first leads us to consider nature as an assemblage of facts, the second as a system of laws: the exclusive employment of the first is English; that of the second, German. If there is a place between these two nations, it is ours. We have extended the English ideas in the eighteenth century; and now we can, in the nineteenth, add precision to German ideas. Our business is to restrain, to correct, to complete the two types of mind, one by the other, to combine them together, to express their ideas in a style generally understood, and thus to produce from them the universal mind.

Section IX.—A Morning in Oxford

We went out. As it ever happens in similar circumstances, each had caused the other to reflect, and neither had convinced the other. But our reflections were short: in the presence of a lovely August morning, all arguments fall to the ground. The old walls, the rain-worn stones, smiled in the rising sun. A fresh light rested on their embrasures, on the keystones of the cloisters, on the glossy ivy leaves. Roses and honeysuckles climbed the walls, and their flowers quivered and sparkled in the light breeze. The fountains murmured in the vast lonely courts. The beautiful town stood out from the morning's mist, as adorned and tranquil as a fairy palace, and its robe of soft rosy vapor was indented, as an embroidery of the Renaissance, by a border of towers, cloisters, and palaces, each enclosed in verdure and decked with flowers. The architecture of all ages had mingled their arches, trefoils, statues, and columns; time had softened their tints; the sun united them in its light, and the old city seemed a shrine to which every age and every genius had successively added a jewel. Beyond this, the river rolled its broad sheets of silver: the mowers stood up to the knee in the high grass of the meadows. Myriads of buttercups and meadow-sweets; grasses, bending under the weight of their gray heads, plants sated with the dew of the night, swarmed in the rich soil. Words cannot express this freshness of tints, this luxuriance of vegetation. The more the long line of shape receded, the more brilliant and full of life the flowers appeared. On seeing them, virgin and timid in their gilded veil, I thought of the blushing cheeks and fine modest eyes of a young girl who puts on for the first time her necklace of jewels. Around, as though to guard them, enormous trees, four centuries old, extended in regular lines;

and I found in them a new trace of that practical good sense which has effected revolutions without committing ravages; which, while reforming in all directions, has destroyed nothing; which has preserved both its trees and its constitution, which has lopped off the dead branches without levelling the trunk; which alone, in our days, among all nations, is in the enjoyment not only of the present, but of the past.

---

[396]M. Taine has published this "Study on Mill" separately, and preceded it by the following note, as a preface:— "When this Study first appeared, Mr. Mill did me the honor to write to me that it would not be possible to give in a few pages a more exact and complete notion of the contents of his work, considered as a body of philosophical teaching. 'But,' he added, 'I think you are wrong in regarding the views I adopt as especially English. They were so in the first half of the eighteenth century, from the time of Locke to that of the reaction against Hume. This reaction, beginning in Scotland, assumed long ago the German form, find ended by prevailing universally. When I wrote my book, I stood almost alone in my opinions; and though they have met with a degree of sympathy which I by no means expected, we may still count in England twenty à priori and spiritualist philosophers for every partisan of the doctrine of Experience.'

"This remark is very true. I myself could have made it, having been brought up in the doctrines of Scottish philosophy and the writings of Reid. I simply answer, that there are philosophers whom we do not count, and that all such, whether English or not, spiritualist or not, may be neglected without much harm. Once in a half-century, or perhaps in a century, or two centuries, some thinker appears; Bacon and Hume in England, Descartes and Condillac in France, Kant and Hegel in Germany. At other times the stage is unoccupied, or ordinary men come forward, and offer the public that which the public likes— Sensualists or Idealists, according to the tendency of the day, with sufficient instruction and skill to play leading parts, and enough capacity to reset old airs, well drilled in the works of their predecessors, but destitute of real invention— simple executant musicians, who stand in the place of composers. In Europe, at present, the stage is a blank. The Germans adapt and alter effete French materialism. The French listen from habit, but somewhat wearily and distractedly, to the scraps of melody and eloquent commonplace which their instructors have repeated to them for the last thirty years. In this deep silence, and from among these dull mediocrities, a master comes forward to speak. Nothing of the sort has been seen since Hegel."

[397]This law has been abrogated by an Act of Parliament.— Tr.

[398]"It is certain, then, that a part of our notion of a body consists of the notion of a number of sensations of our own, or of other sentient beings, habitually occurring simultaneously. My conception of the table at which I am writing is compounded of its visible form and size, which are complex

sensations of sight; its tangible form and size, which are complex sensations of our organs of touch and of our muscles; its weight, which is also a sensation of touch and of the muscles; its colour, which is a sensation of sight; its hardness, which is a sensation of the muscles; its composition, which is another word for all the varieties of sensation which we receive, under various circumstances, from the wood of which it is made, and so forth. All, or most of these various sensations, frequently arc, and, as we learn by experience, always might be, experienced simultaneously, or in many different orders of succession, at our own choice: and hence the thought of any one of them makes us think of the others, and the whole becomes mentally amalgamated into one mixed state of consciousness, which, in the language of Locke and Hartley, is termed a Complex Idea."— Mill's "System of Logic," 4th ed. 2 vols. I. 62.

[399]Mill's "Logic," I. 68.

[400]"Every attribute of a mind consists either in being itself affected in a certain way, or affecting other minds in a certain way. Considered in itself, we can predicate nothing of it but the series of its own feelings. When we say of any mind, that it is devout, or superstitious, or meditative, or cheerful, we mean that the ideas, emotions, or volitions implied in those words, form a frequently recurring part of the series of feelings, or states of consciousness, which fill up the sentient existence of that mind.

"In addition, however, to those attributes of a mind which are grounded on its own states of feeling, attributes may also be ascribed to it, in the same manner as to a body, grounded on the feelings which it excites in other minds. A mind does not, indeed, like a body, excite sensations, but it may excite thoughts or emotions. The most important example of attributes ascribed on this ground, is the employment of terms expressive of approbation or blame. When, for example, we say of any character, or (in other words) of any mind, that it is admirable, we mean that the contemplation of it excites the sentiment of admiration; and, indeed, somewhat more, for the word implies that we not only feel admiration, but approve that sentiment in ourselves. In some cases, under the semblance of a single attribute, two are really predicated: one of them, a state of the mind itself; the other, a state with which other minds are affected by thinking of it. As when we say of anyone that he is generous. The word generosity expresses a certain state of mind, but being a term of praise, it also expresses that this state of mind excites in us another mental state, called approbation. The assertion made, therefore, is twofold, and of the following purport: Certain feelings form habitually a part of this person's sentient existence; and the idea of those feelings of his, excites the sentiment of approbation in ourselves or others."— Mill's "Logic," 80.

[401]Mill's "Logic," 110.

[402]"According to idealist logicians, this being is arrived at by examining our notion of it; and the idea, on analysis, reveals the essence. According to

the classifying school, we arrive at the being by placing the object in its group, and the notion is defined by stating the genus and the difference. Both agree in believing that we are capable of grasping the essence."— Mill's "Logic," I. 127.

[403]"An essential proposition, then, is one which is purely verbal; which asserts of a thing under a particular name, only what is asserted of it in the fact of calling it by that name; and which, therefore, either gives no information, or gives it respecting the name, not the thing. Non-essential or accidental propositions, on the contrary, may be called Real Propositions, in opposition to Verbal. They predicate of a thing, some fact not involved in the signification of the name by which the proposition speaks of it; some attribute not connoted by that name."— Mill's "Logic," I. 127.

[404]Mill's "Logic," I. 162.

[405]"The definition above given of a triangle obviously comprises not one, but two propositions, perfectly distinguishable. The one is, 'There may exist a figure bounded by three straight lines the other. 'And this figure may be termed a triangle.' The former of these propositions is not a definition at all; the latter is a mere nominal definition, or explanation of the use and application of a term. The first is susceptible of truth or falsehoods, and may therefore be made the foundation of a train of reasoning. The latter can neither be true nor false; the only character it is susceptible of is that of conformity to the ordinary usage of language."— Mill's "Logic," I. 162.

[406]Mill's "Logic," I. 211.

[407]Mill's "Logic," I. 218.

[408]Ibid. I. 240.

[409]"For though, in order actually to see that two given lines never meet, it would be necessary to follow them to infinity; yet, without doing so, we may know that if they ever do meet, or if, after diverging from one another, they begin again to approach, this must take place not at an infinite, but at a finite distance. Supposing, therefore, such to be the case, we can transport ourselves thither in imagination, and can frame a mental image of the appearance which one or both of the lines must present at that point, which we may rely on as being precisely similar to the reality. Now, whether we fix our contemplation upon this imaginary picture, or call to mind the generalizations we have had occasion to make from former ocular observation, we learn by the evidence of experience, that a line which, after diverging from another straight line, begins to approach to it, produces the impression on our senses which we describe by the expression 'a bent line,' not by the expression 'a straight line.'"— Mill's "Logic," I. 364.

[410]Mill's "Logic," I. 315.

[411]"We must first observe, that there is a principle implied in the very statement of what Induction is; an assumption with regard to the course of nature and the order of the universe; namely, that there are such things in

nature as parallel cases; that what happens once, will, under a sufficient degree of similarity of circumstances, happen again, and not only again, but as often as the same circumstances recur. This, I say, is an assumption, involved in every case of induction. And, if we consult the actual course of nature, we find that the assumption is warranted. The universe, so far as known to us, is so constituted, that whatever is true in any one case, is true in all cases of a certain description; the only difficulty is, to find what description."— Mill's "Logic," I. 337.

[412]Mill's "Logic," I. 351.

[413]Mill's "Logic," I. 359.

[414]Ibid. I. 360.

[415]Ibid. I. 365.

[416]Mill's "Logic," I. 372.

[417]"If we take fifty crucibles of molten matter and let them cool, and fifty solutions and let them evaporate, all will crystallize. Sulphur, sugar, alum, salt— substances, temperatures, circumstances— all are as different as they can be. We find one, and only one, common fact— the change from the liquid to the solid state— and conclude, therefore, that this change is the invariable antecedent of crystallization. Here we have an example of the Method of Agreement. Its canon is:—

"'I. If two or more instances of the phenomenon under investigation have only one circumstance in common, the circumstance in which alone all the instances agree, is the cause (or effect) of the given phenomenon.'"— Ibid. I. 422.

[418]"A bird in the air breathes; plunged into carbonic acid gas, it ceases to breathe. In other words, in the second case, suffocation ensues. In other respects the two cases are as similar as possible, since we have the same bird in both, and they take place in immediate succession. They differ only in the circumstance of immersion in carbonic acid gas being substituted for immersion in the atmosphere, and we conclude that this circumstance is invariably followed by suffocation. The Method of Difference is here employed. Its canon is:—

"'II. If an instance in which the phenomenon under investigation occurs, and an instance in which it does not occur, have every circumstance in common save one, that one occurring only in the former; the circumstance in which alone the two instances differ, is the effect, or the cause, or a necessary part of the cause, of the phenomenon.'"— Ibid. I. 423.

[419]("A combination of these methods is sometimes employed, and is termed the Indirect Method of Difference, or the Joint Method of Agreement and Difference. It is, in fact, a double employment of the Method of Agreement, first applying that method to instances in which the phenomenon in question occurs, and then to instances in which it does not occur. The following is its canon:—

"'III. If two or more instances in which the phenomenon occurs have only one circumstance in common, while two or more instances in which it does not occur have nothing in common, save the absence of that circumstance; the circumstance in which alone the two sets of instances differ, is the effect, or the cause, or a necessary part of the cause, of the phenomenon.'")— Mill's "Logic," I. 429.

"If we take two groups— one of antecedents and one of consequents— and can succeed in connecting by previous investigations all the antecedents but one to their respective consequents, and all the consequents but one to their respective antecedents, we conclude that the remaining antecedent is connected to the remaining consequent. For example, scientific men had calculated what ought to be the velocity of sound according to the laws of the propagation of sonorous waves, but found that a sound actually travelled quicker than their calculations had indicated. This surplus, or residue of speed, was a consequent for which an antecedent had to be found. Laplace discovered the antecedent in the heat developed by the condensation of each sonorous wave, and this new element, when introduced into the calculation, rendered it perfectly accurate. This is an example of the Method of Residues, the canon of which is as follows:—

"'IV. Subduct from any phenomenon such part as is known by previous inductions to be the effect of certain antecedents, and the residue of the phenomenon is the effect of the remaining antecedents.'"— Mill's "Logic," I. 431.

[420]"Let us take two facts— as the presence of the earth and the oscillation of the pendulum; or, again, the presence of the moon and the flow of the tide. To connect these phenomena directly, we should have to suppress the first of them, and see if this suppression would occasion the stoppage of the second. Now, in both instances, such suppression is impossible. So we employ an indirect means of connecting the phenomena. We observe that all the variations of the one correspond to certain variations of the other; that all the oscillations of the pendulum correspond to certain different positions of the earth; that all states of the tide correspond to positions of the moon. From this we conclude that the second fact is the antecedent of the first. These are examples of the Method of Concomitant Variations. Its canon is:—

"'V. Whatever phenomenon varies in any manner whenever another phenomenon varies in some particular manner, is either a cause or an effect of that phenomenon, or is connected with it through some fact of causation.'"— Mill's "Logic," I. 435.

[421]"The Method of Agreement," says Mill ("Logic," I. 4-14), "stands on the ground that whatever can be eliminated, is not connected with the phenomenon by any law. The Method of Difference has for its foundation, that whatever cannot be eliminated, is connected with the phenomenon by a law." The Method of Residues is a case of the Method of Differences. The

Method of Concomitant Variations is another case of the same method; with this distinction, that it is applied, not to the phenomena, but to their variations.

[422]This quotation, and all the others in this paragraph, are taken from Mill's "Logic," I. 451-9. Mr. Mill quotes from Sir John Herschel's "Discourse on the Study of Natural Philosophy."

[423]Mill's "Logic," I. 526.

[424]See chapter 9, book VI. V. 2, 478, on The Physical or Concrete Deductive Method as applied to Sociology; and chapter 13, book III, for explanations, after Liebig, of Decomposition, Respiration, the Action of Poisons, etc. A whole book is devoted to the logic of the moral sciences; I know no better treatise on the subject.

[425]Mill's "Logic," II. 4.

[426]"There exists in nature a number of Permanent Causes, which have subsisted ever since the human race has been in existence, and for an indefinite and probably an enormous length of time previous. The sun, the earth, and planets, with their various constituents, air, water, and the other distinguishable substances, whether simple or compound, of which nature is made up, are such Permanent Causes. They have existed, and the effects or consequences which they were fitted to produce have taken place (as often as the other conditions of the production met), from the very beginning of our experience. But we can give no account of the origin of the Permanent Causes themselves."— Mill's "Logic," I. 378.

[427]"The resolution of the laws of the heavenly motions established the previously unknown ultimate property of a mutual attraction between all bodies: the resolution, so far as it has yet proceeded, of the laws of crystallization, or chemical composition, electricity, magnetism, etc., points to various polarities, ultimately inherent in the particles of which bodies are composed; the comparative atomic weights of different kinds of bodies were ascertained by resolving, into more general laws, the uniformities observed in the proportions in which substances combine with one another; and so forth. Thus, although every resolution of a complex uniformity into simpler and more elementary laws has an apparent tendency to diminish the number of the ultimate properties, and really does remove many properties from the list; yet (since the result of this simplifying process is to trace up an ever greater variety of different effects to the same agents), the further we advance in this direction, the greater number of distinct properties we are forced to recognize in one and the same object; the coexistences of which properties must accordingly be ranked among the ultimate generalities of nature."— Mill's "Logic," II. 108.

[428]Ibid. I. 378.

[429]Mill's "Logic," II. 95.

[430]Mill's "Logic," II. 104.

[431] See the Posterior Analytics, which are much superior to the Prior—δί αίνίων κα ηρότέρων.

[432] An eminent student of Physical Science said to me: "A fact is a superposition of laws."

[433] Die aufgehobene Quantität.

Chapter Sixth. Poetry—Tennyson

Section I.—His Talent and Work

When Tennyson published his first poems, the critics found fault with them. He held his peace; for ten years no one saw his name in a review, nor even in a publisher's catalogue. But when he appeared again before the public, his books had made their way alone and under the surface, and he passed at once for the greatest poet of his country and his time.

Men were surprised, and with a pleasing surprise. The potent generation of poets who had just died out, had passed like a whirlwind. Like their forerunners of the sixteenth century, they had carried away and hurried everything to its extreme. Some had culled gigantic legends, piled up dreams, ransacked the East, Greece, Arabia, the Middle Ages, and overloaded the human imagination with hues and fancies from every clime. Others had buried themselves in metaphysics and moral philosophy, had mused indefatigably on the condition of man, and spent their lives on the sublime and the monotonous. Others, making a medley of crime and heroism, had conducted, through darkness and flashes of lightning, a train of contorted and terrible figures, desperate with remorse, relieved by their grandeur. Men wanted to rest after so many efforts and so much excess. On the going out of the imaginative, sentimental and Satanic school, Tennyson appeared exquisite. All the forms and ideas which had pleased them were found in him, but purified, modulated, set in a splendid style. He completed an age; he enjoyed that which had agitated others; his poetry was like the lovely evenings in summer: the outlines of the landscape are then the same as in the daytime; but the splendor of the dazzling celestial arch is dulled; the reinvigorated flowers lift themselves up, and the calm sun, on the horizon, harmoniously casts a network of crimson rays over the woods and meadows which it just before burned by its brightness.

Section II.—Portraits of Women

What first attracted people were Tennyson's portraits of women: Adeline, Eleanore, Lilian, the May Queen, were keepsake characters, from the hand of a lover and an artist. The keepsake is gilt-edged, embossed with flowers and decorations, richly got up, soft, full of delicate faces, always elegant and always correct, which we might take to be sketched at random, and which are yet drawn carefully, on white vellum, slightly touched by their outline, all selected to rest and occupy the soft, white hands of a young bride or a girl. I have translated many ideas and many styles, but I shall not attempt to translate one of these portraits. Each word of them is like a tint, curiously deepened or shaded by the neighboring tint, with all the boldness and results of the happiest refinement. The least alteration would obscure all. And there an art so just, so consummate, is necessary to paint the charming prettinesses, the sudden hauteurs, the half blushes, the imperceptible and fleeting caprices of feminine beauty. He opposes, harmonizes them, makes of them, as it were, a gallery. Here is the frolicsome child, the little fluttering fairy, who clasps her tiny hands, who,

> "So innocent-arch, so cunning-simple,
> From beneath her gather'd wimple
> Glancing with black-beaded eyes,
> Till the lightning laughters dimple
> The baby-roses in her cheeks;
> Then away she flies."[434]

Then the pensive fair, who dreams, with large open blue eyes:

> "Whence that aery bloom of thine,
> Like a lily which the sun
> Looks thro' in his sad decline,
> And a rose-bush leans upon,
> Thou that faintly smilest still,
> As a Naiad in a well,
> Looking at the set of day."[435]

Anew "the ever-varying Madeline," now smiling, then frowning, then joyful again, then angry, then uncertain between the two:

> "Frowns perfect-sweet along the brow
> Light-glooming over eyes divine,
> Like little clouds sun-fringed."[436]

The poet returned well pleased to all things, refined and exquisite. He caressed them so carefully that his verses appeared at times far-fetched, affected, almost euphuistic. He gave them too much adornment and polishing; he seemed like an epicurean in style, as well as in beauty. He looked for pretty rustic scenes, touching remembrances, curious or pure sentiments. He made them into elegies, pastorals, and idyls. He wrote in every accent, and delighted in entering into the feelings of all ages. He wrote of St. Agnes, St. Simeon Stylites, Ulysses, Œnone, Sir Galahad, Lady Clare, Fatima, the Sleeping Beauty. He imitated, alternately, Homer and Chaucer, Theocritus and Spenser, the old English poets and the old Arabian poets. He gave life successively to the little real events of English life, and the great fantastic adventures of extinguished chivalry. He was like those musicians who use their bow in the service of all masters. He strayed through nature and history, with no foregone conclusions, without fierce passion, bent on feeling, relishing, culling from all parts, in the flower-stand of the drawing-room and in the rustic hedgerows, the rare or wild flowers whose scent or beauty could charm or amuse him. Men entered into his pleasure; smelt the grateful bouquets which he knew so well how to put together; preferred those which he took from the country; found that his talent was nowhere more at ease. They admired the minute observation and refined sentiment which knew how to grasp and interpret the fleeting aspects of things. In the "Dying Swan" they forgot that the subject was almost threadbare, and the interest somewhat slight, that they might appreciate such verses as this:

> "Some blue peaks in the distance rose,
> And white against the cold-white sky,
> Shone out their crowning snows.
> One willow over the river wept,
> And shook the wave as the wind did sigh;
> Above in the wind was the swallow,
> Chasing itself at its own wild will,
> And far thro' the marish green and still
> The tangled water-courses slept,
> Shot over with purple, and green, and yellow."[437]

But these melancholy pictures did not display him entirely; men accompanied him to the land of the sun, toward the soft voluptuousness of southern seas; they returned, with an involuntary fascination, to the verses in which he depicts the companions of Ulysses, who, slumbering in the land of the Lotos-eaters, happy dreamers like himself, forgot their country, and renounced action:

> "A land of streams! some, like a downward smoke,
> Slow-dropping veils of thinnest lawn, did go;
> And some thro' wavering lights and shadows broke,
> Rolling a slumbrous sheet of foam below.
> They saw the gleaming river seaward flow
> From the inner land: far off, three mountain-tops,
> Three silent pinnacles of aged snow,
> Stood sun-set flush'd: and, dew'd with showery drops,
> Up-clomb the shadowy pine above the woven copse....
>
> "There is sweet music here that softer falls
> Than petal from blown roses on the grass,
> Or night-dews on still waters between walls

Of shadowy granite, in a gleaming pass;
Music that gentlier on the spirit lies,
Than tir'd eyelids upon tir'd eyes;
Music that brings sweet sleep down from the blissful skies.
Here are cool mosses deep,
And thro' the moss the ivies creep,
And in the stream the long-leaved flowers weep,
And from the craggy ledge the poppy hangs in sleep....

"Lo! in the middle of the wood,
The folded leaf is woo'd from out the bud
With winds upon the branch, and there
Grows green and broad, and takes no care,
Sun-steep'd at noon, and in the moon
Nightly dew-fed; and turning yellow
Falls, and floats adown the air.
Lo! sweeten'd with the summer light,
The full-juiced apple, waxing over-mellow,
Drops in a silent autumn night.
All its allotted length of days,
The flower ripens in its place,
Ripens and fades, and falls, and hath no toil,
Fast-rooted in the fruitful soil....

"But, propt on beds of amaranth and moly,
How sweet (while warm airs lull us, blowing lowly),
With half-dropt eyelids still,
Beneath a heaven dark and holy,
To watch the long bright river drawing slowly
His waters from the purple hill—
To hear the dewy echoes calling
From cave to cave thro' the thick-twined vine—
To watch the emerald-colour'd water falling
Thro' many a wov'n acanthus-wreath divine!
Only to hear and see the far-off sparkling brine,
Only to hear were sweet, stretch'd out beneath the pine."[438]

Section III.—Wherein Tennyson is at One with Nature

Was this charming dreamer simply a dilettante? Men liked to consider him so; he seemed too happy to admit violent passions. Fame came to him easily and quickly, at the age of thirty. The Queen had justified the public favor by creating him Poet-Laureate. A great writer declared him a more genuine poet than Lord Byron, and maintained that nothing so perfect had been seen since

Shakespeare. The student, at Oxford, put Tennyson's works between an annotated Euripides and a handbook of scholastic philosophy. Young ladies found him amongst their marriage presents. He was said to be rich, venerated by his family, admired by his friends, amiable, without affectation, even unsophisticated. He lived in the country, chiefly in the Isle of Wight, amongst books and flowers, free from the annoyances, rivalries, and burdens of society, and his life was easily imagined to be a beautiful dream, as sweet as those which he had pictured.

Yet the men who looked closer saw that there was a fire of passion under this smooth surface. A genuine poetic temperament never fails in this. It feels too acutely to be at peace. When we quiver at the least touch, we shake and tremble under great shocks. Already, here and there, in his pictures of country and love, a brilliant verse broke with its glowing color through the calm and correct outline. He had felt that strange growth of unknown powers which suddenly arrest a man with fixed gaze before revealed beauty. The specialty of the poet is to be ever young, forever virgin. For us, the vulgar things are threadbare; sixty centuries of civilization have worn out their primitive freshness; things have become commonplace; we perceive them only through a veil of ready-made phrases; we employ them, we no longer comprehend them; we see in them no longer magnificent flowers, but good vegetables; the luxuriant primeval forest is to us nothing but a well-planned, and too well-known, kitchen garden. On the other hand, the poet, in presence of this world, is as the first man, on the first day. In a moment our phrases, our reasonings, all the trappings of memory and prejudice, vanish from his mind; things seem new to him; he is astonished and ravished; a headlong stream of sensations oppresses him; it is the all-potent sap of human invention, which, checked in us, begins to flow in him. Fools call him mad, but in truth he is a seer: for we may indeed be sluggish, but nature is always full of life; the rising sun is as beautiful as on the first dawn; the streaming floods, the teeming flowers, the trembling passions, the forces which hurl onward the stormy whirlwind of existence, aspire and strive with the same energy as at their birth; the immortal heart of nature beats yet, heaving its coarse trappings, and its beatings work in the poet's heart when they no longer echo in our own. Tennyson felt this not indeed always; but twice: or thrice, at least, he has dared to make it heard. We have found anew the free action of full emotion, and recognized the voice of a man in these verses of "Locksley Hall":

"Then her cheek was pale and thinner than should be for one so young,
And her eyes on all my motions with a mute observance hung.

And I said, 'My cousin Amy, speak, and speak the truth to me,
Trust me, cousin, all the current of my being sets to thee.'

On her pallid cheek and forehead came a colour and a light,

As I have seen the rosy red flushing in the northern night.

And she turn'd— her bosom shaken with a sudden storm of sighs—
All the spirit deeply dawning in the dark of hazel eyes—

Saying, 'I have hid my feelings, fearing they should do me wrong;'
Saying, 'Dost thou love me, cousin?' weeping, 'I have loved thee long.'

Love took up the glass of Time, and turn'd it in his glowing hands;
Every moment, lightly shaken, ran itself in golden sands.

Love took up the harp of Life, and smote on all the chords with might;
Smote the chord of Self, that, trembling, pass'd in music out of sight.

Many a morning on the moorland did we hear the copses ring,
And her whisper throng'd my pulses with the fulness of the Spring.

Many an evening by the waters did we watch the stately ships,
And our spirits rushed together at the touching of the lips.

O my cousin, shallow-hearted! O my Amy, mine no more!
O the dreary, dreary moorland! O the barren, barren shore!

Falser than all fancy fathoms, falser than all songs have sung,
Puppet to a father's threat, and servile to a shrewish tongue!

Is it well to wish thee happy?— having known me— to decline
On a range of lower feelings and a narrower heart than mine!

Yet it shall be: thou shalt lower to his level day by day,
What is fine within thee growing coarse to sympathize with clay.

As the husband is, the wife is: thou art mated with a clown,
And the grossness of his nature will have weight to drag thee down.

He will hold thee, when his passion shall have spent its novel force,
Something better than his dog, a little dearer than his horse.

What is this? his eyes are heavy: think not they are glazed with wine.
Go to him: it is thy duty: kiss him: take his hand in thine.

It may be my lord is weary, that his brain is overwrought:
Soothe him with thy finer fancies, touch him with thy lighter thought.

He will answer to the purpose, easy things to understand—
Better thou wert dead before me, tho' I slew thee with my hand!"[439]

This is very frank and strong. "Maud" appeared, and was still more so. In it the rapture broke forth with all its inequalities, familiarities, freedom, violence. The correct, measured poet betrayed himself, for he seemed to think and weep aloud. This book is the diary of a gloomy young man, soured by great family misfortunes, by long solitary meditations, who gradually became enamoured, dared to speak, found himself loved. He does not sing, but speaks; they are the hazarded, reckless words of ordinary conversation; details of every-day life; the description of a toilet, a political dinner, a service and sermon in a village church. The prose of Dickens and Thackeray did not more firmly grasp real and actual manners. And by its side, most splendid poetry abounded and blossomed, as in fact it blossoms and abounds in the midst of our commonplaces. The smile of a richly dressed girl, a sunbeam on a stormy sea, or on a spray of roses, throws all at once these sudden illuminations into impassioned souls. What verses are these, in which he represents himself in his dark little garden:

> "A million emeralds break from the ruby-budded lime
> In the little grove where I sit— ah, wherefore cannot I be
> Like things of the season gay, like the bountiful season bland,
> When the far-off sail is blown by the breeze of a softer clime,
> Half lost in the liquid azure bloom of a crescent of sea,
> The silent sapphire-spangled marriage ring of the land?"[440]

What a holiday in his heart when he is loved! What madness in these cries, that intoxication, that tenderness, which would pour itself on all, and summon all to the spectacle and the participation of his happiness! How all is transfigured in his eyes; and how constantly he is himself transfigured! Gayety, then ecstasy, then archness, then satire, then disclosures, all ready movements, all sudden changes, like a crackling and flaming fire, renewing every moment its shape and color: how rich is the soul, and how it can live a hundred years in a day! The hero of the poem, surprised and insulted by the brother of Maud, kills him in a duel, and loses her whom he loved. He flees; he is seen wandering in London. What a gloomy contrast is that of the great busy careless town, and a solitary man haunted by true grief! We follow him down the noisy thoroughfares, through the yellow fog, under the wan sun which rises above the river like a "dull red ball," and we hear the heart full of anguish, deep sobs, insensate agitation of a soul which would, but cannot, tear itself from its memories. Despair grows, and in the end the reverie becomes a vision:

> "Dead, long dead,
> Long dead!
> And my heart is a handful of dust,
> And the wheels go over my head,
> And my bones are shaken with pain,
> For into a shallow grave they are thrust,
> Only a yard beneath the street,
> And the hoofs of the horses beat, beat,
> The hoofs of the horses beat,
> Beat into my scalp and my brain,
> With never an end to the stream of passing feet,
> Driving, hurrying, marrying, burying,
> Clamour and rumble, and ringing and clatter...."[441]
> O me! why have they not buried me deep enough?
> Is it kind to have made me a grave so rough,
> Me, that was never a quiet sleeper?
> Maybe still I am but half-dead;
> Then I cannot be wholly dumb;
> I will cry to the steps above my head,
> And somebody, surely, some kind heart will come
> To bury me, bury me
> Deeper, ever so little deeper."[442]

However, he revives, and gradually rises again. War breaks out, a liberal and generous war, the war against Russia; and the big, manly heart, wounded by deep love, is healed by action and courage:

> "And I stood on a giant deck and mix'd my breath
> With a loyal people shouting a battle-cry....
> Yet God's just wrath shall be wreak'd on a giant liar;
> And many a darkness into the light shall leap,
> And shine in the sudden making of splendid names,
> And noble thought be freer under the sun,
> And the heart of a people beat with one desire;
> For the peace, that I deem'd no peace, is over and done,
> And now by the side of the Black and the Baltic deep,
> And deathful-grinning mouths of the fortress, flames
> The blood-red blossom of war with a heart of fire."[443]

This explosion of feeling was the only one; Tennyson has not again encountered it. In spite of the moral close, men said of "Maud" that he was imitating Byron; they cried out against these bitter declamations; they thought that they perceived the rebellious accent of the Satanic school; they blamed this uneven, obscure, excessive style; they were shocked at these crudities and incongruities; they called on the poet to return to his first well-proportioned style. He was discouraged, left the storm-clouds, and returned to the azure sky. He was right; he is better there than anywhere else. A fine soul may be transported, attain at times to the fire of the most violent and the strongest beings: personal memories, they say, had furnished the matter of "Maud" and of "Locksley Hall"; with a woman's delicacy, he had the nerves of a woman. The fit over, he fell again into his "golden languors," into his calm reverie. After "Locksley Hall" he wrote the "Princess"; after "Maud" the "Idylls of the King."

Section IV.—In Memoriam.—The Princess

The great task of an artist is to find subjects which suit his talent. Tennyson has not always succeeded in this. His long poem, "In Memoriam," written in praise and memory of a friend who died young, is cold, monotonous, and too prettily arranged. He goes into mourning; but, like a correct gentleman, with brand new gloves, wipes away his tears with a cambric handkerchief, and displays throughout the religious service, which ends the ceremony, all the compunction of a respectful and well-trained layman. He was to find his subjects elsewhere. To be poetically happy is the object of a dilettante-artist. For this, many things are necessary. First of all, that the place, the events, and the characters shall not exist. Realities are coarse, and always, in some sense, ugly; at least they are heavy; we do not treat them as we should like, they oppress the fancy; at bottom there is nothing truly sweet and beautiful in our life but our dreams. We are ill at ease whilst we remain glued to earth, hobbling along on our two feet, which drag us wretchedly here and there in the place which impounds us. We need to live in another world, to hover in the wide-air kingdom, to build palaces in the clouds, to see them rise and crumble, to follow in a hazy distance the whims of their moving architecture, and the turns of their golden volutes. In this fantastic world, again, all must be pleasant and beautiful, the heart and senses must enjoy it, objects must be smiling or picturesque, sentiments delicate or lofty; no crudity, incongruity, brutality, savageness, must come to sully with its excess the modulated harmony of this ideal perfection. This leads the poet to the legends of chivalry. Here is the fantastic world, splendid to the sight, noble and specially pure, in which love, war, adventures, generosity, courtesy, all spectacles and all virtues which suit the instincts of our European races, are assembled, to furnish them with the epic which they love, and the model which suits them.

The "Princess" is a fairy tale, as sentimental as those of Shakespeare. Tennyson here thought and felt like a young knight of the Renaissance. The mark of this kind of mind is a superabundance, as it were, a superfluity of sap. In the characters of the "Princess," as in those of "As You Like It," there is an over-fulness of fancy and emotion. They have recourse, to express their thought, to all ages and lands; they carry speech to the most reckless rashness; they clothe and burden every idea with a sparkling image, which drags and glitters around it, like a brocade clustered with jewels. Their nature is over-rich; at every shock there is in them a sort of rustle of joy, anger, desire; they live more than we, more warmly and more quickly. They are ever in excess, refined, ready to weep, laugh, adore, jest, inclined to mingle adoration and jests, urged by a nervous rapture to opposite extremes. They sally in the poetic field with impetuous and ever-changing caprice and joy. To satisfy the subtlety and superabundance of their invention, they need fairy-tales and masquerades. In fact, the "Princess" is both. The beautiful Ida, daughter of King Gama, who is monarch of the South (this country is not to be found on the map), was affianced in her childhood to a beautiful prince of the North. When the time appointed has arrived, she is claimed. She, proud and bred on learned arguments, has become irritated against the rule of men, and in order to liberate women has founded a university on the frontiers, which is to raise her sex, and to be the colony of future equality. The prince sets out with Cyril and Florian, two friends, obtains permission from good King Gama, and, disguised as a girl, gets admission to the maiden precincts, which no man may enter on pain of death. There is a charming and sportive grace in this picture of a university for girls. The poet gambols with beauty; no badinage could be more romantic or tender. We smile to hear long learned words come from these rosy lips:

> "There sat along the forms, like morning doves
> That sun their milky bosoms on the thatch,
> A patient range of pupils."[444]

They listen to historic dissertations and promises of a social revolution, in "Academic silks, in hue the lilac, with a silken hood to each, and zoned with gold,... as rich as moth from dusk cocoons." Amongst these girls was Melissa, a child—

> "A rosy blonde, and in a college gown
> That clad her like an April daffodilly
> (Her mother's colour), with her lips apart,
> And all her thoughts as fair within her eyes,
> As bottom agates seem to wave and float
> In crystal currents of clear morning seas."[445]

The site of this university for girls enhances the magic of the scene. The words "College" and "Faculty" bring before the mind of Frenchmen only wretched and dirty buildings, which we might mistake for barracks or boarding-houses. Here, as in an English university, flowers creep up the porches, vines cling round the bases of the monuments, roses strew the alleys with their petals; the laurel thickets grow around the gates, the courts pile up their marble architecture, bossed with sculptured friezes, varied with urns from which droop the green pendage of the plants. "The Muses and the Graces, group'd in threes, enring'd a billowing fountain in the midst." After the lecture, some girls, in the deep meadow grass, "smoothed a petted peacock down"; others,

> "Leaning there on those balusters, high
> Above the empurpled champaign, drank the gale
> That blown about the foliage underneath,
> And sated with the innumerable rose
> Beat balm upon our eyelids."[446]

At every gesture, every attitude, we recognize young English girls; it is their brightness, their freshness, their innocence.

And here and there, too, we perceive the deep expression of their large dreamy eyes:

> "Tears, idle tears, I know not what they mean,
> Tears from the depth of some divine despair
> Rise in the heart, and gather to the eyes,
> In looking on the happy Autumn-fields,
> And thinking of the days that are no more....
>
> "Dear as remember'd kisses after death,
> And sweet as those by hopeless fancy feign'd
> On lips that are for others; deep as love,
> Deep as first love, and wild with all regret;
> O Death in Life, the days that are no more."[447]

This is an exquisite and strange voluptuousness, a reverie full of delight, and full, too, of anguish, the shudder of delicate and melancholy passion which we have already found in "Winter's Tale" or in "Twelfth Night."

The three friends have gone forth with the princess and her train, all on horseback, and pause "near a coppice-feather'd chasm,"

> "till the Sun
> Grew broader toward his death and fell, and all
> The rosy heights came out above the lawns."

Cyril, heated by wine, begins to troll a careless tavern catch, and betrays the secret. Ida, indignant, turns to leave; her foot slips, and she falls into the river; the prince saves her, and wishes to flee. But he is seized by the Proctors and brought before the throne, where the haughty maiden stands ready to pronounce sentence. At this moment

> "... There rose
> A hubbub in the court of half the maids
> Gather'd together: from the illumined hall
> Long lanes of splendour slanted o'er a press
> Of snowy shoulders, thick as herded ewes,
> And rainbow robes, and gems and gemlike eyes,
> And gold and golden heads; they to and fro
> Fluctuated, as flowers in storm, some red, some pale,
> All open-mouth'd, all gazing to the light,
> Some crying there was an army in the land,
> And some that men were in the very walls,
> And some they cared not; till a clamour grew
> As of a new-world Babel, woman-built,
> And worse-confounded: high above them stood
> The placid marble Muses, looking peace."[448]

The father of the prince has come with his army to deliver him, and has seized King Gama as a hostage. The princess is obliged to release the young man. With distended nostrils, waving hair, a tempest raging in her heart, she thanks him with bitter irony. She trembles with wounded pride; she stammers, hesitates; she tries to constrain herself in order the better to insult him, and suddenly breaks out:

> "'You have done well and like a gentleman,
> And like a prince: you have our thanks for all:
> And you look well too in your woman's dress:
> Well have you done and like a gentleman.
> You saved our life: we owe you bitter thanks:
> Better have died and spilt our bones in the flood—
> Then men had said— but now— What hinders me
> To take such bloody vengeance on you both?—
> Yet since our father— Wasps in our good hive,
> You would-be quenchers of the light to be,

> Barbarians, grosser than your native bears—
> O would I had his sceptre for one hour!
> You that have dared to break our bound, and gull'd
> Our servants, wronged and lied and thwarted us—
> *I* wed with thee! *I* bound by precontract
> Your bride, your bondslave! not tho' all the gold
> That veins the world were pack'd to make your crown,
> And every spoken tongue should lord you. Sir,
> Your falsehood and yourself are hateful to us:
> I trample on your offers and on you:
> Begone: we will not look upon you more.
> Here, push them out at gates.'"[449]

How is this fierce heart to be softened, fevered with feminine anger, embitterbed by disappointment and insult, excited by long dreams of power and ascendancy, and rendered more savage by its virginity! But how anger becomes her, and how lovely she is! And how this fire of sentiment, this lofty declaration of independence, this chimerical ambition for reforming the future, reveal the generosity and pride of a young heart, enamoured of the beautiful! It is agreed that the quarrel shall be settled by a combat of fifty men against fifty other men. The prince is conquered, and Ida sees him bleeding on the sand. Slowly, gradually, in spite of herself, she yields, receives the wounded in her palace, and comes to the bedside of the dying prince. Before his weakness and his wild delirium pity expands, then tenderness, then love:

> "From all a closer interest flourish'd up
> Tenderness touch by touch, and last, to these,
> Love, like an Alpine harebell hung with tears
> By some cold morning glacier; frail at first
> And feeble, all unconscious of itself,
> But such as gather'd colour day by day."[450]

One evening he returns to consciousness, exhausted, his eyes still troubled by gloomy visions; he sees Ida before him, hovering like a dream, painfully opens his pale lips, and "utter'd whisperingly":

> "'If you be, what I think you, some sweet dream,
> I would but ask you to fulfil yourself:
> But if you be that Ida whom I knew,
> I ask you nothing: only, if a dream,
> Sweet dream be perfect. I shall die to-night.
> Stoop down and seem to kiss me ere I die.'
> ... She turned; she paused;

> She stoop'd; and out of languor leapt a cry;
> Leapt fiery Passion from the brinks of death;
> And I believe that in the living world
> My spirit closed with Ida's at the lips;
> Till back I fell, and from mine arms she rose
> Glowing all over noble shame; and all
> Her falser self slipt from her like a robe,
> And left her woman, lovelier in her mood
> Than in her mould that other, when she came
> From barren deeps to conquer all with love;
> And down the streaming crystal dropt; and she
> Far-fleeted by the purple island-sides,
> Naked, a double light in air and wave."[451]

This is the accent of the Renaissance, as it left the heart of Spenser and Shakespeare; they had this voluptuous adoration of form and soul, and this divine sentiment of beauty.

Section V.—The Idylls of the King

There is another chivalry, which inaugurates the Middle Ages, as this closes it; sung by children, as this by youths; and restored in the "Idylls of the King," as this in the "Princess." It is the legend of Arthur, Merlin and the Knights of the Round Table. With admirable heart, Tennyson has modernized the feelings and the language; this pliant soul takes all tones, in order to give itself all pleasures. This time he has become epic, antique and ingenuous, like Homer, and like the old *trouvères* of the *chansons de Geste.* It is pleasant to quit our learned civilization, to rise again to the primitive age and manners, to listen to the peaceful discourse which flows copiously and slowly, as a river in a smooth channel. The distinguishing mark of the ancient epic is clearness and calm. The ideas were new-born; man was happy and in his infancy. He had not had time to refine, to cut down and adorn his thoughts; he showed them bare. He was not yet pricked by manifold lusts; he thought at leisure. Every idea interested him; he unfolded it curiously, and explained it. His speech never jerks; he goes step by step, from one object to another, and every object seems lovely to him: he pauses, observes, and takes pleasure in observing. This simplicity and peace are strange and charming; we abandon ourselves, it is well with us; we do not desire to go more quickly; we fancy we would gladly remain thus, and forever. For primitive thought is wholesome thought; we have but marred it by grafting and cultivation; we return to it as our familiar element, to find contentment and repose.

But of all epics, this of the Round Table is distinguished by purity. Arthur, the irreproachable king, has assembled

> "A glorious company, the flower of men,
> To serve as model for the mighty world,
> And be the fair beginning of a time.
> I made them lay their hands in mine and swear
> To reverence the King, as if he were
> Their conscience, and their conscience as their King,...
> To speak no slander, no, nor listen to it,
> To lead sweet lives in purest chastity,
> To love one maiden only, cleave to her,
> And worship her by years of noble deeds."[452]

There is a sort of refined pleasure in having to do with such a world; for there is none in which purer or more touching fruits could grow. I will show one— "Elaine, the lily maid of Astolat"— who, having seen Lancelot once, loves him when he has departed, and for her whole life. She keeps the shield, which he has left in a tower, and every day goes up to look at it, counting "every dint a sword had beaten in it, and every scratch a lance had made upon it," and living on her dreams. He is wounded: she goes to tend and heal him:

> "She murmur'd, 'vain, in vain: it cannot be.
> He will not love me: how then? must I die?'
> Then as a little helpless innocent bird,
> That has but one plain passage of few notes,
> Will sing the simple passage o'er and o'er
> For all an April morning, till the ear
> Wearies to hear it, so the simple maid
> Went half the night repeating, 'must I die?'"[453]

At last she confesses her secret; but with what modesty and spirit! He cannot marry her; he is tied to another. She droops and fades; her father and brothers try to console her, but she will pot be consoled. She is told that Lancelot has sinned with the queen; she does not believe it:

> "At last she said, 'Sweet brothers, yester night
> I seem'd a curious little maid again,
> As happy as when we dwelt among the woods,
> And when you used to take me with the flood
> Up the great river in the boatman's boat.
> Only you would not pass beyond the cape
> That hast the poplar on it; there you fixt
> Your limit, oft returning with the tide.
> And yet I cried because you would not pass
> Beyond it, and far up the shining flood

Until we found the palace of the King.
... Now shall I have my will.'"[454]

She dies, and her father and brothers did what she had asked them to do:

"But when the next sun brake from underground,
Then, those two brethren slowly with bent brows
Accompanying, the sad chariot-bier
Past like a shadow thro' the field, that shone
Full summer, to that stream whereon the barge,
Pall'd all its length in blackest samite, lay.
There sat the lifelong creature of the house,
Loyal, the dumb old servitor, on deck,
Winking his eyes, and twisted all his face.
So those two brethren from the chariot took
And on the black decks laid her in her bed,
Set in her hand a lily, o'er her hung
The silken case with braided blazonings
And kiss'd her quiet brows, and saying to her:
'Sister, farewell for ever,' and again
'Farewell, sweet sister,' parted all in tears.
Then rose the dumb old servitor, and the dead
Steer'd by the dumb went upward with the flood—
In her right hand the lily, in her left
The letter— all her bright hair streaming down—
And all the coverlid was cloth of gold
Drawn to her waist, and she herself in white
All but her face, and that clear-featured face
Was lovely, for she did not seem as dead
But fast asleep, and lay as tho' she smiled."[455]

Thus they arrive at Court in great silence, and King Arthur read the letter before all his knights and weeping ladies:

"Most noble lord, Sir Lancelot of the Lake,
I, sometime call'd the maid of Astolat,
Come, for you left me taking no farewell,
Hither, to take my last farewell of you.
I loved you, and my love had no return,
And therefore my true love has been my death.
And therefore to our lady Guinevere,
And to all other ladies, I make moan.
Pray for my soul, and yield me burial.

Pray for my soul thou too, Sir Lancelot,
As thou art a knight peerless."[456]

Nothing more: she ends with this word, full of so sad a regret and so tender an admiration: we could hardly find anything more simple or more delicate.

It seems as if an archaeologist might reproduce all styles except the grand, and Tennyson has reproduced all, even the grand. It is the night of the final battle; all day the tumult of the mighty fray "roll'd among the mountains by the winter sea"; Arthur's knights had fallen "man by man"; he himself had fallen, "deeply smitten through the helm," and Sir Bedivere, the last of all his knights, bore him to a place hard by,

"A chapel nigh the field,
A broken chancel with a broken cross,
That stood on a dark strait of barren land.
On one side lay the Ocean, and on one
Lay a great water, and the moon was full."[457]

Arthur, feeling himself about to die, bids him to take his sword Excalibur "and fling him far into the middle meer"; for he had received it from the sea-nymphs, and after him no mortal must handle it. Twice Sir Bedivere went to obey the king: twice he paused, and came back pretending that he had flung away the sword; for his eyes were dazzled by the wondrous diamond setting which clustered and shone about the haft. The third time he throws it:

"The great brand
Made lightnings in the splendour of the moon,
And flashing round and round, and whirl'd in an arch,
Shot like a streamer of the northern morn,
Seen where the moving isles of winter shock
By night, with noises of the northern sea.
So flash'd and fell the brand Excalibur:
But ere he dipt the surface, rose an arm
Clothed in white samite, mystic, wonderful,
And caught him by the hilt, and brandish'd him
Three times, and drew him under in the meer."[458]

Then Arthur, rising painfully and scarce able to breathe, bids Sir Bedivere take him on his shoulders and "bear me to the margin. Quick, quick! I fear it is too late, and I shall die." They arrive thus, through "icy caves and barren chasms," to the shores of a lake, where they saw "the long glories of the winter moon":

> "They saw then how there hove a dusky barge
> Dark as a funeral scarf from stem to stern,
> Beneath them; and descending they were ware
> That all the decks were dense with stately forms
> Black-stoled, black-hooded, like a dream— by these
> Three Queens with crowns of gold— and from them rose
> A cry that shiver'd to the tingling stars,
> And, as it were one voice, an agony
> Of lamentation, like a wind, that shrills
> All night in a waste land, where no one comes
> Or hath come, since the making of the world.
> Then murmur'd Arthur: 'Place me in the barge,'
> And to the barge they came. There those three Queens
> Put forth their hands, and took the King, and wept.
> But she, that rose the tallest of them all
> And fairest, laid his head upon her lap,
> And loosed the shatter'd casque, and chafed his hands
> And call'd him by his name, complaining loud...."[459]

Before the barge drifts away, King Arthur, raising his slow voice, consoles Sir Bedivere, standing in sorrow on the shore, and pronounces this heroic and solemn farewell:

> "The old order changeth, yielding place to new,
> And God fulfils himself in many ways,
> Lest one good custom should corrupt the world....
> If thou shouldst never see my face again,
> Pray for my soul. More things are wrought by prayer
> Than this world dreams of....
> For so the whole round earth is every way
> Bound by gold chains about the feet of God.
> But now farewell. I am going a long way
> With these thou seest— if indeed I go—
> (For all my mind is clouded with a doubt)
> To the island-valley of Avilion;
> Where falls not hail, or rain, or any snow,
> Nor ever wind blows loudly; but it lies
> Deep-meadow'd, happy, fair with orchard-lawns
> And bowery hollows crown'd with summer sea,
> Where I will heal me of my grievous wound."[460]

Nothing, I think, calmer and more imposing, has been seen since Goethe.

How, in a few words, shall we assemble all the features of so manifold a talent? Tennyson is a born poet, that is, a builder of airy palaces and imaginary castles. But the individual passion and absorbing preoccupations which generally guide the hands of such men are wanting to him; he found in himself no plan of a new edifice; he lias built after all the rest; he has simply chosen amongst all forms the most elegant, ornate, exquisite. Of their beauties he has taken but the flower. At most, now and then, he has here and there amused himself by designing some genuinely English and modern cottage. If in this choice of architecture, adopted or restored, we look for a trace of him, we shall find it, here and there, in some more finely sculptured frieze, in some more delicate and graceful sculptured rose-work; but we only find it marked and sensible in the purity and elevation of the moral emotion which we carry away with us when we quit his gallery of art.

Section VI.—Comparison of English and French Society

The favorite poet of a nation, it seems, is he whose works a man, setting out on a journey, prefers to put into his pocket. Nowadays it would be Tennyson in England, and Alfred de Musset in France. The two publics differ: so do their modes of life, their reading, and their pleasures. Let us try to describe them; we shall better understand the flowers if we see them in the garden.

Here we are at Newhaven, or at Dover, and we glide over the rails looking on either side. On both sides fly past country houses; they exist everywhere in England, on the margin of lakes, on the edge of the bays, on the summit of the hills, in every picturesque point of view. They are the chosen abodes; London is but a business-place; men of the world live, amuse themselves, visit each other, in the country. How well-ordered and pretty is this house! If near it there was some old edifice, abbey, or castle, it has been preserved. The new building has been suited to the old; even if detached and modern, it does not lack style; gable-ends, mullions, broad-windows, turrets perched at every corner, have a Gothic air in spite of their newness. Even this cottage, though not very large, suited to people with a moderate income, is pleasant to see with its pointed roofs, its porch, its bright brown bricks, all covered with ivy. Doubtless grandeur is generally wanting; in these days the men who mould opinion are no longer great lords, but rich gentlemen, well brought up, and landholders; it is pleasantness which appeals to them. But how they understand the word! All round the house is turf, fresh and smooth as velvet, rolled every morning. In front, great rhododendrons form a bright thicket, in which murmur swarms of bees; festoons of exotics creep and curve over the short grass; honey-suckles clamber up the trees; hundreds of roses, drooping over the windows, shed their rain of petals on the paths. Fine elms, yew-trees, great oaks, jealously tended, everywhere combine their leafage or rear their heads. Trees have been brought from Australia and China to adorn the thickets with the elegance or the singularity of their foreign shapes; the copper-beech stretches over the delicate verdure of the meadows the shadow of its dark metallic-hued foliage. How delicious is the freshness of this verdure! How it glistens, and how it abounds in wild flowers brightened by the sun! What care, what cleanliness, how everything is arranged, kept up, refined, for the comfort of the senses and the pleasure of the eyes! If there is a slope, streamlets have been devised with little islets in the glen, peopled with tufts of roses; ducks of select breed swim in the pools, where the water-lilies display their satin stars. Fat oxen lie in the grass, sheep as white as if fresh from the washing, all kinds of happy and model animals, fit to delight the eyes of an amateur and a master. We return to the house, and before entering I look upon the view; decidedly the love of Englishmen for the country is innate; how pleasant it will be from that parlor window to look upon the setting sun, and the broad network of sunlight spread across the woods! And how cunningly they have disposed the house, so that the landscape may be seen at distance between the hills, and at hand between the trees! We enter. How nicely everything is got up, and how commodious. The smallest wants have been forestalled, and provided for; there is nothing which is not correct and perfect; we imagine that everything in the house has received a prize, or at least an honorable mention, at some industrial exhibition. And the attendance of the servants is as good as everything else; cleanliness is not more scrupulous in Holland; Englishmen have, in proportion, three times as many servants as Frenchmen; not too many for the minute details of the service. The domestic machine acts without interruption, without shock, without hinderance; every wheel has its movement and its place, and the comfort which it dispenses falls like honey in the mouth, as clear and as exquisite as the sugar of a model refinery when quite purified.

We converse with our host. We very soon find that his mind and soul have always been well balanced. When he left college he found his career shaped out for him; no need for him to revolt against the Church, which is half rational; nor against the Constitution, which is nobly liberal: the faith and law presented to him are good, useful, moral, liberal enough to maintain and employ all diversities of sincere minds. He became attached to them, he loves them, he has received from them the whole system of his practical and speculative ideas; he does not waver, he no longer doubts, he knows what he ought to believe and to do. He is not carried away by theories, dulled by sloth, checked by contradictions. Elsewhere youth is like water, stagnant or running to waste; here there is a fine old channel which receives and directs to a useful and sure end the whole stream of its activities and passions. He acts, works, rules. He is married, has tenants, is a magistrate, becomes a politician. He improves and rules his parish, his estate, and his family. He founds societies, speaks at meetings, superintends schools, dispenses justice, introduces improvements; he employs his reading, his travels, his connections, his fortune, and his rank, to lead his neighbors and dependents, amicably, to some work which profits themselves and the public. He is influential and respected. He has the pleasures of self-esteem and the satisfaction of conscience. He knows that he has authority, and that he uses it loyally, for the good of others. And this healthy state of mind is supported by a wholesome life. His mind is beyond doubt, cultivated and occupied; he is well informed, knows several languages, has travelled, is fond of all precise information; he is kept by his newspapers conversant with all new ideas and discoveries. But, at the same time, he loves and practises all bodily exercises. He rides, takes long walks, hunts, yachts, examines for himself all the details of breeding and agriculture; he lives in the open air, he withstands the encroachments of a sedentary life, which always elsewhere leads the modern man to agitation of the brain, weakness of the muscles, and excitement of the nerves. Such is this elegant and common-sense society, refined in comfort, regular in conduct, whose dilettante tastes and moral principles confine it within a sort of flowery border, and prevent it from having its attention diverted.

Does any poet suit such a society better than Tennyson? Without being a pedant, he is moral; he may be read in the family circle by night; he does not rebel against society and life; he speaks of God and the soul, nobly, tenderly, without ecclesiastical prejudice; there is no need to reproach him like Lord Byron; he has no violent and abrupt words, extravagant and scandalous sentiments; he will pervert nobody. We shall not be troubled when we close the book; we may listen when we quit him, without being shocked by the contrast, to the grave voice of the master of the house, who reads evening prayers before the kneeling servants. And yet, when we quit him, we keep a smile of pleasure on our lips. The traveller, the lover of archaeology, has been pleased by the imitations of foreign and antique sentiments. The sportsman, the lover of the country, has relished the little country scenes and the rich rural pictures. The ladies have been charmed by his portraits of women; they are so exquisite and pure! He has laid such delicate blushes on those lovely cheeks! He has depicted so well the changing expression of those proud or candid eyes! They like him because they feel that he likes them. He even honors them, and rises in his nobility to the height of their purity. Young girls weep in listening to him; certainly when, a little while ago, we heard the legend of Elaine or Enid read, we saw the fair heads drooping under the flowers which adorned them, and white shoulders heaving with furtive emotion. And how delicate was this emotion! He has not rudely trenched upon truth and passion. He has risen to the height of noble and tender sentiments. He has gleaned from all nature and all history what was most lofty and amiable. He has chosen his ideas, chiselled his words, equalled by his artifices, successes, and versatility of style, the pleasantness and perfection of social elegance in the midst of which we read him. His poetry is like one of those gilt and painted stands in which flowers of the country and exotics mingle in artful harmony their stalks and foliage, their clusters and cups, their scents and hues. It seems made expressly for these wealthy, cultivated, free business men, heirs of the ancient nobility, new leaders of a new England. It is part of their luxury as well as of their morality; it is an eloquent confirmation of their principles, and a precious article of their drawing-room furniture.

We return to Calais, and travel towards Paris, without pausing on the road. There are on the way plenty of noblemen's castles, and houses of rich men of business. But we do not find amongst them, as in England, the thinking elegant world, which, by the refinement of its taste and the superiority of its mind, becomes the guide of the nation and the arbiter of the beautiful. There are two peoples in France: the provinces and Paris; the one dining, sleeping, yawning, listening; the other thinking, daring, watching, and speaking: the first drawn by the second, as a snail by a butterfly, alternately amused and disturbed by the whims and the audacity of its guide. It is this guide we must look upon! Let us enter Paris! What a strange spectacle! It is evening, the streets are aflame, a luminous dust covers the busy noisy crowd, which jostles, elbows, crushes, and swarms near the theatres, behind the windows of the cafés. Have you remarked how all these faces are wrinkled, frowning or pale; how anxious are their looks, how nervous their gestures? A violent brightness falls on these shining heads; most are bald before thirty. To find pleasure here, they must have plenty of excitement: the dust of the boulevard settles on the ice which they are eating; the smell of the gas and the steam of the pavement, the perspiration left on the walls dried up by the fever of a Parisian day, "the human air full of impure rattle"— this is what they cheerfully breathe. They are crammed round their little marble tables, persecuted by the glaring light, the shouts of the waiters, the jumble of mixed talk, the monotonous motion of gloomy walkers, the flutter of loitering courtesans moving about anxiously in the dark. Doubtless their homes are not pleasant, or they would not change them for these bagmen's delights. We climb four flights of stairs, and find ourselves in a polished, gilded room, adorned with stuccoed ornaments, plaster statuettes, new furniture of old oak, with every kind of pretty knick-knack on the mantle-pieces and the whatnots. "It makes a good show;" you can give a good reception to envious friends and people of standing. It is an advertisement, nothing more; we pass half an hour there agreeably, and that is all. You will never make more than a house of call out of these rooms; they are low in the ceiling, close, inconvenient, rented by the year, dirty in six months, serving to display a fictitious luxury. All the enjoyments of these people are factitious, and, as it were, snatched hurriedly; they have in them something unhealthy and irritating. They are like the cookery of their restaurants, the splendor of their cafés, the gayety of their theatres. They want them too quick, too pungent, too manifold. They have not cultivated them patiently, and culled them moderately; they have forced them on an artificial and heating soil; they grasp them in haste. They are refined and greedy; they need every day a stock of word-paintings, broad anecdotes, biting railleries, new truths, varied ideas. They soon get bored, and cannot endure tedium. They amuse themselves with all their might, and find that they are hardly amused. They exaggerate their work and their expense, their wants and their efforts. The accumulation of sensations and fatigue stretches their nervous machine to excess, and their polish of social gayety chips off twenty times a day, displaying an inner ground of suffering and ardor.

But how quick-witted they are, and how unfettered is their mind! How this incessant rubbing has sharpened them! How ready they are to grasp and comprehend everything! How apt this studied and manifold culture has made them to feel and relish tendernesses and sadnesses unknown to their fathers, deep feelings, strange and sublime, which hitherto seemed foreign to their race! This great city is cosmopolitan; here all ideas may be born; no barrier checks the mind: the vast field of thought opens before them without a beaten or prescribed track. Use neither hinders nor guides them; an official Government and Church rid them of the care of leading the nation: the two powers are submitted to, as we submit to the beadle or the policeman, patiently and with chaff; they are looked upon as a play. In short, the world here seems but a melodrama, a subject of criticism and argument. And be sure that criticism and argument have full scope. An Englishman entering on life, finds to all great questions an answer ready made. A Frenchman entering on life, finds to all great questions simply suggested doubts. In this conflict of opinions he must create a faith for himself, and, being mostly unable to do it, he remains open to every uncertainty, and therefore to every curiosity and to every pain. In this gulf, which is like a vast sea, dreams, theories, fancies, intemperate, poetic and sickly desires, collect and chase each other like clouds. If in this tumult of moving forms we seek some solid work to prepare a foundation for future opinions, we find only the slowly-rising edifices of the sciences, which here and there obscurely, like submarine polypes, construct of imperceptible coral the basis on which the belief of the human race is to rest.

Such is the world for which Alfred de Musset wrote: in Paris he must be read. Read? We all know him by heart. He is dead, and it seems as if we daily hear him speak. A conversation among artists, as they jest in a studio, a beautiful young girl leaning over her box at the theatre, a street washed by the rain, making the black pavement shine, a fresh smiling morning in the woods of Fontainebleau, everything brings him before us, as if he were alive again. Was there ever a more vibrating and genuine accent? This man, at least, never lied. He only said what he felt, and he has said it as he felt it. He thought aloud. He made the confession of every man. He was not admired, but loved; he was more than a poet, he was a man. Everyone found in him his own feelings, the most transient, the most familiar; he did not restrict himself, he gave himself to all; he possessed the last virtues which remain to us, generosity and sincerity. And he had the most precious gift which can seduce an old civilization, youth. As he said, "that hot youth, a tree with a rough bark, which covers all with its shadow, prospect and path." With that fire did he hurl onward love, jealousy, the thirst of pleasure, all the impetuous passions which rise with virgin blood from the depths of a young heart, and how did he make them clash together! Has anyone felt them more deeply? He was too full of them, he gave himself up to them, was intoxicated with them. He rushed through life, like an eager racehorse in the country, whom the scent of plants and the splendid novelty of the vast heavens urge, headlong, in its mad career, which shatters all before him, and himself as well. He desired too much; he wished, strongly and greedily, to enjoy life in one draught, thoroughly; he did not glean or enjoy it; he tore it off like a bunch of grapes, pressed it, crushed it, twisted it, and he remains with stained hands as thirsty as before.[461] Then broke forth sobs which found an echo in all hearts. What! so young, and already so wearied! So many precious gifts, so fine a mind, so delicate a tact, so rich and varied a fancy, so precocious a glory, such a sudden blossom of beauty and genius, and yet anguish, disgust, tears, and cries! What a mixture! With the same attitude he adores and curses. Eternal illusion, invincible experience, keep side by side in him to fight and tear him. He became old, and remained young; he is a poet, and he is a sceptic. The Muse and her peaceful beauty, Nature and her immortal freshness, Love and his happy smile, all the swarm of divine visions barely passed before his eyes, when we see approaching with curses, and sarcasms, all the spectres of debauchery and death. He is as a man in a festive scene, who drinks from a chased cup, standing up, in front, amidst applause and triumphal music, his eyes laughing, his heart full of joy, heated and excited by the generous wine he quaffed, whom suddenly we see growing pale; there was poison in the cup; he falls, and the death-rattle is in his throat; his convulsed feet beat upon the silken carpet, and all the terrified guests look on. This is what we felt on the day when the most beloved, the most brilliant amongst us, suddenly quivered from an unseen attack, and was struck down, being hardly able to breathe, amid the lying splendors and gayeties of our banquet.

Well! such as he was, we love him forever: we cannot listen to another; beside him, all seem cold or false. We leave at midnight the theatre in which he had heard Malibran, and we enter the gloomy Rue des Moulins, where, on a hired bed, his Rolla came to sleep and die. The lamps cast flickering rays on the slippery pavement. Restless shadows march past the doors, and trail along their dress of draggled silk to meet the passers-by. The windows are fastened; here and there a light pierces through a half-closed shutter, and shows a dead dahlia on the edge of a window-sill. To-morrow an organ will grind before these panes, and the wan clouds will leave their droppings on these dirty walls. From this wretched place came the most impassioned of his poems! These vilenesses and vulgarities of the stews and the lodging-house caused this divine eloquence to flow! it was these which at such a moment gathered in this bruised heart all the splendors of nature and history, to make them spring up in sparkling jets, and shine under the most glowing poetic sun that ever rose! We feel pity; we think of that other poet, away there in the Isle of Wight, who amuses himself by dressing up lost epics. How happy he is amongst his fine books, his friends, his honeysuckles and roses! No matter. De Musset, in this wretched abode of filth and misery, rose higher. From the heights of his doubt and despair, he saw the infinite, as we see the sea from a storm-beaten promontory. Religions, their glory and their decay, the human race, its pangs and its destiny, all that is sublime in the world, appeared there to him in a flash of lightning. He felt, at least this once in his life, the inner tempest of deep sensations, giant-dreams, and intense voluptuousness, the desire of which enabled him to live, the lack of which forced him to die. He was no mere dilettante; he was not content to taste and enjoy; he left his mark on human thought; he told the world what was man, love, truth, happiness. He suffered, but he imagined: he fainted, but he created. He tore from his entrails with despair the idea which he had conceived, and showed it to the eyes of all, bloody but alive. That is harder and lovelier than to go fondling and gazing upon the ideas of others. There is in the world but one work worthy of a man: the production of a truth, to which we devote ourselves, and in which we believe. The people who have listened to Tennyson are better than our aristocracy of townsfolk and bohemians; but I prefer Alfred de Musset to Tennyson.

---

[434]Poems by Alfred Tennyson, 7th ed. 1851; "Lilian," 5.
[435]Poems by Alfred Tennyson, 7th ed. 1851; "Adeline," 33.
[436]Ibid. "Madeline," 15.
[437]Poems by Alfred Tennyson, 7th ed. 1851; "The Dying Swan," 45.
[438]Poems by Alfred Tennyson, 7th ed. 1851; "The Lotus-Eaters," 140.
[439]Poems by Alfred Tennyson, 7th ed. 1851; "Locksley Hall," 266.
[440]Tennyson's "Maud," 1856, IV. 1, 15.
[441]Tennyson's "Maud," 1856, XXVII. 1.
[442]Ibid. XXVII. 11, 105.
[443]Ibid, XXVIII. 3 and 4, 108.
[444]"The Princess, a Medley," 12th ed. 1864, II. 34.
[445]Ibid. II. 46.
[446]Ibid. III. 60.
[447]"The Princess, a Medley," 12th ed. 1864, V. 76.
[448]"The Princess, a Medley," 12th ed. 1864, IV. 99.
[449]Ibid. IV. 102.
[450]"The Princess, a Medley," V. 163.
[451]Ibid. V. 165.
[452]"Idylls of the King," 1864; Guinevere, 249.

[453]Ibid.; Elaine, 193.
[454]Ibid.; Elaine, 201.
[455]"Idylls of the King," 1864, 206.
[456]Ibid. 213.
[457]Poems by Alfred Tennyson, 7th ed. 1851; "Morte d'Arthur," 189.
[458]Ibid. 194.
[459]Poems by Alfred Tennyson, 7th ed. 1851; "Morte d'Arthur," 196.
[460]Ibid. 197.
[461]"O médiocrité! celui qui pour tout bien
T'apporte à ce tripot dégoûtant de la vie
Est bien poltron au jeu s'il ne dit: Tout ou rien."

THE END

BOOK V— MODERN AUTHORS

HISTORY OF ENGLISH LITERATURE

Detailed Historical Context

INTRODUCTION

The nineteenth century was a fascinating and vital formative period in Western literature since it provided the fundamental backdrop for the formation and emergence of contemporary literary traditions and styles as we know them today.

The Victorian Period, named after Queen Victoria's reign from 1837 to 1901, was characterised by significant cultural and creative triumphs, social and technological developments, and significant political and economic transformation. It was a time of development and expansion for Britain, as it became the world's largest empire; it was also a time of significant social and cultural transformation in America. Rapid industrialisation and urbanisation resulted in a lively literary environment with a diverse spectrum of genres and styles. Popular literary genres at the time included sentimental novels, gothic novels, and regionalist writing. Additional research, for example, shows that the Romantic, Symbolist, and Realist movements, as well as a variety of social and economic circumstances that dominated the twentieth century, all had their origins and predecessors in the nineteenth century.

MOVEMENTS AND LITERATURE

ROMANTICISM

Romanticism, with its stress on sensation and the irrational, emerged in the nineteenth century as a significant literary and cultural movement. The 18th century, on the other hand, was regarded to be the age of intelligence, reasoning, and the mind. Romanticism, which emerged from the late-nineteenth-century German Sturm und Drang ("Stress and Storm") movement and whose notable members included Goethe and Friedrich Schiller, was marked by a focus on the individual, subjective, mystical, emotional, and inner life.

Writers and poets such as William Wordsworth, Samuel Taylor Coleridge, and John Keats in England, and Johann Wolfgang von Goethe and Friedrich Schiller in Germany, sought to capture the sublime in nature and the depth of human emotion in their works.

The Romantic movement was also marked by a fascination with the past, the mystical, and the exotic. This was evident in the rise of Gothic literature, with novels such as Mary Shelley's 'Frankenstein' (1818) and the poems of

Edgar Allan Poe. Romanticism was not just a literary movement; it also had profound impacts on art and music, inspiring artists like J.M.W. Turner and composers like Ludwig van Beethoven. Ultimately, Romanticism represented a fundamental shift in cultural attitudes, offering a new perspective on the nature of creativity, the purpose of art, and the role of the artist in society.

- *Rousseau*

Jean-Jacques Rousseau was a towering intellectual figure whose ideas shaped the 19th century, despite his death in 1778. His writings profoundly influenced both the Age of Enlightenment and the Romantic movements, creating a bridge between these two key periods. Rousseau challenged the primacy of reason advocated by his Enlightenment contemporaries, arguing that feelings and emotions were also essential in understanding the human experience. His novel, "Julie, or the New Heloise" (1761), is considered a precursor to Romanticism, emphasizing passion and sentiment.

- *Early Romantic poets*

The late 18th and early 19th century Romantic English poets William Wordsworth and Samuel Taylor Coleridge, who released their collection of poems Lyrical Ballads in 1798, are considered the forefathers of this style. As seen by the works of Pushkin in Russia, Ugo Foscolo and Giacomo Leopardi in Italy, José de Espronceda in Spain, and Giacomo Leopardi, the Romantic poetry movement was popular and flourished throughout Europe and beyond.

- *American Romanticism*

American Romanticism, a movement that spanned the mid-19th century, was a reaction against the rationalism of the Age of Enlightenment and a manifestation of the ethos of individualism that was central to the American frontier spirit. It encapsulated a broad range of human experience and played out differently across various genres, exploring themes like the supernatural, the power of nature, and the potential of the individual.

James Fenimore Cooper's historical adventure novels, such as "The Last of the Mohicans" (1826), created a uniquely American kind of Romantic hero - the rugged, self-reliant frontiersman. Edgar Allan Poe took a darker route, delving into the eerie and supernatural in tales like "The Fall of the House of Usher" (1839) and "The Raven" (1845). These works were representative of the Gothic element within Romanticism, exploring the darker recesses of the human psyche.

Walt Whitman, with his groundbreaking collection "Leaves of Grass" (1855), embodied another aspect of American Romanticism. His free verse celebrated the individual, democratic values, and the spiritual significance of everyday life.

Finally, the Transcendentalist movement, led by Ralph Waldo Emerson and Henry David Thoreau, elevated the individual conscience above societal norms. Emerson's essay "Self-Reliance" (1841) became a key text, while Thoreau's "Walden" (1854) documented his experiment in simple living and immersion in nature.

Together, these authors and works shaped the American Romantic movement, offering new perspectives on the human experience and inspiring readers to break free from societal constraints and explore their own individual paths.

- *Second Generation Romantic poets*

To discover the "truth" of things, the Romantics went to people's emotions, which were grounded in and exemplified by interaction with nature and the primordial self, rather than logical inquiry. Second-generation Romantic writers John Keats, Lord Byron, and Percy Bysshe Shelley's writings are good examples of these points of view.

POST ROMANTICISM

- *Parnassianism*

The works of French poets Théophile Gautier and Charles Baudelaire are examples of Parnassianism, which can be considered as an extension of early Romantic viewpoints with its emphasis on aesthetics and the concept of art for the sake of art. Schopenhauer's philosophical ideas had an impact as well. Devotees attempted to address their foreign and old subjects of fascination in a more controlled, formal manner, retreating from the excess passion and sentimentality of the Romantic movement.

- *Impressionism and Symbolism*

Claude Monet and other Paris-based painters contributed to the development of impressionism, which first arose in painting and then in music in France near the end of the nineteenth century. Impressionism was a painting style that attempted to reflect the visual world as accurately as possible by employing the shifting qualities of light and colour as seen via human perception and experience.

Symbolism is characterised as a departure from naturalism and realism in favour of a harsher, more truthful portrayal of the world, with a concentration on the ordinary rather than the extraordinary. Symbolist poets, such as Gustave Kahn and Ezra Pound, employed imagery to "evoke" rather than portray or describe.

THE GOTHIC NOVEL

The Gothic Novel, a vibrant subgenre of Romantic fiction, emerged in Europe towards the end of the 18th century. Pioneers in this field include Horace Walpole with his ground-breaking novel "The Castle of Otranto" (1765), and Ann Radcliffe, whose work "The Mysteries of Udolpho" elevated the genre. The term 'Gothic' is derived from Gothic architecture, a common setting in these novels, characterized by crumbling castles, haunted monasteries, and dark forests, which lent an eerie atmosphere to the narratives.

Distinct from typical supernatural tales, Gothic novels often dealt with themes of ancestral curses and past sins haunting the present, exploring the darker recesses of the human psyche and the effects of terror and horror on it. This was further explored in the 19th-century through seminal works such as Mary Shelley's "Frankenstein" (1818), Sir Walter Scott's "Bride of Lammermoor" (1819), E.T.A. Hoffmann's "The Devil's Elixirs" (1815), Emily Bronte's "Wuthering Heights" (1847), Robert Louis Stevenson's "The Strange Case of Dr. Jekyll and Mr. Hyde" (1886), and Bram Stoker's "Dracula" (1897).

Even beyond these iconic pieces, the influence of the Gothic novel can be seen in many well-regarded Victorian works. Charles Dickens' "Bleak House" (1852-1853) and "Great Expectations" (1861), for example, both incorporate elements of the Gothic tradition, reflecting its broad impact on the literature of the time. This genre, with its exploration of the sublime, the uncanny, and the spectral, significantly contributed to the richness and depth of 19th-century literature.

POPULAR PHILOSOPHY

- *German Idealism*

German Idealism, a significant philosophical movement of the late 18th and early 19th centuries, was pioneered by figures such as Johann Gottlieb

Fichte. Building upon the metaphysical insights of Immanuel Kant, Fichte proposed a dynamic conception of the self as a constantly evolving entity. Georg Wilhelm Friedrich Hegel further extended this idea by emphasizing the importance of historical and dialectical thinking in understanding the self. In contrast, Arthur Schopenhauer diverged from Hegel's path and argued for a return to Kant's transcendental philosophy.

- *Marxism*

The philosophical and political ideology known as Marxism was born out of the intellectual partnership of Karl Marx and Friedrich Engels. Their seminal work, "The Communist Manifesto" (1848), presented a critique of capitalism, asserting its inherent instability and predicting its eventual replacement by socialist and, subsequently, communist systems. This work laid the foundation for the later international communist movement.

- *Positivism*

The philosophical position of Positivism was proposed by August Comte, advocating the belief that genuine knowledge is inherently empirical and verifiable. Comte argued that such knowledge derives from observable phenomena and subsequent logical and mathematical reasoning, excluding innate knowledge or metaphysical speculation

- *Social Darwinism*

The concept of Social Darwinism sought to apply the biological principles of natural selection and survival of the fittest, as outlined in Charles Darwin's "On the Origin of Species", to societal and political contexts. Proponents included Francis Galton, who maintained that cognitive abilities were as heritable as physical characteristics, and advocated for societal intervention in reproductive practices to prevent the over-breeding of "less fit" individuals. Similarly, Herbert Spencer, in his work "The Social Organism" (1860), likened society to a living organism, evolving and adapting according to Darwinian principles.

SOCIAL, ECONOMIC AND POLITICAL IMPACTS

- *The Industrial Revolution*

The Industrial Revolution, which took place between the late 18th and a time between 1820 and 1840, was a time of great social, political, and economic uprisings and change that involved the challenging transition from largely manual production methods to mechanical manufacturing methods, particularly in the fields of textiles, steam power, iron making, and the invention of machine tools. Agriculture had previously been the foundation of the European economy, and it was also a time when basic political, scientific, and religious ideas were unravelled to their core.

As a result of this mechanisation, a considerable number of people were transported from rural villages to metropolitan regions, resulting in a significant increase in population and the establishment of new, larger cities. The advancement of new technology resulted in the establishment of factories, a dehumanising and horrifying method of labour, particularly child labour, and a capitalist way of life. Because cities were unable to accommodate the rapidly rising population, there were overcrowded slums and terribly deplorable living conditions, as described in books such as Friedrich Engels' *The Condition of the Working Class in England*, published in 1844.

Elizabeth Barrett Browning's The Cry of the Children, Thomas Hardy's Tess of the D'Urbervilles, and works by author and philosopher Thomas Carlyle warned of the threat to society posed by these inhumane conditions and the profit-focused, materialistic ideals of what Dickens referred to as the "mechanical age" in his novels Hard Times and Oliver Twist.

- *Slavery and the Abolionist movement*

The 19th century in the United States was a time of great political upheaval and moral conflict. At the heart of these struggles was the question of slavery - the practice of owning human beings as property and forcing them to labor for the benefit of their owners. Slavery was deeply entrenched in the southern states, where it was seen as essential to the region's economy and way of life. But in the north, a growing abolitionist movement called for the immediate and unconditional end of slavery, seeing it as a fundamental violation of human rights and a stain on the nation's conscience.

These debates over slavery were not just academic or theoretical - they were deeply intertwined with the politics and culture of the time. The question of whether or not to allow slavery in new territories was a key issue in the lead-up to the Civil War, which ultimately erupted in 1861 and tore the nation apart. But even before the war, tensions over slavery were high, and political leaders grappled with how to address this thorny and divisive issue.

While the United States grappled with the practice and morality of slavery within its own borders, across the Atlantic, the United Kingdom was undergoing its own transformation in the 19th century regarding slavery. In

1807, the UK took a decisive step with the passage of the Slave Trade Act, which outlawed the transatlantic slave trade. This was followed by the Slavery Abolition Act of 1833, effectively ending slavery throughout the British Empire, except for areas under the administration of the East India Company, and in the territories of Ceylon (now Sri Lanka) and Saint Helena. This Act marked a critical turning point in the global fight against slavery.

This momentous development was not without its influences. Several influential works published during this period galvanized public opinion and shaped the discourse on slavery and abolition. Thomas Clarkson's 'An Essay on the Slavery and Commerce of the Human Species' (1786) offered a thorough critique of slavery, leading to its expanded edition in 1808. Another influential work, 'The History of Mary Prince' (1831), was the first account of a black woman's life published in the UK, detailing her experiences as an enslaved person in Bermuda, which sparked public interest and became a tool in the hands of abolitionists.

In tandem, anti-slavery sentiment was reflected in the literary world as well. For instance, Elizabeth Barrett Browning's influential poem, 'The Runaway Slave at Pilgrim's Point' (1847), powerfully condemned the institution of slavery.

- *The Rise of Nationalism and Imperialism*

The 19th century marked a pivotal period in global history, as it saw the rise of two influential ideologies: Nationalism and Imperialism. Both had profound implications for the world, reshaping political, economic, and social landscapes.

Nationalism emerged as a potent political force, rooted in the belief that individuals sharing a common language, culture, or ancestry constituted a nation. This ideology played a critical role in the unification of fragmented regions into cohesive nation-states. The unification of Italy in 1861 and Germany in 1871 stand as two of the most significant examples of nationalism's impact. Both unifications were driven by charismatic leaders— Camilo di Cavour in Italy and Otto von Bismarck in Germany— and the shared desire of the people to form a unified national identity. The emergence of nationalism also led to a rise in independence movements in various parts of the world, leading to the downfall of old empires and the birth of new nations.

Imperialism, on the other hand, was driven by the ambitions of the powerful Western nations to expand their influence and control over other parts of the globe. Rooted in a belief in cultural and racial superiority, as well as economic motivations, imperialism led to the colonization of large parts of Africa, Asia, and the Pacific. Key events during this period include the scramble for Africa (1881-1914), where European powers divided the continent among themselves, and the Opium Wars (1839-1860), which marked the beginning of Western imperial control over China.

The expansion of the British Empire, which, at its height, was the largest empire in history, is another prominent example of 19th-century imperialism. This period also witnessed the rise of the United States as an imperial power, with its acquisition of territories in the Caribbean and Pacific, notably following the Spanish-American War in 1898.

Both nationalism and imperialism had profound and lasting impacts on global politics, economics, and societies, the effects of which continue to be felt into the present day. They shaped national identities, redrew the world map, and sowed the seeds for many of the conflicts and power dynamics of the 20th century.

- *Science and influential Non-Fiction works*

Throughout the nineteenth century, Victorians' drive to understand and categorise the natural world played an important part in the development of scientific theory and understanding. Charles Darwin's works, such as the well-known On the Origin of Species (1859), would have a dramatic and far-reaching impact due to their innovative idea of evolution, which contradicted many of the time's established notions and religious beliefs.

The French Revolution: A History, published in 1837, and On Heroes, Hero-Worship, and the Heroic in History, published in 1841, are two other important non-fiction works from the period that influenced political thinking in the mid-nineteenth century.

KEY HISTORICAL EVENTS

- *The Acts of Union and Treaty of Amiens*

After the turmoil of the French Revolution and the Irish Rebellion, the Acts of Union in 1800 unified Britain and Ireland, creating the United Kingdom. This was a pivotal step in British history, aiming to stabilize and consolidate power in the region.

The Treaty of Amiens in 1802, albeit short-lived, ended the Second Coalition French Revolutionary War and temporarily eased tensions between France and the United Kingdom. However, peace was short-lived as the Napoleonic Wars commenced in 1803, reshaping European geopolitics.

- *US expansion*

In the early 19th century, the United States, newly independent, made a significant territorial expansion with the Louisiana Purchase in 1803. This acquisition, bought from the French First Republic for $15 million, doubled the nation's size and significantly increased its influence over the Mississippi River. It also brought the U.S. into closer contact with numerous Native American tribes, who were the primary inhabitants of the region, setting the stage for future conflicts and negotiations.

- *Napoleonic Wars*

Napoleon Bonaparte's military prowess was on full display in 1805, decisively defeating Russian and Austrian forces. However, his ambitions to invade England were thwarted at the Battle of Trafalgar, where Admiral Nelson's victory solidified British naval supremacy.

The disastrous Russian campaign of 1812 marked a turning point, with catastrophic losses for the French army. Napoleon's subsequent defeat in the War of the Sixth Coalition in 1814 led to his abdication and exile to Elba, marking the end of his reign and reshaping European politics.

- *British and Russian empire expansion*

The 19th century witnessed the ascension of Britain and Russia as global superpowers. Russia expanded its influence into Central Asia and the Caucasus, while Britain extended its colonial reach to include Canada, Australia, South Africa, and parts of Africa. The Indian Rebellion of 1857, a significant uprising against British rule, led to the dissolution of the British

DETAILED HISTORICAL CONTEXT

East India Company and the establishment of the British Raj, signifying a new era of direct British governance in India.

- *Opium wars*

By the mid-nineteenth century, China experienced severe opium problems as a result of the opening of trade with the West and the illicit trafficking in the drug coordinated by British entrepreneurs seeking to earn money at the trading ports. On the basis of free trade principles, Britain resisted the emperor's attempt to outlaw its sale, resulting in the First Opium War and the Treaty of Nanking in 1842, which permitted the drug trade to continue while handing over control of Hong Kong to the British.

The Taiping Rebellion of 1856 set the stage for the second Opium War, in which France and Britain collaborated. The 1860 Peking Convention, which legalised the opium trade and forced the surrender of additional provinces, resulted in the early nineteenth-century demise of the Qing dynasty.

- *The 1848 Revolutions*

The 1848 Revolutions, also known as the Springtime of the Nations, were a series of political upheavals that occurred in Europe and the rest of the world in 1848. The main purpose of these uprisings was to abolish previous monarchical authority and establish free nation governments.

Nationalists in Italy organised revolutions in Sicily and the Italian peninsula republics in order to construct a liberal government and break free from Austrian domination. The February Revolution in France occurred in Paris following the crackdown on the campagne des banquets, a violent insurgency against the monarchy that resulted in King Louis Philippe's overthrow. Germany, Denmark, Hungary, Galicia, Sweden, and Switzerland were among the other countries that revolted against the Habsburg Monarchy.

- *Abolitionism and the end of slavery*

Abolitionism, the movement to end slavery, gained momentum throughout the 19th century, driven by a combination of moral, economic, and political factors. In the United States, the abolitionist movement was intertwined with religious fervor, particularly among Quakers and other religious groups who viewed slavery as a profound moral evil. Key figures like Frederick Douglass, a former slave turned prominent activist, and Harriet

Tubman, who led many slaves to freedom via the Underground Railroad, played pivotal roles in advocating for abolition.

The British Empire's move to abolish slavery was equally significant. The Slavery Abolition Act of 1833, which followed years of tireless campaigning by abolitionists like William Wilberforce, marked a turning point in the global perception and legality of slavery. This act provided for the emancipation of slaves in most British colonies and significantly impacted the global slave trade.

In the United States, the abolitionist movement was a major factor leading up to the Civil War. The conflict between abolitionist northern states and pro-slavery southern states reached a climax with the war, which ultimately led to the passage of the Thirteenth Amendment in 1865. This amendment formally abolished slavery throughout the United States, marking a monumental victory for the abolitionist cause and a crucial step in the nation's history.

- *Women's Suffrage movement*

The women's suffrage movement was a decades-long struggle for the right of women to vote and participate in government. It was part of a larger women's rights movement that sought to achieve equal rights for women in various aspects of society.

In the United States, the movement began to take shape in the mid-19th century. The Seneca Falls Convention of 1848, organized by women's rights activists like Elizabeth Cady Stanton and Lucretia Mott, marked the first women's rights convention and the start of the organized women's suffrage movement in America. The Declaration of Sentiments, modeled after the Declaration of Independence, was adopted at this convention and outlined the injustices faced by women and the demand for equal rights, including the right to vote.

Key feminist literary works, such as Margaret Fuller's 'Woman in the Nineteenth Century' (1845), which advocated for women's independence and equality, and Sarah Grimké's 'The Equality of the Sexes and the Condition of Women' (1838), helped shape the discourse surrounding women's rights.

Despite facing significant opposition and slow progress, the movement continued to grow. Leaders like Susan B. Anthony, Sojourner Truth, and later Alice Paul and Lucy Burns, played crucial roles. The suffragists employed various strategies, from peaceful protests and lobbying to more radical tactics like hunger strikes and civil disobedience, particularly in the early 20th century.

In the United Kingdom, the movement was spearheaded by figures like Emmeline Pankhurst and her daughters Christabel and Sylvia. Founded in 1903, the Women's Social and Political Union (WSPU) led by Pankhurst was known for its militant tactics, including hunger strikes, demonstrations, and even acts of vandalism as forms of protest. These actions were pivotal in drawing public attention to the suffrage cause.

The suffrage movement's persistent efforts eventually led to legislative victories. In the United States, the Nineteenth Amendment, granting women the right to vote, was ratified in 1920. In the United Kingdom, the Representation of the People Act 1918 granted voting rights to women over 30, and the Equal Franchise Act of 1928 extended this right to all women over 21, finally achieving equal suffrage with men.

.

The edits and layout of this print version are Copyright © 2024+ by Century Bound.

Printed in Great Britain
by Amazon